12-99

WITHDRAWN

ISRAEL HOROVITZ

Collected Plays Volume IV

TWO TRILOGIES:
The Growing-Up-Jewish Trilogy
The Alfred Trilogy

ISRAEL HOROVITZ

Collected Plays Volume IV

TWO TRILOGIES:
The Growing-Up-Jewish Trilogy
The Alfred Trilogy

CONTEMPORARY PLAYWRIGHTS
SERIES

SK
A Smith and Kraus Book

A Smith and Kraus Book
Published by Smith and Kraus, Inc.
PO Box 127, Lyme, NH 03768

Manufactured in the United States of America
Cover and Text Design by Julia Hill
Cover photo © Gaëla Blancy, Paris. Used with permission.

First Edition: June 1998
10 9 8 7 6 5 4 3 2 1

The Library of Congress Cataloging-In-Publication Data
Horovitz, Israel.
Israel Horovitz: Collected plays volume IV / two trilogies. —1st ed.
p. cm. —(Contemporary playwrights series)
ISBN 1-57525-144-2 ISSN 1067-327X
I. Title. II: Title: Collected plays. III.Title: Two trilogies.
IV. Series: Contemporary playwrights series.
PS3558.069176 1993
812'.54—dc20
93-46378
CIP

c-/

CONTENTS

THE GROWING-UP-JEWISH TRILOGY

THE ALFRED TRILOGY

THE GROWING-UP-JEWISH TRILOGY

Based upon the book
A Good Place to Come From by Morley Torgov

INTRODUCTION

"THE GROWING-UP-JEWISH TRILOGY"
Today, I Am A Fountain Pen, A Rosen By Any Other Name,
and *The Choping Playoffs*

Growing up Jewish in Wakefield, Massachusetts, seemed to me like not grow-ing up Jewish at all. My father's "Pah'k yo'r ca'h" accent twanged like John F. Kennedy's. Our local synagogue, a converted garage, was several miles away in a neighboring town. Our rabbi was a part-timer. He was a full-time dentist. There were only a few Jewish families in our town. I had three Jewish friends: Richie, Jimmy, and Buzzy. My sister Shirley married Buzzy's older brother Arnold.

Preparation for my *Bar Mitzvah* was an ordeal. We found a Hebrew teacher—Mr. Copeland—who was a full-time high school English teacher in Gloucester, marathon distance away from Wakefield. Sometimes, Mr. Copeland came to our house to give his lessons. Sometimes, we few Jewish lads were driven to odd places to meet him. I recall being driven to Mr. Copeland's car, once. It was parked on Route #128. Our mothers shopped while we few Jewish lads prepared to become a few Jewish men…in the dis-comfort of Mr. Copeland's '51 Olds.

When I read stories about growing up Jewish, by the likes of Singer or Malamud or Roth, I felt like a bogus Jew. Experiences reported by these big-city Jewish writers were so unlike my own small-town-in-the-minority Jewish experiences, I was certain I would never write about mine. My Jewish back-ground seemed too odd, too against the expected. During the late 1970s, I had the occasion to visit Canada—Toronto, specifically—with some remark-able frequency. My play *The Primary English Class* had found success in that city, possibly because of Canada's French-versus-English struggle… probably because of Toronto's great ethnicity and vibrant immigrant spirit. Whatever the cause, the effect was splendid: *The Primary English Class* became the longest-running play in Canada's history. As playwrights have a tendency to visit their hits, I found myself in Toronto, and often. The late and great stage-director John Hirsch was, then, Head of Television Drama for the Canadian Broadcasting System. He'd called me in to discuss the possibility of my writ-ing/developing a comedy series for the CBC to be called "Rimshot." I hadn't any interest in the project, but had enormous interest in working with Hirsch, and with the CBC. Somebody had given me a collection of stories to read at the airport. Planes in and out of Toronto were invariably delayed in winter, because of heavy snowfall. Written by Morley Torgov, a Toronto lawyer, the stories were reminiscences of childhood in Sault Ste. Marie, Ontario, a rather undistinguished place…not exactly Canada's garden- spot…not at all unlike my own hometown, Wakefield, Massachusetts.

My plane back to NYC was delayed, *comme d'habitude*, so I cracked open the Torgov book for a browse. My plane came and went. I read the book from cover to cover, and then read it, again. I taxied back into Toronto and met with Hirsch and his CBC staff. Within a few hours, we had set up a project for three films, based upon Torgov's witty, wise stories: *Today, I Am A Fountain Pen; A Rosen By Any Other Name,* and *The Chopin Playoffs.*

In truth, the three teleplays weren't so much based on Torgov's stories as they were inspired by them. I was amazed to find that another writer had had my sort of Growing-Up-Jewish experience. It was as if the very existence of Torgov's stories gave me *permission* to write about my own childhood, but, through the lives of Morley Torgov's characters. The intermingling of Torgov's background with my own was a fascinating experiment. I recently found a dog-eared notebook dated 1978, in which I had noted that the writing of these plays was, for me, *psychoarchaeology*. Of the three teleplays, *Today, I Am A Fountain Pen* came closest to being a straight-forward adaptation. In the main, the teleplay was directly based on Torgov's most successful story, *Semper Annie*. The characters of the parents were greatly renovated, however, and the character of old Ardenshensky was totally original/invented.

A Rosen By Any Other Name was, by contrast, a totally original story, not found at all in Torgov's book. When I was thirteen, I belonged to a Jewish boys club, the A-Z-A (a Hebrew-letter fraternity: Aleph-Zadik-Aleph), in my mother's birthplace, Medford, Massachusetts. As my maternal grandparents were then still alive and living in Medford, my parents were quite willing to drive me to my club's meeting, once weekly, and visit their family while I did whatever I did.

One of the things I did in A-Z-A was compete in an oratory contest. I won. As club Oratory Champ, I went on to compete in the New England Region contest, which I also won. I then competed, *internationally, yet,* in the USA/Canada contest, held that year in Starlight, Pennsylvania. The contest was in a two-section format: a prepared speech, followed by an extemporaneous speech…meaning, a subject was handed to each contestant a scant ten minutes before they returned to the podium to orate/emote. My prepared speech was based upon Roosevelt's lofty notion that "We have nothing to fear but fear, itself". (I have since learned, of course, that we have much to fear beyond fear, itself. But, that's quite another essay.) The subject handed to me for my extemporaneous speech was "Name-changing." As luck would have it, not two weeks before the contest, an A-Z-A buddy had changed his name from a Jewish-sounding name to a not-Jewish-sounding name. Well, actually, his *parents* changed his name…but he went along with the deal, didn't stop it. And, I, Israel Arthur Horovitz, was shocked and amazed. My speech, entitled "From Kalitsky to Kay," was passionate and mercurial. It was also not bad. It was also the direct outline for *A Rosen By Any Other Name,* a play that *N.Y. Post* drama critic Clive Barnes would call "The best thing I have seen from Horovitz, yet. Triumphant!" As Barnes had probably reviewed some twenty-five Horovitz plays, by that point, I figured he had a right to his opinion. By the bye, the oratory contest, itself, went on to be the backbone of still another play of mine, *Unexpected Tenderness,* written in 1995 (and published in *New England Blue: Collected Works — Volume II). Psychoarchaeology über alles.* In this play, as in the actual contest, the boy (*moi-même, bien sûr*) walks to the podium to make his speech, but discovers that he is too short to be seen by the audience. Undaunted, he walks in front of the podium, microphone in hand, Sinatra-style, faces the audiences, croons, wins.

The Chopin Playoffs returns to Morley Torgov's book, borrowing the brilliant central image of Oscar Levant versus George Gershwin for Irving and Stanley's war: competition. But, more than anything else, *The Chopin Playoffs* is a play about leaving home…something I had done at age seventeen…and the pain of, uh, love…I was married at seventeen, and divorced at nineteen, one child in the grave. To this day, I cannot see or read the final moments of *The Chopin Playoffs* without tears staining/betraying my real-man face.

The three teleplays were filmed and presented to all of Canada with great success. And that seemed to be, as they say, that. Friends in the USA would only know about these films if I either screened the videos for them, or gave them the scripts to read. So, five years later, when I read about a prize being offered by the National Foundation for Jewish Culture for plays "written on a Jewish theme," I contacted the appropriate people, quickly, and offered not one but three proposed plays, and the three videotapes as support of my plan. My project was accepted and I won the prize. I used the money for family food/rent for nearly two months, while I sketched out rough drafts of the three new stage-plays, which I gave to Stanley Brechtner, artistic director of the American Jewish Theatre, where a stage adaptation of my novel *Cappella* had been produced a few years prior. I asked Brechtner if he would set up readings of the trilogy, so that I could "see if the plays worked." He contacted me within a few days, offering to fully produce the work. Flattered, I still asked for the readings, to which he agreed.

In their early drafts, the three plays of the trilogy filled two evenings, not three. *Today, I Am A Fountain Pen* and *A Rosen By Any Other Name* were both one-hour one-acts, to be paired together; and *The Chopin Playoffs* was a self-sustaining two-act play. The readings went well. There was obvious work to do, but within a context of something that would probably please its audience and author. Brechtner and I agreed to open the plays during AJT's 1985/86 season. Stephen Zuckerman signed on as director. Stephen and I had worked together on one of the early Gloucester-based plays *Firebird at Dogtown* at the WPA Theatre in Manhattan. He was a director I'd long wanted to work with, and he seemed delighted to sign on with me for this intimate, demanding project. Together, we decided to build a Jewish acting company. (Actually, this idea came from the legendary Broadway producer Robert Whitehead, who'd read the plays and reported to me that he'd found them to be "...charming, intelligent, moving, and totally noncommercial.") Sam Schact, Sol Frieder, Marcia Jean Kurtz, and Peter Riegert were among actor-friends I'd previously worked with who signed on.

Early rehearsals were a kind of nightmare for me. Everybody seemed happy...but me. Marcia Jean, Sam, Sol, and Josh Blake (the miracle of a kid we'd found to play Irving) all nailed their characters, early on, fully. *Today, I Am A Fountain Pen* was working, clearly, but, *A Rosen By Any Other Name,* for me, didn't work at all as a one-act. it seemed jokey and cartoonish...not at all the serious (funny) play I'd planned. It seemed to me that I hadn't spent two years of my life on this project in Canada, only to make less of it at home. I suggested that we shut down shop, so I could revise the plays. And then, like sent from God, Riegert got a movie. Head down, he reported the offer, saying he didn't know what to do. To his amazement, Steve and I gleefully screamed "Do it, Peter, do the movie! We'll wait for you!" I'll never forget Riegert's response. Undone by our generosity, he smiled, meekly..."You guys are being so understanding...*Why?*"

I wanted to rewrite *Today, I Am A Fountain Pen* and *A Rosen By Any Other Name* and make them full-length plays that could occupy their own evenings. Steven and I went to Stanley Brechtner, who was a model of understanding and support. We told the *Today, I Am A Fountain Pen* actors to take six weeks off, and I went home to write and rewrite. The *A Rosen By Any Other Name* cast went home with instructions to "wait until we call you."

Having done a lot of one-act plays in my early career, I can report that a double-bill has its own special energy: Usually, the cast of Play "A" feels that it is in competition with the cast of Play "B." The *Today, I Am A Fountain Pen* cast had felt like undisputed winners all through initial rehearsals. Sam

Schact, on hearing that *Today, I Am A Fountain Pen* had been expanded, announced with certainty, "You are taking a gem and ruining it!"

On that note, I began to bring new pages into rehearsals. Marcia Jean and Sam were not happy. Every new line seemed to prick Marcia Jean's skin. Every *changed* line was unthinkable. In fairness to all concerned, the actors were already off-book, when we halted initial rehearsals. They were ready to open. And actors of Sam's and Marcia Jean's talents find a magnificent loyalty to a text. It is something rare. And for me, of all people, *the playwright, yet*, to shake that faith and loyalty, and to announce, "It's no good! I'm taking it away from you! I'm going to change it! Fix it!" was, for them, unbearable.

A word here about Sol Frieder. Sol is one of America's great actors, and I state this from the point of view of somebody who has worked with some very good actors—Pacino, Dreyfuss, Keaton, Cazale, etc. I can report that Frieder is one of the very best. If he didn't have an Eastern European ["Jewish"] accent, his career would have been quite different. Let's say it simply: Were Sol Frieder British, not Yiddish, he would have had a career like Olivier's. And Sol's reaction to my we're-closing-down announcement was, "Do what you have to do. I'll be home. Call me when you want me."

Today, I Am A Fountain Pen was, of course, a wonderful success. I'm told that the first preview—the first time the play went in front of a live audience—was a triumph. I wouldn't know, because I wasn't there. I was in Gloucester, Massachusetts, holding Gillian's hand at Addison-Gilbert Hospital, while she gave birth to our twins, Hannah and Oliver. Three plays and two children began on the same night. Quite a night.

Riegert came back from his film-job, read the new, full-length version of *A Rosen By Any Other Name* and called me by phone, speaking with typically Riegertian succinctness…"Now, *this* is a play!" Stanley Brechtner, still supportive as ever, announced, "This is the play I've been waiting seven years to find and produce."

Steve Zuckerman's work on *A Rosen By Any Other Name* was nothing short of brilliant. Riegert was splendid as Barney, as were Maddie Corman and Peter Smith as Fern and Stanley, as was Barbara Eda-Young as Pearl, and Michael Ornstein as Manny. But the triumph was Sol Frieder's, hands (as they say) down. Every NYC drama critic agreed, as well. The day that the Al Hirschfield cartoon of Sol appeared in the *New York Times*, I felt that being a playwright was a holy thing…to be able to create roles for people like Sol Frieder... Mel Gussow, the *Times* drama critic wrote, "Move over, *Star Wars*, this is a trilogy with dimension!" And, as mentioned earlier, Clive Barnes's review in the *New York Post* was headlined "THE BEST ISRAEL

HOROVITZ PLAY YET!"… I was happy for the word "yet," in both the headline and the body of the work. Since 1985/86, such plays as *North Shore Fish, Unexpected Tenderness, My Old Lady, Lebensraum, One Under, Barking Sharks* and *Captains and Courage* have somehow issued forth from my imagination/pen/laptop…and "The best Horovitz play" has "yet" to be written. But, for the moment, we're in 1985/86, and the run of *A Rosen By Any Other Name* was extended and extended and extended, and, finally, had to close to make room for the opening of *The Chopin Playoffs*.

The Chopin Playoffs brought back the exquisite Maddie Corman, as an older, more beautiful, more experienced, more dangerous Fern…and Sol Frieder as Ardenshensky (and nearly everybody else in the play). Sam and Marcia Jean returned as the Yanovers, and two talented high school boys were found for Stanley and Irving, Nicky Strouse and Jonathan Marc Sherman. (During the run of *The Chopin Playoffs,* Jonathan showed me the first draft of his first play, typed on pink scrap-paper. In recent years, he has become, of course, Jonathan Marc Sherman, the famous, young playwright…with a bit of time out to act in plays like *Unexpected Tenderness*…)

By the time *The Chopin Playoffs* went into rehearsal, both Zuckerman and I were exhausted, physically drained from our work on the prior two shows. Also, like houseguests who have stayed too long, we'd worn out our welcome at the American Jewish Theatre. In retrospect, we would have done much better if we'd postponed *The Chopin Playoffs* until the next season, but we didn't. Stephen and I were determined to open the entire trilogy in one season. We both felt that something would go wrong if we waited…the steam would go out of the pot…the Jewish-catastrophe would strike. So, exhausted, we forged ahead.

The Chopin Playoffs was, at that point, the least reworked text. We'd all assumed, since the beginning, that *The Chopin Playoffs* was the surefire hit of the trilogy. It was, after all, a romantic comedy, without heavy or serious underpinning…

The first inkling that I had of any trouble surrounding *The Chopin Playoffs* was when both Riegert and Barbara eda-Young declined to return to the company. Peter said he was tired, and Barbara said she was short of money. Both things were true…but, additionally, the roles of the parents were now secondary, small.

I allowed *The Chopin Playoffs* to open in its original two-act format. Both *Today, I Am A Fountain Pen* and *A Rosen By Any Other Name* had been rewritten and shaped into a 90-minute-intermissionless format. And now, *The Chopin Playoffs* arrived, the least serious of the three plays…and, somehow, the longest. On its opening night, *The Chopin Playoffs* didn't hold a candle to its two siblings. Even though the reviews were mostly favorable and the audience was loyal and smiling, I cut some thirty minutes from the play and removed the intermission. In the end, many people who came late in the run of *The Chopin Playoffs* actually *preferred* this play to either *Today, I Am A Fountain Pen* or *A Rosen By Any Other Name.*

I have no preference. For me, the three plays compose one long work about growing up Jewish some thirty-five hundred miles from the disaster known as World War II. It's also about the affluence and competitiveness that followed the War, which is to say, *in Peace*. It's also about Jews who survived, which is to say, stayed alive. And, for me, mostly, it's about growing up, leaving a loving home, Jew or Gentile…about friendship and human love.

I know that when I began writing the project—the original teleplays— nearly two decades ago, my impulse was to write something large that was good for Jews. I was disgusted by the stereotypical stage-Jews I'd seen in play after play, Kosher Amoses and Andys. My own family was not a family of shruggers. We did not talk directly to God, nor did we roll our eyes to Heaven, excessively. Our sentences rarely ended in question marks, unless we were asking questions. Our men were not slaves to hard, domineering women. To my thinking, the concept of "Jewish Princess" was totally odious and totally untrue. I simply did not know Jewish women like that. I set out to create plays that featured Jews like the Jews I'd known and loved: thoughtful, loving people, full of passion, full of wit, full of lust, full of fun…people of positive spirit…team players. We've all seen and read enough about the difficulty one has leaving an unhappy home. But what about the difficulty one has leaving a *happy* home? I wasn't a deeply religious person while growing up, so I had no need to proselytize with these plays, but, I did certainly want to *celebrate* being Jewish. As a kid, I *adored* being Jewish. For me, it was *cool*…it was important to be *different*, to be on the *outside*. When the sister-school kids grabbed me and yelled "You killed Christ!" my commitment deepened. When Hitler led the German nation to do what it did, my commitment deepened even further.

I knew then, as I know now…Writing three plays about growing up Jewish (or about anything else) will never cure Cancer or replace Night Baseball, but these three plays—*Today, I Am A Fountain Pen, A Rosen By Any Other Name,* and *The Chopin Playoffs* —do form a small, detailed report of what life was like on one tiny corner of the planet Earth, in our time. I do have faith in literature. I do have faith in theatre. These plays will be seen and heard. And it's obvious—as you're the one holding this book—their future is now in your hands.

ADDENDUM: In September of 1992, Sol Frieder telephoned to say that he'd been asked to star as Ardenshensky in an upcoming production of *Today, I Am A Fountain Pen* at a Jewish theatre in Detroit. I was thrilled. To my amazement, Frieder went on to say that he'd thought it over felt the role and "...might possibly be just a bit short to excite an actor such as me into playing such a snowy place in winter." I asked him how much new material he would need to brace himself against possible foul weather. "Possibly a lengthy new scene between Ardenshensky and the boy" was Frieder's major negotiating point. My back to the wailing wall, I created a two-act version of the play by writing two new scenes...the first to end Act One, and another to begin Act Two, both, of course, featuring Ardenshensky. Frieder read the new scenes, throught they were "not bad," played Ardenshensky at JET in Detroit, to standing ovations, nightly. *Today I Am A Fountain Pen* was a triumph, and my popularity in Detroit leaped to a high. This new (optional) material is included in this edition, printed for the first time, anywhere, and dedicated to Sol Frieder...with my unending love.

I.H. April, 1998.

Today, I Am
A Fountain Pen

For Hannah and Oliver Horovitz,
who were born during
the first public performance
of *Today, I Am A Fountain Pen.*
Thank you for giving your Daddy
an opening night
that no other playwright will ever top.

ORIGINAL PRODUCTION

The world premiere of *Today, I Am A Fountain Pen* was presented by the American Jewish Theatre (Stanley Brechner, Artistic Director) in New York City, January 2, 1986. It was directed by Stephen Zuckerman; the set design was by James Fenhagen; the costume design was by Mimi Maxmen; the lighting design was by Curt Ostermann; the sound design was by Aural Fixation; the casting was by Darlene Kaplan; the production photographer was Gerry Goodstein; the production stage manager was Michael S. Mantel; the production coordinator was Neal Fox. The cast was as follows:

Irving Yanover	Josh Blake
Emil Ilchak	Stephen Prutting
Ardenshensky/Ukrainian Priest	Sol Frieder
Mrs. Ilchak	Dana Keeler
Esther Yanover	Marcia Jean Kurtz
Annie Ilchak	Melissa Leo
Moses Yanover	Sam Schacht
Pete Lisanti	Grant Shaud

Today, I Am A Fountain Pen was originally commissioned by The Community Theatre Project of the National Foundation for Jewish Culture.

Today, I Am A Fountain Pen was produced on the off-Broadway stage by Lou Kramer, Kenneth Waissman and Robert A. Buckley in association with Louis Scheeder, Road Works Productions, Michael Lonergan. The original cast transferred with the play, with the following exceptions: Barbara Garrick played Annie, Stan Lachow played Ilchak, and Danny Gerard played Irving.

THE PEOPLE OF THE PLAY

ESTHER YANOVER: thirties; small, somewhat round; Irving's mother.

MOSES YANOVER: late thirties; a kindly face; Irving's father.

IRVING YANOVER: ten years old; small, thin.

ANNIE ILCHAK: fifteen years old; classic Ukrainian looks.

PETE LISANTI: eighteen years old; athletic, Italian looks.

EMIL ILCHAK: forty; muscular, Ukrainian looks.

MRS. ILCHAK: thirties; strong-backed, Ukrainian looks.

ARDENSHENSKY: an old Jew.

UKRAINIAN PRIEST: an old Ukrainian (also plays Ardenshensky).

THE TIME OF THE PLAY

1941, during the early stages of the War in Europe

THE PLACE OF THE PLAY

The action of the play takes place in and around the home and store of the Yanover family, in Sault Ste. Marie, Ontario, Canada.

Today, I Am A Fountain Pen

The lights in the auditorium fade out. In the darkness, we hear the sound of a child playing a Chopin étude on a piano. A spotlight fades up on Jacob Ardenshensky, an old Jew, who speaks directly to the audience.

ARDENSHENSKY: I heard that! *(He points to man in audience.)* Not a word out of my mouth yet and that one turns to his wife and says "I hate it already"... *(Calls out to rear of auditorium.)* What's the matter? You've never seen a Canadian before? *(Smiles at man in audience.)* Tonight's play is called *Today, I Am A Fountain Pen*... *(Points at someone in audience who has laughed.)* You know the joke? *(Smiles.)* My name is Jacob Ardenshensky and I'm the oldest living man in the Soo...I beg your pardon. I said the Soo. *(To another man.)* ...not "the Zoo"! The "Soo" is our nickname for Sault Ste. Marie, Ontario. That's in Canada. You've heard of Canada... *(To another woman.)* Don't worry, madame, we speak English... *(Shrugs to man in rear.)* I'm sorry, but we speak English... *(To all.)* My landsman up there said "Oyy, English." *(To Old Yiddle.)* It's a very easy English...Sault Ste. Marie, Ontario, is just across the Lake from Sault Ste. Marie, Michigan. It is now early 1941. There is a war in Europe, and the news from the front is just beginning to drift home to Canada. On the other side of the Lake, American hepcats are still cuttin' the rug to "The Flat Foot Floogee with the Floy Floy." *(Shrugs.)* ...Americans. *(Lights up to glow on stage. Esther Yanover in second spotlight. Irving continues to play piano. Moses Yanover is in the store, below.)*

ARDENSHENSKY: The boy at the piano is Irving Yanover. He's ten. The boy's father, Moses Yanover, is working downstairs, in the family's drygoods store. I bought a defective sheet from Yanover many years ago, but, that's another story. Irving's mother, Esther Yanover, has something to say to you about happiness... *(To Esther.)* Are we ready? *(Esther nods. Ardenshensky speaks to audience.)*

ARDENSHENSKY: I think we're ready. *(Smiles.)* I'll be back later. *(Ardenshensky exits. Esther looks at audience, speaks. Music in: Chopin, played lightly on a piano by a child. Auditorium lights fade out. In a pinspot, we see the anguished face of Esther Yanover.)*

ESTHER: You want to know what happiness is. I'll tell you what happiness is:

Happiness is *help*…neither of which am I getting… *(Pauses.)* Buttttt, you'll never hear *meee* complain!

(Lights up full. The setting: the front rooms of the Yanover family apartment above the Yanover family store. Sault Ste. Marie, Ontario, 1941. Living room with overstuffed furniture, old-fashioned upright piano, oversized dining table; kitchen visible upstage center. Child's bedroom also visible. Downstairs, to one side, the store. A funnel-mouthpiece at each end of a tube creates a homemade intercom between home and store. Two smallish bells, spring-mounted, joined by lightweight chainlink, create the intercom signal. At the play's opening, Moses Yanover, fortyish, pulls the chain, causing the bell to ring in the kitchen above. Esther Yanover stands at the dining table, stuffing a chicken, enthusiastically. Yells across to mouthpiece.)

ESTHER: I can only put my two hands in one place at one time.

(The bell rings again.)

ESTHER: Stop ringing, Mosie! Stop ringing!

MOSES: Whhaaaat?

ESTHER: I said "stop ringing!"

MOSES: I stopped!

ESTHER: I'm busy stuffing tonight's chicken. Do you want help in the store, now, or supper, tonight? Make a choice!

MOSES: Help, now, and supper, later!

ESTHER: *(Suddenly yells at Irving, who sits at piano, reading a comic book.)* Irving, for God's sakes, *play!*

(Irving snaps into action. Without thought, Irving launches into Chopin Black Keys Étude. This is clearly not the first time.)

MOSES: Are you coming? We've got customers!

ESTHER: Three minutes! *(Esther works faster. She is aware of Irving's piano playing. She pauses to enjoy his talent.)* You play like an angel.

IRVING: Angels play harps. This is a piano…

ESTHER: You can't take a compliment, Mr. Wiseguy?

IRVING: I'm sorry.

ESTHER: But, Stanley Rosen: He plays like God himself.

IRVING: That's a compliment for me to take?

ESTHER: That's a *fact* for you to take!

IRVING: Stanley Rosen's four months older than me and he's a mile taller and he's been studying longer…

ESTHER: So, make excuses and Stanley Rosen will be playing a Steinway Grand at Carnegie Hall, New York City, and who will be his tuner?

IRVING: Great! That would make me happy. I love a good tune.

ESTHER: If your father or I had your Mister Wiseguy/Mister Give-Up-Easy Attitude, where would the store be? Where would the money for Friday night stuffed chickens be? And where, Mr. Einstein Yanover, would the money come from to pay for your pianos? *(Listens.)* What is that you're playing, please.

IRVING: Well, I only know scales and Chopin. I'm not playing scales, so…?

ESTHER: Such a mouth on you… *(Sniffs, alarmed.)* What's burning? *(She runs into kitchen; disappears momentarily.)*

IRVING: Smells like bacon.

ESTHER: *(Reappears; worried by Irving's remark.)* Are you crazy? Bacon in this house?

IRVING: I didn't say it *was* bacon. I said it smelled like bacon.

ESTHER: How would you know what bacon smells like?

IRVING: It's the little red bits in the Chinese food we eat at the Ritz Cafe…

ESTHER: Who told you that?

IRVING: God, himself: Stanley Rosen…

ESTHER: Mr. Rosen is having bad dreams. Whatever it is you smell, I can assure you, does not smell like bacon to you, because you have never once smelled bacon!

IRVING: I ate bacon at Freddy Folger's. You know that.

ESTHER: A blocked memory, believe you me…Eating bacon is against the law, Mr. Jesse James, and this house does not break the law…

IRVING: Oh yeah, well, if the law ever changes, I would love to eat some more bacon…for the first time!

ESTHER: *(Turns suddenly and grabs a smoldering pot holder; throws same into sink.)* Pot holder!

(Lights fade up in store again.)

MOSES: *(At intercom.)* Essie, for God's sake! I'm full of customers here!

ESTHER: I can't be everywhere, Mosie, dammit! If we had a new girl, she could be here and I could be there!

MOSES: What are you doing?

ESTHER: I'm fixing dinner and putting out fires, what do you think I'm doing?

MOSES: *(From the store below.)* What fires?

ESTHER: And keeping an eye on a boy who's throwing his talent *down the drain!*

IRVING: Okay! *(Throws his magazine down and starts playing again at once.)*

ESTHER: Potatoes! *(She grabs a burning pot from the stove; places under water.)* I cannot do it all alone!…

MOSES: *(From the store below.)* *What fires, Essie?* What are you *doing?*

ESTHER: There was a fire and it's out, Moses. Trust me! *(To Irving.)* Louder!
(To Moses.) Happiness is help, Mosie, and I want both!

MOSES: *(From the store below.)* Me, too!
(Moses runs to back of store, he exits, in disgust. As he moves upstage, lights fade out in store, below.)

ESTHER: That man is a genius!

IRVING: Daddy?

ESTHER: No, Chopin!
(The lights black out. Lights shift to Pete Lisanti and Annie Ilchak, teenaged. They are walking to Annie's house, holding hands, along apron of stage.)

PETE: What if he sees us?

ANNIE: It's Wednesday. He won't be home 'til seven-thirty...

PETE: I guess you probably want another kiss...

ANNIE: Yeah, I do...

PETE: God! Never enough...
(They kiss. They are almost instantly observed from "inside the house" by Annie's father, Emil Ilchak, forty-five, powerfully built.)

ILCHAK: *(Ukrainian accent is very heavy.)* What the hell is going on here?
(Annie and Pete leap away from one another. Annie swallows a scream.)

PETE: It's not Wednesday! It's Thursday!
(Pete runs off. Ilchak "opens the door"; speaks to Annie, harshly, deep-throated anger.)

ILCHAK: *(Thick accent.)* Get in there, you!
(The lights shift to Ilchak, Annie, and Elsa, Ilchak's wife. Yanover living room is now Ilchak living room. A screen/curtain covers piano. We hear: a Caruso recording playing on old-fashioned phonograph. Annie and Elsa prepare dinner.)

ANNIE: Can't you speak to him for me? Please?

ELSA: We have made up...our mind.

ANNIE: Pete was just walking me home, mama, that's all...

ELSA: That's all?

ANNIE: That's all...

ELSA: You can lie to your papa...you can lie to yourself...but, you can't lie to me, Anja. What I see, I see... *(Ilchak turns, faces women. He motions to Annie.)*

ILCHAK: Sit. I want you to listen...
(Annie sits; listens.)

ANNIE: It's beautiful, papa...

ILCHAK: I'm trying to stop my anger with something beautiful. I am thinking about what you did to me...

ANNIE: Papa, please. I didn't do anything to you. Pete was just walking me home.

ILCHAK: Don't you open your mouth to me, you! *(To Elsa, in Ukrainian, angrily.)* Tell her!

ELSA: Just listen to your papa, please...just listen...

ANNIE: I'm sorry, papa...

ILCHAK: In this family, we've got rules. I told you you could never again go on any date with Pete Lisanti...and what do you do?

ANNIE: It wasn't a date, papa...

ILCHAK: *(Screams.) What do you dooo?*

ANNIE: I'm sorry, papa...

ILCHAK: Of course, you're sorry. You're sorry you got caught!

ANNIE: No, papa, please, listen...

ELSA: Anja!

ILCHAK: *(Screams.)* Pete Lisanti is *nothing* to you!

ANNIE: Yes, papa...

ILCHAK: I have decided. School ends for you in June, anyhow, so you will stop going to school, as of yesterday, and start working in a nice home, as soon as we can place you...

ANNIE: *(Sobs.)* Noooo... *(Sobbing.)* Mama, please, mama...

ILCHAK: You cry today, but, in ten years, you'll say "I had real parents..."
(Elsa stares at her husband wordlessly. Annie sobs.)

ILCHAK: I'll let it be known that you're looking for work in a good family's house...
(The scene shifts back to Yanover rooms. Lights up at once on Irving, standing beside piano. Moses is in chair, reading the newspaper. Esther is sewing. Esther notices Irving first. Irving prays, soft voice; a murmur. He rocks back and forth, enthusiastically.)

ESTHER: What are you *doing?*

IRVING: Praying.

ESTHER: Praying?

IRVING: Praying.

MOSES: *What* is he doing?

ESTHER: He's praying.

IRVING: I'm praying.

MOSES: Praying?

IRVING: Praying.

ESTHER: Praying.

(There is a pause. Irving continues to mumble his prayer and "duven"—rock and sway, as might an old Jew in prayer.)

MOSES: I don't mean to interfere. I mean, what goes on between you and God is private business…

ESTHER: He's driving me crazy!

MOSES: Irving, what are you praying for?

IRVING: For a nice person.

ESTHER: Of *course* she's a nice person.

IRVING: Is Mrs. Berkowitz's niece Rosie a nice person?

ESTHER: A very nice person and you shouldn't forget it!

IRVING: Nice enough to sleep with?

ESTHER: *(Holds back laugh.)* What are you saying?

MOSES: *(Holds back laugh.)* What is he saying?

IRVING: This person you've hired is going to sleep with me, right?

ESTHER: Not *"with"* you…

MOSES: Next to you…

IRVING: Same thing.

ESTHER: In the same room…

IRVING: It's the same thing! *(Pauses.)* If I hired some stranger to work for me who was going to sleep with you, wouldn't you pray…?

MOSES: *(Interrupting.) Definitely!* I would definitely pray!

IRVING: Stanley says she's from Cabbagetown…

ESTHER: From what?

IRVING: That's what he said: She's from Cabbagetown, and she's going to smell bad…

ESTHER: Stanley Rosen said that?

(Esther and Moses exchange a glance.)

IRVING: That's not all he said. But you don't want to know the rest…

MOSES: You're absolutely right. Annie Ilchak is a superb young lady. I've met her twice. I've also met her mother and her father and her six brothers and sisters…

IRVING: Six?

MOSES: Six.

ESTHER: She's an old hand around little Mr. Know-It-All-Big-Mouths…

IRVING: *(Horrified.)* She *hits* kids?!

ESTHER: Who said "She hits kids!?"

IRVING: You did! *(Looks to Heaven.)* Do you hear what's coming into my bedroom? Do you hear what they're putting in there?

(A knock on the door. Esther and Moses stand. Irving talks to heaven.)

IRVING: Pay attention, please.

ESTHER: Stop that!

MOSES: Irving, stop praying!

ESTHER: I'll get it.

MOSES: *I'll* get it! *(Stops.)* We'll all get it. Come.

(They all go to door, open same. And there stands Annie Ilchak, a fifteen-year-old Ukrainian girl, pale, thin, shivering, cold; scared. Irving prays and rocks again, more enthusiastically than ever before.)

ESTHER: Oh my God! Don't tell me you *walked?*

MOSES: In the snow?

ESTHER: Didn't your father drive you?

MOSES: I would have picked you up! *(A small silence.)* Well, come innn!

ESTHER: Come innnnnn!

(Annie steps into the room. Moses and Esther clear to one side: out of her way. Irving is able to see Annie for the first time. He is standing with his eyes clenched closed. Annie enters the room, sees Irving, stops. Irving opens his eyes, looks at Annie. They hold eye-contact for a moment. Annie smiles. Irving looks to heaven again. Irving smiles. He looks to heaven, once again.)

IRVING: *(To God.)* Thank you.

(Blackout. Music: Chopin. Lights up on Yanover family, Irving, Esther, and Annie seated at table having tea and cake. Esther pours the tea. Moses stands, Irving is in his chair.)

ESTHER: Irving is our resident stand-up comedian…

IRVING: I'm sitting down…

MOSES: Show her…stand up. *(Pulls Irving up; sits in chair.)*

IRVING: *That* was funny.

ESTHER: Every other Jewish family in Sault Ste. Marie is raising a doctor or a lawyer. Here at 7 Queen Street, we are growing ourselves a regular Fred Allen…

MOSES: A ten-year-old Jack Benny…

ESTHER: He's only ten…

MOSES: Ten, going on forty…

ESTHER: He's an only child. That's what happens…

ANNIE: *(To Irving.)* Are you really going into show business?

ESTHER: Over my dead body. I have a cousin on my father's side who sang in nightclubs, thank you…

MOSES: Irving plays piano.

(Irving stands and stares at Annie.)

IRVING: *(To Annie.)* You've got Italian eyes.

ANNIE: *What?*

IRVING: Are you all Ukrainian, or, part Italian, too?

ANNIE: Oh, gosh, all Ukrainian…absolutely totally all Ukrainian. *(She giggles.)*

ESTHER: *(To Irving.)* What kind of a question is that, young man?

IRVING: Our last girl was part Italian and part Swiss. My mother used to call her "Miss Cheese with Holes." She taught me some really nifty Italian words, though. Do you know how to say "Kiss my behind" in Italian?

ANNIE: Uh, no.

MOSES: Ten years old with a mouth like a truck driver. *(Smiles.)* This he gets from my wife's family.

ESTHER: Two comedians in one house.

IRVING: Before "Miss Cheese with Holes" we had an all-Croatian girl, "Miss Spinach Pie." She taught me some really neat words, too. Maybe you could teach me some Ukrainian words?

ANNIE: Uh, well, sure, maybe, sure…

IRVING: Oh, swell! We once had an all-Ukrainian girl here, but she quit after a week. I only learned one thing from her… *(Here Irving speaks an obscenity, in Ukrainian language.)* "Sirroco e-pee-da do-chorda."
(Annie blushes and looks away. There is an astonished glance between Esther and Moses.)

ESTHER: Did you just say something filthy to this girl?

IRVING: *(This never occurred to him before.)* Me? I…filthy?

MOSES: Did you, Irving?

ESTHER: *(To Annie.)* What did he just say to you?

ANNIE: Nothing, really. Just an old-fashioned expression.

ESTHER: Is it filthy, Irving? Answer me, Mr. Has-A-Mouth-Like-A-Truck-Driver! It is filthy what you just said to this girl?

IRVING: *(Panicked; he doesn't know.)* I don't know, dammit!

ANNIE: *(Lying.)* No, nooo, it wasn't filthy. It was just…surprising…to hear Irving suddenly speaking like my father.

ESTHER: You never know what's coming out of this one's mouth next. You simply never know. *(To Irving.)* You owe an extra hour's practice for that scare, Mr. Foreign-Language-Speaker!

IRVING: I do not! That isn't fair, I…

MOSES: Don't talk back to your mother, please!

IRVING: You talk back to your mother! *(To Annie.)* He does. Sometimes he screams at my grandmother: loud, too.

MOSES: Your grandmother is deaf. I *have* to scream…

IRVING: Oh, yeah, well, how do I know that my very own mother isn't [dah-bahhhh]… *(This last word/sound is barely audible.)*

ESTHER: That your mother isn't *what?*

IRVING: *(Screams.)* Deaf!

MOSES: Irving Yanover!

(Irving runs to piano.)

IRVING: I'll practice! I'll practice!

(Lights cross fade. The Chopin continues, but on tape, through the auditorium speakers. Lights up in the bedroom. Irving is lying atop his bed; Annie is arranging things on her dresser-top. The music fades under the scene, lightly.)

IRVING: Do you hate sharing a bedroom?

ANNIE: I'm used to sharing a *bed.*

IRVING: I guess that's okay if the bed's big.

ANNIE: It was pretty big…

IRVING: My mother and father's bed is *great.* Maybe we could share that sometime.

ANNIE: *(Looks at Irving; smiles.)* Do you do well in school?

IRVING: If I didn't, I'd be dead. You'd have the whole bedroom to yourself. I got seven "Excellents" and one "Very Good"… *(Pauses in disgust.)* Stanley Rosen got eight "Excellents."

ANNIE: You really hate him, huh?

IRVING: You'll see. When you meet him, you'll hate him, too. He's a twirp and a jerk.

ANNIE: Oh, yuh. I hate twirps and jerks.

(Irving giggles approvingly.)

IRVING: Hey, maybe I could get him here for supper with his parents and you could slip some poison onto his brisket. *(Pauses.)* I'm planning to murder Stanley Rosen.

ANNIE: I can see why. Eight excellents. What a twirp!

IRVING: *(Pleased.)* Do Ukrainians really eat weird things?

ANNIE: What kind of weird things?

IRVING: Oh, well…like cabbage?

ANNIE: Cabbage isn't weird.

IRVING: How about bacon?

ANNIE: You think bacon is weird?

IRVING: I think bacon is wonderful, but it is totally illegal for Jews. Pig food.

ANNIE: Pig food?

IRVING: Pig food.

ANNIE: Pigs eat bacon?

IRVING: Pigs *are* bacon.

ANNIE: Right. Well, if cabbage and bacon is weird food, then I guess Ukrainians eat weird food… *(Annie reties the twine around her dilapidated suitcase.)*

IRVING: How come you had twine tied around your suitcase? When you first came here I noticed your suitcase was tied together with twine…but, when you opened it, there wasn't much in there…to fall out, I mean…

ANNIE: *(Looks at Irving; pauses.)* Better safe than sorry, I guess…

IRVING: How come you brought so little? The last girl needed two whole drawers, she had so much stuff.

ANNIE: I guess she was fancy.

IRVING: Nawww. She wasn't fancy. I heard my mother talking to my father about her, after she quit. She forgot some of her underwear and my mother said it was really filthy… *(Pauses.)* Do you think I'm really funny?

ANNIE: When I first got here I noticed your big eyes, right away, and I thought "What big eyes this little boy has!"…and then I got to hear your big mouth, and I thought "What a big mouth for a little boy!" Now, I've found out that you also have inordinately big ears—they hear *every*thing, right! So, I guess it stands to reason that you've gotta have the big head you've got…'cause you are really the Big Head of all time!…but, you've gotta have a big head, right? 'cause it's got to lug all that other *big stuff around!*

IRVING: *(Looks up to heaven.)* Why meee?

(Blackout. Lights fade up in store, below. Esther yells up to Annie, over intercom.)

ESTHER: Annnieee! I forgot to tell you that the saucepans are milk-and-meat, too. It isn't just the silverware. Are you listening? Are you listening?

(Lights fade up in Yanover home. Annie stands talking on telephone, while at the same time, trying to talk with Esther, who stands at the intercom, below, in store screaming up to Annie.)

ANNIE: *(Into telephone: quietly.)* Of course, I want to see you, too…but… When? Where?… *(Pauses; then, in a hushed voice.)* Pete? Please, Pete…*Peeeeeeeete.*

ESTHER: Annie, are you listening to me?

ANNIE: *(Yells out.)* Yes, Mrs. Yanover, I'm listening! *(Into telephone.)* I have to go, Pete…

ESTHER: My grandmother—*Alivoh, Shalom*—knew a woman in Pinsk, who dressed impeccably, but kept a wreck of a saucepan for her gravies…

ANNIE: Please, Pete, let me call you back…

ESTHER: Annnie, are you talkingggg? Annnieee?

   (Esther pulls the bell-cord, below, the bell rings in kitchen.)

ANNIE: *(Yells out.)* I'm not talking, Mrs. Yanover. I'm listening to you! *(Into telephone.)* Pete, I have to go, *please!*

ESTHER: It sounded like you said something.

ANNIE: I'm listening! *(Into telephone.)* 'Bye, Pete. I miss you… *(Hangs up; yells out.)* Whhhhat-ttt, Mrs. Yanoverrrr? I can't hear youuuu!

ESTHER: *(Over intercom.)* Shh. Not so loud, Annie! There are customers! Did you hear what I said about separate milk and meat saucepans?

ANNIE: *(Continues to yell into intercom.)* Oh I heard most of it.

ESTHER: *(Into intercom, as well.)* You didn't hear all of it?

ANNIE: I was dusting in the front room…

ESTHER: I gave an entire Kosher-lesson…

ANNIE: Well I heard *most* of it…

ESTHER: You have to know it *all!* You can't make mistakes in a Kosher home! *(Pauses; listens.)* Why isn't Irving practicing? It's after three-thirty!

ANNIE: I think he's in the bathroom.

ESTHER: Is he sick?

ANNIE: He might be reading.

ESTHER: Go look.

ANNIE: I'll call him.

ESTHER: You tell him I said that school holidays are not holidays from practicing. His closest friend, Stanley Rosen, you can assure him for me, is not in the bathroom, at this time. Stanley is at the piano and he is playing *scales! Can you hear me, Annieee?*

ANNIE: *(Starting to frazzle.)* I hear you, Mrs. Yanover! *(Annie, in Esther Yanover's spirit, screams out to Irving.)* Irvvvinnnnnnnng! Get out of the bathroom, now!

   (The door pops open, and Irving, frightened, looks at Annie; Irving and Esther, simultaneously.)

IRVING: Jesus, Annie, what's the matter?

ESTHER: *(From downstairs.)* Not so loud, Annie! We've got customers!

   (There is a pause. The telephone rings. Annie turns, horrified, and stares at the telephone. It rings again.)

ESTHER: Who's on the phone? *(No reply.)* Who's on the phone?

(Annie, in a panic, picks up the receiver and, immediately, hangs up, without answering.)

ANNIE: *(Calls out to Mrs. Yanover.)* Wrong number! *(To Irving; an authorial scream.)* Practice your scales, now! That was *not* Pete Lisanti!

(Irving, terrified, plays scales. Esther calls to Annie, from store below.)

ESTHER: Annnieeee, please, come down here now…

(Lights fade out in Yanover home; fade up in store. Annie runs around the set and enters store, breathlessly, still carrying dishtowel. Esther greets her, smiling. The Kosher-lesson continues.)

ESTHER: It's quiet in the store. We can go on with our lesson, face to face…

(Hands Annie a pencil and paper.) Maybe you should take notes…

ANNIE: I'll remember…

ESTHER: No, no, no. My mother made me take notes and I remembered. These laws have survived for thousands and thousands of years because young women were made to take notes…

ANNIE: I'll take notes…

(Annie stands poised with pencil and paper. Esther gathers her thoughts.)

ESTHER: Now these dietary laws were first devised by the Jews, because the Pagans used to slaughter animals and offer them in sacrifice in the animal's own mother's milk…

ANNIE: They *what?*

ESTHER: I know. I remember when my mother first told me. I thought she was making it up…are you writing?

ANNIE: They killed the animals in the animal's own mother's milk?

ESTHER: It's hard to believe that people can be so cruel. Believe me, Annie, life is not like the moving pictures. Life does not invent such happy endings…

ANNIE: *(Lost in thought; a word escapes.)* Yessss…

ESTHER: What "yes"?

ANNIE: Hmmm?

ESTHER: You said "yes"…

ANNIE: Oh, nothing, I was just concentrating hard on the Kosher lesson…

ESTHER: *(Delighted.)* You were?

ANNIE: I was.

ESTHER: It's nice having a girl in the house, Annie. Girls pay attention…

ANNIE: It's nice being in a house with so few children. When I told Irving that I have four brothers and two sisters, he said to me "there are too many children in your family."

ESTHER: He's got such a mouth on him!

ANNIE: Nooo, I think he's right!

ESTHER: Let me tell you what my grandmother told me. My grandmother would never count up the number of grandchildren she had. She thought it was bad luck. When anybody would ask her how many grandchildren she had, she would say "A lot of grandchildren." *(Smiles; remembers.)* When Mr. Yanover and I were getting married, I asked my grandmother what she thought would be the ideal number of children for a family to have…and she said "Estellah, the ideal number of children to have is the number of children you will get." I was panicked. "Grandmother, what does that mean?" And she said "It will become obvious." And she was right. *(Touches Annie's shoulder, lightly.)* My family is ideal and your family is ideal…and with you staying here with this family, it's even more ideal…

(The two women exchange a loving glance.)

ESTHER: Let me tell you the truth: The main reason we keep Kosher today is because our parents would *kill* us if we didn't. And this is reason enough…

ANNIE: Should I write that down?

ESTHER: No. There are some things that should *never* be written down.

ANNIE: And that's one of them?

ESTHER: And that's one of them…

(Blackout. On the radio, playing in room, softly, we hear: "The Fred Allen Show." After it is established, we hear Moses' voice, offstage, calling to Irving.)

MOSES: *(In dark.)* Irving Yanover, it's a quarter-to-nine on a school night! I want that radio turned off!

IRVING: *(In dark.)* It's Fred Allen, poppy!

MOSES: *(In dark.)* Did you hear me?

IRVING: *(In dark.)* Okay, okayyy!

(The radio switches off. There is a moment of silence, and then lights up in living room. Irving at piano; Annie housecleaning.)

ANNIE: *(Yelling into intercom.)* Yes, Mrs. Yanover! I did it already, Mrs. Yanover…

(Annie stuffs her dish towel into intercom; looks over at Irving, who laughs, conspiratorially.)

IRVING: Annie?

ANNIE: What?

(He sits on table.)

ANNIE: Off the table!

IRVING: *(He sits on chair.)* You know who I want to be like when I grow up?

ANNIE: *(Sits.)* Who?

IRVING: More than anybody in all of Canada…in all the world…in the whole solar system!

ANNIE: Who?

IRVING: *(Simply.)* Horowitz.

ANNIE: *(Simply.)* Who's Horowitz?

IRVING: Who is Horowitz? Are you kidding me? Horowitz is just the single greatest pianist on the Planet Earth, that's all…

ANNIE: Oh, right. Horowitz. There's a Horowitz on the hockey team with my friend Pete…

IRVING: That's Berkowitz. Fat Rosie Berkowitz's cousin, Arnold. He plays hockey, yuh… *(Pauses.)* There's a problem.

ANNIE: Huh?

IRVING: My growing up like Horowitz. Horowitz looks like a bird.

ANNIE: So do you…

IRVING: Yuh, but I've got big muscles. Horowitz is skinny as a rail. You should see him…

ANNIE: How'd you get to meet him?

IRVING: I didn't! I saw him in a newsreel at the Algoma Cinema…I love movies. You?

ANNIE: Oh, I do.

IRVING: If I push my arm up, like this, my muscles aren't bad. Stanley Rosen has got arms like turds…Fingers like turds, too. He's disgusting. A real stinker!… *(Irving giggles.)*

ANNIE: Irvingggg, shushhhhh! *(She giggles, too.)* Do your parents take you to the movies a lot?

IRVING: *(Ironically.)* Oh, yuh sure… *(Pauses.)* Twice, maybe, in my life. They are always working or else they go out to supper with the Rosens. Working and eating: That's about it…and yelling at me… *(Pauses.)* I went with my class. There was a movie about Chopin and a short with Horowitz playing Chopin. It was excellent.

ANNIE: Your parents aren't against you going to the movies?

IRVING: Naw, they're too busy working, eating, and yelling… *(Pauses.)* Are you thinking what I'm thinking?

ANNIE: I think so. We could ask her.

IRVING: *Him,* ask him. If you ask her, she's liable to say "It would have been okay with me, but, your father said no"…and then he'll back her up. But, if you ask him first, he'll say "yes" and she'll have no choice… *(Explains.)* They both hate to be the one who says "no"…but he hates it much much more than she hates it. It's exhausting, figuring these things out… *(Pauses.)* Can you keep a secret?

ANNIE: What do you think?

IRVING: I think you can, but, you've got to say it yourself, or you're not bound.

ANNIE: I promise.

(He moves close to Annie.)

IRVING: It's about my piano playing…

ANNIE: You really hate it?

IRVING: Opposite. I would rather be playing piano than anything else in life. But, you can't let my parents know this, okay?

ANNIE: I don't get it.

IRVING: Well, think about what my parents make me do when they punish me for something bad…

ANNIE: *(Smiles.)* Oh, you are very smart.

IRVING: If they knew, I'd be washing dishes, taking out garbage…

ANNIE: You mean the things I do…

IRVING: You get paid. I just get yelled at…Do you know Mr. Ardenshensky?

ANNIE: Who's he?

IRVING: The oldest living person in the Soo, next to his wife.

ANNIE: His wife is older?

(He puts his arm around Annie.)

IRVING: Many years older. I just heard about it. Mr. Ardenshensky married a woman ten years older than him…and it worked out great. They just had their sixtieth anniversary…

ANNIE: Sixtieth. My goodness. Let's see. Twenty-five is silver, fifty is gold… what's sixty?

IRVING: I think sixty is bacon.

ANNIE: *(Laughs; hugs Irving.)* You are the funniest boy in the whole world, Irving. The funniest.

(Footsteps are heard on stairs in kitchen.)

IRVING: *(Suddenly.)* Oh, God!

(He whips around and starts playing Chopin. Annie grabs the dish towel from the funnel. Esther Yanover enters the kitchen from downstairs.)

ESTHER: Could you not hear me yelling?

ANNIE: Did you call?

ESTHER: Could you not hear me?

ANNIE: Maybe Irving's practicing too loudly—

IRVING: What? You say something? Oh, hiii, mama. I didn't hear you come in…

ESTHER: Mr. Lies-to-His-Own-Mother! You heard me! *(Goes to intercom.)* What is the matter with this thing? It was completely dead. I couldn't hear a peep; and I screamed into it fifty times… *(Ear to intercom.)* I can hear customers…

(She rings bell, testing it. Moses goes to intercom, downstairs in store.)

MOSES: What? I'm busy with customers…

ESTHER: Testing, one two three four…

MOSES: Why are you playing games? We've got customers!

ESTHER: Cancel the call, Mosie. Go back to the customers…

(He does; Esther turns to Irving.)

ESTHER: One extra hour of practice.

(Irving playacts great anger. He punches the keyboard six times, shouts.)

IRVING: *No No No Nooooooo!*

ESTHER: Yes, yes, yes yesssssssss!

(Annie turns away; giggles.)

IRVING: This is the most unfair thing on the Planet Earth!

ESTHER: One more word from you and it goes up to one hour and fifteen minutes.

IRVING: *You wouldn't dare!!!*

ESTHER: *(Shocked.)* I wouldn't what???

IRVING: You heard me!

ESTHER: And I'll continue to hear you: practicing…for one hour and thirty minutes, until the store closes at five P.M.

(The bell rings at intercom.)

MOSES: *(From downstairs.)* Essie, for God's sake! It's packed down here…

ESTHER: Coming, Mosie. I'm going to tell you something about your son…if you dare to listen! *(She turns to Irving.)* I dare…and he will dare.

IRVING: An hour and a half?

ESTHER: An hour and a half. Want to try for two?

(Irving covers his mouth with one hand, to prevent himself from talking…so to speak. With the other hand, he plays Chopin. Esther nods triumphantly to Irving, and then to Annie. And then she exits. Irving continues to practice with one hand. He stares at Annie. Annie stares at Irving. She is dumbfounded. She holds back her laugh for a count of four…and then she explodes into laughter. The lights cross fade to store. Moses is stocking shelves. Annie enters with a glass of tea and a biscuit. She is prepared to outsmart Moses.)

ANNIE: I'd like to talk with you about Irving, Mr. Yanover.

MOSES: *(Looking up.)* Oh. Certainly, Annie.

ANNIE: I like him a great deal, you know.

MOSES: And he you. I can tell.

ANNIE: I think that Irving stays inside too much. With you and Mrs. Yanover in the store all the time, he just stays upstairs, by himself…never in the air…and all.

MOSES: It's true, Annie…

ANNIE: I was thinking that I should include him in on some of my plans… maybe even think things up that he and I could do together…outside… in the air and all…

MOSES: Sounds good. What sort of things, for example?

ANNIE: …Walks. We could walk together. I have an idea! Irving and I could walk to the movies on Saturday. He said he loves the movies. And I'm sure he wouldn't mind walking down and back. And I wouldn't mind going at all…

MOSES: That sounds fine…

ANNIE: There's an excellent double bill playing at the Algoma on Saturday. We could be back in plenty of time for me to help with supper…

MOSES: Fine. I think that's a fine idea…

ANNIE: You do?

MOSES: Yes I do. I'll treat you both.

ANNIE: You will?

MOSES: Absolutely. My pleasure…Have you mentioned this plan to Mrs. Yanover?

ANNIE: Oh, not yet. Should I?

MOSES: Uh, no…I'll handle it. Sometimes there's a way of introducing a new idea to people without actually announcing it. The trick is to make them think the idea is theirs, and not yours… *(Smiles.)* It's a system that's worked quite well over the last ten years with Irving, especially…When I want him to read a particular book, I never say "Irving, read this, it's great!" That would guarantee that he'd read five pages and hate it. Instead, I usually say something like "What a great book! It's way too hard for a ten-year old. But you might want to take a peek at it in five or six years!" *(Smiles.)* He'll have the book read, cover to cover, by noon, the next day… *(Pauses; exact same "reading" as Irving's of same line.)* It's exhausting, figuring these things out… *(Smiles.)* I'll take care of the movie, okay?

ANNIE: Okay.

(Annie exits. The Chopin continues, lightly, the lights cross fade again to living room; Esther, reading. Moses enters from store.)

MOSES: I had a very interesting talk with Annie, earlier…

ESTHER: And?

MOSES: She thinks Irving's looking a little pale.

ESTHER: Pale?

MOSES: Well he isn't rosy-cheeked…

ESTHER: It's Canada. It's twenty below zero…

MOSES: He is indoors all the time…

ESTHER: It's the middle of the winter…

MOSES: Some kids skate or play hockey…

ESTHER: What are you saying, Moses? Didn't Elsa Berkowitz's son fall through the ice?

MOSES: I'm not suggesting he take up hockey…

ESTHER: I didn't think so!

MOSES: Walks…

> *(Esther looks up.)*

MOSES: We're indoors all the time. He could go for walks.

ESTHER: With who?

MOSES: Annie volunteered…

ESTHER: To walk with Irving?

MOSES: To the movies…

ESTHER: An outdoor movie?

MOSES: To the Algoma, on Saturday. There's a John Wayne and a Roy Rogers on a double bill, for young people…

ESTHER: Well, I personally wouldn't allow it, but, if you've said "yes" already, I'll go along…

> *(Moses starts to speak, thinks better of it. Esther and Moses look at one another. A brief pause. The music stops. The lights cross fade to bedroom to Irving and Annie atop their beds. Irving is ecstatic.)*

IRVING: I can't believe you got permission! Did you have to lie?

ANNIE: I don't lie.

IRVING: Never?

ANNIE: Never.

> *(And with that, Annie leans over and switches out the bed lamp between them. Lights out. There is a pause. Annie switches light on again. Irving is startled.)*

ANNIE: Irving.

IRVING: What?

ANNIE: I did lie a little.

IRVING: I was worried, 'cause I lie a lot...all the time! What did you lie a little about?

ANNIE: Pete Lisanti...

IRVING: Who's Pete Lisanti?

ANNIE: My boyfriend. He's going to the movie with us...

IRVING: *(Not the best news he's ever heard.)* He is?

ANNIE: I left that part out with your father...

IRVING: With me, too...

ANNIE: Is it okay?

IRVING: I guess. If he's *your* boyfriend, he's my boyfriend, too...

ANNIE: My parents would kill me if they found out...

IRVING: Why?

ANNIE: They made me promise I wouldn't go out with him...

IRVING: You're going to break your promise?

ANNIE: Well, yuh...sometimes you get pushed into making promises you really never want to make in the first place...

IRVING: Sure, well, *sure.* But, a promise is a promise...

(Pete appears on stage, downstage of Annie and Irving, in the shadows. N.B. Room will soon become the cinema. Neither Annie nor Irving acknowledge Pete's presence, as yet.)

ANNIE: It's different. Pete's my boyfriend...

IRVING: I guess.

ANNIE: I mean really my *boyfriend.*

(Pete steps upstage to Annie, touches her cheek with his hand. She doesn't turn, but, instead, reaches up and touches his hand on her cheek.)

IRVING: You mean *dates!*

ANNIE: Dates. Dances...long walks...

IRVING: I know about those things...

ANNIE: Pete's a genius.

IRVING: Pete's a genius?

ANNIE: At hockey. He played for Tech until he graduated last year. His line was the best, two years straight, and he was the highest scorer, too...

IRVING: Did he go to the university?

ANNIE: Nooo, silly. He works nights at Algoma Steel, and he practices and plays during the daytime. He starts for the James Street Aces...He's the youngest starter...

IRVING: With Arnold Berkowitz.

ANNIE: When he makes the Detroit Red Wings, we're going to get married and move out of the Soo.

(Irving now turns and stares at Pete.)

IRVING: Does Pete like you a lot?

ANNIE: I think so.

IRVING: I like you a lot, too, you know…

ANNIE: Pete likes me in the romantic way…

IRVING: Oh, right…

(Annie and Irving walk from bedroom, put on coats, move downstage to Pete in area designated as lobby of Algoma Cinema. Lights shift with them. In the background, we hear the soundtrack from a segment of "Movietone News.")

ANNOUNCER'S VOICE: *(Offstage.)* "English and Canadian troops are known for their serious fighting spirit, but not so for our friends from down-under in Australia. Wherever the Aussie troops have gone, they have given rise to stories of their high spirits and high jinks…"

ANNIE: Irving, this is Pete; Pete, this is Irving…

IRVING: Annie talks about you all the time…She's told me *every*thing…

PETE: Don't believe it.

IRVING: I shouldn't have. You're a lot shorter than I thought…

ANNIE: Irving's got a lot of crust…

PETE: You're a lot tougher than I thought…

IRVING: This'll be rich… *(Sees the joke coming.)* How so?

PETE: I always thought of kids who play the piano in a certain way.

IRVING: Sissies?

PETE: Well, no, I wouldn't say "sissies," exactly…

IRVING: Jerks?

PETE: That's it: jerks. You must be a dinger of a pianist.

ANNIE: Oh, he is, Pete, really. You've just got to hear Irving play…

IRVING: You would?

PETE: You'd better believe it. I'll make a deal. I get to hear you play piano and you get to watch me play hockey…

IRVING: Great!

ANNIE: Pete's a genius at hockey! And Irving's a genius at piano, Pete, he really is…

PETE: Well, this is an historic meeting, two geniuses shake…

(They pump hands. Irving laughs. Lights flicker. We are now in the movie theatre. Irving slides between Annie and Pete. We hear: the sound of a John Wayne movie on tape, and the lights flicker on the three of them, brightly, as

they watch the movie, seated in a straight line, eyes straight ahead, staring widely. Pete's arm sneaks out around Annie. Irving sees; leans back against it. The film's soundtrack continues. Irving turns, discreetly, and stares at Pete's hand on Annie's shoulder, next to Irving's young face. Irving looks up at them as Annie and Pete face one another and kiss, deeply, passionately. Irving stares at them. Annie breaks from the kiss, somehow aware of Irving's staring. Pete pulls back, surprised. They whisper to one another.)

ANNIE: Are you hungry?

PETE: You want some popcorn?

IRVING: I wouldn't mind.

PETE: My treat.

IRVING: You sure?

PETE: Sure, I'm sure...

VOICE: *(From the darkness.)* Shhhhhh.

SECOND VOICE: *(From the darkness.)* Shhhhhh...

IRVING: *(Takes money.)* I'll be right back...

(Irving stands and walks out of the "row," whispering "Excuse me" as he goes. The lights (film) continue their flicker. The soundtrack continues, softly. Annie and Pete kiss again, now certain that Irving isn't with them, staring. Their kiss is long, deep, passionate. Their hands search each others' bodies. The lights cross fade to the living room. Irving sits reading a comic book. Esther stands ironing shirts.)

ESTHER: To me, a movie in the daytime is like eating chicken for breakfast.

IRVING: What's wrong with chicken for breakfast?

ESTHER: Don't talk disgusting.

IRVING: I think it's important for people to be prepared to eat new things...That's how you got me to eat squash. I hated squash, but, you convinced me to try...

ESTHER: I thought you still hated squash.

IRVING: That's not the point.

ESTHER: Tomorrow morning you get two scrambled eggs and one drumstick...

IRVING: Did you ever break a promise, Mama?

ESTHER: I would rather break an arm than a promise. Why?

IRVING: You never *ever* broke a promise?

ESTHER: Not a promise that counted...

IRVING: What promises count and what promises don't count?

ESTHER: What are you getting at, Mr. Beat-Around-The-Bush? What have you done?

IRVING: I'm just asking.

ESTHER: About what?

IRVING: Bacon.

ESTHER: You ate bacon?!

IRVING: I didn't! I didn't! I'd just like to know why I can't!

ESTHER: You have a funny way of asking...

IRVING: Why can't I?

ESTHER: Because my mother, your grandmother—*Alivoh, Shalom*—and your father's mother, your own grandmother, both made me promise that I would keep a Kosher home and to bring you up Jewish, and I promised, and that promise counts...So there'll always be Jews.

IRVING: There'll always be Jews, Mama, with or without bacon...

ESTHER: Mr. Know-It-All. You've read the papers? You know what's happening in Europe?

IRVING: You mean to tell me, mama, that if I eat bacon, there will be no more Jews in Europe?

ESTHER: Europe...North America, South America...the Planet Earth. That, my son, is exactly, what I mean to tell you... *(Suddenly.)* Are you watching the time?

(Irving runs into kitchen, looks at clock.)

IRVING: Oh, God, I'm late!

(Irving stands and runs to his coat. Esther helps bundle him up against the cold. Lights cross fade again: Lights and sound full again now in "cinema." Pete and Annie break from their embrace. Annie looks around for Irving. Irving squeezes into "row" carrying box of popcorn. He sits beside Annie. She smiles at him; leans over, kisses his cheek. Pete tousles Irving's hair. The three of them—Pete, Irving, Annie—stare straight ahead, wide-eyed, into the flickering light, and final dialogue of film, watching the film play out to its conclusion. Lights shift to stage apron. Irving, Pete, and Annie walk home from Algoma Cinema. Irving walks ahead, chatting, happily. Pete and Annie hold hands, nuzzle, giggle, absorbed in one another, somewhat oblivious to Irving's chirping chat.)

IRVING: That was my third movie with John Wayne...

PETE: My second...

ANNIE: *Our* second...

PETE: *Our* second.

IRVING: In all three movies he gets married at the end, but, to different women. You would think he could just stick with one, huh? My parents say that a man shouldn't get married unless he has one thousand dollars in his bank account. How much do you have in yours, Pete?

PETE: Well, not *quite* a thousand...

ANNIE: A thousand dollars?

PETE: *(Ironically.)* I may have to work some overtime at the plant.

ANNIE: *(Smiles.)* I could save up a thousand, easy. 'Course it'd take me about six-and-a-half years...

IRVING: Yuh, I'm nowhere near a thousand myself. I've got forty-three dollars and thirty cents saved, but that's going to piano lessons in Montreal. I'm going to study piano in Montreal, after university...You need a lot of money for university, too. That's why you shouldn't have too many children. How many children do you want, Pete?

PETE: Oh, I dunno, fifty...sixty...

ANNIE: *Peeeeeetttte!*

PETE: Why? I *like* kids!

IRVING: Come on, Pete, get serious. You could never have fifty or sixty kids. You'd wreck your hands, spanking them all... *(Giggles.)* I'll bet Pete's gonna spank his kids, huh?

ANNIE: Pete would never!

IRVING: Me, neither...

PETE: There's no need to hit a kid when all's ya hav'ta do, really, is turn him upside-down... *(Pete lifts Irving upside-down, holds him by his feet.)*

IRVING: Nice...

ANNIE: Pete!

IRVING: I really hate this...

PETE: *(Self-announcing.)* And Pete Lisanti, ladies and gentlemen, turns the kid right side up, quick as a Shick! *(Pete rights Irving.)*

IRVING: You'll make tremendous amounts of money, when you're a pro. I've read that many hockey players earn more than two thousand in just one season...

PETE: Oh, that's for sure. Eddie Shore made nearly ten thousand dollars last year alone...

IRVING: *(Whistles.)* Ten thousand dollars? Whewwww! You could get married five time more than John Wayne! Got your scarf!

(Irving grabs Pete's scarf; runs off. Pete chases. Lights cross fade to Emil Ilchak. Ilchak talks to Annie from across stage.)

ILCHAK: So, do you like your job, Anja?

(Annie stands, moves to her father, who enters carrying lunch-pail; end of workday.)

ANNIE: Yes, I do, very much…

ILCHAK: So, your papa knows something, yes?

ANNIE: Oh, yes, it was a good idea.

ILCHAK: And the Yanovers? It's a good family?

ANNIE: A *wonderful* family.

ILCHAK: I knew, from the beginning, that this job was going to work out. You cried and your Mama yelled, but I knew. A father knows what is best for his Annie.

(Father and daughter embrace. Lights shift to store. Moses Yanover is stocking a shelf with boxes of fresh, new merchandise. It is Sunday. Irving is off-stage, at the start of the scene, about to enter from the store's inventory closet with an armload of boxes. Moses calls off, to his son.)

MOSES: Spending my Sundays stocking shelves is one of my least favorite things about being in the dry goods business. I need you to read the number on this box for me. My eyes are gone…

(Irving enters, carrying boxes, which he places on counter.)

IRVING: Which shelf?

MOSES: Top shelf,…

IRVING: 640.

MOSES: Are you *kidding?* 640 is women's support hose and garter belts…*Oy vay*…Middle age is no picnic. First, the eyes; then, the mind…

(Irving reads number on box; laughs.)

MOSES: It's not funny.

(Moses takes boxes down from shelf. Irving giggles.)

MOSES: Imagine when Mr. Weisman gets home with what he thinks are his "usual" boxer shorts and Mrs. Weisman unpacks…

IRVING: *(Interrupting, happily.)* What? What? Ladies tights?

MOSES: Worse! *(Laughs.)*

IRVING: A garter belt?

MOSES: A dozen garter belts!

(Irving and Moses share a long laugh.)

MOSES: I'm glad that you spend Sundays with me. Otherwise, the day would be wasted… *(Smiles.)* But, this I like: just the two of us: two fellas… every Sunday morning…

IRVING: Can I ask you a question, Poppy? Fella to fella?

MOSES: Sure.

IRVING: How can you tell when somebody's in love?

MOSES: Somebody?

IRVING: Somebody. How can you tell?

MOSES: Oh, sometimes somebody's knees can get all wobbly when somebody looks at the somebody somebody's in love *with*. 'Course, it depends on a lot of things. I mean, there's Love and there's *Love*.

IRVING: Oh, I mean *Love*. People who get married sort of thing, like you and Mama. Do your knees go all wobbly when you look at her?

MOSES: Well, I…sometimes, sure.

IRVING: But not all the time?

MOSES: No, I would have to say no. But, this is strictly fella-to-fella talk…I mean, I wouldn't mention to your mother that I said that my knees didn't wobble all the time when I looked at her…and then there's the matter of your mother's knees, which certainly don't wobble every time she looks across at me, either…

IRVING: So, love is a now-and-then wobble?

MOSES: That's it, precisely…

IRVING: I thought so.

MOSES: You know, it's wonderful for me, Irving…watching you…being with you. *(Smiles.)* Some day, you will be quite a fountain pen.

IRVING: Yuhh… *(Looks up; admits.)* …I don't get it. *(Pauses, exclaims.)* Fountain pen?

MOSES: You mean you don't know the story? Your cousin Quentin?

IRVING: Who's cousin Quentin?

MOSES: He's really *my* cousin. Your second cousin on my mother's side of the family…a real *schmendrick,* Quentin. What Stanley Rosen is to you, Quentin Becker was to me.

IRVING: A bedbug.

MOSES: Two bedbugs.

(Irving giggles.)

MOSES: My uncle Sam Becker made money, so when *schmendrick* Quentin was *Bar Mitzvahed,* it was a huge affair. Every Jew in Toronto, plus most of the gentiles. My own Bar Mitzvah was thirty-five Jews at a dollar a head, so I was a little jealous…Anyway, the standard Bar Mitzvah present in those days was a fountain pen. I don't know why. It was the custom. If forty people came to your Bar Mitzvah, you could count on getting thirty fountain pens…which you would exchange in the shops later for something you wanted. Quentin must have gotten two hundred and fifty fountain pens.

IRVING AND MOSES: *(In unison; Moses stays put; Irving crosses to bedroom.)* That sounds like an exaggeration, but he certainly had his pockets crammed full of fountain pens when he stood up to make his speech…

(Lights cross fade, to bedroom. Irving takes over the telling of the story, nearing its completion. He enters bedroom, where Annie is in her bed ready for sleep. When Irving reaches his bed, he will snap on the bed lamp, so as to be certain that the best part of the story is heard properly by his audience: Annie.)

IRVING: You wouldn't know this on your own, but, it's the tradition that every Bar Mitzvah boy makes a speech to the congregation which has to start with the words: "Today I am a Man," because on the day of a boy's Bar Mitzvah, he, legally, in the Jewish laws, becomes a man. He becomes a full member of the congregation. He gets to sit downstairs with the men, because he's one of them. *(Suddenly.)* Are you awake?

(Irving leans over to Annie, who has been drifting into sleep.)

IRVING: Annie!

ANNIE: I'm listening! I'm listening!

IRVING: I'm just getting to the best part.

ANNIE: I'm listening.

IRVING: *So.* There's Quentin...pockets stuffed with pens...standing up in front of five hundred people...sweating like a disgusting pig and he screams out with this dopey voice of his, "Todayyyy...I ammm...a *fountain pennn!*"

ANNIE: He didn't?

IRVING: He did!

(Annie and Irving roar with laughter.)

ANNIE: It sounds like you and your father had a wonderful time together...

IRVING: Oh, yuh, we always do...It's more than wonderful. It's actually *two*derful.

ANNIE: *(Laughs.)* I think you're *ten*derful.

IRVING: Oh, yuh, well then you're *twent* derful...

(They both laugh again.)

IRVING: What's Pete?

ANNIE: Oh, Pete's a *hundra*ful...

IRVING: *(Slightly depressed by this computation.)* Yuh, I guess... *(Pauses.)* How come your father doesn't like Pete?

ANNIE: 'Cause Pete's Italian. My father thinks the Italians keep the Ukrainians poor. The Italians control all the work at Algoma Steel and force Ukrainians into terrible jobs...

IRVING: Is that true?

ANNIE: I don't think it's true... *(Pauses.)* God, don't ever let on I said that! Can you keep a secret?

IRVING: Do I look like I can't?

ANNIE: I know you can. *(Whispers.)* I think my father's totally wrong. I think the Italians are fine people. I've met Pete's mother and father and his brother Robert, and his sister Carmella, and they're really all fine people.

IRVING: So, why don't you bring your father to meet them?

ANNIE: Oh, don't talk crazy! My father won't have anything to do with anything that's Italian, period.

IRVING: I thought you said he loves opera?

ANNIE: He loves opera more than he loves me or my mother or anything else in the whole world...on the Planet Earth!

IRVING: But, all the great operas are Italian!

ANNIE: No they're not, silly! They're Canadian...

IRVING: They are not. They're Italian.

ANNIE: Irving, don't say that. My father would never listen to an opera if it were Italian...

IRVING: Annie, I should know, right. Music is my middle name...

ANNIE: Irving, are you trying to kid me? Because, if you are, this isn't very funny!

IRVING: I swear to you: Verdi, Puccini...all of them: Italians.

ANNIE: The names *sound* Italian...

IRVING: Because they're Italian. I swear to you. I promise never to eat bacon when I grow up, if I'm lying. *(Pauses; whispers.)* I'm planning to eat a great deal of bacon when I'm a man on my own...which is something *my* parents made *me* promise not to do...like your not seeing Pete, ever...

ANNIE: Oh, God, this is incredible news...

IRVING: I'm glad I was able to tell you...

ANNIE: Me, too. I really owe you a lot, Irving... *(Pauses.)* Irving?

IRVING: What?

ANNIE: You must never, ever in a million years let on that it was me who let on, but, your parents eat bacon all the time...

IRVING: Don't talk crazy! My mother would rather fall through the ice...

ANNIE: It's in the Chinese food they eat at the Ritz Cafe with the Rosens every Saturday night...

IRVING: That's what the brain-damaged *putz* Stanley Rosen said, but, he was just trying to get me in trouble...

ANNIE: It's true. It's the little red bits...

IRVING: No *wonder* I love the red bits! No *wonder!* God, Annie! How could they just *lie* to me? How could they just look me straight in the eye and lie to me? *How could they?*

ANNIE: They didn't exactly lie…It was more like, sort of breaking a law than a lie…like driving a little too fast?

IRVING: But they knew it was bacon: They knew they were breaking the law. If you break the law, you break the law. You don't break laws "a little"…That's a lot of crap!

ANNIE: Irving!

IRVING: Well, it is! How come they lied to me? How come?

ANNIE: I think we just have to accept the fact that sometimes parents have impossible sets of rules.

IRVING: You mean like with bacon?

ANNIE: Well, yes…like with bacon. Or the way my parents are with me…and Italians. They think that I should hate all Italians, just because they do…

IRVING: Except for the Italians in opera.

ANNIE: *(Suddenly.)* Do you think I should stop seeing Pete? Do you agree with my father?

IRVING: I think you should keep Pete Lisanti as your friend. That's what *I* think.

ANNIE: Irving, if you promise not to tell I did it, I'm going to get you a real meal of bacon. More bacon than you've ever seen… *(Pauses; then quickly.)* I think that children should have their own sets of rules… according to what *they* think is right and wrong, not their parents.

IRVING: What happens if parents find out about certain children having their own certain rules? Won't certain children get their behinds beaten black and blue?

ANNIE: Well, certain parents don't have to ever find out. It is possible for secrets to be kept secret, right?

IRVING: If you will cook me a bacon meal and never tell my parents, I will be your friend for life!

ANNIE: *(In Ukrainian.)* "Te brechaca mene."

IRVING: What does that mean?

ANNIE: That is "Kiss my behind" in Ukrainian.

IRVING: *That's* "Kiss my behind" in Ukrainian? "Te brechaca mene?" So, what's [Ukrainian words spoken at her arrival.]…what I said to you on your first day?

ANNIE: You don't want to know.

IRVING: Oh, God, I do, I really do!

(Annie whispers horrifying obscenity into Irving's ear: a shared private moment. Shocked and thrilled.)

IRVING: I said *that???*

(He faints. Blackout. Lights up in store. Mrs. Ilchak enters. Mrs. Yanover notices her.)

ESTHER: Can I help you?

MRS. ILCHAK: Hello.

MOSES: *(Realizes.)* You are Annie's Mother! Of course! That face. I know that face...Come, come. We'll go upstairs and have some tea. Annie will be delighted...

MRS. ILCHAK: *(Frightened.)* No please! I'll see Annie at home next Sunday. *(Mrs. Ilchak produces a large pudding.)*

ESTHER: What's this?

MRS. ILCHAK: This is for you, for your family. We are pleased, Mr. Ilchak and myself, that you took our Annie in your home. We want you to have this, from us.

ESTHER: That is very nice of you... *(Looks under cloth cover of bowl at pudding.)* Uh, what is this, exactly?

MRS. ILCHAK: A pudding.

ESTHER: A pudding! How very sweet! Thank you...

MOSES: That's very nice of you, Mrs. Ilchak...

MRS. ILCHAK: You're both so wonderful to Annie. She tells me things. I thank you both. *(Smiles; nods to pudding.)* I wish it could be more.

ESTHER: Don't be silly. A pudding is wonderful...

MOSES: It looks delicious...

MRS. ILCHAK: I must go.

ESTHER: Whenever you're in the neighborhood, shopping, please, stop in...

MOSES: Please, do...

(Mrs. Ilchak smiles, shyly; exits the scene.)

MOSES: Such a nice face, huh? Just the spitting image of Annie...

ESTHER: A pudding yet...

MOSES: *(Reaching across for a taste.)* Let me try some...

ESTHER: Are you crazy? You would put a Ukrainian pudding in your mouth?

MOSES: You can't just throw it out.

ESTHER: I'll give it to Annie.

(Blackout. Lights up on Pete, Annie, and Irving, staring out front, across an imagined Lake Superior, apron of stage.)

PETE: See those lights—out *there!* That's the United States...

ANNIE: It's still called Sault Ste. Marie…It's probably not very different from our Sault Ste. Marie…

IRVING: Ah, yes, but Sault Ste. Marie, Michigan, doesn't have a King in England who quit…

PETE: Now, that is true…

ANNIE: How did you know that, Irving?

IRVING: I hear. I read…My father read a book on King Edward the Second that he thought was great, but way too hard for me. He left it in the living room, by accident… *(Proudly.)* He was nuts. The book was a cinch. I only had to look up five or six words in the dictionary…"Abdicate," "Monarchy," "Despotic," uhhh, "Xenophobic" and a couple of others… *(Annie and Pete stare, amazed.)*

IRVING: What are you staring at? *(Blows into his hands.)* How come we're parked here?

ANNIE: No reason.

IRVING: You two wanna do more smooching?

ANNIE: Irving!

PETE: Yuh.

IRVING: For how long?

PETE: Six minutes' worth…

IRVING: I'll take a walk…

PETE: You will?

IRVING: Yuh, sure…

ANNIE: Keep your mittens on.

IRVING: Yuh, sure… *(Tightens his coat around him.)* I could die doing this…six minutes in the dark forty below zero, wind raging across Lake Superior… *(Shrugs.)* …buttt, you'll never hear *meee* complain…
(Blackout. After a moment, lights up in living room. Moses sits reading the Sunday newspaper; Esther cooks the Sunday meal. The radio plays news from the Front under scene.)

MOSES: I don't like what I read in my Sunday paper…
(Esther looks across; smiles.)

RADIO ANNOUNCER: *(Under scene.)* The Suez Canal is seriously threatened by a surprise Nazi attack. The first meeting of German and British armies is being fought now on the deserts of North Africa. On these same grounds, the British forces had their first victory, just last winter, with a three hundred mile mechanized march across Italian Libya, capturing and killing one hundred thousand Italians…

MOSES: And I don't like what I hear on my radio, either…

(Esther goes to radio, switches it off. She then goes to Moses and takes newspaper from him; kisses him, playfully.)

ESTHER: Smile, Mosie, it's a nice day, the house is clean, the store is doing well…we've got lots to smile about.

MOSES: Is this Esther Yanover I'm hearing?

ESTHER: My spirits are high. It's true.

(Moses sits at dining table. Esther sits on his lap. She smiles seductively.)

MOSES: *(Suspiciously.)* Well, what's cooking, Esther?

ESTHER: There's nothing cooking…

MOSES: Except?

ESTHER: Except I'm feeling good…I'm glad that it's sunny out and I think you're a good looking fellow.

MOSES: Whoa!

ESTHER: "Whoa" is for horses…

MOSES: "Hay" is for horses…When you tell me I'm a good looking fellow, I know you've got something important. So *say!*

ESTHER: I was thinking, that since Annie has worked out so well, maybe she should wear a uniform. You know, nothing fancy, just a plain black dress.

(Moses looks up at his wife again, facing her fully.)

ESTHER: And, also, I was thinking that maybe we should get a little apron for her…white…and maybe a white collar for the little black dress…

(Pause. Moses has looked away, pensively.)

ESTHER: Are you listening?

MOSES: I'm listening.

ESTHER: Don't say "no" yet, please.

MOSES: I won't say no.

ESTHER: I was also thinking we could get a little brass bell for the dining room table. It's nicer than calling her. It's not just because Pearl Rosen is doing all these things. It's because it would be like a *promotion* for Annie…from live-in-girl to…like a live-in-…well…maid.

MOSES: Is that it?

ESTHER: That's it.

MOSES: Over my dead body! I will *not* have a maid in a uniform in the house and that's *it!*

ESTHER: *(After a pause.)* So, that means "no"?

MOSES: Yes, Esther, that means "no"… *(After a long pause.)* Well, am I still a good looking fellow?

(There is a pause.)

ESTHER: I've seen better.

(Blackout. Lights up in living room. Moses standing near the door. He holds winter coats, about to go out for the evening. Jive music plays on radio. Annie is drying dishes, sways to the music.)

MOSES: Esther, it's almost twenty after. We're going to be late...

(Irving is at table reading comic book. He sways to music as well.)

IRVING: Ohh, are you going out, Poppy?

ESTHER: *(Entering, adjusting earring.)* We're going out to eat with the Rosens. You know that. What's the surprise? And why are you not practicing? Did you hear me, Mr. Wax-Gets-In-Your-Ears?

IRVING: In a second I'll practice...I promise...

ESTHER: I'll promise that when we honk our horn at the Rosens, we'll hear Stanley, upstairs, at the keyboard...

IRVING: Yuh, sure. He waits for the honk and then he plays...

ESTHER: This, Stanley Rosen does not do. Stanley Rosen is dedicated to his piano...

IRVING: Stanley Rosen is the only person in life I truly detest...

ESTHER: Irving!

MOSES: Irving!

IRVING: *(To Annie, in kitchen doorway.)* You've heard of Hitler?

(Annie nods.)

IRVING: *Much* nicer than Stanley Rosen...

ESTHER: Irving!

MOSES: Irving!

ESTHER: You checked the back door?

MOSES: I checked the back door...

ESTHER: You checked the side window?

MOSES: I checked the side windows. A burglar would have to break into this house with a *tank*.

ESTHER: Bite your tongue! *(To Irving.)* Thirty minutes of scales or no *Fibber Magee. (To Annie.)* And absolutely no *The Shadow Knows* under any circumstance, do you understand?

ANNIE: I would never...

ESTHER: I wouldn't want any more nightmares in this house.

ANNIE: I would never.

ESTHER: You hear me Irving Yanover?

IRVING: Don't worry, don't worry.

ESTHER: Kiss your father...

MOSES: Kiss your mother...

(Esther and Moses kiss Irving; and they exit.)

ESTHER: Lights out at nine and no talking.

ANNIE: I promise.

IRVING: I promise. Do I have to practice scales?

ESTHER: Young man!

IRVING: Okay, okay…

(The Yanovers exit. There is a beat. Irving goes to the window; looks out.)

IRVING: They're in the car…he's starting the engine…they're backing out…they're going!

(Irving runs to the radio, switches station. We hear: "Who knows what evil lurks in the hearts of men? The Shadow knows" Annie snaps radio off, and Annie and Irving snap into action. They are preparing a meal of bacon for Irving. Annie lights the stove, Irving runs into the bedroom and runs back into the kitchen carrying a package of bacon, which he tears open. Bacon was hidden outside bedroom window.)

ANNIE: Careful where you throw the wrapper! No evidence!

(Irving stows wrapper under his bed.)

IRVING: Oh, God, this is going to be great! This is going to be *great!*

(Annie puts the strips of bacon on to the skillet. Irving bounces up and down in joyous anticipation. We hear: the sound of bacon frying. Irving bounces, enthusiastically.)

IRVING: Once, I had chocolate-covered orange slices which got me very excited, until I ate them. It wasn't chocolate-covered orange slices at all. It was chocolate covered orange-*peel,* which is disgusting… *(Sudden ecstasy.)* Smell it! Smell it! *(Sudden panic.)* It's not burning, is it?

ANNIE: It's fine. It's perfect! Here's the first piece… *(She brings a slice of cooked bacon to Irving, dancing around him in tantalizing fashion: cruel master and kindly pup.)*

IRVING: What an odor, Annie! God—You've got to be the best cook in the whole world…on the Planet Earth! *(Takes a bite; realizes.)* I just burned my mouth, terribly.

ANNIE: I'll get you some water…

IRVING: Oh, God, no. Not with bacon! You'll spoil the taste!

ANNIE: You like it?

IRVING: Oh, God, I love it? You know something, Annie?

ANNIE: What?

IRVING: I have never seen the advantages of growing old as clearly as I do tonight.

ANNIE: What are you talking about?

IRVING: To be able to shop what you want, to be able to cook what you want, to be able to eat what you want: That's worth growing old for... *(Smiles.)* Have a smell. Isn't it beautiful?

ANNIE: It's a little heavy...Maybe I should open a window?

IRVING: No! I want the smell to linger. Mmmmmmm mmmmmm. What a treat, Annie, what a treat. Sitting here, Annie, with this smell of perfect bacon in my nostrils, I am very happy, Annie...I am a very happy young man...

(Suddenly, the sound of door closing in distance; then we hear: footsteps on stairs. Suddenly.)

IRVING: *What's that noise?*

ANNIE: *What's what noise?*

(The sound of somebody on the staircase.)

IRVING: *They're coming back!*

ANNIE: *They're coming back!*

IRVING: They're coming back.

ANNIE: They're coming back.

(Annie and Irving scurry about, trying to wash the pan, clear the plate, etc.)

IRVING: *Oh, my God!*

ANNIE: *Oh, my God!*

IRVING: *What are we going to do?*

ANNIE: *What are we going to do?*

(They run into the bedroom. Annie throws pan out of window.)

IRVING: Into bed, into bed!

ANNIE: Into bed! Into bed!

(They leap under covers.)

IRVING: Go to sleep. Maybe God will be kind! *(Sniff.)* The house smells like a pig.

(There is a pause. Esther enters. She calls out.)

ESTHER: I'm back. Your father forgot his wallet. Irving, I... *(Stops; sniffs.)* It smells like a pig in here... *(Realizes.)* Oh. my God... *(She turns and runs to the window, yells.)* Mosie, get in here!

IRVING: Oh, God, oh, God, oh, God...

ESTHER: Irving Yanoverrrr! Annabell Ilchakkkkk! Get...into...this... kitchennn...immediatelyyyyy!

(Irving pulls the covers from his head, looks at Annie, who pulls the covers from her head. Moses enters the kitchen, from the staircase. He carries pan that Annie threw out of window.)

MOSES: What? What is this?

ESTHER: Sniff, why don't you?

MOSES: What? *(Sniffs.)* What the hell is that? It smells like a pig in here.

ESTHER: Uh huh.

MOSES: Is it?

ESTHER: It certainly is.

MOSES: Irving Yanoverrrr!

(Irving and Annie stand in bedroom doorway.)

ANNIE: Please, Mrs. Yanover, it was really all my fault...

MOSES: Do you know the meaning of the word "trust"? Either of you? Do you?

ANNIE: Please, Mr. Yanover, it's really all my fault. It is really all my fault...

ESTHER: Bacon, today; tomorrow, what? *What?* My mother is spinning in her grave...

MOSES: *My* mother is spinning in *Toronto!*...

ESTHER: I should have known when I first set eyes on you, Annie Ilchak. I should have known! I will have to think about whether you can stay in this house with this family, young lady. I will have to think...

MOSES: A boy who is dishonest and untrustworthy to his own mother and father: That's what you are, Irving Yanover. I am going to have to think about this. Now, go to bed... *(Yells.)* Both of you! *Quickly!*

(Annie and Irving leap into their beds; terrified. Esther and Moses pace the floor of the bedroom: a chorus of complaint. They complain in unison.)

MOSES: You know how I hate to lose my temper, you two, but, I have. It's gone. There is a war in Europe and Hitler is doing terrible terrible things to Jewish people. This is no time for you to be untrustworthy. You gave us your word and your word was believed...*trusted.* You make me feel foolish for giving you so much trust...permission and money for movies, too, *movies!* You have upset your mother, terribly! Terribly! I'm not complaining for me, but for your mother, Irving. For Mrs. Yanover, Annie. She has given you a great deal of her time and a great deal of her faith...her *trust!* I don't care for myself, so much, about these things, but I will not have Mrs. Yanover's feelings hurt! Are you listening? Are you listening?

ESTHER: It's not like me to lose my temper, as you well know, but *I am furious!* A *milchadicha* frying pan used for bacon, yet! Bacon! After the lessons I gave you, Annie Ilchak! After the years of upbringing, Irving Yanover. What if the Rosens came in here and sniffed? They would have known? What if your grandmother made a surprise visit. What if my own mother—*Alivoh, shalom*—looked down upon such a scene from

Heaven??? It's not for me I'm so angry, but for your father, Irving…For Mr. Yanover, Annie! That man trusted you both. That man gave you money for the movies! Have you even been *going* to the movies? *Hmmmmmm?* Are you listening? Are you listening?

(They cross through the bedroom a final time, and exit. After a pause, Irving turns on bedlamp. Annie is weeping and Irving is weeping.)

ANNIE: She's going to fire me, isn't she?

IRVING: She won't. I know she won't.

ANNIE: She fired all the others!

IRVING: My mother never fired anybody. They all quit. My mother would never fire you, Annie.

ANNIE: That's how she sees me: like "Miss Cheese" and the others…

IRVING: No, she doesn't!

ANNIE: She does! Irving, she does!

IRVING: How can he call me dishonest when he was on his way to eat bacon at the Ritz Cafe, *himself?* How can he, Annie?

ANNIE: How can my father lie to me about Italian opera?

IRVING: I wasn't going to tell you, but the man who discovered the stars was Italian. We studied him at school. Italians are really great people!

ANNIE: *(Weeps.)* You see? Irving, you see?

IRVING: I think you should see Pete whenever you want and I should eat bacon whenever I want. And that's the truth!

ANNIE: To hell with their goddamn rules!

IRVING: To hell with their goddamn rules! *(Giggles.)* I never heard you swear in English before…

ANNIE: I can swear in three different languages…

IRVING: English…Ukrainian…

ANNIE: …and Italian…

IRVING: Oh, right…

ANNIE: *Ah bah fah Napola!*

IRVING: What's that?

ANNIE: "Go to Hell" in Italian…

IRVING: *(Giggles.)* That is so nifty! *(Suddenly.)* You know something Annie? You could bring Pete here, to my parents' house, to visit and all…

ANNIE: Oh, noooo…

IRVING: But, you could. They've no rules against Italians here…

ANNIE: I would never dare…But, you know something, Irving? I could take you to my house for a totally legal bacon meal. You could come home with me some Sunday…if you dare…

IRVING: If I dare? Are you kidding? I dare...You're a genius, Annie. *(Pauses thoughtfully.)* You know something, Annie. I'm going to stop talking to my parents. I'm never going to talk to them again, not until they tell me why they can eat bacon and I can't...

(Irving moves into living room. Lights shift with him. Esther and Moses stand at kitchen door, worried, smiling. Irving walks silent past them.)

MOSES: You're going to school?

(Irving gets his coat, wordlessly.)

MOSES: You're still not talking?

(Irving puts on his cap; mittens, arranges his bookbag. Esther offers a polished, red apple.)

ESTHER: Would you like to take an apple, for later?

(Irving is tempted. He silently fetches the apple.)

ESTHER: You're still not talking?

(Irving calls across the house—and across his parents—to Annie.)

IRVING: I'm off for school. Bye, Annie...

ANNIE: *(Calls from bedroom.)* Bye, Irving...

(Irving exits the house, out front door, slamming same. There is a pause. Esther and Moses turn, at the same time, look at one another.)

ESTHER: He's still not talking.

MOSES: He's still not talking.

(Annie exits bedroom, crosses into kitchen. Moses is at left of kitchen door.)

MOSES: Irving's just left for school...

ESTHER: *(Right of kitchen door.)* We'll be going down to the shop to open up...

(Annie passes them, wordlessly, shoving them aside. She begins washing Irving's breakfast dishes in kitchen. To Moses: a whisper.)

ESTHER: She's still not talking, either...

MOSES: She's still not talking, either...

(Lights shift to store. Irving enters, starts stacking boxes. Moses calls across to him and moves to store; enters.)

MOSES: It's very nice of you to help out in the store; even though you're not talking...

(Irving continues to stack boxes, wordlessly. Moses crosses to Esther, who sits at table. Esther is reading a book.)

MOSES: He still won't talk to me.

ESTHER: *(Not looking up.)* He will, sooner or later.

MOSES: Why do you say that?

ESTHER: *(Not looking up.)* Because he will...

MOSES: How do you know that?

ESTHER: Because it stands to reason...

MOSES: Well, it's almost a week now...

ESTHER: You think I don't know that?

MOSES: It doesn't seem to upset you...

ESTHER: You didn't notice my book is upside down?

(He turns her book right-side-up.)

MOSES: I noticed... (Sighs.) It's really quite simple. He knows we've lied to him. He knows we have a double standard. He knows we've punished him severely for something we do ourselves.

ESTHER: (Taps table with fingernail ends, for emphasis.) But not in the house!

MOSES: That's a pretty complicated notion for a ten-year-old. Now that I think about it, it's a pretty complicated notion for a forty-one-year-old...

ESTHER: You're forty-two...

MOSES: (Slaps hand down on tabletop, in disgust.) Please, don't do that!

ESTHER: So? What do you suggest? You're the man. I'm just the woman...

MOSES: That is so *annoying* when you do that!

(Mr. Ardenshensky "knocks on door" to store. He is extremely old. He carries a brown paper bag. He is drenched from the rain.)

ARDENSHENSKY: (Offstage.) Yanover? Are you here or are you closed?

(Moses calls down from front window.)

MOSES: It's a little late. Who is that?

ARDENSHENSKY: Ardenshensky. It's freezing down here. There is ice on my eyebrows!

MOSES: (To Esther.) It's old Ardenshensky... (To Ardenshensky.) I'll be right down, Ardenshensky...

ESTHER: Good. We can talk to Ardenshensky. He knows everything. You keep him amused till I get there. I'll make some tea.

(Lights shift as Moses crosses to shop. Jacob Ardenshensky enters, dripping wet.)

MOSES: Here, Ardenshensky, wipe off with this towel...

ARDENSHENSKY: I should wipe off with new merchandise?

MOSES: It's last year's model. You shouldn't worry, Ardenshensky. You'll catch your death. Wipe...

ARDENSHENSKY: A man of my age doesn't *catch* his death. Death, to a man of my age, is an easy grounder. You just fall on it.

MOSES: What are you talking about, Ardenshensky?

ARDENSHENSKY: Baseball, Yanover, baseball...

MOSES: What do you know from baseball? A man like you...

ARDENSHENSKY: What do you know from death? A man like *you.*

MOSES: What brings you out in a storm?

ARDENSHENSKY: I ripped my sheet.

MOSES: You only have one?

ARDENSHENSKY: How many should I have? I'm not in the sheet business, *you are!*

MOSES: Was it defective?

ARDENSHENSKY: Possibly.

MOSES: Are you sure that you bought it from me, Ardenshensky? I haven't seen you in the store for twenty years…

ARDENSHENSKY: *(Slams bag down on countertop.)* That's the sheet!

MOSES: That's the sheet?

ARDENSHENSKY: It ripped. Sarah was making our bed and it ripped. About fifteen minutes ago. I fired right on over here.

(Displays sheet, in brown paper bag. Yanover holds back a laugh.)

MOSES: What can I do for you? I'll be happy to give you a refund…

ARDENSHENSKY: Did I say anything about a refund?

MOSES: What can I do for you?

ARDENSHENSKY: I'm back in the market.

MOSES: *(Smiles.)* Oh. I have here a sheet that is fortified with pure nylon. This sheet's guaranteed for thirty years or double your money back…this sheet is built for hard use…

ARDENSHENSKY: I'm seventy-seven years old, Yanover. What kind of "hard use" are you talking? In thirty years, I won't be needing double my money, I'll be needing a *miracle!* How much?

MOSES: Forget it, it's a gift.

ARDENSHENSKY: In this life, Yanover, if you *take* a gift, you have to *give* a gift. I would prefer not to get involved, thank you. What's your best price?…

MOSES: For this sheet? Six dollars.

ARDENSHENSKY: A first price is never a best price.

MOSES: *(Laughs lovingly.)* Ah, but for you, Ardenshensky, I started right at the bottom…But I can go lower. Make me an offer…

ARDENSHENSKY: There is a philosophical-Talmudical question afoot here, Yanover: Should a man of seventy-seven get involved with a sheet that is designed for thirty years? Or have you got something that is, maybe, one-sixth as good—that will last one sixth the time and cost one-sixth the price?

MOSES: A *dollar?*

ARDENSHENSKY: I'm not a rich man, Yanover…

MOSES: Cash or charge…

ARDENSHENSKY: Charge is *Goyim-nachas.* Jacob Ardenshensky pays cash…

MOSES: One dollar, cash…

(Esther enters, hands him a glass of tea.)

ESTHER: Good to see you, Mister Ardenshensky…

ARDENSHENSKY: *(Smiles at Esther.)* You look very well, Mrs. Yanover…

ESTHER: Thank you. You're looking very well yourself, Mr. Ardenshensky. You also look drenched. Here, dry off… *(Passes a towel to Ardenshensky.)*

ARDENSHENSKY: No, I'm dry as a bone, already.

ESTHER: No, no. Just in case…wipe your hair again. It couldn't hurt…

ARDENSHENSKY: For you, I'll do it. I don't know how you've made a living, the way you both waste new towels…and your husband's letting sheets go way below cost…

ESTHER: Well, easy come, easy go, Mr. Ardenshensky. And how is Mrs. Ardenshensky? Anything new?

ARDENSHENSKY: Very little beyond this sheet, Mrs. Yanover…

MOSES: We sold him inferior goods…many years ago.

ARDENSHENSKY: Anything new with you, Mrs. Yanover?

ESTHER: Well, Mr. Ardenshensky, I'm glad you should ask, I think we're having a little trouble with our Irving…

ARDENSHENSKY: Schoolwork?

ESTHER: Bacon.

MOSES: Irving insists on eating bacon…

ARDENSHENSKY: A Jewish boy insists on eating bacon?

ESTHER AND MOSES: *(In unison; in shame.)* I know…I know…

ARDENSHENSKY: So, tell him not to…

MOSES: Jacob, it's a mess…

ESTHER: We lied to our son…

MOSES: Esther!

ESTHER: Well, it's true, we did. He wanted to eat bacon and we told him that Jews don't, but, he found out we do…in the fried rice and the egg foo yong at the Ritz Cafe…

ARDENSHENSKY: Oh, the Ritz Cafe. Nothing but "traif," the worst…

MOSES: Nevertheless, we all eat there…

ARDENSHENSKY: *(In shame.)* I know, I know…

ESTHER: He found out…

ARDENSHENSKY: Well, really, I mean, this is 1941…It's not so terrible, really, I mean really, it's only in the egg foo yong and the fried rice…

MOSES: We know it's not so terrible, but children have other ideas.

ARDENSHENSKY: Oh, well, children…

MOSES: That's not the worst.

ARDENSHENSKY: Oh. Tell me the worst.

MOSES: He and the live-in girl did it together...

ARDENSHENSKY: *What?*

ESTHER: We caught them...

MOSES: We came home early...

ESTHER: Mosie forgot his wallet...we turned around...

MOSES: We caught them at it...

ESTHER: In the kitchen...

ARDENSHENSKY: In the kitchen?

MOSES: They ran into the bedroom...

ARDENSHENSKY: How old is the girl?

ESTHER: Fifteen...

ARDENSHENSKY: And your son?

MOSES: Ten and a half...

ARDENSHENSKY: Ten and a half years old? That's all?

ESTHER: He's bright for his age...

ARDENSHENSKY: Doing it? In the kitchen? With the live-in girl?

ESTHER: Cooking bacon, Mister Ardenshensky, cooking bacon!

ARDENSHENSKY: Cooking bacon?

MOSES: What the hell did you think we were telling you?

ARDENSHENSKY: I'm not sure...

ESTHER: The house was full of smoke...

MOSES: It smelled like a pig in there...

ARDENSHENSKY: So, what did you do?

MOSES: We punished them.

ESTHER: We threatened terrible things and we punished them...

ARDENSHENSKY: Was it before or after the Ritz Cafe information reached him?...

MOSES: After. But he must have known, before. That's why he probably felt free to cook the bacon...

ESTHER: He's stopped talking...

MOSES: Her, too...

ESTHER: Both of them...

ARDENSHENSKY: Not a word?

MOSES: A few words...

ESTHER: It's been nearly a week.

ARDENSHENSKY: Well, getting children to keep strictly Kosher in this day and age...I don't know...Things are changing, Yanover. My own grandson ate a pork chop and my son, Allen, took a strap to him. It was exactly the same thing. My Allen is a shellfish eater. The boy knew... *(Pauses.)* I'll tell you what I told Allen...

MOSES: Please, Mr. Ardenshensky, I'm desperate. My son won't talk to me...

ARDENSHENSKY: I told Allen "Being Jewish is bigger than a pork chop..."

MOSES: *(After a long pause.)* I see what you mean, Mr. Ardenshensky. Thank you very much, Mr. Ardenshensky, thank you.

ARDENSHENSKY: So, you'll let me exchange this sheet? *(He holds up paper bag.)*

MOSES: Keep the nylon-fortified and take two more from the same range. It's not a gift, it's an even exchange. A good piece of advice is well worth three sheets... *(Laughs, waves sheets away.)*

ARDENSHENSKY: Very very generous. When your husband opened this store, I said to my wife "Yanover is a fine boy. He'll go far." Luckily, you're still young and there's still time...

ESTHER: *(Into intercom.)* Don't either of you move! We're coming right up!
(Lights shift to Annie and Irving in living room, frightened.)

IRVING: Be tough, Annie. You know what it says in the newspaper: "War Is Hell"...

ANNIE: Just don't you start being a wiseacre!

IRVING: *Me?* Oh, God, here they come!
(Esther and Moses enter the living room. Irving and Annie move silently about the room, pretending to busy themselves in activity: Annie dusts, Irving stacks his piano scores, etc. Esther starts to speak; loses her courage.)

ESTHER: Your father will speak for both of us.

MOSES: *(Amazed; looks at Esther who shrugs; looks at Irving; speaks.)* There have been certain misunderstandings that want to be cleared up. You mother and I are sure that you and Annie are both sorry that you cooked bacon in this house, and your mother and I are both sorry that we lost our tempers. We love you both and we want you to talk. We would like life to continue as normal. If you will accept *our apology,* we will accept yours. *(There is a silence.)*

ANNIE: I accept. Thank you.
(Irving is silent; Annie yells at him.)

ANNIE: Irving!

IRVING: *(Talks for the first time in a week.)* Okay. It's a deal. But, on one condition.
(Esther and Moses exchange a smile. Irving and Annie exchange a smile.)

IRVING: On Sunday, when Annie goes home for dinner with her family, she was thinking it might be fun for me to come along for the visit with her…since you two are always pushing me toward trying new things and I've never been in Annie's house before…

MOSES: That sounds like a great idea. We could drive you ourselves when we go over to eat with the Rosens…

ESTHER: We're going to their house! Not to the Ritz Cafe.

MOSES: Right…Have you checked with Annie?

IRVING: Uh would it be alright with you if I came along with you on Sunday? To your parents' house to visit and all?

ANNIE: Sure, that'd be great. My parents are dying to meet you…

ESTHER: And how about *my* permission?

IRVING: Are you giving permission?

ESTHER: Only if you're giving kisses…

IRVING: Blackmail?

ESTHER: Precisely…

IRVING: Then, I've got no choice… *(He kisses his mother; giggles.)* How come you eat bacon in restaurants and then punish me for eating it at home? *(There is a small silence.)*

ESTHER: Ask your father.

IRVING: Poppy, how come you yourself eat bacon in restaurants and then you…

MOSES: *(Interrupting.)* I heard the question.

IRVING: You like me to keep talking?

MOSES: Is this what I think it is?

IRVING: Precisely.

MOSES: *(Sighs.)* Go get your coat. We're taking a walk. The subject for tonight's walk is "The Double Standard"…Get my coat and your coat. *(Annie smiles. Irving runs for the coats. Esther looks at her husband; smiles happily.)*

ESTHER: He's talking.

(Moses starts to talk, thinks better of it; shrugs. Irving hands him his coat, which he puts on.)

MOSES: Forty-below-zero and I'm stepping outside to tell my son I can't be trusted. *(To Irving.)* You ready?

IRVING: Let's hit it.

(Music: Chopin. Irving and Moses exit. Annie crosses to Pete, opposite side of stage. Irving joins them. Light shift during move. Irving talks to Pete and Annie, chirping enthusiastically. Annie seems depressed, secretive, mysterious.)

IRVING: This is the most nifty weekend of my life, really…Us all going to the movies today, and Annie and I going to her parents' tomorrow for you-know-what. No work in the store, but I still get my dollar-fifty… *(Realizes Pete and Annie are depressed.)* What's with you two? Something wrong?

PETE: I think you'd better go to the movies without us, Irving…

IRVING: How come?

PETE: Annie and I have got a lot to talk about…

IRVING: We can skip the movies. We can just go someplace else, where talking's okay…

PETE: We want to talk, alone, Irving…

IRVING: Without me?

PETE: Yuh.

IRVING: How come? Did I do something wrong?

PETE: Uh uh…We just have to talk…All right?

IRVING: *(Sees that Annie is weeping.)* Is Annie crying?

PETE: No…Annie is not crying.

ANNIE: I'm not crying, Irving. Pete and I just have to talk about something. You go in. We'll be waiting right here on the sidewalk as soon as the movie's over…

IRVING: I don't wanna go in alone…

ANNIE: Please, Irving…

IRVING: *(Sternly.)* I don't think that Annie should be unhappy, Pete…

ANNIE: I'm not unhappy, Irving. Thank you for worrying, but I'm really fine. Really. Please, go in…

IRVING: I don't like this… *(He backs toward movie theatre, away from Pete and Annie.)*

ANNIE: Thanks, Irving…

PETE: Thanks, kid…

IRVING: I really hate this…Tomorrow's still on, right?

ANNIE: Of course, Irving…

IRVING: It better be…

(Irving is about to cry. Instead, he turns and runs away from Annie and Pete. He runs to his bed, hops under the covers. Lights shift with him. Annie goes to her bed, gets under covers. Pete exits. There is a moment's pause. In the darkness we hear Irving's voice; whispered.)

IRVING: Annie?

ANNIE: What?

IRVING: You mad at me or something?

ANNIE: No, 'course not!

(Irving turns on the bed lamp. Lights up in bedroom, Irving leans across from his bed to Annie, who lies atop her bed, wide awake.)

IRVING: What's the matter?

ANNIE: I'm just nervous about going to my parents' house...tomorrow.

IRVING: You shouldn't be nervous. It's totally legal. No bacon in *this* house. Eating bacon at your parents' house isn't in *this* house, so...

ANNIE: That's not it, Irving. It's something else...

IRVING: Are you and Pete fighting with each other?

ANNIE: Pete and I have some really big news that is making us both really nervous...

IRVING: Oh, *great!* Did he get picked by the Red Wings?

ANNIE: Irving, this is the deepest darkest secret I've ever told you, so you better not even breathe a *hint*, okay?

IRVING: Sure, Annie, sure! What is it?

ANNIE: Pete and I are getting married, very very soon...

IRVING: Very very *sooon?* Why, Annie, *why?*

ANNIE: Irving, for *some* things, you're just really too young, okay?
(Annie leans back on her bed, hands behind her head, worried. Irving leans back on his bed, heartbroken; betrayed. He turns away from Annie; faces front. He stands, crosses to piano. Lights cross fade to living room. Music in, immediately. The sound of Irving practicing Chopin, on tape. Esther and Moses enter, exhausted, in bathrobes.)

ESTHER: *(Calls out to Irving.)* So early you're practicing?

MOSES: *(Calls out to Irving.)* So early you're practicing?

ESTHER: *(Looks at clock.)* It's only six A.M. and on a Sunday morning!
(Irving is crying. He pounds his fists down on keyboard.)

IRVING: I'll stop, okay? *(Pound.)* Okay, okay... *(Pound.)* I'll stop... *(Pound.)* Okay? Okay...
(Irving puts his head down on the keyboard. He tries to stop his sobbing. Esther and Moses listen; look at one another. Esther calls out.)

ESTHER: What's with you? *(To Moses.)* What's with him?
(The lights fade out. Music in, immediately. On tape, we hear Caruso, singing an aria from Rigoletto. *The lights fade up on the dining area and kitchen. We are now in the Ilchak home. Annie's father, Emil Ilchak, sits looking at Irving and Annie. Annie's mother works at the stove, upstage. The music is quite prominent and Ilchak takes delight in it.)*

ILCHAK: So, this is the little Jew-boy they never let eat pork, eh? Well, today's going to be your big day...

IRVING: It's bacon that I like. Pork I don't think I like so much.

ILCHAK: You like Caruso? I hear you like music.

IRVING: I *love* music. I have a Caruso record like this…"La Donna è Mobile" from *Rigoletto,* right?

ILCHAK: *(To all, smiling.)* He's a very smart young man, this one…

ANNIE: I've been learning a great deal about music, too, Papa…Caruso is Italian and so is the man who wrote *Rigoletto.* I'm starting to think that all the really *great* opera composers and opera singers are Italian, don't you, Papa?

ILCHAK: Some Italians write good music, and some sing good, too… *(He stands, turns off record. Music stops. He calls to his wife.)* Let's get this meal, huh? Who's got all day to wait?

MRS. ILCHAK: *(In Ukrainian.)* Who the hell do you think you're talking to that way, huh?

ILCHAK: *(In Ukrainian.)* You're taking all day. I've got work to do, right? The kid's got to get home, too…

MRS. ILCHAK: *(In Ukrainian.)* I'm getting it now!

IRVING: *(Frightened.)* Maybe you went too far?

ANNIE: It's nothing. They're always like this…

MRS. ILCHAK: *(To Irving; in Ukrainian.)* I'll bring your food right away. I'm sorry there's this confusion. Cooking two meals…we ate already, ourselves…

IRVING: *(Panicked.)* What did she say to me?

ANNIE: She said your bacon's coming. Whenever she gets nervous, she forgets how to speak English. She's nervous now…

ILCHAK: *(Smiling.)* We ate our meal already. This is special for Annie's friend, yes?

(Mrs. Ilchak puts a platter with cooked bacon strips on table.)

MRS. ILCHAK: Hot.

ILCHAK: A whole week's supply, huh?

IRVING: Oh, God, it's beautiful…

ILCHAK: Good bacon? You like?

IRVING: This is the very best bacon I've ever eaten in my entire life! Oh, God, it's great!

(Irving chomps and chatters. Everyone watches and listens.)

IRVING: I've only had bacon four times in my life before this. Once at Freddy Folger's, my friend's…Twice at the Ritz Cafe, but that was just little red bits in soupy sauce and stuff…Once for real at home, but we don't talk about that, do we, Annie?…

(Annie laughs.)

IRVING: This, I can safely say, is my very favorite meal. Well, almost my favorite. Maybe tied. Lately. I have been loving spaghetti almost as much as bacon. Annie's boyfriend takes me for spaghetti all the time. He's going to take me to a place where they sell spaghetti with bacon and an egg right on top of it…

ILCHAK: *(Stunned.)* *Which* boyfriend?

IRVING: *(Terrified to do what he is about to do.)* Pete Lisanti.

ANNIE: *(Horrified.)* Irving!

(Irving stands; runs from the table and into his bedroom. He leaps into bed and hides under the covers out of sight.)

ILCHAK: *(In Ukrainian.)* You lied to me! You lied to me!

(Annie runs downstage: outside. Her mother follows. Annie is sobbing.)

MRS. ILCHAK: *(In Ukrainian.)* Let me look at your face. Look at me…

ANNIE: *(Faces her mother.)* It's too late, mama…

(Annie runs from downstage up, through the dining area, to the other bedroom. The lights cross fade to bedroom. Annie sits on bed, faces the lump on the other bed that is Irving, hiding. The bed lamp is on. It is night. They are home at the Yanovers'.)

ANNIE: *Why?!* *(No reply.)* I know you're awake, Irving. I want to know why. I *deserve* to know why. You gave me your sacred word. *(No reply.)* You could start crying now if you want…or you could be a decent human being and tell me why you betrayed me… *(No response.)* Irving?

(Irving, without lifting his head from his pillow, answers: staring off to the wall, weeping; frightened and ashamed.)

IRVING: I always thought you were kidding when you said you and Pete were getting married. When you told me you were really going to do it…I…I wanted to stop it, I guess…

ANNIE: Irving, pay attention. I am pregnant and Pete and I are getting married, okay?

IRVING: Okay.

ANNIE: So, that's clear to you?

IRVING: Yes.

ANNIE: So, there you go.

IRVING: If you marry him you'll never get out of Sault Ste. Marie…Pete's not going to be a Detroit Red Wing, Annie. He's not good enough…

ANNIE: Maybe I don't want to…get out of Sault Ste. Marie!

IRVING: *(Sits up, sharply, amazed.)* Annie!

ANNIE: I like it. It's my home.

IRVING: Everybody good in Sault Ste. Marie has to leave. You have to go to

Montreal…Toronto…New York…The world, Annie. You're going to be *famous!* You can't stay here!

ANNIE: Pete Lisanti is a good hockey player…only good. I know that. But he's going to be a good husband, too, Irving. He never lies. He'll never drink: He promised me that and I believe him. He'll never go off with other women…He's honest and strong and handsome and he loves children…

IRVING: He'll never have money…

ANNIE: We'll have enough. We're not Jewish, you know, I mean it's not like we're going to need two sets of dishes and two sets of silverware, right? *(She leans closer to Irving.)* I'm never going to be famous, Irving…never. I'm Annie Ilchak from Bayview. I want a clean house and a nice husband and a small family: two children at the most. *They* can leave Sault Ste. Marie. I don't want to. *(Pauses; softly.)* You can. I have no reason.

IRVING: There was the other Ukrainian girl: She left. And Roseanne, the half-Italian: She left…and the other Annie, too. They *all* left! You can't leave me, too, Annie! Please stay!

ANNIE: I won't ever be far away, Irving. If you ever need to talk, I won't be far away…

(Does not finish…Irving buries his head in his pillow, sobbing. Lights cross fade downstage, to Emil Ilchak, wearing heavy mackinaw. He faces Pete Lisanti, who wears a tweed coat, team scarf.)

PETE: I love Annie, Mr. Ilchak. I'll be a good husband. I swear this to you…

ILCHAK: Why shouldn't I just break your neck?

PETE: You'll see. I'll take care of Annie. I'll be a good husband. I swear it to you…

ILCHAK: Emil Ilchak will have an eye on you, believe me…

PETE: Mr. Ilchak, Annie and I are getting married no matter what. You and I can be friends, or it could go the other way. That decision is yours…but, Annie and I are getting married…and it's not because we *have* to, it's because we *want* to.

ILCHAK: What are you? Nineteen?

(Pete nods.)

ILCHAK: You think at nineteen you know what you want?

PETE: Didn't you?

ILCHAK: When I was nineteen, I had one baby already and another one coming. I knew nothing.

PETE: Are you sorry?

ILCHAK: I'm sorry that I'm forty and I look fifty and I feel a hundred! I'm sorry that there never was one single week in twenty years when I really and truly knew I was going to earn enough money to put enough food on the table…or to pay off the loan payments on a house that's too small and too ugly to be worth a man's life of work…

PETE: Annie and I are only going to have two children. One next year and the other one in two more years…after we have the down payment on a house.

ILCHAK: I see.

PETE: Mr. Ilchak, you're going to be really proud of both of us.

ILCHAK: What about your hockey?

PETE: *(After a pause.)* I can play…sometimes. I can make a little extra money at it too, you know. Last week, we split a purse of nearly thirty dollars…two dollars a man.

ILCHAK: Two dollars buys peanuts when you have a family.

PETE: *Extra* peanuts…for a small family.

(Ilchak studies Pete's face a moment.)

ILCHAK: I warn you, Lisanti…no funny business while I'm alive. And after I'm dead, I'll *still* be looking over your shoulder.

PETE: I swear to you, Mr. Ilchak: no funny business.

ILCHAK: *(Sharply.)* You like opera?

(Pete shows his palms, shakes them, making a "so-so" comment. Ilchak is disgusted, rolls his eyes to heaven in a "why me?" gesture. Lights widen, suddenly: The entire stage brightens. Irving plays start of The Wedding March *on piano. Annie enters, downstage right, in a simple white wedding dress, with her mother and an elderly Ukrainian priest (Ardenshensky); joined by Pete, and Ilchak, in ill-fitting suits; (pre-dressed under mackinaws). They all form a wedding tableau. They stand frozen in place, downstage left. As soon as they are in position, Irving stops playing, bangs his hand down on the piano. With the bang, a light switches on in piano area. Light remains on as well, downstage.)*

IRVING: I'm not going! I'm not going!

(Esther pops her head out of bedroom, she is dressing: fancy dress-up dress and hat.)

ESTHER: What's this?

IRVING: *(Ripping off necktie. Throws same on floor.)* I'm not going!

ESTHER: That is a pure silk tie that costs two dollars and fifty cents, young man!

IRVING: *(Picks it up.)* This cost *two fifty?*

ESTHER: Cash.

IRVING: I'm *still* not going!

ESTHER: *(Calls out.)* Mosie!

MOSES: *(Enters from bedroom, tying his tie.)* I heard. *(To Irving.)* It took me ten minutes to tie that thing. Why'd you take it off?

ESTHER: He's not going.

MOSES: What does this mean?

IRVING: I'm not going. What could "I'm not going" mean? It means *I'm not going!*

MOSES: Why aren't you going?

IRVING: Why is Annie marrying Pete? *Really,* why?

ESTHER: Well, Irving, that's…

MOSES: That's quite a complicated question…

IRVING: What's complicated about it? Why is Annie marrying Pete Lisanti? Really?

ESTHER: Well, Irving, it's commmplicateddd beecaussee…

MOSES: *(Interrupting.)* Annie is pregnant. That's one of the major major major reasons she's marrying Pete Lisanti. She is pregnant.

IRVING: I know *that.*

ESTHER: You know that?

MOSES: You know that?

IRVING: I know that.

MOSES: So, why are you making us stand here, embarrassed, blushing, sweating…?

IRVING: By why doesn't Annie's father stop it?

MOSES: The wedding?

IRVING: The being pregnant. I understand that a pregnant woman should get married, but, if Mr. Ilchak hates Pete so much, why doesn't he simply insist that Annie stop being pregnant?

ESTHER: I seee. Mr. Know-It-All is really Mr. *Almost*-Know-It-All…

IRVING: I know a lot!

ESTHER: So, listen, and you'll know a little more. When a woman is pregnant, she stays pregnant…for nine months, no matter what…until the baby is born…

IRVING: *(Shocked.) Baby?* What baby? What baby, Mama?
(An angel flies by the window: There is a pause.)

ESTHER: Mosie!

MOSES: Irving, supposing you and I bundle up and walk to the wedding, just the two of us…two fellas…We should talk about this. Your mother will drive the car and meet us there…

IRVING: If you think.

MOSES: I think.

ESTHER: I'll get your coat. You don't want to miss the whole wedding ceremony… *(Esther turns upstage; goes to Irving's jacket on hook.)*

IRVING: Did Chopin have a wife, Poppy?

MOSES: Ask me outside. I'll tell you.

IRVING: Promise?

MOSES: I promise…

IRVING: A promise is a promise…

MOSES: Take your necktie. We'll tie it on the road…

IRVING: Papa, why do men wear neckties, anyway?

MOSES: I don't know why men wear neckties, Irving. I really don't. Neckties
neither keep your neck warm nor comfortable. They are silly-looking, a
waste of time to tie, and get ruined by soup. Furthermore, they are
expensive.

IRVING: How come you wear a necktie then?

MOSES: Because my father did. And his father before him. I never broke the
family habit. If you would like to, be my guest. You could be the first
Yanover man to never wear a necktie. *(Pauses.)* There are many things
about this family you have the power to change…believe you me.

IRVING: Maybe I'll keep it in my pocket…just in case… *(He puts necktie in
his pocket.)*

MOSES: Remember the story I told you about my cousin Quentin?

IRVING: The *schmuck* with all the fountain pens?

MOSES: *(Winces at word "schmuck.")* Shhh, your mother…

ESTHER: *(Shocked.)* What's this?

MOSES: *(Teams with Irving.)* Man's talk…

IRVING: *(Giggles.)* Two fellas…

(Moses kneels, buttons Irving's coat; hugs Irving.)

MOSES: Quentin was thirteen and, I'll tell you the truth, he was *not* a fountain pen. But, you, Irving, at ten years old, you are really and truly a
fountain pen…

IRVING: I am?

(Esther looks out front, to audience.)

ESTHER: This genius he gets from my side of the family…

*(*The Wedding March *plays enthusiastically, on tape. Pete and Annie kiss.
Esther and Moses embrace Irving. Ilchak and Mrs. Ilchak hug each other;
the priest smiles. The lights fade to black. As soon as audience applauds,
lights to full. The actors bow once, then, suddenly Ardenshensky, who is, of*

course, costumed as the Ukrainian priest, holds up a hand, talks to audience, confidentially.)

ARDENSHENSKY: It's me: Ardenshensky… *(Lifts off headdress.)* You thought maybe I was a Ukrainian Priest? *(Smiles.)* I'm an actor. I'm working… *(Looks at watch.)* See? It didn't take so long, this play? It's only [time of day]… *(Smiles.)* I should leap ahead a little and tell you what became of some of us… *(Looks at Annie.)* Annie and Pete had a boy who they named Enrico Irving Lisanti…Enrico for Caruso, and Irving for the fountain pen…Five years later they had a daughter, Elsa Esther Lisanti. Pete quit Algoma Steel and opened a sporting goods store on Queen Street which he and Annie co-managed. According to Annie, it did "a nice business."…Emil Ilchak died from silicosis at age fifty-two, but was extremely close to his son-in-law Pete, and taught his grandson Enrico to sing the first two choruses of "La Donna è Mobilé"…in Italian. Elsa Ilchak moved in with Annie and Pete and lived to the ripe old age of eighty-one…As for Irving and Esther and Mosie Yanover, they have two more plays to go… *A Rosen by Any Other Name*, starring none other than Irving's dearest enemy, Stanley Rosen; and *The Chopin Playoffs*, starring three Yanovers, three Rosens, and two Steinways… *(Smiles.)* As for me, Jacob Ardenshensky, I never lived, so, I never died. I'm just a character in a play with a very happy ending.

(Wedding music plays to conclusion. The lights fade to black.)

The play is over.

ADDENDUM: If an intermission is required in *Today, I Am A Fountain Pen*, the following scenes may be inserted for such an act break. The following new Act One Irving/Ardenshensky scene is to be inserted immediately after the blackout ending the existing Irving/Annie/Pete scene. Ardenshensky's new Act Two speech will, of course, immediately follow the intermission. Use of this new material is also suggested if producing groups wish to enlarge the role of Ardenshensky. These additions to my play were recently negotiated by my old friend Sol Frieder, a genius of an actor, to whom these new scenes are forever dedicated, with my love. I.H.

(*Irving walks to park bench, where discovers Mr. Ardenshensky sitting alone, bundled in an old tweed overcoat.*)

IRVING: Hi.

ARDENSHENSKY: Hi.

IRVING: Quite a storm.

ARDENSHENSKY: Don't tell *me* about snow! I'm an old man!

IRVING: Aren't you Mr Ardenshensky?

ARDENSHENSKY: Who wants to know?

IRVING: I'm Irving Yanover.

ARDENSHENSKY: Are you related to the dry goods Yanover?

IRVING: He's my father. I've seen you in the shop.

ARDENSHENSKY: Your father sold me a defective sheet.

IRVING: I heard.

ARDENSHENSKY: How did you hear?

IRVING: My bedroom's right over the shop. You were screaming.

ARDENSHENSKY: I never scream. I project. I'm an actor.

IRVING: Where do you act?

ARDENSHENSKY: In Poland.

IRVING: Recently?

ARDENSHENSKY: If I acted in Poland, recently, I'd be dead. And if I were dead, you'd be talking to the Ghost of Allen's Father.

IRVING: Who's Allen?

ARDENSHENSKY: My son.

IRVING: Oh, right. I get it. I'm very interested in things like acting. I'm going to be a concert pianist. Like Horowitz. Do you know Horowitz?

ARDENSHENSKY: The man or the matzoh?

IRVING: The man. He's the greatest pianist on the planet Earth.

ARDENSHENSKY: Better than Arnold Paterofsky?

IRVING: Who's Arnold Paterofsky?

ARDENSHENSKY: My nephew in Winnipeg.

(Ardenshensky sees Irving's mittens aren't on his hands.)

ARDENSHENSKY: My dear young Mr Yanover, you'd better put something warm on your hands, unless you're planning to play the piano with your toes. Here…take my gloves.

IRVING: I have mittens!

ARDENSHENSKY: Where? Did you lose them?

IRVING: Oh, no, they're right here! *(Shows Ardenshensky his mittens hanging from his mitten-clips.)* It's not possible for me to lose my mittens, unless, of course, I lose my whole coat, which *has* happened, but, not a lot.

ARDENSHENSKY: And a good thing, too.

(Ardenshensky studies Irving's mitten-clips as Irving puts his mittens on his hands.)

ARDENSHENSKY: Isn't that clever? I should have things like that for my gloves. I mostly lose right hands. Last year, alone, I lost three right hands! I have a cigar box full of left hands. It makes me sick to look in the box!…What are they called, those things?

IRVING: These? Mitten-clips.

ARDENSHENSKY: Mitten-clips? You see that? Jews are the best inventors in the world!

IRVING: I'm sure that's true, but, how do you know for certain that a Jew invented mitten-clips?

ARDENSHENSKY: Just say the word: "mitten-clips."

IRVING: It does *sound* Jewish.

ARDENSHENSKY: Would a Protestant invent anything called *mitten-clips?*

IRVING: I see what you mean. I've always assumed that mitten-clips were an English invention, because the words "mitten" and "clips" are both English.

ARDENSHENSKY: You think "mitten" and "clips" are *English?* Are you a *meshuggena?* I suppose you think "box-kite" is English!?

IRVING: "Box-kite"? Oh, right…the kind of kite you fly that looks like a box…Stanley Rosen has a box-kite that he flies in the park with his mother. Rosen's a jerk. *(Says "box-kite" aloud, slowly and thoughtfully.)* "Boxxx-kiiiite." *(Smiles.)* I see what you mean, Mr Ardenshensky. I never really thought about whether or not a box-kite was a *Jewish* invention, before now. Are there many other Jewish words in the English language, Mr Ardenshensky?

ARDENSHENSKY: You must be joshing! The English language is *full* of Jewish words!

IRVING: Like what?

ARDENSHENSKY: There are a million of them!…uhhh, *Bedraggled… Conniption… Fear-laden.* (That's one of my favorites: fear-laden.) Also, the thing you scoop soup with …

IRVING: A ladel!

ARDENSHENSKY: Exactly! You think an Irish Catholic came up with a *ladel!?* …And, while we're talking soup, how about "lentil"?

IRVING: Oh, "lentil" is *definitely* Jewish!

(Irving giggles.)

ARDENSHENSKY: What? Something funny?

IRVING: My mother always adds "garnish" to the fruit salad. "Garnish" *has* to be Jewish, right?

ARDENSHENSKY: "Garnish"? *Voo den?*

IRVING: Oh, I like this! Name some other Jewish words!

ARDENSHENSKY: "Foible."

IRVING: What does "foible" mean?

ARDENSHENSKY: Nobody knows.

IRVING: How about "dental" and "mental."

ARDENSHENSKY: What do you think?

IRVING: Definitely Jewish! I can't imagine two more Jewish-sounding words… "dental"…"mental" …. Ooooo, how about "snuggle"?

ARDENSHENSKY: "Snuggle" is Jewish.

IRVING: *(Suddenly remembers.)* Oh, God! Have we been talking more than six minutes, Mr Ardenshensky?

ARDENSHENSKY: Why? You've got a time-limit on talking?

IRVING: I do, sort of. I promised Annie and Pete I'd take a walk, so they could smooch for six minutes, but, then, I'm supposed to come back and get them, so we can leave and get home by seven o'clock.

ARDENSHENSKY: Are they the two smoochers on my bench over there?

IRVING: That's *your* bench?

ARDENSHENSKY: My *favorite* bench. I was sitting on it, reading my newspaper, when they drove up. I came over here to watch the ferryboat coming in from Michigan. When I went back to my bench, they were sitting on it, smooching. My newspaper's tucked in the bench-slats beside them, but, I didn't feel I should interrupt such goings-on…So, that's why I'm stuck waiting here…til they stop smooching. If you can go make them stop smooching and leave, I can get my paper and go home, before my *kishkas* freeze, altogether!

IRVING: I'll go get them to stop smooching and leave, right away. *(Starts off; stops.)* It was very nice chatting with you, Mr Ardenshensky.

ARDENSHENSKY: Likewise.

IRVING: Do you think "smooch" is a Jewish word?

ARDENSHENSKY: What do *you* think?

IRVING: *Voo den?...* Good night, Mr Ardenshensky.

ARDENSHENSKY: Tell your father I'll be knocking on his door with my defective sheet.

IRVING: I'll tell him.

(Irving exits.)

ARDENSHENSKY: *(To audience.)* Nice boy. He takes after his mother...We'll take an intermission here. Fifteen minutes. No smooching!

(The lights fade to black.)

End of Act One.

ACT TWO

(Ardenshensky walks out on stage, calls to the Stage Manager, offstage.)

ARDENSHENSKY: House lights out, please. *(House lights begin to fade out. Ardenshensky calls to audience.)* Settle, please! We're starting the second act!...Unwrap all your Act Two hard candy, now, please. Otherwise, you'll do it during a quiet, dramatic moment, slowly, thinking you're being discreet, but, everybody around you will hear the noise of your candy-wrapper, which sounds like a mouse scratching, and they'll think that the [name of theatre] has got a mouse problem. *(Calls to Stage Manager.)* May I have my spotlight, please?...(Spotlight finds Ardenshensky, who is suddenly bathed in pink light. Smiles to audience, ironically.)* Very nice, this color...if I were dancing in *Swan Lake!* *(Ardenshensky flashes nasty look toward Stage Manager's booth. Spotlight-color changes to green. Disgusted.)* You *can't* be serious! I'm not playing Dracula! *(Spotlight-color changes to soft flattering neutral tone. Ardenshensky smiles.)* Thank you. *(Ardenshensky now talks to audience, directly.)* So, here we are, again...It's now 1942, and the hideous war is in full swing. Concentration camps are fixtures on the European landscape, like monuments to the Devil, himself. Jews and Gypsies and homosexuals are being exterminated like vermin. The French are fighting side by side with the Allies, but, on the sly, they are selling Hitler their bubbliest Champagne, their smoothest *foie gras,* and many thousand lovely French Jews. In divided Italy, brothers are fighting against brothers, but, soon enough, the black-shirted brothers aligned with Mussolini will overpower all...and Italy and Germany will stand with Japan, against Jews and Gypsies, homosexuals and the rest of the world. It seems unbelievable, now, doesn't it? Well, *believe it,* my friends, *believe it!* Because, if we don't...if we allow ourselves to forget these horrors of real-life, we will be condemned to re-live them, again!...George Santayana and Jacob Ardenshensky swear this to be true! *(Smiles.)* Real life...Oy vay! Luckily, tonight, we are not dealing with real life!... *(LIGHTS FADE UP in Yanover living room, behind Ardenshensky. MOSES sits in his easy-chair, reading the Sunday Newspaper. Radio is on table next to MOSES. ESTHER is in kitchen, readying Sunday meal.)* ...We are in the theatre, watching a very nice play about a very nice Jewish family, the Yanovers, who live in Sault Ste Marie, Ontario, Dominion of Canada, three thousand five hundred miles away from the hideous War. *(Calls to Moses.)* We're almost ready, Mr Yanover. *(Moses smiles at Ardenshensky. Ardenshensky says his* *good-bye to the audience.)* I think you'll enjoy the second act even more than the first act. It's more *conclusive.* The first act wanders a bit; the second act moves dramatically…it's lean. To use a Jewish word…it's *svelt. (Remembers.)* Oh, yes… You'll be seeing me, again, in the second act. I washed the defective sheet Yanover pawned off on me in Dreft, the Jewish detergent, and the sheet fell apart, altogether. This, I cannot live with! *(Ardenshensky nods to Moses.)* Okay, Mr. Yanover…hit it! *(Ardenshensky exits, as lights shift to Moses. Radio Announcer's voice fades in, under scene.)*

RADIO ANNOUNCER: The Suez Canal is seriously threatened by a surprise Nazi attack. The first meeting of German and British armies is being fought now on the deserts of North Africa…

MOSES: I don't like what I read in my Sunday paper!

RADIO ANNOUNCER: …On these same grounds, the British forces had their first victory, with a three-hundred-mile mechanized walk across Italian Libya, capturing and killing one hundred thousand Italians…

MOSES: And I don't like what I'm hearing on my radio, either!

NOTE: Play now continues as printed.

A Rosen By
Any Other Name

For my father, Julius Horovitz,
who drove a truck until he was fifty,
went to law school, nights, and became a lawyer.

ORIGINAL PRODUCTION

A Rosen By Any Other Name received its world premiere production at the American Jewish Theatre in New York City (Stanley Brechtner, Artistic Director; Leda Gelles, Managing Director) on March 4, 1986. It was directed by Stephen Zuckerman; the set design was by James Fenhagen; the costume design was by Mimi Maxmen; the lighting design was by Curt Ostermann; the sound design was by Aural Fixation; the casting was by Darlene Kaplan; the technical director was Floyd R. Swagerty, Jr.; the production stage manager was Evanne Christian; and the production coordinator was Neal Fox. The cast was as follows:

Fern. . . . . Maddie Corman
Pearl Rosen. . . . . Barbara eda-Young
Red Brechtman, Ardenshensky, Farentelli,
Pottstein, Judge Brown, Edelman, Kravitz & Clerk. . . . Sol Frieder
Manny Boxbaum . . . . Michael Ornstein
Barney Rosen. . . . . Peter Riegert
Stanley Rosen . . . . Peter Smith
Toronto Rosen. . . . . Cat

A Rosen By Any Other Name was originally commissioned by The Community Theatre Project of the National Foundation for Jewish Culture.

NOTE: Certain scenes in this play were inspired by passages in Morley Torgov's book, *A Good Place To Come From*. The remainder of the play is based upon "From Kalitsky to Kay," a speech written and delivered by I.H. to win the Dist. #l A-Z-A Oratory Contest, Camp B'nai B'rith, Starlight, Pa., May, 1952.

A NOTE ON THE SETTING

A living room is the major setting, center, with piano upstage by kitchen door; dining table and chairs, center. Barney's armchair, downstage left.

Stanley's bedroom is up three steps from living room, stage left. Barney and Pearl's bedroom is upstage of living room, across small corridor from Stanley's bedroom. Therefore, from living room, up three steps and turn left into Rosen bedroom, or straight ahead into Stanley's bedroom.

Pearl and Barney's room has double bed, dresser, bed lamp with pull-chain on/off.

Stanley's bedroom has twin beds parallel to auditorium. Stanley's bed is upstage against wall; Manny's bed is downstage, closest to audience.

Barney's store is downstage right, formed by counter, shelves, and racks with stock (suit, shirts, etc.). There is a breakable windowpane alongside main window. Main window and door are painted "Barney Rosen Menswear".

Reb Brechtman's study is downstage left. There is shelving with books, a small wooden desk, appropriate prints and paintings on wall.

Fern's window is upstage right, above Barney's store. The window should be covered with scrim, so that Fern can appear or disappear as if by Stanley's dreaming.

Other settings—Edelman's photography studio, Judge Brown's study— will be created by use of costume and props and will "double" in exiting sets.

THE PEOPLE OF THE PLAY

JACOB ARDENSHENSKY: an old actor.

PEARL ROSEN: age forty-five, Stanley's mother.

BARNEY ROSEN: age forty-six, Stanley's father.

STANLEY ROSEN: age twelve years and nine months through his thirteenth birthday.

MANNY BOXBAUM: age nineteen, extremely thin, aesthete.

REB BRECHTMAN: an old Rabbi.

TORONTO ROSEN: an old, old house cat.

KRAVITZ: an old signpainter.

MR. POTTSTEIN: a neighboring Jewish shopkeeper.

INFORMATION CLERK: an old court employee.

JUDGE BROWN: a Protestant judge.

EDELMAN: a photographer.

FERN: a twelve-year-old bombshell.

FARENTELLI: an Italian sculptor.

N.B. One actor plays Brechtman, Ardenshensky, Farentelli, Pottstein, Kravitz, Information Clerk, Judge Brown, and Edelman. There should be no particular attempt to hide this fact: no change of character, accent, etc.

THE PLACE OF THE PLAY

The home and store of the Rosen family, Sault Ste. Marie, Ontario, Canada.

THE TIME OF THE PLAY

Three months in 1943; mid-World War II.

A Rosen By Any Other Name

Ardenshensky enters, speaks directly to audience.

ARDENSHENSKY: Good evening, ladies and gentlemen. My name is Jacob
   Ardenshensky, and I am the oldest living man in the Soo… *(Pauses.)* I
   said the "Soo" not the "Zoo." Maybe you didn't see our last play? *(Looks
   at audience member who giggles.)* What's so funny? You've never seen a
   Canadian before? The Soo is our nickname for Sault Ste. Marie,
   Ontario. That's in Canada. You've heard of Canada, yes? *(Smiles.)* Our
   town is just across the Lake from Sault Ste. Marie, Michigan… *(Pauses.)*
   Tonight's play is called *A Rosen By Any Other Name.* You don't think
   that's funny? *(Confidentially.)* You're not the only one, believe me…
   (Smiles.) Three years have passed since *Today, I Am A Fountain Pen.*
   Now, *that* was a title! *(Pauses.)* The year is 1943, right in the middle of
   World War II. The month is October, and Naples has just fallen to the
   Allied Forces. But, luckily, we're not in Italy, tonight: we're in Sault Ste.
   Marie… *(Smiles; nods to Stanley Rosen.)* The twelve-year-old boy at the
   piano is Stanley Rosen. In three months' time, he'll have his Bar
   Mitzvah… *(Nods to Barney.)* That's the father right there in the easy
   chair, Barney Rosen. I bought an inferior topcoat from Rosen, many
   years ago, but, that's another story… *(Smiles.)* Rosen's come up from his
   menswear store, early tonight. That's Toronto, on Barney's lap. The
   house cat. He's sixty-three years old. Not Barney: Toronto. Sixty-three,
   in cat years. I'm seventy-nine, myself…in Canadian years. In cat years,
   I'm five hundred forty-nine…but, who is counting? *(Smiles.)* That's the
   mother over here: Pearl Rosen. Before our story begins, Mrs. Rosen has
   something to say to you about hysteria… *(To Pearl.)* Are you ready?
   (Pearl smiles; nods.)

ARDENSHENSKY: She's ready…Oh, yes, there's one more thing. From time to
   time, I'll be playing a few extra parts…walk-ons. Normally, I would
   never do such a thing, believe me…but, this is the [name of theatre playing play], so, I can't help myself… *(Shrugs helplessly.)* I just thought I
   should warn you, in case you should see me on stage and somebody calls
   me "Judge Brown" or "Reb Brechtman," you shouldn't get confused…Of course, the likelihood of your being able to recognize me

playing another part is, well, very, very, very slim: I am a master of disguise. *(Nods to Pearl.)* Mrs. Rosen…hysteria.

(Ardenshensky smiles; exits. The lights cross fade to Pearl. Stanley continues to play Chopin on the piano, lightly. Barney continues to read his newspaper. A tight spot on the face of Pearl Rosen. She talks to the audience, directly.)

PEARL: You want to know what hysterical is? I'll tell you exactly what hysterical is. Hysterical is discovering that Mr. Farentelli, the Italian sculptor who is carving the chopped liver statue for your only son's Bar Mitzvah, has bought fifty-seven pounds of ham salad instead, and tells you, straight-faced, "Tell me the truth, Mrs. Rosen? Who's going to really know the difference??" *(Pauses; nods.)* That, from me to you, is hysterical.

(The piano playing stops. The lights widen to include the Rosen family home. Like the Yanover set, we see Living Room/Dining Area featuring piano. We see Stanley's bedroom, twin beds. We see small section of family store below, a rack of menswear: suits, sports coats, trousers. NOTE: It is essential that a store sign and small section of storefront window is available. (This will be replaced, nightly.) It would be useful to design the window in two separate panels, so that the reverse lettering "Barney Rosen Menswear" can be seen but is NOT on the same panel of storefront glass that will be broken and need replacing, nightly. There is a second bedroom, this one for the parents, with a double bed. This bedroom replaces the kitchen area in the Yanover set. Otherwise, the Yanover and Rosen settings remain the same, redressed with different fabrics, cushions, pictures on the walls. A wedding photograph sits atop piano. Stanley Rosen, thin, small aesthete, sits at piano. He has stopped his playing. Stanley is thirteen years old, almost…and he is not happy. Barney sits reading paper. He is not happy. Pearl to Stanley…suddenly; away from the audience. The play has begun.)

PEARL: Why have you stopped? I assure you Irving Yanover hasn't stopped. He is practicing, Stanley. *Practice, Stanley!*

STANLEY: *(Fist punches down on word "not.")* I will *not* be a chopped liver statue!

PEARL: I beg your pardon.

STANLEY: *(Another punch of piano's keyboard.)* I will *not* be a chopped liver statue! *(And another.)* I will *not!* I will *not!* I will *not!* I will *not!* *(Another for good luck.)* I will *not!*

BARNEY: *(Without looking up.)* Stop that, Stanley! I'm trying to read…
(Stanley, disgusted, stops pounding.)

PEARL: Do you know what I'm thinking about?

STANLEY: In fact, I do…

PEARL: You do?

STANLEY: I do.

BARNEY: *(Slaps paper.)* Do you know what they're saying in *The Forward* about Franklin Delano Roosevelt?

STANLEY: He hates Jews.

BARNEY: Have you read the article?

STANLEY: Just a very lucky guess on my part…

BARNEY: Imagine…The President of the United States… *(To Stanley.)* How'd you guess? Did you hear something at school?

STANLEY: No.

BARNEY: So, how? How is it my son suspects the President of the United States of Jew hating?

PEARL: And how is it my son claims to know his mother's unspoken thoughts?

STANLEY: Because every time my mother opens her mouth and talks to me, she tells me about another grotesque idea to embarrass me at my Bar Mitzvah: chopped liver statues, a strolling accordion in front of me, dancing with all the women…

PEARL: There was a strolling accordion at the Coronation Party for the King of England, thank you very much…

STANLEY: …orrrr, she yells "Practice, Stanley!"

PEARL: *(Interjects.)* Practice, Stanley!

STANLEY: Or, when my father finally talks to me, he tells me about another Jew-hater who's going to attack us. Today, it's the President of the United States; yesterday, it was my Hebrew teacher, who snuck into a parking space ahead of him…

BARNEY: I couldn't see in the snow!

STANLEY: It was my Hebrew teacher!

BARNEY: I could not see in the snow!

IRVING: What couldn't you see? It was clearly Reb Brechtman, in his '39 DeSoto, two-door with…

BARNEY: Let me tell you something, young man. Every word that comes back from Europe tells us that they are rounding up the Jews…

PEARL: *Barney! You promised me!*

STANLEY: What are you saying, Poppy?

BARNEY: Practice, Stanley! *(To Pearl.)* May I see you in the kitchen for a moment, please? *(Exits.)*

STANLEY: *(To Pearl.)* What is Poppy saying, Mama? Are the Nazis coming to Canada?

PEARL: You heard your father: Practice, Stanley!

(Pearl exits into kitchen. Stanley suddenly moves downstage center. Lights shift with him. He talks, straightforwardly, as if on telephone.)

STANLEY: I know it's late, Fern, but, I've got to talk with you...

(Lights fade up on Fern in her bedroom. She also talks as if on telephone, whilst polishing nails. NOTE: Fern is probably placed behind scrim.)

FERN: Did I not tell you to never call after eight? What is the *matter* with you?

STANLEY: I promised to call you at six and I forgot...we're having a crisis in our house...

FERN: There's no excuse for calling me after eight...

STANLEY: I thought you'd be upset if I didn't call at all...

FERN: Why should I be?...

STANLEY: Because we talk every night. Because, we never miss a night...

FERN: Miss all the nights you want. I'd never notice.

STANLEY: Fern, I have to ask you a really personal question...*Please.*

FERN: Okay, but make it snappy...

STANLEY: Do you think kids at school hate me because I'm Jewish?

FERN: That's not why the kids at school hate you, Stanley...

STANLEY: Oh, that's great. I'm so relieved...

FERN: I'm going to hang up now, Stanley...

STANLEY: Sure, I understand. Swell talking to you, Fern...I'll see you in my dreams...

FERN: That's a grotesque idea, Stanley.

STANLEY: Will you dream of me, Fern?

FERN: Of course not!

STANLEY: Good night, Fern...

FERN: Good night, Stanley...

(Lights widen again on stage. Suddenly we hear: Air Raid Alert. Barney and Pearl rush to pull curtains over windows. Stanley calls out in fear.)

STANLEY: Are they bombing us?

PEARL: Air raid drill!

BARNEY: Air raid drill!

PEARL: Close the black-out curtains!!

BARNEY: Stanley, help me close the black-out curtains!

(Stanley does. Toronto squeals loudly in the dark.)

STANLEY: Oh, God, I think I almost squashed Toronto!...Poppy, are they bombing us? What's happening?

(Toronto squeals again.)

BARNEY: Dammit, Pearl, I almost tripped on your cat!...It's only practice, Stanley! Nobody's bombing!

STANLEY: How do you know it's only practice, Poppy?

BARNEY: Because I know.

STANLEY: But, how?

BARNEY: Stanley!

PEARL: Do you hear bombs?

STANLEY: Oh, God, mama. That's how we'll know when they're actually dropping bombs? We'll *hear* them? We won't know *before* that?

PEARL: No one is bombing Canada, Stanley!

BARNEY: Not *yet*…

PEARL: Barney, for God's sake…

BARNEY: The Soo will be an excellent strategic position, in fact…

STANLEY: You see?

BARNEY: Canada is the gateway to the United States…

STANLEY: You hear that, Mama? The *gateway!*

PEARL: Barney!

BARNEY: You're damn right, the gateway! And once Germany controls Canada and the United States, Mexico and South America will fall in an instant!

STANLEY: Oh, my God, Mama! Germany's getting Mexico and South America, too!

PEARL: Barney, what are you doing?

BARNEY: I'm being realistic. Algoma Steel will be an important target…

STANLEY: Oh, my God! Algoma Steel is walking distance from here!

PEARL: We are perfectly safe in Canada, Stanley. This is all your father's imagination, that's all!

STANLEY: Are you sure, Mama?

PEARL: Of course, I'm sure…

(Barney looks at Pearl.)

PEARL: Barney!

BARNEY: Okay, fine. I'm going to have a look…

PEARL: No! Close the curtains!

BARNEY: *(Blows out candle flame.)* There. It's totally dark in here. I'm going to have a peek…

STANLEY: Me, too…

(Barney pulls back curtains. They all peek outside. Spotlights sizzle through the darkness. A beam illuminates their faces, then disappears.)

STANLEY: God! Look at the searchlights!

BARNEY: Oh, yes. There's really a war on…

STANLEY: Here?

PEARL: Not here! *Barney!*

BARNEY: The war's not here, Stanley. The war's in Europe. Here, it's just practice…

STANLEY: For when the war comes here?

PEARL: The war is not coming to Canada, Stanley! I promise you and your father promises you!

BARNEY: Pearl!

STANLEY: You can't make promises for the Nazis! Poppy, what if Canada goes to war against the Jews, like Germany?

PEARL: That's not going to happen, Stanley…

STANLEY: Yuh, but, what *if?* Whose side am I supposed to fight on, huh?

PEARL: You see what you're doing to him, Barney? You see?

STANLEY: I hate this goddamn war!

PEARL: A war is no excuse for a filthy mouth, young man!

STANLEY: Huh?

REB BRECHTMAN: *(Offstage.)* Could we try it one more time, Mr. Rosen, if you please…

(Stanley moves downstage left to Reb Brechtman's study. Reb Brechtman enters, carrying "yamulka" and "tallis" for Stanley, which Stanley puts on. Reb Brechtman is preparing Stanley for his Bar Mitzvah. As the scene begins, Stanley is singing his "Half-Torah": practicing. Reb Brechtman sings along, mouthing the words, silently. Once and again, when Stanley goes far astray from the suggested melody, Brechtman will interject and correct. By contrast to Stanley's high-pitched voice, Reb Brechtman's voice is deep-throated, fully professional, perhaps even a tad showbiz. Stanley completes the passage; looks up.)

REB BRECHTMAN: Well, Mr. Rosen? How do you think it went?

STANLEY: Oh, well, I think it went…uh, not good, not good. Not *terrible*, but, I can do better…

REB BRECHTMAN: Would you like to try it again, Mr. Rosen?

STANLEY: My heart's not in it, Reb Brechtman. I'm sorry…

REB BRECHTMAN: Is there something troubling you, Mr. Rosen?

STANLEY: How come you call me "Mister," Reb Brechtman? I mean, in the whole world, nobody ever called me "Mister" before I started Hebrew lessons with you? How come the "Mister"?

REB BRECHTMAN: Should not a man be called "Mister"?

STANLEY: Yuh, well, sure: a *man*…

REB BRECHTMAN: And how old is a man, Mr. Rosen?

STANLEY: A man is older, bigger.

REB BRECHTMAN: How old is a Jewish man, Mr. Rosen?

STANLEY: Oh, I seeeeee. You mean that once I'm Bar Mitzvahed, I'm a member of the congregation…I'm a *man*. I get it.

REB BRECHTMAN: And that was troubling you?

STANLEY: Oh, no, it's my parents. My father sees Jew-haters everywhere he turns.

REB BRECHTMAN: Really?

STANLEY: He's so worried about it, he imagines *everybody* hates Jews.

REB BRECHTMAN: And you don't think these are times for Jews to worry?

STANLEY: I do, I do. But, he's taking it too far?

REB BRECHTMAN: This we do not know for certain, do we?

STANLEY: It's really my mother who's troubling me.

REB BRECHTMAN: And what is your mother doing to you, Mr. Rosen?

STANLEY: She wants to feature me in chopped liver.

REB BRECHTMAN: To feature you in chopped liver in what sense, Mr. Rosen?

STANLEY: Carved. In a statue at my Bar Mitzvah reception.

REB BRECHTMAN: *(Smiles.)* I seeee. Well, say nothing of this, but, the Potemkins featured their Randolph in ice cream, set afire with cognac… compared to flaming ice cream, a chopped liver statue might even be considered, you'll excuse the expression, *tasteful*.

STANLEY: Flaming ice cream? Didn't it melt?

REB BRECHTMAN: What's your guess?

STANLEY: *(Laughs.)* Musta been a real mess!

REB BRECHTMAN: What do *you* think?

STANLEY: Why do you always answer questions with questions, Reb Brechtman?

REB BRECHTMAN: Which teaches you more, Mr. Rosen? Making answers, or asking questions?

STANLEY: Which teaches me more? *(Serious pause.)* Asking questions.

REB BRECHTMAN: *(Smiles.)* Shall we take it from the top, Mr. Rosen?
(Lights up on Fern, in window.)

FERN: Okay, go ahead, Stanley: Ask me your question.
(The lights narrow down to pinspot on Stanley. He talks to Fern, as if on telephone.)

STANLEY: Fern, answer me as honestly as you possibly can. Spare me no pain, please; because I really have to know the truth. Fern, if Canada went to war against the Jews and you were fighting for Canada and I was fighting for the Jews, and we met on the front line and you had a gun and I didn't…would you shoot?

FERN: *What?*

(There is a pause, and then Fern laughs at Stanley. A flashbulb goes off. Lights up, on cue. Stanley stands with Pearl, being photographed by Mr. Edelman, downstage center. Stanley wears "tallis" and "yamulka." Pearl wears bright red dress and matching shoes and hat. Mr. Edelman, who was not a moment ago Reb Brechtman, now wears a powder blue artist's smock and a matching blue beret. Stanley reacts to flash, immediately.)

STANLEY: You've devised a great, great plan: Blind me, totally, I won't be able to see the chopped liver statue, the strolling accordionist, the…

PEARL: *(Through clenched teeth.)* We're not alone, Stanley!

MR. EDELMAN: Now, one of the Bar Mitzvah boy and his mother…

PEARL: Do you think?

MR. EDELMAN: Hurry, Mrs. Rosen, please. Spontaneity is the name of my game. Quickly, into position and smile!
(Pearl hurries, sits next to Stanley; poses, smiling out front. Mr. Edelman focuses his camera from under black cloth.)

MR. EDELMAN: Smile, Stanley.

PEARL: Smile, Stanley.

STANLEY: I'm smiling, I'm smiling!

MR. EDELMAN: That's not a smile, Stanley: That's a grimace.

PEARL: Mr. Edelman says that's not a smile; that's a grimace.

STANLEY: What is this? A foreign movie? I can understand Mr. Edelman…

MR. EDELMAN: Smile! Hold it!

STANLEY: Hold what? I think Mr. Edelman just said something dirty, mama…

PEARL: What?
(Flash goes off.)

PEARL: Dammit, Stanley, you ruined the shot!

STANLEY: Oh, yuh, if not for me, we would have been on the cover of *Life*…now, they'll probably use Roosevelt…the Jew-hater.

MR. EDELMAN: *(Emerging from under black cloth.)* That, Mrs. Rosen, will be a picture to paste down and keep. *(He frames his hands in a rectangle and stares at Pearl and Stanley through the hands.)* If you ask me, the invitation should have this picture and not just the son…

STANLEY: The invitation is going to have a picture?

PEARL: Oh, nooo…The Bar Mitzvah Boy and Mother? No Father? I don't *thinkkk* so…Do you *reallly*?

STANLEY: What does this mean?

PEARL: Shhhah, Stanley.

MR. EDELMAN: The photo-invitation.

STANLEY: The photo-invitation? *(To Pearl.)* Over my dead body, mama!

MR. EDELMAN: Have you thought to carry through with the photo-motif on the souvenir matchbooks and the dinner napkins?

PEARL: Can dinner napkins be done in good taste with a photo motif?

MR. EDELMAN: Well…in a *certain kind* of good taste… *(French.)* …absolument!

PEARL: Let me mull it over for a while Mr. Edelman.

STANLEY: Mama! What is this?!?

(Flash bulbs pop off on all sides of the stage, blinding Stanley, Pearl, and the audience, momentarily. When the lights restore, Pearl and Stanley walk into living room.)

PEARL: I read in a magazine about a party that had a literary motif. The guests all got the names of authors, and their places at the table were marked with names of books. So the guest had to match their authors with their books, to find out where they sat.

STANLEY: At my Bar Mitzvah reception?

PEARL: It's clever, isn't it? James Joyce sits at *Ulysses*. Tolstoy sits at *War and Peace.*

STANLEY: At my Bar Mitzvah reception?

PEARL: I think it could work, Stanley.

STANLEY: Mama, if you gave James Joyce to Auntie Goldberg and told her she couldn't sit down 'til she found his book, she wouldn't sit down for a year! I've got to get away from you! You're driving me crazy!

(Stanley bolts away from Pearl, he looks up and talks to Fern, as if on telephone. The lights narrow to spot on Stanley and on Fern.)

STANLEY: It's the same old problem, Fern. My mother's making a Bar Mitzvah reception that's gonna be about as simple as Fibber McGee and Molly's closet…statues of me, invitations of her…

FERN: Rise above it, Stanley.

STANLEY: Huh?

FERN: Rise above it. My parents wanted me to take toe-tap…they insisted. I hated toe-tap, but the more I said "No," the more they insisted. But…I rose above it.

STANLEY: You did-yes take toe-tap, or you did-no-not take toe-tap? I don't quite follow.

FERN: Oh, Stanley, you are so *young*…

(Lights cross fade to Barney in store.)

STANLEY: Where do you want the 38s?

BARNEY: Shorts, longs, or regulars?

STANLEY: *(Sees tags.)* Oh, longs. I know where they go.

BARNEY: You know, Stanley, this could possibly be the only thing that makes Sundays bearable for me, Stanley…knowing that we work together, side by side…that we have a chance to talk…

(Stanley joins Barney in store, moves stack of overcoats. He puts stack to one side.)

STANLEY: I wish we'd talk about what's going on?

BARNEY: The War?

STANLEY: The Bar Mitzvah reception.

BARNEY: Oh, well…that's strictly your mother's department. I really shouldn't mix in…

STANLEY: I think you really *should*…

BARNEY: Oh, I don't know, Stanley. The decisions about your Bar Mitzvah are your mother's to make…not mine…

STANLEY: Not mine, either… *(Motions to stack. Stanley stacks clothing.)* How come mama gets to make all the big decisions?

(Barney laughs, seemingly out of context.)

BARNEY: I get to make all the big decisions, Stanley.

STANLEY: The Bar Mitzvah is a big decision.

BARNEY: You know Mr. Ardenshensky?

STANLEY: The old, old guy?

BARNEY: The old, old guy, right. About a year ago, Ardenshensky and his wife were celebrating their sixty-second or sixty-third wedding anniversary. He was in here getting his annual topcoat repair. We were kibitzing, so I asked him how it was that he and his wife could have stayed married so happily for so long… *(Imitates Ardenshensky.)* "It's because Sara lets me make all the big decisions, while she's content to make the little decisions…" *(As himself, to Stanley.)* Like what, I ask…what are the little decisions she makes? *(Imitates Ardenshensky again.)* "Whether we should buy a new house, or a new car, or, whether we should send our son Allen to university…" *(As himself, to Stanley.)* "Wait, wait, hold it, Ardenshensky!" I yell. "If those are the *little* decisions your wife makes, what are the big decisions *you* make?" *(Imitates Ardenshensky again.)* "Whether Canada should enter the War." *(Laughs; looks at Stanley.)* Do you get it?

STANLEY: I get it, I get it. Mama decides everything about my Bar Mitzvah, and you decide about the Annexation of Czechoslovakia.

BARNEY: Not *me*, Stanley…*Ardenshensky!* (Barney smiles at his son's cleverness.)

I don't know if I've ever told you this straight out, before, but, you, Stanley Rosen, are my Lucky Star.

STANLEY: Really?

BARNEY: Really…

STANLEY: Would you consider thanking your Lucky Star by putting in a word against the chopped liver statue?

BARNEY: Stanley, please, ask me anything else…

STANLEY: How about killing the photo-invitations?

BARNEY: Keep going.

STANLEY: The photo-matches?

BARNEY: Keep going?

STANLEY: *(Rolls eyes to heaven.)* Oh, God…

(The lights widen to include living room. Pearl sits at table, sketching invitation copy. Stanley at piano, playing Chopin Raindrop Prelude. *Toronto meows. Pearl calls across to Barney and Stanley.)*

PEARL: Did anyone feed Toronto?

BARNEY: I did.

STANLEY: I did.

(Toronto meows again. Pearl talks to him.)

PEARL: You got them both to feed you? Keep it up. We'll loan you out to the circus!

(Toronto meows; exits. Pearl calls after him.)

PEARL: Are you finished helping in the store?

STANLEY: Yuh, I guess…

PEARL: Everybody says they "cordially invite." Maybe we should "request the pleasure of your company." I mean, Jane Austen requested the pleasure of your company…it's more…elegant. Don't you think so, Stanley?

STANLEY: *(Slams piano; runs to Pearl.)* Oh, my God, the invitations, *again!* Mama, listen to me, please…Couldn't I just have a simple, quiet straightforward, Bar Mitzvah…no photo-invitations, no photo-matches, no photo-napkins, no chopped liver statues, no literary games…just me, God, ten Jews and a Torah?

PEARL: Don't blaspheme, Stanley!

STANLEY: Blaspheme! What the hell is blaspheme?

PEARL: You listen to me, Stanley Rosen! This is the Bar Mitzvah that I deserve, and you will have it! *Do…you…understand?*

STANLEY: Who couldn't understand something as simple and clear as what you just said?

PEARL: And don't you forget it! Let me tell you something else, young man: There is another Bar Mitzvah being planned as we speak...

STANLEY: *(Interjects.)* Please, don't...

PEARL: Yours is hardly a shoo-in for best Bar Mitzvah in Sault Ste. Marie, believe you me...

STANLEY: This is embarrassing!

PEARL: Don't tell me what is embarrassing! I'll be the judge of what's embarrassing in this house, thank you very much! Tell him about Irving Yanover, please, Barney...*Barney!*

BARNEY: *(Looks up, absently.)* What, Pearl?

PEARL: Tell your son about Irving Yanover...

STANLEY: *(Absently.)* Quite a boy that Irving...

BARNEY: Quite a boy that Irving...

STANLEY: Four months younger than you.

BARNEY: Four months younger than you...

STANLEY: Same grade in school...

BARNEY: ...Same grade in school...

STANLEY: ...Plays Chopin like Chopin himself...

BARNEY: ...Plays Chopin like Chopin himself...

PEARL: The *Bar Mitzvah,* Barney!

BARNEY: What about it?

PEARL: Without Stanley's full cooperation, will Irving's Bar Mitzvah be better than ours? I mean, realistically speaking, in ten years' time, will people be talking about Irving Yanover's Bar Mitzvah or *my* Bar Mitzvah.

BARNEY: Oh, Pearl, that *is* embarrassing!

PEARL: "Embarrassing" is a word that hasn't been spoken in this home, *ever!* Tonight, inside of three minutes, two mentions...

STANLEY: What's another word for "embarrassing"?

(The telephone rings.)

BARNEY: Stanley!

STANLEY: I'll get it! *(Stanley runs downstage, to "telephone" position.)*

PEARL: I'm not going to get myself upset over any of this...

BARNEY: Good, Pearl.

(Manny Boxbaum's voice is heard, on telephone, over speakers in auditorium.)

STANLEY: Hullo?

MANNY: *(Offstage.)* Who's this?

STANLEY: This is Stanley...

MANNY: *(Offstage.)* Hi-ya, "pischah," this is your cousin, Manny Boxbaum...

STANLEY: Manny Boxbaum's in the War...

MANNY: *(Offstage.)* Not anymore, he isn't! Manny Boxbaum's in Ottawa and he'll be coming to your house to stay for awhile in about four days' time…

STANLEY: He *is?* You *are?* Is this really you, Manny?

MANNY: *(Offstage.)* Does corn flakes come in boxes?

STANLEY: It soitenly does!

MANNY: *(Offstage.)* And I soitenly am! I'll be there a week from Saturday. I'll call back with the exact train…

STANLEY: Oh, God, Manny this is such great news. You're coming just in time to save my life, Manny! I am *so completely happy!* Manny?

MANNY: *(Offstage.)* What?

STANLEY: *(Offstage.)* How tall are you now?

MANNY: *(Offstage.)* Normal height: six-ten, six-eleven…

(The lights shift back to the Living Room.)

BARNEY: *(Reading* Life *magazine; looks up.)* There's an article in this week's *Life* about Protestants painting stars on Jewish homes in Gloucester, Massachusetts!

PEARL: Barney, please read quietly…

BARNEY: The Katzbachs summer in Gloucester. Nine hours from Montreal by car, that's all…

PEARL: Barney, *please!*

BARNEY: It gets closer and closer and closer…

PEARL: *Barney!*

STANLEY: *(Runs back on.)* Momma, Poppy, you'll never guess in a million years who that was!

PEARL: Who?

STANLEY: On the phone…a big surprise.

BARNEY: So, who?

STANLEY: Cousin Manny Boxbaum. He's out of the War…You hear that, Toronto: Manny's out of the War!

PEARL: Yes, he said he might be coming to stay with us for awhile.

STANLEY: You knew he might?

PEARL: Not for sure. He said he'd call. I'm delighted.

BARNEY: How does Manny…sound?

STANLEY: He sounds perfect and he's tall, too!

BARNEY: So, when's he coming?

STANLEY: A week from Saturday. This is great! How long do you think he'll stay, mama?

PEARL: Manny Boxbaum can stay in our house as long as he wants. Isn't that right, Barney?

BARNEY: Manny Boxbaum is a wonderful boy…absolutely. *(A worried tone; to Stanley.)* But, Stanley, you're going to have to go easy on Manny for awhile…

PEARL: Nothing but rest for Manny…for awhile.

STANLEY: Why? Is he tired?

BARNEY: Manny is coming here because he needs a lot of rest…

STANLEY: Why? What's wrong with Manny?

BARNEY: He's what they call "shell-shocked"…

STANLEY: What's shell-shocked?

BARNEY: Oh, well…shell-shocked has to do with being around too many, uh, well, *guns*…

PEARL: Manny is very nervous. It's a nervous kind of illness.

STANLEY: You mean Manny is *crazy?*

(Simultaneously.)

BARNEY: Noooo…

PEARL: Noooo…

BARNEY: Just nervous…

PEARL: Just a little nervous…That's all.

BARNEY: And he's coming here because he needs a lot of rest.

(Lights out, suddenly, we hear the air raid siren.)

PEARL: Air raid drill.

BARNEY: Air raid drill.

STANLEY: Air raid drill.

(They all run to close the curtains. Darkness on stage. They all step on Toronto. The sound of three shrill cat screams, and an equal number of human cries.)

(Stanley, Pearl, and Barney, simultaneously.)

STANLEY: Toronto, dammit!

PEARL: Toronto!

BARNEY: Pearl! Your cat!

(Lights up on Manny Boxbaum in bedroom. He is unpacking his suitcase. Stanley calls from offstage.)

STANLEY: *(Offstage.)* Hey, *Mannyyyyy?*

(Manny turns and smiles. Stanley bursts into the room.)

STANLEY: Hey, Manny!

MANNY: Hey, Stanleyyy! *(Laughs.)* Look at you. You grew two more feet…

STANLEY: *(Looks down his legs.)* What would I do with two more feet? I can hardly get along with the two I've got...

(Manny forms hands into cow's udder: Stanley "milks" Manny's thumbs. Both make Three Stooges' "Nuh nuh" sound; laugh.)

STANLEY: I'm sorry I'm late. I've got this friend I have to walk home, every day...you know...

MANNY: I guess you mean *girl,* huh?

STANLEY: Oh, yuh, sure. Her name's Fern. You won't say anything to my parents, okay?

MANNY: "Say Nothing" is my middle name...

STANLEY: Great. Yuh, well, she insists on me walking her home every day, calling her at all hours of the night. All that stuff. Maybe I'll introduce you... *(Looks Manny over.)* You look okay. You don't look, you know... *not* okay.

MANNY: I *am* okay. I'm out of the Navy. That's okayyyy! How are you?

STANLEY: I'm okay. I'm okay. Manny?

MANNY: What?

STANLEY: Are you crazy? I kinda heard...

MANNY: Whattt? Who told you that?

STANLEY: Nobody said that directly. There were *hints.* Is shell-shocked crazy or what?

MANNY: Shell-shocked is definitely not crazy. A little *nuts* maybe, but never crazy... *(Simply.)* Once in awhile, I pick up kids and toss them, but that is it.

(Manny picks up Stanley and tosses him on to the bed. Stanley squeals, delighted.)

STANLEY: I'm glad you're here, Manny. I really need your help.

MANNY: I'm glad I'm here, too, Stanley. Why do you need my help?

STANLEY: How do you feel about chopped liver statues at Bar Mitzvah receptions?

MANNY: Ahhh, yessss, there's a Bar Mitzvah coming soon.

STANLEY: So? What's your feeling about chopped liver statues?

MANNY: It depends on who's carved in liver; and whose reception it is.

STANLEY: If it were your reception and you were carved in chopped liver, what would *you* do?

MANNY: Welll, Stanley...a complex and unique question like that takes some thought...

STANLEY: Off the top of your head, what?

MANNY: Off the top of my head...that would work...

(Stanley looks up at his cousin.)

MANNY: That's a good idea. *(Smiles.)* I would get to the reception early and bite off the top of the statue's head…and then nobody would know who the statue was.

(Stanley giggles, ecstatically.)

STANLEY: Thank *God* you're here!

(Stanley "milks" Manny's thumbs. Both yell "Nuh nuh!" The lights cross fade to store. Lights up in the store and in the living room: and, dimly, in the bedroom. On tape, we hear: Stanley playing Chopin, lightly. Manny is taking a nap. In the store, below, Barney and Pearl are fitting an overcoat to Mr. Ardenshensky, an old Jew.)

ARDENSHENSKY: Snow! Why God figured we needed such a thing as snow, I'll never know if I live to be four hundred twenty-six. Maybe in Alaska, they can use snow. *That*—I can see. I mean if you live in an igloo and there is no snow you could be possibly ruined, but in Canada it's not needed! Achhh, snow! Don't tell me about snow. I have seen it all. White snow, black snow, red snow, it's never any good; snow, believe you me. Snow is never what it promises to be. Just last night, I told my son Allen…

(Pearl finishes stitching coat.)

PEARL: It looks lovely…

BARNEY: Lovely. A solid tweed topcoat like this could last you another forty years, Ardenshensky…

ARDENSHENSKY: Don't talk crazy, Rosen. I'm seventy-nine years old. I'm not worrying about another forty years for my tweed topcoat. I'm just worrying about getting through the winter!

BARNEY: I will guarantee the winter, Ardenshensky…

ARDENSHENSKY: For me or my topcoat?

BARNEY: For the topcoat, Ardenshensky. For a guarantee for yourself, you'll have to go to a higher menswear store… *(Points to Heaven.)*

PEARL: *I'll* guarantee you the winter, Mr. Ardenshensky…I'm a very good judge of what lasts and what doesn't last…

ARDENSHENSKY: I hope you're a better judge than this one… *(Nods to Barney.)* I never would have overpaid, except for Barney Rosen's word…He promised me for this tweed topcoat a lifetime of use…

BARNEY: That was fifteen years ago, Ardenshensky…

ARDENSHENSKY: A promise is a promise…

BARNEY: I kept my promise. Didn't I? Don't I repair this coat for you, every year, free of charge?

ARDENSHENSKY: Ten dollars of my hard earned money in your bank at two percent compound interest for fifteen years…Is that what you call your "free of charge repair service" Rosen?

BARNEY: I charged you ten dollars for the topcoat, period, Ardenshensky!

ARDENSHENSKY: That's my point, exactly!

BARNEY: *What's* your point, exactly? You were the first customer in my store, ever. I didn't know what I was doing. To tell you the truth, I sold you the coat for a dollar less than it cost me, myself.

ARDENSHENSKY: You haven't done such a bad business over the years, Rosen, have you?

BARNEY: No thanks to you, Ardenshensky, really. One topcoat at a dollar under cost plus fifteen years of upkeep…

PEARL: We're happy to do it, Mr. Ardenshensky… *(Flashes a look to Barney.)* Barney…

BARNEY: It's true. We are…

ARDENSHENSKY: Of course, you are. Having Jacob Ardenshensky's name number one on your customer list has meant something, has it not?

BARNEY: A great deal…

PEARL: A great deal…

ARDENSHENSKY: Maybe you want me to take my business to Sears and Roebuck…

BARNEY: There's no need…

ARDENSHENSKY: *(Looks in mirror; turns around.)* You don't think it's too tight under the yoke?

BARNEY: The yoke is perfect…

ARDENSHENSKY: Well, okay…if you say so. *(Smiles.)* A man has got to trust his tailor…

PEARL: Why don't you stay for lunch, Mr. Ardenshensky? Stanley will be home from school for lunch and I'm sure he'd love to practice his half-Torah for you…

ARDENSHENSKY: Very kind of you to offer, Mrs. Rosen, but, I've got a million errands… *(Taps paper bag.)* I shouldn't say this too loud, as I know he and Yanover are friends, but Yanover sold me inferior goods…I'm very upset and so is Sara…

PEARL: I'm sure Mosie Yanover will make good on it for you.

ARDENSHENSKY: I hope to God he will. I'm not a rich man. I had a terrible argument with Silversweig this morning… *(Remembers.)* You heard about the rock through Silversweig's window?

BARNEY: What?

PEARL: What?

BARNEY: Al Silversweig, the plumber?

ARDENSHENSKY: No! Of course not! Dave Silversweig, the furrier. Would I argue with a plumber?

BARNEY: You see, Pearl? You see? Queen Street, Sault Ste. Marie! Queen Street! Not Poland, not Czechoslovakia! Queen Street, Dave Silversweig's fur shop!

PEARL: Somebody threw a rock through his window?

ARDENSHENSKY: As big as a fist, glass shattered, everywhichway…

PEARL: *Voof…*

ARDENSHENSKY: Lucky for Silversweig, the fur business is seasonal.

PEARL: No customers in the store…

ARDENSHENSKY: That's my point, exactly…

BARNEY: You see, Pearl? It's started: The pattern is forming: a rock through a Jewish window every other day. The day before yesterday, it was Maury Ginsburg, the Chemist; today, it's Dave Silversweig, the furrier…

ARDENSHENSKY: Yesterday.

BARNEY: Who, yesterday? Oh, my God, it's every *day!* Who got it yesterday?

ARDENSHENSKY: You said "Silversweig was today." Silversweig was yesterday. There were no rocks thrown today…

BARNEY: Yet.

ARDENSHENSKY: *(Nodding.)* Yet.

PEARL: What are you two *saying?* Don't be silly…

BARNEY: "Silly"? Tell her, Ardenshensky: "Silly"…go ahead! Hahahaha…in your words, no prompting from me…tell her.

ARDENSHENSKY: Well, actually, Mrs. Rosen, last night my son Allen and I…

BARNEY: *(Interrupting.)* Two rocks in one week through two windows, and both windows belong to Jewish merchants, and you think this is a *coincidence,* Pearl?

PEARL: Oh, please, Barney, of *course,* it's a coincidence. Most of the merchants on Queen Street are Jewish.

BARNEY: *(Interrupting.)* Are you blind, Pearl? You mark my words: Canada and the United States will do the same thing to their Jews that Germany is doing to its Jews. You mark my words!

PEARL: Barney, this is simply not true. Tell him, Mr. Ardenshensky. No prompting from me. Tell him…

ARDENSHENSKY: Well, Barney, as a matter of fact, last night for three hours…

PEARL: *(Interrupting.)* You won't be satisfied until you have Stanley frightened to walk the streets in his own hometown. Do you think Mosie Yanover is doing such a thing to their Irving? Do you? Tell him, Mr. Ardenshensky, tell him!

BARNEY: No, tell *her,* Mr. Ardenshensky…

PEARL: Go on, tell Mr. Ardenshensky.

ARDENSHENSKY: *(Taking off overcoat. Outraged; exasperated; furious.)* I absolutely will not tell anything to either one of you! Every time you tell me to talk, you won't let me. You interrupt me! Only my worst enemies should try to give you some advice. You think I've got nothing to do with my time? You think I'm an old man who doesn't have a million errands?

(Suddenly, without warning, an eight-ounce rock crashes through the window. Pearl screams, Barney leans against the counter, sickened. Upstairs, Stanley and Manny hear the crash.)

ARDENSHENSKY: My God, somebody threw a rock! I'll go see!

(The Old Man runs offstage. Barney is ashen. He picks up the rock.)

BARNEY: Do you see this, Pearl? Do you see this? Is this my imagination now, Pearl? Is this your crazy husband's crazy imagination, or is this a rock? Answer me! Answer!

ARDENSHENSKY: *(Offstage.)* Did you see anything, Pottstein? *(Answers as Pottstein.)* Two kids—there!

BARNEY: Answer me, Pearl!

PEARL: *(Quietly.)* It's real, Barney. It's a real rock…

BARNEY: Mmmmm… *(Smiles.)* Mmmmmmmmmmm…

ARDENSHENSKY: *(Reenters.)* It was just two kids from the sister-school. In their uniforms. Pottstein saw them throw it. Everything okay in here?…

PEARL: *(Relieved.)* Oh, yes, we're just fine, thank you, Mr. Ardenshensky…

(Pearl takes broom, sweeps broken glass. Barney is near catatonia. He stares at rock in his hand)

ARDENSHENSKY: I fired off after them, myself, but they got away…

PEARL: That was very brave of you to chase them, Mr. Ardenshensky, very brave. Did you hear that, Barney: "Just two kids from the sister-school," that's all…

BARNEY: That's all, right, that's all…

PEARL: Barney, for the love of God, that is all!

BARNEY: Two more for *Hitler,* that's all! *(Pauses; looks at rock, then at Pearl.)* It's started, Pearl. You mark my words. *It has started!*

(Barney exits into house, carrying rock in his hand. Ardenshensky exits. In blue light, Pearl sweeps up broken glass, exits into kitchen, and almost immediately reenters, carrying food for dinner. Barney paces in bedroom. Stanley

stares at it all, frightened. Lights up full in dining area and bedroom. Manny and Stanley sit at the table in silence. There are two other places, one for Barney and one for Pearl. Barney is in bedroom; sitting in silence. Pearl enters from offstage, from kitchen, carrying casserole. She serves food to Manny and to Stanley.)

PEARL: Eat. *(Looks off, to Toronto.)* You eat, too.

    (Cat meows.)

STANLEY: This is weird.

PEARL: It's just meatloaf…

STANLEY: I mean now…eating without Daddy… *(To Manny.)* I never eat without him…

PEARL: Daddy's too upset to eat.

STANLEY: The rock?

PEARL: The rock, the war, everything…

STANLEY: Me, too?

PEARL: Hmmm?

STANLEY: Do you mean that Daddy stopped talking because of me, too?

PEARL: No, of course not, Stanley! Your father is refusing to speak because he's…well…he's overwrought.

STANLEY: Do you think we should call Dr. Sternberg?

PEARL: And have it known all over town?

    (Barney, in bedroom, stands, goes to door, turns handle. Pearl hears this.)

PEARL: Shush! I think he's coming.

STANLEY: *(As Barney enters room.)* Hi, Poppy.

MANNY: Hi, Uncle Barney.

PEARL: Hi, Barney. Hungry?

    (Barney "drifts" to the meatloaf. His eyes seem unfocused. He seems a bit bewildered.)

BARNEY: This looks like an excellent meatloaf, Pearl…

PEARL: It's not bad, Barney. We like it…

MANNY: The meatloaf's great, Uncle Barney.

STANLEY: Great!

PEARL: So, sit, Barney, we'll have a nice family meal. We'll talk…

BARNEY: I am remaining silent until I have figured out "What to do." I'll thank you to respect my silence. *(Barney exits dining room, carrying the pan of meatloaf with him; plus a large serving spoon. He enters bedroom, locks door behind him, sits. He eats from pan with spoon, absently.)*

STANLEY: He took the meatloaf…

PEARL: He's hungry. I'll fix you something else…

MANNY: He looks like I did, a month ago…

STANLEY: He took the entire meatloaf…He's acting so *crazy!*

PEARL: Your father and I have known each other for nearly twenty years, Stanley. We've seen the best and the worst of each other, believe you me…

STANLEY: Is this Daddy's worst?

PEARL: Not yet. Close. But not yet…

STANLEY: My life is not as much fun as it used to be, mama…

PEARL: Fun? What's fun?

(Light fades up on Fern, in her window.)

FERN: *(Picks up telephone; speaks.)* If this is who I think it is, I am *furious!*

(Stanley moves downstage, "talks" to Fern. Barney, rock in hand, goes to bedroom, puts rock on dresser; sits, staring into space, frightened. Pearl completes the sweeping up of the glass; pauses a moment, weeps. She has a strong sense of what is coming. She exits the store, carrying the dustpan and broken glass through the living room, into the kitchen. The lights shift to Stanley, in hot telephone-light, downstage. Barney paces in bedroom, in blue light, staring into space, in background)

STANLEY: *(Talking to Fern as if on telephone.)* My father's stopped talking to me, Fern…He marches from room to room, totally silent…

FERN: There, you see that, Stanley? Even your own *father* has stopped talking to you!

STANLEY: Not just to me, Fern, to *everybody!* My mother says he thinks that Canada's going to turn in the Jews to the Nazis, like they did in Poland. He's gone totally silent. He's stopped *talking.*

FERN: Are you sure?

STANLEY: Of course I'm sure.

FERN: He's totally silent?

STANLEY: Not a peep.

FERN: And he's awake?

STANLEY: On his feet, moving…

FERN: God, Stanley. What a family!

(The lights fade out on Fern and Stanley as Stanley turns and moves into dining room. Pearl and Manny enter dining room, in blue light. Pearl carries meatloaf; sets table. The sound of Fern "hanging up" her telephone.)

STANLEY: Hullo? *(Pauses. Stanley goes to Barney's bedroom door; knocks.)* Poppy? Poppy? It's me: Stanley: your son. Please come out, Poppy. I'm a little frightened…

(Barney goes to door, starts to turn knob. Stanley notices, runs back to the table.)

STANLEY: He's coming out! He's coming out!

(Barney opens door; faces Pearl and Stanley.)

PEARL: Hello, Barney.

STANLEY: Hi, Poppy…

BARNEY: I am sure you have both noticed that I have been silent since this morning.

PEARL: I noticed, yuh.

STANLEY: I noticed.

BARNEY: This morning, when the rock smashed my store window, I was, I dunno, lost, *panicked*…I said to myself "Barney, try to figure out what the great scholars would do in a crisis situation like this…" I studied and I found that they all used silence. They stopped all talk until they knew what they were actually going to do…And so did I. *(Pauses; smiles.)* I've stopped my talk. *(Smiles.)* I know exactly what we're going to do. *(Pronouncement.)* We're going to change our name.

PEARL: What?

STANLEY: Huh?

BARNEY: Of course, there's a Talmudiacal–philosophical question afoot here: Is a Jew with a Gentile name still a Jew? I answer "Emphatically, *yes!*" This family will still be Jewish, no matter what our name *seems* to be… But, we have suffered enough insults, enough rocks through our windows…In the simplest possible terms, there are maniacs out there gunning for people with Jewish-sounding names. We're changing our name.

STANLEY: We're changing our name? To *what?* To *what?*

BARNEY: If you want to be a help, you'll think of names for the family…

STANLEY: Are you kidding?

BARNEY: I am most definitely not kidding…

PEARL: I think your father and I should have a serious talk, Stanley…

STANLEY: Without me? I'd like to be in on it…

PEARL: Go to bed, Stanley…

BARNEY: Go to bed, Stanley…

STANLEY: Go to bed? Like I'm six years old? Go to bed?

PEARL: Go to bed, Stanley…

BARNEY: Go to bed, Stanley…

STANLEY: You said that he was close to the worst, but not there yet. Is this it? Is this the worst?

PEARL: *Much* closer.

STANLEY: You mean it could be worse?

BARNEY: There is nothing so bad that it can't grow worse. There's no *limit* to how bad things can be! This is precisely what I am trying to teach you about life…

PEARL: This is what you teach a twelve-year-old?

BARNEY: Yes, Pearl, this is precisely what you teach a twelve-year-old: *my* twelve-year-old…my beloved twelve-year-old son, yes, if I can open his eyes, yes. And if I can open *your* eyes, yes, you, too…

STANLEY: I'm going to bed. *(Exits.)*

PEARL: I'm going to bed. *(Exits.)*

(Stanley crosses to bedroom, gets into bed. The lights cross fade with Stanley. Manny sits on the end of his bed, looking out the window at the night. Stanley pulls the covers up to his chin, talks quietly to Manny. N. B. The lighting should now be night-lighting.)

STANLEY: Do you stay up all night, Manny?

MANNY: Most of the night.

STANLEY: How come?

MANNY: I dunno. It's just easier for me to sleep in the daytime…

STANLEY: How come you look out of the window?

MANNY: Because it beats looking *in* the window—it beats looking at *you!*

(Stanley giggles.)

MANNY: How are you doing with the name-change game?

STANLEY: It's not funny, Manny! It's really serious. I heard my mother tell Mrs. Yanover that he's going to see a judge about changing our name…

MANNY: Really?

STANLEY: Really. If that putz Irving Yanover gets wind of the name-change, he'll never let up.

MANNY: Who?

STANLEY: The Yanovers have a brain-damaged son, Irving, who always tries to get my goat. (Pause.) …I don't get it, Manny. I always thought Rosen was very Canadian. I mean, no offense, but, Rosen isn't *Boxbaum!*

MANNY: *(Playacts toughguy's voice.)* You ain't just whistling "Dixie," m'boy!

STANLEY: *(Giggles.)* I dunno, Manny. The older I get, the less I know.

MANNY: Watch out, kid. By the time you're fifteen, you'll know nothing at all; and by the time you're seventeen, you'll owe knowledge!

STANLEY: *(Giggles again.)* I need you to talk sense to them for me. My parents will listen to you. They used to call you "The Prince," you know that?

MANNY: They did?

STANLEY: Honest to God.

MANNY: Not for awhile, I'll bet.

(Lights cross to Barney downstage at "phone." He talks as if on telephone.)

BARNEY: *(Pauses.)* Mosie? Hello, Mosie. It's Barney Rosen. Oh, no, nothing's wrong. I was just thinking about something, and I thought I'd call you to chat about that something. No, no, everything's fine…How's Essie? Good, fine, wonderful. And Irving? Good, fine, wonderful…Pearl's fine. Stanley's wonderful…Yes… *(Pauses.)* Oh, no, Toronto's fine, too. Really, Mosie, we're all doing very well…under the circumstance… *(Pause.)* The circumstance of having obviously Jewish names when the world is out there persecuting Jews… *(Pauses.)* Please, Mosie, let me explain, Mosie…Did you know that Jack Benny's real name is Benny Kubelski. Kubelski…Mosie, did you ever think that "Yanover" was a lot to lug around…? The name: Yanover. *(Pauses.)* …Do you think anybody ever would have even heard of Jack Benny if he kept his Jewish name? And, Mosie, did you ever think that changing "Yanover" to a name that was less obviously Jewish might be, a little *safer? (Pauses.)* I don't see why you're laughing. I don't see why you think this is *funny… (Pauses.)* No, I am definitely not kidding, Yanover…

(Pauses; listens. Yanover has hung up. Barney clicks the receiver, hangs up, turns around, sees Pearl listening. He snaps at Pearl.)

BARNEY: Yanover thinks it's too serious a discussion to have over the telephone. He thinks we should continue the discussion face-to-face…

(Pearl guffaws. Barney snaps at her.)

BARNEY: They say the privacy goes first, then the tenderness, then the marriage…

PEARL: Who says?

BARNEY: Me. I say…Think about this the next time, before you eavesdrop on my private conversations.

(Barney moves downstage to an Information Officer at the courthouse. The word "INFORMATION" is probably printed on the wall of the theatre's proscenium arch. Tight light on Officer (same actor as always) creates the setting. Barney calls out to Officer as he turns from Pearl, no pause wanted.)

BARNEY: Am I in the right courthouse for name changing?

OFFICER: Why?

BARNEY: Why? Because I want to change my name, that's why…

OFFICER: Why? What's your name?

BARNEY: What's my name?

OFFICER: Yes, I am curious to know what name could be so *odious* as to cause anyone to wallow through the strangle of bureaucratic red tape...to go to the unfathomable trouble of actually changing that name...

BARNEY: My name is Benny Kubelski.

OFFICER: *(Suddenly serious; understanding.)* ...Second floor, Room 209, center staircase, straight ahead...

BARNEY: Thank you...

(We hear Fern's voice, as light fades up on her, in her window.)

FERN: *(Into telephone.)* Have you wigged out completely, Stanley? It's after midnight!

(Barney exits. The light goes out on Officer and up on Stanley talking to Fern as if on telephone.)

STANLEY: I know you'll be shocked to hear this, Fern, but sometimes, I think my cousin Manny is really creepy...

FERN: Why should I be shocked?

STANLEY: Because Manny is brilliant...he's handsome, he's tall...he's a war hero...

FERN: But, he's your cousin, right?

STANLEY: Right. My father's sister's son: my first cousin...

FERN: Right. So, why should I be shocked to hear that he's creepy. He's related to you...

STANLEY: Oh, I get it. That's right. *I'm* creepy and he's my cousin, so that makes him creepy...

FERN: Exactly.

STANLEY: Very funny...

FERN: *I* don't think it's funny...

STANLEY: Right, listen, Fern, it's been swell chatting with you, but, I've got to ring off now...

FERN: Oh, sure, as soon as the conversation becomes *truthful,* you've got to go, right?

STANLEY: Okay, Fern, 'bye... *(Looks at audience.)* Women: What the hell do they *want?*

(The lights shift to Pearl and Barney, in their bed, in their bedroom. Pearl stares silently at Barney, who is reading law books, bed lamp on. He is mumbling, audibly. Pearl speaks quietly.)

PEARL: What are you doing, Barney?

BARNEY: I am studying the Canadian Laws governing the changing of an unwanted or unsavory name.

PEARL: Does this mean you're staying up?

BARNEY: If you want to sleep, sleep.

PEARL: It's extremely difficult sleeping beside a maniac who mutters. *(She takes box of invitations and envelopes from night table.)* You mutter and I'll address. We will have ourselves a night.

BARNEY: *(Listens to Pearl's pen scratching.)* If you continue to scratch, it is hardly likely that I'll actually be able to comprehend what I'm reading…

PEARL: I'm doing fine.

BARNEY: *(Puts book down, picks up scrapbook.)* I could have married Estelle Sugarman. She was extremely fond of me…

PEARL: What are you saying? Estelle Sugarman got killed by a car, two years ago. You know that…

BARNEY: That's exactly my point…

PEARL: That is mentally *sick!*

BARNEY: I'm sorry…

(They kiss again. Pearl pulls back and smiles at Barney.)

PEARL: Do you wanna? *(She smiles again, seductively.)*

BARNEY: Yes, I wanna, no, I won't. I'm studying…

PEARL: *(Sees scrapbook.)* What's the scrapbook for?

BARNEY: I have to go back five generations and prove conclusively that I am really a Rosen…

PEARL: Maybe you'll find out you're not…then you can change your name to Rosen…

BARNEY: *(He looks at another page.)* My God, look at this. Look at this, Pearl: Cousin Hershie Rosen. Look at him.

PEARL: He's the one who died?

BARNEY: *(Quietly.)* He's the one who died. Poor Hershie. He could spit farther than any of us! *(Laughs.)* Look, Pearl, you: pregnant…

PEARL: Lemme see! *(Sees.)* Oh, my God!

BARNEY: Stopp! You were beautiful… *(Giggles, looks at Pearl lovingly.)* You still are, Pearl, even more…even more beautiful…

PEARL: So, now that I've got three hundred invitations and an open ink bottle on the bed, now, you wanna, right?

BARNEY: *(Shrugs.)* You don't wanna?

PEARL: *(Shrugs.)* There's only one man on the face of this Earth with whom I wanna, and his name is Barney Rosen… *(Spells.)* Capital *R*, small *o*…

BARNEY: Don't spoil it, Pearl…

PEARL: *(Giggles.)* I wouldn't *dream…*

(They kiss. The lights cross fade to boys' bedroom. Stanley is asleep in his bed. Manny is in the throes of a nightmare, in his bed, sweating, groaning. Suddenly, we hear Toronto, the cat, freak. A cat scream cuts through the

*night. Manny leaps awake, terrified, his eyes wild. He screams out. Pearl and
Barney stop their kissing and sit up in bed, frightened.)*

MANNY: Medic! Medic! He's bleeding! Medic!

(The lights cross fade to the boys' bedroom.)

STANLEY: Manny?

MANNY: …Medic!

STANLEY: Hey, Manny, you okay…

MANNY: Ooooohhhh…Medic!

STANLEY: Hey, Manny, you're having a bad dream!

MANNY: Oooohhhh…He's bleeding, medic!

(Stanley shakes Manny, wakes him.)

STANLEY: Manny, come on, wake up!

(Manny awakes, in a panic.)

MANNY: What? *(Manny is in a sweat.)*

STANLEY: God, Manny, you're really sweating. You okay?

MANNY: More than anything, I am incredibly embarrassed…

STANLEY: I'll call Dr. Sternberg.

MANNY: No, Stanley, really…It's not at all necessary. I got a little too confi-
dent, lately…I cut myself down on my medication, that's all. I'll go back
to the normal amount…

STANLEY: Those pills you take?

MANNY: Those pills I take.

STANLEY: I thought they were vitamins. You take so many!

MANNY: Six: two yellow and two sizes of white.

STANLEY: And they stop you from dreaming?

MANNY: Yeah, that's what they do, Stanley…

(There is a pause.)

STANLEY: I hate this whole goddamn War.

MANNY: Yuh, me, too…

STANLEY: *(Calls out.)* If Hitler invaded Canada and I had a chance to get to
Switzerland where it's safe, would you go with me, Fern?

(Light fades up on Fern in her window, on telephone.)

FERN: No…

*(Stanley moves downstage, looks up as he goes, "talking" to Fern, as if on tele-
phone. Light fades out on Manny.)*

STANLEY: How about if Hitler were killing everybody—not just Jews—and
your life was in danger and by going to Switzerland with me you could
save yourself? Would you go with me then, Fern?

FERN: I don't know, Stanley. I'd have to really think about it…

STANLEY: I understand. I do. It's a huge trip…

FERN: It's not the trip, Stanley…

STANLEY: You don't have to decide now. Take your time. Think about it…

(Fern's light fades out.)

MANNY: *(Calls out from bedroom. W.C. Fields.)* She walks…she talks…she crawls on her belly like a reptile!

STANLEY: *(Answers Manny, completing joke.)* She has more hair on the palm of her hand than Mae West has on her…

MANNY AND STANLEY: *(In unison.)* Go away, son, ya bother me…

(Lighting shifts to bedroom. It is morning.)

STANLEY: Hey, Manny. You okay?

MANNY: Never better. I'm really sorry about last night.

STANLEY: That's okay. How shell-shocked are you, Manny?

MANNY: Pretty shell-shocked, I guess…

STANLEY: Shell-shocked is more scared than crazy, right?

MANNY: *(In unison with Stanley, imitating Manny.)* You ain't just whistlin' "Dixie," m'boy!

STANLEY: *(Laughing.)* I could see it on your face. You really looked scared.

MANNY: It comes and goes…

STANLEY: You don't look scared now.

MANNY: I'm not.

STANLEY: Good, 'cause I really need you to keep your promise to talk sense to my parents. I don't want to be selfish or anything. I mean, if you're still feeling shell-shocky or anything…don't feel you have to do me the favor, but, if you're really feeling better and you think it won't upset you…

MANNY: *(Smiling.)* Stanley, I'm okay, really…I'm a man of my word. I'll talk to your mother this morning…

STANLEY: Make your comments about the chopped liver statue your own…I mean, don't tell her I hate it…let it be you who hates it, okay?

MANNY: How so?

STANLEY: If she thinks it's me who hates it, she'll close down her mind on the subject. But, if she thinks it's you who hates it, she's liable to keep her own mind open… *(Pauses.)* That's the way people are, Manny. It's exhausting, figuring these things out…

MANNY: I'll do the best I can, Stan, my man…

STANLEY: I know you will…I just hope your best is tough enough to wipe out her worst…I'm running out of time, Manny.

MANNY: I'll do my best…I'm sorry I scared you, last night…

STANLEY: I wasn't scared...the War's driving *everybody* crazy. I can tell. I was just talking with my girlfriend...Guess what she's after me to do...

MANNY: What?

STANLEY: Run away to Switzerland with her...

MANNY: You are joshing...

STANLEY: Not at all. Switzerland's not on either side, right?

MANNY: So they say...

STANLEY: Well, Fern's got it in her head to have us run away there.

MANNY: To elope?

STANLEY: Yeah, sort of?

MANNY: Before or after your Bar Mitzvah?

STANLEY: Are you kidding? My mother would gun us both down if we ran away before...What's "elope," exactly?

MANNY: Run away and get married...

STANLEY: Yuh, that's what I thought...

MANNY: Never ask the fruit salesman's daughter to run away with you and get married. You know why?

STANLEY: Why?

MANNY: She'll say she can't elope!

STANLEY: Cantelope! Oh, my God, that's so *rich!* I'll be right back okay...

(Stanley rushes downstage, calls up to Fern, talking as if on telephone. Light fades up on Fern, in window. She talks into telephone as she polishes nails.)

STANLEY: You know why I never would, Fern?

FERN: Because she'll say "I can't elope"...You are so *young*, Stanley...

STANLEY: Why do you say that?

FERN: Because that joke's so *old!* The first time I heard that joke I laughed so hard the tears ran down my *bib!*

STANLEY: I'll call you later, Fern...

FERN: I may be out...

STANLEY: That's okay...

(The lights cross fade to kitchen, where Pearl stands at table, kneading dough. Manny walks to her, talking as he goes. When he arrives at table, he sits in kitchen chair, looking up at his Aunt Pearl.)

MANNY: It's not that Stanley actually hates the idea, it's just that he fears that maybe the reception might be...a little gauche. Gauche is all I'm trying to say here...

PEARL: Of course, it'll be gauche.

MANNY: Really?

PEARL: Why shouldn't it be?

MANNY: Well…I don't know.

PEARL: I grew up one of twelve children, Manny. I lived in eighteen different places by the time I was ten. Eighteen…and none of them were so terrific, believe-you-me. I started working after fifth grade…in a bakery… rolling out pie dough…Imagine. Fifth grade: I was ten. My father, God rest his soul, thought five years of school for a girl was an indulgence. An indulgence. But, he loved me, so he let it go past the usual three years… *(Pauses.)* I loved my father, but I loved school, too, Manny. I missed it so much. *(Pauses; smiles.)* I've never stopped studying, Manny. I've read every nineteenth-century novel in the Sault Ste. Marie library and most of them twice, including all of Dickens and I love him. I…love… Dickens. *(Pauses.)* Believe-you-me, Manny Boxbaum, I am a woman who knows gauche from not-gauche, and I ask you: For once in the life of a wife and mother who has worked every minute of every day of her entire life since fifth grade, shouldn't there be one big gauche party full of all her friends and family? Just one?

MANNY: *(After a long pause.)* Stanley is going to hate that chopped liver statue.

PEARL: Maybe not, Manny.

> *(Pearl smiles. Manny eats a piece of the dough. Lights cross fade to Stanley, downstage, "talking" to Fern, as if on telephone.)*

STANLEY: Fern, I have two questions, that's all…

> *(Fern's light fades up.)*

FERN: Please, Stanley, hurry, I have to keep the line open…

STANLEY: Is your father expecting a call?

FERN: No, Stanley, *I* am. What are your questions?

STANLEY: If you knew that there was going to be a statue of me at my Bar Mitzvah reception, carved out of chopped liver, would you refuse to go to my Bar Mitzvah with me?

FERN: Stanley, I never once said that I was going!

STANLEY: I know that, Fern, but if you had said you were going, would the statue put you off?

FERN: Chopped liver?

STANLEY: Chopped liver.

FERN: Would people eat it afterwards?

STANLEY: I never thought of that.

FERN: I mean, would they actually eat different parts of you?

STANLEY: Oh, God, Fern, I never thought of that…

FERN: *(Giggling.)* Hurry, Stanley, what's your other question? I have to go call Rosie Berkowitz…

STANLEY: Why Rosie Berkowitz? You swore to me that this conversation was a secret between us, Fern!

FERN: It is! Now, Stanley: What is your final question?

STANLEY: What would you think if my name wasn't Stanley Rosen but Stanley Rose hyphen North?

(Fern and Pearl say the exact same line in unison.)

FERN AND PEARL: The stupidest thing in the whole world…

(The lights cross fade to living room. Stanley goes to piano, sits, plays a Bach étude, lightly. Barney paces, carrying notebook and pen. Pearl sits at desk, addressing invitations.)

BARNEY: Okay, okay, Barney Rose-North is out, okay. Barney *Randall?* Boring… okay…Barney *Randolph.* Not bad huh? You've got to admit, Stanley, that Barney Randolph is not bad! Okay, okay. Barney Richards? It's very calm, the Barney with the Richards. It has a certain *je ne sais quoi,* huh? *(Pause.)* You hate it.

(Stanley looks at Pearl, who looks at Stanley.)

STANLEY: I hate this whole *month!*

(Stanley goes to metronome, on piano, starts the thing clicking. Stanley clicks his head from side to side in same rhythm, annoying his parents, intentionally. Stanley is trapped in the house with them. He is bored. Pearl and Barney both yell: "Stop that, Stanley!")

PEARL AND BARNEY: *Stop that, Stanley!*

(Stanley stops metronome; moves to table.)

PEARL: Eaton's says a cummerbund must never be worn with tails.

STANLEY: What's a cummerbund?

PEARL: It's nothing, nothing. For you to wear to the reception…nothing.

STANLEY: That's what you want me to wear to my Bar Mitzvah reception? Nothing?

PEARL: That's right. Totally nude with a cummerbund. That's *exactly* what I want. Alright?

STANLEY: Very nice.

PEARL: Look, while you're here, I want to go over some last minute invitations with you.

STANLEY: Who, now, mama? We must be up to a thousand.

PEARL: Three hundred and sixty-one.

STANLEY: *(Weak-kneed.)* Oh, my *God!*

PEARL: One quick question: Mr. and Mrs. Jared Rossetti?

STANLEY: Mr. Rossetti? My Social Studies teacher? You're inviting Mr. Rossetti to my Bar Mitzvah?

PEARL: That's my question: him, or him, and her? Could I get away with just him?

STANLEY: How can I ever stand up and sing in Hebrew in front of my Social Studies teacher? No! Uh uh! No!

PEARL: But he'll feel left out, Stanley! We have to invite him!

STANLEY: He'll miss being with our family?

PEARL: He'll miss being with the other teachers...

STANLEY: They've all been invited?

PEARL: And they've all accepted.

STANLEY: I'll never live to see fourteen. I will be the first human being in the history of the world to actually die of embarrassment!

PEARL: Believe me, every teacher in Sault Ste. Marie will be at Irving Yanover's Bar Mitzvah, and he is nothing but pleased...

STANLEY: He is nothing but brain-damaged...

PEARL: Stanley Rosen, that is a terrible terrible thing to say about your closest friend!

STANLEY: *My closest friend?* What are you? Crazy?

PEARL: You would open a mouth like that to your own mother?

BARNEY: I have it!

STANLEY: You have what, Poppy?

PEARL: I think I know!

BARNEY: Quiet! Everybody listen!

PEARL: Every night I hear another hundred! *(To God.)* Why?

BARNEY: The great ideas are always obvious! *(Barney goes to Stanley.)*

STANLEY: What are you talking about, Poppy?

BARNEY: *(Hands on his son's shoulders; simply.)* Stanley Royal.

STANLEY: Hmmm?

(Barney goes to Pearl and places his hands on her shoulders, standing behind her.)

BARNEY: Pearl Royal...

PEARL: Like the *typewriter?*

BARNEY: And I am Barney Royal Menswear...That settles it. Royal is short, memorable, melodic, yet extremely safe. So, what do you think? I'm waiting. I am waiting.

(Pearl and Stanley are silent. They look like they've just been made to eat socks. There is a small and disgusting noise upstage center. It sounds like "EKKKK." We hear the same sound, twice more.)

BARNEY: What is that?

(Stanley runs upstage; opens kitchen door, looks.)

STANLEY: Oh, God! Toronto is throwing up!

PEARL: You see, Barney, how your family feels? Toronto Royal is throwing up. *(Lights up in boys' bedroom. Manny lies atop bed, reading. Stanley crosses into bedroom from piano, talking to Manny as he crosses.)*

STANLEY: I don't agree, Manny. I don't think this is a philosophical question. It's a legal question: If my name gets changed to Stanley Royal before my Bar Mitzvah then who, legally, gets Bar Mitzvahed? Stanley Rosen, or Stanley Royal?

MANNY: Definitely Stanley Royal.

STANLEY: But Stanley Royal isn't even Jewish, Manny! Stanley Royal is an Englishman!

MANNY: What's this? Englishmen can't be Jewish? What about Disraeli?

STANLEY: What are you saying, Manny? Wasn't Disraeli the Englishman who converted?

MANNY: Oh, yuh, I think you're right...

STANLEY: *Great* example, Manny. Very thoughtful. Thanks a lot...

MANNY: You know, Stan, I been thinking...I dunno...maybe your father's not so far off base? Maybe things would've been easier for me if I hadn't been Manny *Boxbaum*...

STANLEY: That is *demented!* You went into the war because you were Manny Boxbaum, period...

MANNY: Yuh, so, what did it get me?

STANLEY: Jesus, Manny...

MANNY: You know, sometimes you do things 'cause you...I dunno...'cause you *just do*... *(Pauses.)* There was a war, it was against Canada, it was against Jews, it was against Mama and Papa. And I wanted to get out of University anyway, because I think I would have been the worst dentist on the face of the Earth, Stanley. The absolute worst. *(Pauses.)* I dunno, Stanley. I'm just trying to figure out why I *really* did what I did...why I went into the war to begin with...whether it was, I dunno, *worth it.* *(Pauses.)* Stanley, I used to be really sure about a lot of things. Lately, I'm not too sure about anything. I'm pretty confused, Stanley: That's about the only thing I'm sure of.

STANLEY: What the hell are you saying, Manny?

MANNY: I'm not saying, Stanley: I'm thinking...maybe for the first time about some of this. I don't know...

STANLEY: Jesus, Manny! If *you're* confused, I'm gonna end up with my goddamn name changed, that's what! Jesus, Manny!

(Stanley crosses into living room to piano, dejectedly. He bangs at piano,

once, twice, three times. And then he pounds the keyboard violently…Pearl runs out from kitchen, sees her son.)

PEARL: Stanley, Stanley, darling, calm yourself, calm yourself.

STANLEY: How the hell can I calm myself, mama? Daddy's gonna change our name!

PEARL: I will handle your father. Trust me. I've figured out how to get him to change his mind about changing our name…

STANLEY: You *have?*

PEARL: I have.

STANLEY: Thank God…

PEARL: Trust me…

STANLEY: How will you do it, mama? How will you convince daddy not to change our name?

PEARL: There's only one way, but, it will accomplish exactly what you and I both want… *(Pauses; then the Pronouncement.)* I will fight fire with fire! *(Pearl looks at Stanley, squarely, as though she has just made sense.)* A word to the wise is sufficient.

(Pearl exits into the bedroom. Stanley looks out front, rolls his eyes to heaven. He gets his schoolbook from the top of the piano, goes to the table, sets up to study. Manny enters from kitchen with milk and cookies; pauses a moment with Stanley en route to easy chair.)

MANNY: Hey, kid, how goes it?

STANLEY: Oh, great, never better…

MANNY: Great. *(Sits in easy chair.)*

STANLEY: My mother says she's going to fight fire with fire…

MANNY: What's that mean?

STANLEY: I dunno. Can't be good. What do you think?

MANNY: Can't be good.

STANLEY: Wanna know who I'm gonna be? I'll tell you who I'm gonna be. I'm gonna be Stanley David Royal, a schmuck with earlaps who's carved in chopped liver in front of every teacher in his school. I will have to leave Sault Ste. Marie, immediately and join the Foreign Service…I will have to leave, Canada! Oh, my God, Manny! We are talking *Life, itself!*

(Blackout. Lights cross fade to Barney and Pearl's bedroom. They are in bed. The bed lamp is off at start of scene. As they argue, Barney will turn bed lamp on, Pearl will turn it off…to underscore what each is saying: threatening.)

BARNEY: *(Switches on the light.)* Pearl Protestant?

PEARL: Pearl Protestant. You got it. *(Switches off light.)*

BARNEY: *(Switches light on.)* That's supposed to be funny?

PEARL: Nope. That's going to be my new name: Pearl Protestant.

(She switches light off. We now see Stanley, in shadows, outside door, eavesdropping. He slaps his forehead with his palm. Barney switches light on.)

BARNEY: I'm not going to take this seriously…You, changing your name to Pearl Protestant. *(Laughs, switches light off.)* I'm not taking it seriously, Pearl, I'm warning you!

PEARL: And I'm warning you, Barney: You'd better take it damned seriously…from now on, you are Royal; and I am Protestant. And that is that! *(Waits a moment, suddenly sits up, switches light on.)* You are a crazy person!

BARNEY: You want crazy? I'll give you crazy. If you go against me on this, I swear to you that I will… (1) not pay a penny toward your precious Bar Mitzvah. (2) I will not attend the Bar Mitzvah under any circumstance, and (3) I will live separately from this house…and that is that. If you want reasons four through seven, I'll give them to you…

PEARL: That's blackmail, Barney!

BARNEY: Yes, Pearl, that is precisely what this is: blackmail.

PEARL: *(Pauses; stares at him, weeps.)* I hate this, Barney.

(Stanley scoots back to his own bedroom, having eavesdropped on the conversation between his parents. Pearl turns away from Barney, weeping. Barney lies awake, hearing his wife's sadness. The lights cross fade to Stanley's bedroom. It is morning. The boys are dressed; making their beds.)

STANLEY: My father says he will become Royal, and my mother just said she will become Protestant! So what the hell does that make me?

MANNY: You're going to have to calm down, Stanley. Really…There's a way to work this through…

STANLEY: How? For God's sakes, how? The Bar Mitzvah is less than a week away…she's got the whole town coming to see me in chopped liver!…and he's changing my name into a comedy routine: *(Does an announcer's voice.)* Ladies and Gentlemen, we proudly present the Royal Family. *Vay ist mier!* What am I going to do, Manny, what am I going to do? Please help me, please help me, please help me. I am twelve-point-nine years old and I am losing my mind!

MANNY: Okay. Now, let's see what's possible here. First off, that your father's the one to work on.

STANLEY: My father will never change his mind. He's the most stubborn man on the earth. Once, he wanted me to swim in the lake and there was a crocodile in the lake and he wanted to go anyway…

MANNY: A crocodile in the lake?

STANLEY: I think so. It was a long time ago…

MANNY: I guess I owe it to you.

STANLEY: You do, Manny, you do. Manny, Irving Yanover, that brain-damaged putz, drew a crown on my gym locker. A *crown*, Manny. Royal… Crown…*get* it?

MANNY: Are you positive it was Yanover?

STANLEY: If I were to tell you that he called me over and made me stand and watch him draw the crown…that he said "See that, Royal: a crown!" and then he walked away, laughing like a brain-damaged putz, would you believe me then, Manny? Huh?

MANNY: I'll talk to your father, right away, Stanley.

(Manny crosses to Barney, in store. Lights cross fade. Barney, stocking shelves, talks sharply to Manny.)

BARNEY: What are you saying, Manny? For God's sakes, you of all people should understand. I've heard stories of how in the army soldiers with Jewish names are treated…

MANNY: I'm in the Navy…

BARNEY: Whatever.

MANNY: It was rough, sometimes…

BARNEY: "Rough"? I heard if you didn't keep your eyes open, you could get beaten up.

MANNY: If you didn't keep your eyes open, you could get *shot!* It's a war, Uncle. It's bigger than Jews and Gentiles…

BARNEY: I will not have rocks thrown through my window!

MANNY: The world is always going to have a few lunatics, Uncle…even in a town like Sault Ste. Marie…changing your name doesn't change the way people are…or who they are…or what they are.

BARNEY: Manny, you're a nice boy, but, you're just like your mother. I love you both, very much, but, the world is a lot worse off than either of you think it is… *(Pauses.)* This family has suffered enough for its Jewish name.

MANNY: *(Screams.)* Uncle Barney, listen to me! I have just come from a War that is being fought, in part, over Jews…Jews who are proud to be Jews…

BARNEY: *(Outraged, screams.) I am a Jew!* But, I see no reason to print it on my forehead, or my wife's forehead, or my innocent son's forehead! And that is my decision…*my decision.*

MANNY: My God, I thought *I* was confused…

BARNEY: Manny, do you think I'm some kind of idiot? Do you think I've given this no thought? I see what's coming. Today, in Canada, it's rocks through the windows. Tomorrow, in Canada, it's going to be rocks through the skulls... *(Rationally, calmly. Doesn't complete his thought; pauses; speaks coldly, clearly.)* This family is changing its name from Rosen to Royal, and that, Nephew, is that.

(Barney turns his back on Manny and begins jotting notes into his inventory register. Manny pauses a moment, helplessly, then, without warning, exits the store. Barney senses that Manny has gone. He turns and looks, to be certain. He then bows his head, extremely upset. Unnoticed at first, Kravitz, an old Jew, a sign painter, enters. N.B. Same actor who plays Ardenshensky plays Kravitz. He wears a painted-spattered coverall upon which is printed: "Kravitz Signs". He carries a sign-painter's kit: open pots of paint, brushes, rags, solvents, etc., all easily accessible. He calls softly to Barney to get his attention. He senses Barney's upset.)

KRAVITZ: Barney? Hey Barney? Are you alright?

BARNEY: Hello, Kravitz...Yes, I'm fine. I appreciate your coming on such short notice...

KRAVITZ: Oh, listen, with this war on and no work around, I'm delighted to be called on any notice: short, long, medium, you name it...Well, what can I do for you? Another sale?

BARNEY: No, this is big. I want a new window, a new main sign and maybe some new cards.

KRAVITZ: Really? What's the problem? My old window looks fresh still...

BARNEY: *(Motions with his hands.)* Barney Royal Menswear...

KRAVITZ: Who?

BARNEY: Royal is in. Rosen is out.

KRAVITZ: Oh my, you told me business was down, Barney...but, oh, my... *(Hand on Barney's shoulder.)* This is really bad news. The Soo is losing a great man and a great menswear store. And that is the truth!

BARNEY: No, no, Kravitz. It's okay. Don't fret! I am Royal: me.

KRAVITZ: They made you a good price?

BARNEY: Kravitz, listen! I am Royal: me...

KRAVITZ: You're a partner with the new owner?

BARNEY: I *am* the new owner. I never sold. You said that, not me. I am Royal: Barney Royal. I am changing my name, that's all.

KRAVITZ: You are changing your what?

BARNEY: My name, my name...

KRAVITZ: But, why?

BARNEY: Come on, Kravitz, you haven't noticed there's a war on?

KRAVITZ: I noticed there's a war on, but I didn't notice that they were fighting over your name!

BARNEY: I don't have time for this! Are you or are you not going to paint my sign?

KRAVITZ: Oh, I see what's going on here. *(Takes brush from paint-box.)* I'll show you what I'll paint... *(Kravitz paints a Jewish star on his own coverall, on his own chest; slowly, bright yellow paint.)* If you're smart, you'll hire me to paint the same thing on your window...but, if you need a new sign painted, Mr. Royal, you're going to have to get yourself a new boy... *(Kravitz stands staring at Barney a moment, silently.)* Oh, come on, Barney, hmmm, you haven't noticed there's a war on?

(Lights shift to dining table. Pearl and Stanley sit at table. Newspaper open in front of Stanley.)

STANLEY: It's in the paper?

PEARL: *(Points to advertisement in paper.)* It's in the paper.

STANLEY: Oh, God. It's in the paper.

(Manny crosses to table; sits.)

PEARL: It's in the paper.

STANLEY: It's in the paper.

MANNY: It's in the paper? *(Looks; reads.)* It's in the paper.

STANLEY: You really let me down, Manny. You were my only hope. Now I've got no hope at all... *(Pounds table with fist.)* Dammit, Manny! Dammittt!

(The lights cross fade as Manny, humiliated, moves into bedroom; stands, center of room, head bowed. We hear: a siren blaring the alert for an air raid drill. At the sound of the siren, all of the family snaps into action...except Manny, who seems frozen in humiliation.)

STANLEY: Air raid drill!

PEARL: Air raid drill...

BARNEY: Air raid drill!

STANLEY: Turn out the lights!

BARNEY: Stanley, pull the curtains!

PEARL: Turn out the lights!

(Stanley runs into bedroom. Manny is drenched in perspiration, terrified. Stanley doesn't notice. Yells at Manny.)

STANLEY: Air raid drill, air raid drill! Pull the blackout curtains closed!

(Stanley shuts off lights in the bedroom. Pearl and Barney shut off lights in the rest of the house.)

BARNEY: Stanley, help me close the blackout curtains! Pearl, turn out the lights!

STANLEY: Are they out there? Look! Are the Nazis out there?

PEARL: There are no Nazis out there, Stanley! *(To Barney.)* Do you see, Mr. Royal, how scared you've made your son?

(Manny, in bedroom, is streaked with lights as searchlights cut across window in air raid practice outside. Manny, soaked and frightened, suddenly screams aloud, crazed.)

MANNY: *Hitttt ittttttt! Hit the deck! The sky is full! Five o'clock! Hit... the... deckkkk! Hit itttt!*

(And with that, Manny leaps on to floor, under bed. The lights all black out. The siren continues, and then, suddenly, there is darkness and silence. Lights up on Reb Brechtman and Stanley, at table, which is now Reb Brechtman's study.)

REB BRECHTMAN: Well, Mr. Rosen, what did Doctor Sternberg say after that?

STANLEY: He said if Manny stayed in bed, he'd feel better. His nerves are still shot...

REB BRECHTMAN: And *your* nerves, Mr. Rosen?

STANLEY: My nerves are fine.

REB BRECHTMAN: So, why is it, after such good news about your cousin, you are still so depressed that you sing your *half-torah* like an Anglican?

STANLEY: Oh, well, depressed? Mentally, you mean?

REB BRECHTMAN: Mentally, yes, wouldn't you say mentally? If you were physically depressed, Mr. Rosen, would you not be on the floor?

STANLEY: Oh, it's nothing, Reb Brechtman. The usual. Family problems, a little bit, but, nothing, nothing... *(Sighs.)* Oh, God...

REB BRECHTMAN: Well, Mr. Rosen? You could talk to me and I might be able to help. Or you could hold it inside, and I could sit here wondering why it is a young man like you doesn't have the courage to face what is making him suffer. But it's up to you, isn't it, to pick one way or the other?

STANLEY: *(After a long pause.)* My mother has invited all of my teachers, not to mention all of my friends and their parents...but that's not it.

REB BRECHTMAN: That's not it?

STANLEY: There's worse.

REB BRECHTMAN: *Vay ist mier!* So what is the worse?

STANLEY: Reb Brechtman, my father is changing my name to Royal!

REB BRECHTMAN: Royal Rosen?

STANLEY: No, no! My family name! All of us! From Rosen to Royal. Stanley Royal, Barney Royal, Barney Royal Menswear, Pearl Royal, and so on.

REB BRECHTMAN: "And so on?" There are more at home?

STANLEY: Just Toronto, the house cat… *(Sighs, again.)* Oh, God.

REB BRECHTMAN: Why would he do such a thing?

STANLEY: So people won't know…won't know…so people won't know… we're…well…Jewish.

REB BRECHTMAN: I beg your pardon, but are my ears playing me tricks?

STANLEY: Oh, God!

REB BRECHTMAN: This is Barney Rosen, who was President of our congregation once and secretary-treasurer of the Brotherhood? This is the man of whom you are speaking?

STANLEY: He isn't converting us…he just thinks a Jewish name will get us in trouble in Canada, like it's doing for Jews in Poland. He thinks he's saving our lives…He's already published legal notices in the paper. Thank God, nobody reads them !

REB BRECHTMAN: Uhhhhhh. I seeeeee…He's afraid that the Jews here will…? *(He doesn't, for once, finish his question.)* Oyyy…This is a problem, isn't it? *(There is a small silence.)* Mr. Rosen it is written in the Talmud that "a child must treat his parents as though they were his King and Queen…" *(He thinks some more.)* Also "Let us be grateful for our parents: Had they not been tempted, we would not be here." (He thinks a moment; smiles.) Tell me, Mr. Rosen, there are laws about the changing of names. How far along is your father in this?

STANLEY: The court hearing is at four-thirty…

REB BRECHTMAN: And it seems that you do not want your name changed?

STANLEY: Oh, no! I mean, yes, I do not want my name changed. I don't want to hide from being a Jew, Reb Brechtman. I can understand why my father is frightened and all, but I think he's…wrong.

REB BRECHTMAN: Wrong? Do you think that he's "wrong," or that he has yet to see the "correct choice"?

STANLEY: What I really mean is that he's stubborn! I know he knows what's correct. But he's so stubborn! Once he's decided on something, he's like a great lake…

REB BRECHTMAN: …The wolf does not fear the dog, but fears his bark. He who can only cringe, can only move forward by creeping…It is worse to live on your knees than to die on your feet. Mr. Rosen, do you know what logic is?

STANLEY: Well, yes, I think so.

REB BRECHTMAN: What is logic, Mr. Rosen?

STANLEY: Logic is…uh…being sensible…I don't know how to say it, exactly…

REB BRECHTMAN: To say it exactly? Very good, Mr. Rosen...To not know how to say it exactly, absolutely, is to not know how to say it logically. It's all in the Talmud...a very good book that I might recommend to you... *(He thinks a moment.)* "For instance" is not proof. *(He thinks a moment.)* Every "why" has a wherefore. Lust is the enemy of logic. Mr. Rosen, in this life, one can never accept being a victim of anyone or anything. One must fight for control...to agree or disagree. Without fight, there is no life. That is a lesson in life that even the Jews must study well...if we are to continue in the face of...what seems to be going on... *(He is lost for a moment. Then he looks to Stanley; smiles.)* Well, Mr. Rosen, any ideas? After all, in a few days you will be a man.

STANLEY: *(Slowly.)* I...I'm going to fight, Reb Brechtman...I'm going to fight—with logic and with truth—I'm going to tell them why I want a Jewish name—what it means to me...That's what I'm going to do, Reb Brechtman. Okay?

REB BRECHTMAN: Do you think it's okay?

STANLEY: Oh, God, Reb Brechtman, why do you always always always answer questions with questions? Questions! I get so sick of your questions!

REB BRECHTMAN: Really?

STANLEY: Really.

REB BRECHTMAN: *(After a pause.)* Which questions in particular?
(Reb Brechtman looks at Stanley; smiles. The lights shift. Fern's light fades up. She is in her window, holding inevitable phone. Stanley turns and "talks" to Fern, as if on telephone.)

FERN: What, Stanley? What could be so important, Stanley? It's so late! I'll get killed for this!

STANLEY: Fern, please, please...

FERN: Well, whhhhhattt?

STANLEY: Please, Fern! What I have to ask is very...difficult...and when you're in a snit, I don't think I can ask it...

FERN: I am not in a snit, Stanley Rosen! For your information, your friend Irving Yanover keeps calling me and calling me. He's probably rung this telephone fifteen times tonight and my parents are furious...

STANLEY: What the hell is Yanover calling you about?

FERN: I think that's my personal business, don't you? If you want to ask me a question, Stanley, please do it *now!*

STANLEY: *(Quietly; quickly.)* If I were to pick you up now at your house, would you run away with me and get married and live in Ottawa?

FERN: No.

STANLEY: Vancouver?

FERN: No.

STANLEY: How about Jasper? It's beautiful.

FERN: No.

STANLEY: I see. You won't marry me?

FERN: No, Stanley, I won't.

STANLEY: Will you just run away with me?

FERN: No.

STANLEY: If I were to run away and then send for you, would you follow me later?

FERN: No.

STANLEY: Do you love me more than words can say?

FERN: No.

STANLEY: Oh, God! Fern, let me just get this straight, you won't run away with me?…

FERN: No.

STANLEY: You won't follow me, or marry me?

FERN: No, no!

STANLEY: Are you in love with Irving Yanover?

FERN: Oh, my God, Stanley, don't be *disgusting!*

STANLEY: *(Giggles.)* Great talking with you, Fern…

(Lights shift to Judge Brown's "study" which is the same desk used by Reb Brechtman, downstage left Barney and Pearl enter. Stanley joins them, wearing winter coat.)

BARNEY: Are you Judge Brown?

JUDGE BROWN: *(Offstage.)* I am…

(The actor who plays Reb Brechtman, etc., re-enters, now wearing a curly white wig and black robes. The costume is traditional: absurd.)

BARNEY: We were sent in here by the clerk outside…It's our turn…

JUDGE BROWN: Do you have an attorney?

BARNEY: No, I…We're here to change our family name…

JUDGE BROWN: Oh, yes, Mr. Rosen…I have your file… *(Judge Brown rummages through pile of papers on desk, finds file.)* Do you have your application with you?

BARNEY: Here…

(Hands envelope to Judge Brown, who speaks to them coldly, flatly, as he inspects documents. His accent is British.)

JUDGE BROWN: Have you published your intention? I don't see any clippings in your file?

BARNEY: *(Hands clipping to Judge Brown.)* Here are the clippings, Judge Brown. These are from the Sault Ste. Marie *Star,* these are from the Ontario *Gazette...*

JUDGE BROWN: Oh, yes, thank you... *(Looks file over.)* This seems to be in order. *(Looks up at Barney.)* Are there any persons here as objectors? *(Looks around room; smiles.)* I suppose it's just us here, isn't it?

STANLEY: *(Quietly.)* I object.

BARNEY: Huh?

STANLEY: Uh, excuse me, uh, sir, uh, but, uh, I, uh, uh, object.

JUDGE BROWN: I beg your pardon.

STANLEY: I object to the name change.

PEARL: Stanley.

BARNEY: What is this?

STANLEY: Jews are caught in a war and Manny is fighting for them so that they can have their names and my father is just being stubborn and I object! I object!

BARNEY: Shut your mouth, Stanley!

STANLEY: *(To Barney.)* No, I won't shut my mouth! I'm not afraid of you! Just your bark! *(To Pearl.)* If I cringe, mama, I'll only be able to move forward by creeping...

BARNEY: What is this? Are you working for your mother?

PEARL: Shush, Barney.

BARNEY: Don't you shush me, Pearl!

STANLEY: I...am not...afraid...of my...parents! *(Suddenly quiet, collected, eloquent. To Pearl and Barney.)* You are my King and my Queen. I am grateful to you for being tempted.

PEARL: What are you *talking* about, Stanley?

JUDGE BROWN: Excuse me, young man...Stanley...

STANLEY: *(To Judge.)* Please, listen to me, sir. I'm not doing this because I think my father is wrong. It's just that he hasn't seen the correct choice! *(Quietly.)* Sir, don't let him change my name. If he wants to change his own, that's for him to decide. *(To Barney.)* I would never change your name on you, Poppy. I never would! *(To Judge.)* I'm getting Bar Mitzvahed on Saturday in front of everybody and I want to be Bar Mitzvahed as Stanley Rosen. That's who I am: a Jew with a Jewish name...

PEARL: *(A whisper.)* Oh, my God, Barney...

BARNEY: Stanley, dammit!

STANLEY: I object, oh, I object, I really do! This is my name! Mine! I'm proud to be a Jew and I want it stamped all over me…I want everybody to know that we've been around since the beginning of time and we're smart and we're nice and we have the Talmud, mama, which I'll bet is even better than Oliver Goddamned Twist! *(To Judge.)* Can you see, sir, logically, that I, Stanley Rosen, am a person and I have rights!!! I…am…not a victim! I have rights! What are my legal rights, your honor?

BARNEY: *(Through clenched teeth.)* Excuse me, your honor…

JUDGE BROWN: I'm afraid, Stanley, that under the Laws of the Dominion of Canada, a thirteen-year-old is still an "Infant Child." You have no rights…not in this particular matter of the changing of a name…

STANLEY: What do you mean: no rights?

JUDGE BROWN: Until you reach the age of fourteen, you are legally…an infant.

STANLEY: An infant? All the time I'm thirteen? Infant?

JUDGE BROWN: An infant.

STANLEY: But, on Saturday, I will become a man—by Jewish law.

JUDGE BROWN: That may well be…

STANLEY: Oh…my…God!

(Stanley turns and runs out of the "courtroom," up the stairs and into the dining room of the Rosen family home. The lights cross fade with him. Barney and Pearl run after him, into the dining room.)

BARNEY: Stanley! Stop!

PEARL: Stanley!

BARNEY: This is the worst thing you've ever done, Stanley Rosen! Explain yourself, Stanley!

STANLEY: But didn't you listen to what I just said in there?

BARNEY: Didn't I listen? *Didn't I listen?* Stanley David Rosen, *you* listen: That man is a judge. *A judge!* Who are you to start such a commotion?…To cause such an embarrassment?

STANLEY: But I don't want to change my name, Poppy!

BARNEY: *You are my son and you will change your name!* I am *telling* you now… *Telling you!*…you…will…change…your name! And that is *that!*

STANLEY: *(Choking back tears)* Is this it?…Mama? Do you want me to, change my name, too?

(Pearl bows her head, silently. She weeps.)

STANLEY: *(Angrily; to Pearl.)* I assume you mean "yes," right? I assume you're on his side, right? Teamed up against me, right? *(He yells at his parents.)* I don't want to be your son! You hear me? You hear me? I wish I weren't your son!

(Without thought, without warning, Barney slaps Stanley's face. It is a sudden shocking blow. The boy reels backwards, trips, falls, stands immediately. Stanley's moves should be awkward, graceless, touching. Pearl is astonished. She spits a whisper at her husband.)

PEARL: How dare you? *How…dare…you?*

(Stanley covers his mouth with both hands, as though creating a sort of surgical mask with his fingers. He turns from Barney and Pearl and runs across the stage to his room. Barney chases after him, crossing through the set. Pearl follows, head down, weeping. Barney raps sharply on Stanley's bedroom door. Stanley is inside, with Manny. Stanley is frightened, goes to door, pauses.)

BARNEY: Stanley, open the door! Stanley! *Stanley!*

STANLEY: *(Opens door a crack.)* I am staying silent until I have an answer to "What to do"—I'll thank you to respect my silence. *(Closes door.)* Please help me, Manny. You're so much smarter and older than I am! *(Pauses.)* I'm sunk, truly *sunk!* It's Tuesday, the Bar Mitzvah is Saturday. I've only got three days.

MANNY: Three days? God created half the Universe in three days.

STANLEY: Don't crack wise, now, Manny, okay? I've got a headache…

MANNY: Sorry…

STANLEY: If I had a *minyan*—if I had ten Jewish men—then the Torah could be opened and read, right?

MANNY: Right…

STANLEY: So, all I've got to do is find ten Jewish men who'll side with me, right?

MANNY: I don't know what you're asking me, exactly…

STANLEY: No, Manny…you don't know what I'm asking you, *logically…* *(Slowly, confidently, seriously.)* No matter what I seem to be doing, Manny, I need you to trust me. Can you trust me?

MANNY: *(Groucho voice.)* Does tuna fish come in cans?

STANLEY: *(Same voice.)* It soitenly does…

MANNY: *(Same voice.)* I soitenly do…

(The two young men do their "moo" handshake, their "honk" signal…and then, they embrace.)

STANLEY: Wish me luck, Manny…

MANNY: You don't need luck. You're Stan-the-Man…

STANLEY: Not yet, Manny, but, that's my plan…

(Stanley crosses to Reb Brechtman's study. The lights cross with him. Stanley stands in front of Reb Brechtman, who seems perplexed.)

REB BRECHTMAN: But, Mr. Rosen, today is Wednesday, tomorrow is already

Thursday! How could I ever find a *minyan* of ten such Jewish men in one day's time?

STANLEY: I have spent the night awake, silent, thinking, Reb Brechtman, I have used logic from start to finish. I know how to do this exactly... *(Pauses.)* Ten thirteen-year-old men are ten men, yes? A *minyan,* yes?

REB BRECHTMAN: Yes.

STANLEY: If the Torah is opened and read, then it's legal, yes?

REB BRECHTMAN: Yes. And if ten such men can be convinced to join our cause, I will have to offer my services, because I am a Rabbi...

STANLEY: You can give me a list of the men you've Bar Mitzvahed in the last year or so, both from Sault Ste. Marie, Ontario, and from Sault Ste. Marie, Michigan, across the lake, yes?

REB BRECHTMAN: Yes, I could do that, yes...

STANLEY: And the ferry is running these days, yes?

REB BRECHTMAN: Yes, the ferry is running, yes.

STANLEY: You won't go away, Reb Brechtman, yes? You'll be here tomorrow, yes?

REB BRECHTMAN: Yes, Mr. Rosen. I'll be here...

STANLEY: Thank you, Reb Brechtman...

(Reb Brechtman exits. Stanley walks downstage and "talks" as if on telephone.)

STANLEY: Hullo, Al Rubenstein? This is Stanley Rosen. I'm on the Canadian side. Hullo, Alvy Singer? This is Stanley Rosen. I'm on the Canadian side. Hullo, Harvey? This is Stanley. Barney Rosen Menswear, Queen Street? *Hiiii.*

(Music in. We hear: the sound of ten young men singing in Hebrew, lightly. The singing increases in volume and intensity. Reb Brechtman joins Stanley in pinspot. Stanley looks out front, excitedly. Thrilled.)

STANLEY: They all showed up, Reb Brechtman! They all came to help me!

REB BRECHTMAN: Jews can be like that, Mister Rosen.

(Reb Brechtman helps Stanley into his "tallis" and "yamulka": prayer shawl and skullcap. Stanley walks to table, stands beside Reb Brechtman, and begins to chant his half-Torah, from the scriptures. The chanting continues, lightly, under. The lights cross fade to Stanley's bedroom, where Barney and Pearl are distraught, facing Manny, and Stanley's empty bed.)

BARNEY: Manny, where's Stanley?

MANNY: He left.

BARNEY: How can this be? It's six-thirty in the morning! He can't have gone to school...Pearl. Six-thirty!

PEARL: What time did he leave, Manny?

MANNY: He left at two o'clock.

BARNEY: And you didn't stop him?

MANNY: No. I didn't stop him… *(Hopefully.)* Maybe he's staying with a friend…

(The sound of the chanting grows louder.)

BARNEY: I'm going to call the Yanovers…

PEARL: Call the police, Barney.

MANNY: No, Aunt Pearl, that's not necessary. I know you're upset, but, for what it's worth, I'm not worried about Stanley. He's very smart and I myself used to stay up all night, many a night. When you're thirteen, it's fun…

PEARL: *(Yells at Barney; suddenly.) I blame you! (Sobs.)* What have you done to this family, you? When I call the police, what name do I give them, you? I'm talking to you, Mr. Royal! You have driven him, and everyone around him, absolutely *crazy!* If anything happens to my son, Barney, I… Call the police, please. *(Yells.)* Now, please…

(The lights cross fade downstage to "synagogue," where Reb Brechtman makes short speech.)

REB BRECHTMAN: We are gathered here to witness the Bar Mitzvah of Stanley David Rosen, who is ready to become a member of our congregation today. Some of you gentlemen have come all the way across the Lake by ferry to help Stanley accomplish his Bar Mitzvah. Now, really, why, in 1943, in the midst of world war, do we take the time and trouble to Bar Mitzvah our young men? *(Pauses.)* The Bar Mitzvah, I think, is our most civilized ritual and rite. To initiate our young men into our ranks, we do not knock out a front tooth or two. We do not give them their own guns with which to shoot people and other animals. We do not take Stanley, or any other Bar Mitzvah *brochah,* to Montreal, or Toronto, or Ottawa, for a city weekend with ladies of pleasure. To qualify for membership in our Jewish club, Stanley Rosen has had to do little more than master an old alphabet and learn enough of an ancient language to be able to read from this holy book. His manliness is associated with handwritten scrolls still studied in a spirit of reverent pleasure. Stanley Rosen cannot help but be shaped by this moment of Bar Mitzvah…by this celebration of his becoming a Jew…by this celebration of you, Stanley David Rosen, Jewish Man…

STANLEY: I am Stanley David Rosen, my name is Rosen, forever…Rosen is a fine Canadian Jewish name. That is my name. I shall never leave

Canada, and I shall never leave Judaism. I didn't know that, yesterday. Almost. Not quite… *(Pauses.)* Today…I am…a man.

(The singing continues lightly. Reb Brechtman exits; slowly; as Manny, Pearl and Barney step forward, excitedly. Lights shift to living room, again.)

MANNY: He's home!

BARNEY: Stanley!

PEARL: It's Stanley!

(Stanley enters living room.)

MANNY: Stanley.

PEARL: Where have you been?

BARNEY: Where have you been? We've been calling all over…

STANLEY: Shul…

BARNEY: Shul?

STANLEY: Shul…

PEARL: Practicing?

STANLEY: Uh, worse…maybe you'd better sit down, Mama…I've already been Bar Mitzvahed, Mama…

MANNY: You're joshing!

STANLEY: I'm not joshing, Manny. I've been Bar Mitzvahed.

BARNEY: You what?

PEARL: You what?

STANLEY: I had myself Bar Mitzvahed…legally…at 8:00 this morning. It's over.

PEARL: *(Weeps, nearly in a swoon.)* How could you do this to me, Stanley?

STANLEY: It's okay. You can still have the reception. I didn't have that! I just had the Bar Mitzvah ceremony! Nothing has changed…Really…And if you want to change our name, Poppy, go ahead. It's fine…really. I've been Bar Mitzvahed as Stanley Rosen and I'll be Stanley Rosen until I die. After all, in the eyes of Jews, I'm a man… *(Pauses.)* I'm not really an infant, you know. I have ideas, just like you had when you were thirteen. I have feelings, too…

(Pearl goes to Stanley, hugs him. Barney goes downstage, "talks" to Judge Brown, as if on telephone. Stanley will eavesdrop during midpoint of Barney's "conversation" with Judge Brown. He moves downstage.)

BARNEY: Is this Judge Brown? I'm so sorry to wake you up. Well…sir…I read an ad in the paper that said I should contact you if I objected to a Barney Rosen of Sault Ste. Marie, Ontario, changing his name to Barney Royal, and I do…object.

(Stanley arrives at Barney's side. Barney sees Stanley; turns. Barney is weeping. Suddenly…)

BARNEY: Oh God, Stanley, Stanley…I love you so much…

STANLEY: I love you so much, too, Poppy.

BARNEY: Can you forgive me, Stanley?

STANLEY: You're my father.

(Barney and Stanley embrace. The lights cross to Manny, in bedroom. Stanley crosses to Manny; Barney exits.)

STANLEY: A cutaway?

MANNY: A cutaway… *(Manny holds up jacket to formal cutaway tuxedo.)* The box came from Eaton's in Toronto, this morning…Your mother wants you to try on the pants…right away…Look at the stripe. Very sexy stuff!

STANLEY: *(Taking off pants.)* At least the color's appropriate.

MANNY: Black?

STANLEY: Black is appropriate.

MANNY: For your Bar Mitzvah reception?

STANLEY: For my funeral…Yesterday, I became a man. Today, I'm becoming a *dead* man. I'm contemplating suicide, Manny. Oh, God! How do they look? Too baggy?

MANNY: No. They're nice. You look like the Head Usher at the Algoma Cinema.

STANLEY: *(Total depression.)* Oh, God…

MANNY: Why the nervous breakdown?

STANLEY: If I say it out loud, I might make it real…

MANNY: Try whispering…

STANLEY: *(Inaudibly.)* I've got no date… *(Full-voiced.)* Oh, God…

MANNY: Stanley, I heard the "Oh, God," but, I didn't hear whatever came after the "I got no…" You've got no what?

STANLEY: *(Inaudibly.)* Date.

MANNY: What?

STANLEY: *(Screams.)* DATE! I've got no goddamn date! Okay? *(Moans.)* …I'm about to become the first living human being in the history of the world not to have a date for his very own Bar Mitzvah reception…

MANNY: Fern turned you down, eh?

STANLEY: If my mother gets wind of this, she'll have fat Rosie Berkowitz on my arm in ten seconds flat. And that brain-damaged putz, Yanover, will be drawing demented drawings of me dancing with Blimp Berkowitz on every goddamn locker in the goddamn school! Oh, God, Manny! Why is life without hope?

MANNY: You know, Stanley, I've been listening to most of your telephone conversations with Fern and I think, well, I might be able to give you a couple of ideas about handling, well, *women…*

STANLEY: *You will, Manny?* I will be your slave for life if you can turn this all around for me!

MANNY: Turning your telephone approach to women around is exactly what I plan on doing, Stanley…

(The lights fade up on Fern. Manny whispers a line to Stanley for him to speak to Fern. Stanley speaks the line at precisely the same time. We are seeing a sort of Semitic John Alden/Pocahontas scene being played out.)

MANNY AND STANLEY: *(In unison.)* I'm really sorry about this, Fern…

FERN: But, when did you meet her?

MANNY AND STANLEY: *(In unison.)* She just moved to the Soo, about three weeks ago…

FERN: Three weeks? Three entire weeks and you haven't mentioned her to me, even once? That is sooo cruel, Stanley! Stanley, that is so…*secretive!*

MANNY AND STANLEY: *(In unison.)* I wanted to, Fern, but, you've been, well, a little hard to talk to…

FERN: That is hardly any excuse for seeing somebody else behind my back!

MANNY AND STANLEY: *(In unison.)* Look, Fern, I really feel terrible about this. If you really want to be my date, I could, I dunno…I could say *something* to her…If you really want to be my date…

(Fern enters. She is twelve years old and she is adorable. She wears a fabulous dress with shoes to match. Heavenly music plays. Stanley moves to Fern and we now see that Fern is several inches taller than Stanley. We hear the sound of an angel chorus: Bach, probably.)

FERN: How could you ever doubt that I wanted to be your date, Stanley, hmmmm?

(Fern gives Stanley a "come here, let's kiss" signal. After a brief "who, me?" response, Stanley flashes Manny a look of triumph and a salute of gratitude. Manny returns the salute and exits. Fern and Stanley embrace and kiss. They are, for all intents and purposes, "making out." The angel chorus segues into something heroic: trumpets announcing the arrival of something magnificent. Farentelli, the sculptor, enters, pushing a wheelable table upon which is placed a life-sized statue of Stanley carved in chopped liver. A cloth covers the statue. Pearl and Barney enter, proudly. They are totally overdressed for any occasion. Barney wears a tux and then some. Pearl wears golden robes. Manny follows. The trumpets build to an extraordinary moment of tension. Stanley is horrified. He and Fern face the statue, as do Manny, Pearl and

Barney. It is a moment of great expectation. Mr. Farentelli plucks the cloth from the statue and there it is, for all to see. Stanley, the Bar Mitzvah boy, carved in chopped liver. It is a masterpiece. The music swells, Pearl kvells, the audience yells…The lights black out. A moment of applause. Lights immediately up, as if for curtain calls. Farentelli steps forward, rips off his beret and reveals himself to be none other than Jacob Ardenshensky. He calls out to an amazed audience.)

ARDENSHENSKY: It's me: Ardenshensky. You thought maybe I was Farentelli, the famous Italian sculptor? *(Pauses; smiles.)* I'm an actor. I'm working… *(Pauses.)* Little voices get heard. That is the most wonderful thing about life: the voices of children, of house cats, or little families whose lives have no real impact on history, just on each other—these voices, some-how, get out, and sometimes a world listens… *(Smiles; nods to audience.)* You listened. *(Pauses.)* The war in Europe finally ended. Luckily, people have memories, they don't forget. Sometimes, they even learn. This is what we call "Hope." And this is why we stay alive, why we have chil-dren—in the face of what we also know to be true… *(Smiles.)* I'd better wrap this up and tell you what became of some of us… *(Pauses.)* The war of the Rosens ended, too…Manny Boxbaum married a nice girl from Vancouver, they had two boys for whom Pearl supervised the Bar Mitzvah receptions, complete with statuary. Manny Boxbaum died in his sleep, peacefully, at the age of eighty-one… *(Smiles to Fern.)* Fern Fipps stayed in love with Stanley Rosen, *buttt*…she also stayed in love with Irving Yanover!

STANLEY: *(Angry; shocked.)* What?

(Stanley turns his back on Fern, in a rage. And then he and Fern laugh; look again at Ardenshensky.)

ARDENSHENSKY: But, you'll be able to see this for yourself. There will be another play: *The Chopin Playoffs,* starring Fern and her family, three Rosens, three Yanovers and two Steinways… *(Remembers.)* Oh, yes, Toronto. Toronto was killed by a truck on the Trans-Canada Expressway at the age of 176 years old. I guess her time was up. *(Smiles.)* Oh, I should tell you a little story about Barney. A salesman who shortened his name from Silberstein to Silber asked Barney what his name had been before he shortened his name to Rosen, and Barney answered…

BARNEY: *(Finishing sentence.)* …Before Rosen, most recently, our name was Royal…

ARDENSHENSKY: So, that's everybody. Oh, yes, as for me, Jacob Ardenshensky, I never lived, so I never died. I'm just eight characters in a play about a very nice family, the Rosens, who, by any other name are still, now and forever, the Rosens…

(Music and lights swell to full, as Pearl and Barney, and Stanley and Manny and Fern bow; and then the curtain falls.)

The play is over.

The Chopin Playoffs

For my darling Gillian.

ORIGINAL PRODUCTION

The Chopin Playoffs received its world premiere production at the American Jewish Theatre in New York City (Stanley Brechtner, Artistic Director; Leda Gelles, Managing Director) on May 15, 1986. It was directed by Stephen Zuckerman; the set design was by James Fenhagen; the costume design was by Mimi Maxmen; the lighting design was by Curt Ostermann; the sound design was by Aural Fixation; the casting was by Darlene Kaplan; the production associate was Evanne Christian; the production stage manager was Neal Fox; the technical director was Floyd R. Swagerty, Jr.; the production coordinator was Elyse Barbell; and the stage manager was Celestine. The cast was as follows:

Fern Fipps . . . . Maddie Corman
Ardenshensky, Uncle Goldberg, Mr. Wong,
Reb Brechtman. . . . . Sol Frieder
Esther Yanover. . . . . Marcia Jean Kurtz
Pearl Rosen (also voice of Mrs. Fipps) . . . . Karen Ludwig
Barney Rosen (also voice of Mr. Fipps/Emcee) . . Richard Portnow
Moses Yanover. . . . . Sam Schacht
Irving Yanover . . . . Jonathan Marc Sherman
Stanley Rosen . . . . Nicholas Strouse

The Chopin Playoffs was originally commissioned by The Community Theatre Project of the National Foundation for Jewish Culture.

THE PEOPLE OF THE PLAY

JACOB ARDENSHENSKY: an old Jew.
UNCLE GOLDBERG: an old Jew (N.B. Same actor as Ardenshensky).
IRVING YANOVER: sixteen, small, thin, handsome.
MOSES YANOVER: fortyish, Irving's father; large, friendly.
ESTHER YANOVER: fortyish, Irving's mother; small.
FERN FIPPS: sixteen, thin, small: a beauty.
VOICE OF PEGGY FIPPS: played by actress who plays Pearl or Esther.
VOICE OF MICHAEL FIPPS: played by actor who plays Barney or Moses.
STANLEY ROSEN: sixteen, small, thin, handsome.
BARNEY ROSEN: fortyish, Stanley's father; small.
PEARL ROSEN: fortyish, Stanley's mother; tall.
WAITER IN RITZ CAFE: an old Oriental (N.B. Same actor as Ardenshensky.)
VOICE OF EMCEE AT PLAYOFF:, tweedy, old scholar (N.B. Same actor as Ardenshensky.)

THE PLACE OF THE PLAY

The front rooms of the Rosen family home and the front rooms of the Yanover family home, and both family stores; Sault Ste. Marie, Ontario, Canada; plus, high school auditorium.

THE TIME OF THE PLAY

The final weeks of the school year, 1947.

A NOTE TO THE DIRECTOR
AND DESIGNER

The setting should have three essential elements: the Yanover home, the Rosen home, and the park and parkland. It is my vision that *The Chopin Playoffs* be full of springtime and blossom. Thus, I imagine the two homes "growing" out of the flowery, busy parkland. Realistically, two home units—each featuring piano, table, dining chairs, easy chair—should frame the stage, one on each side. There should be a channel of parkland, with bench, center. There should be a downstage apron of stage that can accommodate the Ritz cafe, Rosen's store, Capy's Grille, etc.

Changes in time and place should be established by the lighting.

The play is to be played without an intermission.

There should be no stage-waits whatsoever. Each scene is designed to flow into the next. If possible, overlap entrances and exits to move the action even more quickly. The spirit of the presentation should be magical: theatrically heightened storytelling.

A stern note on casting this play. It is my intention that the Rosen parents and Yanover parents be cast with youthful, attractive actors. Stereotypes are to be avoided, entirely. Additionally, Yiddish or Eastern European accents—or stereotypically "Jewish" intonation—are also forbidden in the casting of the parents. By contrast, Ardenshensky should be cast authentically old, optimally with an experienced Yiddish theatre comedian; certainly with a European-born actor. It is my intention to contrast the parents and Ardenshensky as modern vs. ancient world figures.

I.H.
N.Y.C.—Gloucester, January, 1985 – April, 1987

The Chopin Playoffs

ACT I

The lights fade out in the auditorium. In the darkness, we hear the sound of two pianos playing Chopin, lightly: the Raindrop Prelude, *which should serve as theme for the play. An old Jew, Jacob Ardenshensky, enters. He speaks to audience, directly, after "hushing" them.*

ARDENSHENSKY: Shhhh. Good evening, ladies and gentlemen…I feel that we can now speak together as friends… *(Smiles.)* My name is Jacob Ardenshensky… *(Singles out audience member.)* What's the matter? You've never seen a Canadian? *(Singles out section of audience.)* Either you're still laughing at the same joke, or you missed the first two plays… *(Smiles; to all.)* Tonight's play is called *The Chopin Playoffs*. The year is 1947, and the last of Canada's soldiers have returned home from Occupied Germany. Mackenzie King is Prime Minister and he has just stood side by side with Harry Truman in Ottawa and proclaimed "a new era of prosperity for the Dominion"…Free enterprise is booming and the word of the year is "competition"… *(Pauses.)* And this particular word has spread loudly and clearly to the "Soo"… *(Smiles.)* Oh, I forgot. You missed the first two plays…The Soo is our nickname for our town, Sault Ste. Marie, Ontario. We're just across the Lake from Sault Ste. Marie, Michigan. But, the competition in tonight's play has little to do with the automobile industry or the steel industry… *(Smiles.)* Tonight's competition is between the Yanovers and the Rosens…You've heard of the Hatfields and the McCoys? It's sort of the same thing, only different…In this corner, we have the Rosens…

(A prizefight bell rings.)

ARDENSHENSKY: *(Points to Rosens, who stand left.)* Barney, Pearl, and Stanley… I bought a topcoat from Rosen, but, that's another story… *(Points to Yanovers.)* And in this corner, ladies and gentlemen, the Yanovers… *(A prizefight bell rings, again.)* Mosie, Esther, and Irving…I bought a bad sheet from Yanover, but, I won't bore you with those details, either… *(Remembers.)* I am the oldest living man in the Soo. Pearl Rosen has an idiot uncle—a real *hoocchem* named Goldberg, who pretends to be older than me. Rumor has it that he's moving back and *he* will be the oldest living man in the Soo, and I will be the next-to-the-oldest… *(With quiet hostility.)* As if I could care less… *(Smiles.)* Before we begin, I've asked both Mrs. Rosen and Mrs. Yanover to say a word to you about competition. *(Remembers.)* Oh, one more thing. From time to time, I may play an extra part or two. Normally, I would never do such a thing, but, since this is [Name of theatre]… *(Shrugs.)* So, what could I do? *(Pauses.)* I'm just mentioning this in case somebody calls me "Uncle Goldberg" or "Mr. Wong" or somesuch. You shouldn't get confused. Of course, the likelihood of your being able to recognize me playing another role is, frankly, very, very, *very* slim. As some of you already know, I am a master of disguise… *(Smiles to Esther Yanover.)* Mrs. Yanover, you first, please…

ESTHER: *(Directly to audience; simply.)* You want to know what competition is? I'll tell you what competition is. Competition is Pearl and Barney Rosen seeing that we've bought a new DeSoto four-door sedan and a new Philco floor-model console, going out and buying themselves a new DeSoto 4-door sedan and a new Philco floor-model console. That, from me to you, is competition.

ARDENSHENSKY: *(Smiles to Pearl Rosen.)* Mrs. Rosen, now, you…

PEARL: *(Directly to audience; simply.)* You want to know what competition is? I'll tell you what competition is. Competition is Esther and Mosie Yanover seeing that Barney and I have bought a new Westinghouse refrigerator and range suite and running out and buying—you guessed—a new Westinghouse refrigerator and range suite. Now, *that,* from me to you, is competition.

ARDENSHENSKY: *(To audience.)* And now, from me to you, *The Chopin Playoffs*…is begun…

(We hear prizefight bell clang again. Ardenshensky exits. The Rosens exit. The lights dim and then rise, center. Stanley moves downstage into light. He "talks" to Fern, as if on the telephone. A light fades up on Fern, in her window.)

FERN: This phone call had better be important, Stanley Rosen! My father is going to kill me.

STANLEY: You hear the rain, Fern?

FERN: It's raining? That's why you called for the umpteenth time?

STANLEY: Listen. Isn't it beautiful?

FERN: Naturally, I perm my hair and what does it do?

STANLEY: When Chopin wrote the *Raindrop Prelude,* he imagined that he drowned in a lake, and drops of water were falling on his naked, dead chest. And when he told George Sand the story…about imagining himself drowned and the water on his chest, George Sand laughed at him and said "It's raining out. You're just hearing rain hitting the roof!" What an astonishing bitch, huh?

FERN: *(Laughs.)* God, Stanley, you believe any cock-and-bull story anybody throws at you. As long as it's anything about Chopin, you believe it. You are so *gullible.*

STANLEY: Why do you say that, Fern?

FERN: Because it's true! Last year, you told me this completely nuts story that *I'm Always Chasing Rainbows* is based on something Chopin wrote called *The Waltz of the Little Dog…*

STANLEY: But, it's true! *Waltz in D-Flat…*opus 64, number 1. I learned it when I was twelve…

FERN: Oh, God, Stanley, *really…*I've listened to Chopin's *Waltz in D-Flat* and it sounds absolutely nothing like *I'm Always Chasing Rainbows…*

STANLEY: Okay, fine. I'd better get dressed, Fern…What are you wearing tonight? I want to make sure we…you know…match.

FERN: Blue, definitely blue.

STANLEY: Great. I'll go blue, too…

FERN: Stanley, not *dark* blue, okay? At least, not your sport coat…at least, not dark blue on your *shoulders,* okay?

STANLEY: How come?

FERN: Ask me no questions and I'll tell you no lies, Stanley…See you at quarter-to-eight, sharp.

STANLEY: See you, Fern.

(Fern hangs up the telephone. Stanley looks wistfully out front. We hear: Waltz in D-Flat played softly, on a single piano. It is of course "I'm Always Chasing Rainbows." The lights cross fade to Yanover livingroom.)

ESTHER: *(To Moses, whose head is hidden in the newspaper he is reading.)* Listen to this incredible news, Mosie…It's in the paper. In New York City, New York, there is a boy named Arthur Burger who married a girl named Naomi Siegel. Not only is Arthur Burger a doctor; Naomi Siegel is also a doctor. Double *nachas.* Two doctors in one family…

(Irving enters. He wears casual 1940s clothing; white buck loafers. His hair is in a pompadour, slicked with tonic.)

IRVING: There could be *six* doctors, as far as I'm concerned. I have no interest in medical school, whatsoever.

ESTHER: Did anyone insinuate anything?

MOSES: It sounded that way to me.

IRVING: Nawww, not at alll. Did I insinuate that you insinuated?

MOSES: It sounded that way to me.

ESTHER: Discussing something and demanding something are two different matters, young man...

IRVING: Why do I feel we've had this conversation, already?

ESTHER: If you don't want to be a doctor, don't be a doctor. Your life is your life. I was only reading an article in a newspaper...

IRVING: Last night, it was an article in *Life* magazine about twin brothers who are lawyers...

MOSES: Is there anything wrong with lawyers? You have to be *some*thing. Lawyers become judges...

IRVING: It was a story about identical twins! You want me to study to be an identical twin?

MOSES: It was only a story in a magazine!

IRVING: Last week, you left a three-foot stack of accounting journals on my bed. I hopped into bed in the dark and nearly broke my back...

MOSES: I did no such thing...

ESTHER: There's something wrong with the accountancy profession?

MOSES: You put books in his *bed?*

IRVING: I nearly broke my back!

ESTHER: Next time, don't sneak in after hours with the light out...Mr. Skulks-Thru-The-House-Like-A-Cat-Burglar!

MOSES: Hey!!! Sault Ste. Marie's in the Jewish *Forward*...Did you ever hear of Cyrus Drinkwater?

IRVING: No, but I heard Cyrus peeing, afterwards.

ESTHER: This is a mouth you open at home, Mr. Talks-Filthy-To-His-Own-Mother-And-Father?

IRVING: I couldn't resist.

ESTHER: Try.

MOSES: It's a music contest with a money prize...

IRVING: What are you talking about?

MOSES: It's announced here in the *Forward*...A full university scholarship, up to four thousand dollars in fees and expenses...Cyrus Drinkwater... born here in the Soo...moved away, made millions...It's his money... *(Looks up at Irving.)* This is great. You can pay for university yourself. I'm off the hook.

IRVING: I'm delighted to pay for university myself as I've just saved you a fortune... (I assume you're feeling grateful.) So, I wanna ask you a favor, fella to fella...may I borrow the car tonight?

MOSES: Fella to fella, the question should be "May your mother and *I* borrow the car!"

ESTHER: You couldn't double-date with Stanley Rosen? I know he's got the *Rosen* DeSoto tonight. That's why we're going to *them*...

IRVING: I would rather have a tumor on my lip.

ESTHER AND MOSES: *(In unison.)* Irving Yanover!

IRVING: *(Leans even closer; whispers softly.)* It's a very, very big date for me, Papa...

MOSES: Okay, but, you have to help me with inventory Monday night.

ESTHER: How will we get to the Rosens?

MOSES: It's a nice night and we can use the exercise...

IRVING: It's a three-minute walk...

MOSES: I think a simple "thank-you" will suffice, young man.

IRVING: Thank you... *(Whispers to Moses.)* It's really a big big *big* date, Papa. Thanks...

ESTHER: What is going on here?...Mr.-Secret-and-His-Son?

MOSES: Esssieee, *shush!* A son's got to be able to talk to a father...

ESTHER: Now he's "shushhing" me?

IRVING: I'll be home by eleven. I won't drive fast. I'll do extra practice, tomorrow. I'll kiss my mother good night. All those things.
    (He does. Esther isn't smitten.)

IRVING: And Mama, I really appreciate that you've kept your promise here. I know that you're dying to ask, and I know your stomach's in knots, and I want you to know that I really and truly appreciate the courage you've shown in keeping your promise and not asking the big question.

ESTHER: She's not Jewish?

MOSES: *Esther!*
    (Irving runs out the door, which he slams shut. There is a pause.)

ESTHER: My mother would get a straight answer and my father would never shut her up and I myself do not like the way that things have changed in family life and that is that.
    (Moses smiles at Esther. Moses shrugs. We hear: a dog barking, fiercely. The lights cross fade to spotlight, downstage left. Irving stands downstage left facing door to Fern Fipps's home. Window overhead. Irving is being sniffed by an imaginary big dog, which the Fipps love, dearly. Fern's parents call down to Irving from window. They are unseen.)

MR. FIPPS: *(Offstage.)* Porchop won't hurttt youuu...

MRS. FIPPS: *(Offstage.)* Don't be frightened of Porkchooopppppp...
    (We hear: Porkchop growling fiercely.)

IRVING: Oh, Jesus, grab your dog!

(We hear: Porkchop growling.)

MR. FIPPS: *(Offstage.)* Whack her on the snout, smartly. Do you have a newspaper?

IRVING: No.

MR. FIPPS: *(Offstage.)* Use your open palm. Trust me...

(Irving whacks imagined dog, smartly. Dog screams, runs off...for the moment.)

MR. FIPPS: *(Offstage.)* Well done. Now then, what can we do for you, son?

IRVING: I'm sorry to cause such a, uh, rumpus. I'm Irving Yanover: Fern's date tonight. I've just come to pick her up. *(Pauses.)* Is she...ready?

(There is a pause.)

MR. FIPPS: *(Offstage.)* Why, uh, she's gone out already...

MRS. FIPPS: *(Offstage.)* With Stanley Rosen...

MR. FIPPS: *(Offstage.)* Maybe you've got the wrong night. I've done that myself...

MRS. FIPPS: *(Offstage.)* They're over at the "Y" dance. Why don't you join them?

IRVING: I will, thanks so much, Mr. and Mrs. Fipps. I'm so sorry to have bothered you...

(Simultaneously.)

MR. FIPPS: *(Offstage.)* Not at all, son. Good night, now...

MRS. FIPPS: *(Offstage.)* No trouble at all. Good night...

IRVING: *(Sadly.)* Night. *(Walks two steps; sudden terror.)* Oh, shit!

(Porkchop growls, suddenly Irving leaps backwards, protecting his, uh, future. We hear: Dance Music in, lightly: "Sweet Sue." A light fades up across stage on Stanley and Fern, dancing, cheek-to-cheek. Irving stands watching them a moment, shielding his eyes, stooping forward: peering. Stanley spins and dips Fern. Irving watches from the sideline. He is disgusted. N.B. He stands in blue light. The music ends. Stanley and Fern kiss. Irving watches. He is deeply disgusted. Stanley and Fern break from the kiss. Fern is aware of being watched. They whisper, loudly.)

FERN: Somebody's staring at us...

STANLEY: What do you mean?

FERN: Over by the side there, behind the grandstand. There's some pervert *gawking* at us. He's been gawking for the past hour.

STANLEY: You're *joshing*...

FERN: Look for yourself! Don't turn quickly! Look out of the corner of your eye...you *see*?

STANLEY: I see the bastard! I'll thrash him…

FERN: No! Don't! No fighting! You promised.

STANLEY: I'll just scare him off…

FERN: Be careful…

(Stanley walks to Irving. Lights shift as Stanley crosses stage, dimming slightly on Fern, leaving Stanley and Irving in bluish light. The two young men square off.)

STANLEY: Irving Yanover.

IRVING: Stanley Rosen.

(At exactly and precisely the same moment, both Irving and Stanley throw a punch at the other. Both hit at exactly and precisely the same time. Both stagger backward, both hold jaws, grimacing from blow. The boys now charge at one another, wrestling. Their obscene epithets overlap.)

STANLEY: Brain-damaged putz!

IRVING: Turd-faced, no-balled Chihuahua!

(They hop to their feet and square off, one final moment.)

STANLEY: Eat my caca and die, Yanover!

(At precisely the same moment, each throws a punch, each hits his opponent squarely on the nose, each gets a nosebleed. Stanley staggers to Fern; Irving staggers to Ardenshensky, who sits alone on park bench.)

FERN: Oh, God, Stanley, are you alright?

STANLEY: I got him good!

FERN: Who was that pervert?

STANLEY: Big guy…out-of-towner…old: maybe twenty…

FERN: My God, Stanley! You fought with him?

STANLEY: I got him good!

FERN: You've got blood on your nose!

STANLEY: Kiss me, Fern. Kiss me and my blood…

FERN: Stanley Rosen, you are so *disgusting! Uchhh!* I truly loathe people who *fight!* What is the *matter* with you? Have you flipped your wig, *completely???*

(Stanley looks at Fern, helplessly. The lights cross fade to Irving, sitting alone with Ardenshensky, on park bench. Irving's head is back. His nosebleed has stopped: just.)

ARDENSHENSKY: I thought the war was over. It started up again?

IRVING: (Thought he was alone on bench; surprised.) What? Huh? Oh, hullo, Mr. Ardenshensky. Lovely night.

ARDENSHENSKY: I've seen better… (Pauses.) How did you know my name?

IRVING: You shop in my father's store.

ARDENSHENSKY: Are you the Rosen boy? Did your father sell me a defective topcoat?

IRVING: No, I'm the Yanover boy. My father sold you a defective bedsheet.

ARDENSHENSKY: So, Yanover, what's with your nose?

IRVING: You should see the other guy.

ARDENSHENSKY: Oyyy, fighting?

IRVING: He jumped me.

ARDENSHENSKY: He jumped on your nose?

IRVING: My nose is fine, Mr. Ardenshensky, really. Thank you for your concern. I'm fine. Completely restored. *(Sniffs loudly, as if to prove something.)* See?

ARDENSHENSKY: So, why are you alone on a Saturday night, mentally depressed? You've got no girlfriend?

IRVING: I've got a girlfriend.

ARDENSHENSKY: *(Looks about.)* She's hiding in the trees?

IRVING: No, she's…busy tonight. We don't, uh, go steady. I mean, we, uh, go out with other people…

ARDENSHENSKY: You're out with me. Who's she out with?

IRVING: I…I'm not positive.

ARDENSHENSKY: A girl who is everybody's girlfriend is nobody's girlfriend…
(There is a small, painful pause here.)

IRVING: *(Ironically.)* It was really very lucky bumping into you like this, Mr. Ardenshensky. Really very lucky… *(Starts to leave, thinks better of it, turns and faces Ardenshensky.)* I heard that you're not the oldest living man in the Soo, anymore, I heard that Mrs. Rosen's Uncle Goldberg is coming home and he's even older than you…

ARDENSHENSKY: *(Angrily.)* You think that bothers me? You think I could care less about being the oldest living man in the Soo? What is the matter with you??? Can't an old man sit alone peacefully in the park??? *(Magnanimously.)* You keep the bench.
(Ardenshensky exits, in a huff, Irving is alone a moment. Fern calls across stage to Irving who will move to school lockers [probably imagined], open his locker and remove books, as he smiles at Fern, vaguely interested, heroically aloof.)

FERN: I'm really sorry about the confusion on Saturday night…

IRVING: Oh, hey, don't even think about it.

FERN: I'm sorry, Irving. I really am. I really thought it was for next week that we'd agreed.

IRVING: Hey, really, don't worry.

FERN: I don't want to miss out.

IRVING: *(Amazed.)* In what sense?

FERN: I want to make sure that we get to go out next Saturday night. I don't want to miss out.

IRVING: *(Smiles as little as he can.)* Oh...well...sure, we can do that. I'll have to break a *thing*...but...sure...we can. *(New attitude here.)* So...Fern... How's Rosen? Good dancer?

(They stop a moment.)

FERN: Stanley Rosen? Good dancer? Yes. Stanley's a *good* dancer, but, not a *great* dancer...

IRVING: Oh, sure, I understand. It must have been a little, I dunno...embarrassing for you, dancing with him all last night...

FERN: One makes do, Irving.

IRVING: Oh, yes, Fern, one does... *(Pauses; smiles and then looks at Fern seriously.)* Uh, Fern, is there anything about Rosen that you think is, I dunno, particularly *horrible?* From your particular point of view, I mean...

FERN: From my particular point of view? He fights. That's horrible. I hate that.

IRVING: Mmm, yuh...Anything else?

FERN: *(Pauses; confidentially.)* Horrible? No...oh, well, he has a little dandruff. I wouldn't call it *horrible,* but it's a definite imperfection

IRVING: Dandruff, huh? Poor Rosen, huh? Poor guy.

FERN: Isn't it wonderful news about the contest? About the scholarship and all. It's such a fabulous chance for us...for you I mean...with your talent. Do you think you could win it?

IRVING: The contest? Me? Win it? Positive. Sure. I can win it. I'm the best musician around, right?

FERN: You shouldn't be immodest, Irving. It's immature. It's also *unattractive.*

IRVING: I'm just looking at the facts, coldly, Fern, as though I weren't me...immodesty is, well, different. My view is cold, clinical, flatly realistic...I'm simply the best musician in the Soo...

FERN: What about Stanley?

(Stanley walks behind Irving; faces Fern obliquely, puts fingers behind Irving's head, discreetly, forming horns of a beast.)

IRVING: Rosen? What about him?

FERN: *(Nervously.)* Well, he uh, he, uh...Stanley plays, uh, pretty well, too... *He's with us!* Hello, Stanley.

(Irving spins about; faces Stanley.)

IRVING: Rosen.

STANLEY: *(Nods.)* Yanover. Fern.

FERN: *(Trying to ease the unbearable tension.)* Are you trying out for the contest, too, Stanley?

STANLEY: Does a bear pee in the woods?

FERN: That is so completely *uncouth*, Stanley Rosen…

IRVING: *(Happily.)* Very little couth, Rosen…It's true… *(Looks at watch.)*

STANLEY: Right, Yanover, you ought'a know…

IRVING: I ought'a know what, exactly, Rosen? It's a little difficult to follow the twistings and turnings of your unique mind…

STANLEY: Fat lip is what springs to my unique mind, Yanover.

FERN: Is that a threat of violence, Stanley Rosen? Because, if it is, I'm going straight home.

IRVING: No, you stay, Fern. *I'll* go! I've got to practice. There's no magic to perfection. It's all in the honing of genius… *(Smiles. To Fern.)* I'll call you, usual time, Fern… *(Starts off; stops.)* Oh, yuh…Playing *pretty* well is not playing *very* well, Fern. *(To Stanley.)* Fern said you play pretty well, Rosen, but, Irving Yanover plays very, very well. This is a hard cold fact of life. I'll call you, Fern. It's always a pleasure, Rosen… *(Irving looks at Stanley's shoulder and then looks up at the sky; then back at Stanley again.)* Bizarre, huh, snowing at this time of year. Ah, well, that's Canada…

STANLEY: What's this, Yanover?

FERN: It's not snowing, Irving…

IRVING: Then, what the hell's on Rosen's shoulder?

FERN: Irving Yanover! That is *so* cruel!

(Irving reaches across and brushes dandruff from Stanley's shoulder. Stanley punches Irving, who staggers backwards and then rushes at Stanley. Fern is horrified.)

FERN: Stop! Stop it, you two, stop!

(Simultaneously.)

STANLEY: Brain-damaged putz!

IRVING: Turd-faced, no-balled Chihuahua!

FERN: This is mortifying! Stop it!

(The boys now wrestle. Music in: Chopin. The same piece is played, out of synch, by two single pianos. Fern runs offstage. The lights black out and then fade up at once in both living rooms, focused on both pianos. The boys break from one another and reel backwards, each settling down at a piano. They both begin to practice, "locating" the music. Both sets of parents will be awakened. Both fathers will enter, half-awake, prodded into action by both

mothers, who both lie abed, offstage, exhausted and annoyed. For the moment, both Stanley and Irving play Chopin, with great gusto.)

ESTHER: *(Offstage.)* Mosie, will you talk to your son?

MOSES: It's midnight, Irving!

IRVING: Once more through, Poppy, please…

MOSES: But, it's midnight…

ESTHER: *(Offstage.)* It's midnight, Irving!

IRVING: Just once more through…*please!*

(Moses exits into kitchen through swinging-door. Without missing a beat, as door swings downstage, Barney enters, dozey, goes to Stanley.)

BARNEY: One more time through, Stanley, and that is that.

(Pearl yells "Barney!" from offstage.)

BARNEY: I am very, very fatigued.

(Pearl, offstage, yells "Barney!")

BARNEY: I can understand your wanting to win, but, Stanley, getting sleep is vital to life, Stanley, vital…

PEARL: *(Offstage.)* Barney!

BARNEY: *Stanley is playing one more time through, Pearl!!!* *(Calmly; to Stanley.)* Without sleep, you become cranky, irritable. Good night, Stanley…

STANLEY: Good night, Papa…

(Barney "swings" off, Moses "swings" onstage; goes to Irving. Lights shift.)

MOSES: You are practicing like your life depends on your winning, Irving. Your life does not depend on your winning, you know. In this life, you don't have to beat *every*body…

IRVING: I'm not trying to beat everybody, Papa. There's only one man in Sault Ste. Marie who could possibly be serious competition for me…and it is he who I am practicing seriously to beat.

MOSES: You mean…?

IRVING: Yes, Papa. I mean.

ESTHER: *(Yells.) I am beginning to hate Chopin!*

MOSES: I'm going back to bed now.

IRVING: Thanks, Poppy.

MOSES: Don't mention it.

(The lights shift to Rosen home. It is now daytime. Uncle Goldberg, an old Jew, played by the same actor who plays Ardenshensky. In contrast to Ardenshensky, Uncle Goldberg is expensively dressed, obviously rich. In a phrase, Uncle Goldberg exudes wealth. Four handsome matched suitcases surround Goldberg.)

GOLDBERG: I could have hired somebody to help us from the station, Stanley. I'm not a poor man…

(Stanley runs in, grabs two suitcases, runs off again. All of Stanley's moves here are triple-time. He has a date and is already late.)

STANLEY: There's no need, Uncle Goldberg. I'm happy to help. It's just that I'm running late…I'll put these in the back bedroom with the rest of your stuff…

(Stanley runs offstage. Goldberg chirps happily.)

GOLDBERG: I was delighted to find you waiting for me at the train, Stanley. It's a lonely thing for an old man to come home—even a very wealthy man, like me. After all these years, well…it's not easy. Places grow much more beautiful in the memory than they do on the Earth…in reality. I was very happy to see you at the station, waiting. I can see you're a busy fellow, and it was very generous of you…

STANLEY: Not at all, Uncle Goldberg. I was happy to be there, but, the train was a little late…

GOLDBERG: Very generous, indeed…In the Book of Proverbs, 11:25, I believe, it says "The generous man will be enriched; but the man who waters himself will be watered." So. Here it is: Sault Ste. Marie…Home. Lake Street, Churchill Avenue, Elizabeth, Pine…I used to know all the streets in order, from the Park to Algoma Steel, you'll help me relearn them.

(Goldberg pauses. Stanley re-enters.)

GOLDBERG: So. Look at you: all grown and handsome. I hear you're quite a musician…And I hear the town is all abuzz about some music contest. What are your chances?

STANLEY: Not bad. Let me take those!

GOLDBERG: Rest a second! Maybe you'll play for me tonight?

STANLEY: Oh, well, I'm sorry, Uncle Goldberg. I've sorta got something else planned.

GOLDBERG: A woman?

STANLEY: Sort of.

GOLDBERG: Are you a ladykiller, Stanley?

STANLEY: Me? Noooo…

GOLDBERG: You know what it says in the Talmud, "Be careful not to make a woman weep, for God counts her tears."

STANLEY: Oh, it's nothing like that, Uncle Goldberg. Please, let me take those. I'm kinda in a hurry. I'll put them on the bed for you… *(Stanley runs frantically grabbing remaining two suitcases. He sprints into back room, runs back to Uncle Goldberg; smiles. He is winded.)*

GOLDBERG: You'll give yourself a heart attack, running like that, Stanley!

STANLEY: No, I'm fine! Soooo, you're all set up. My folks are working in the store, downstairs, and they're expecting you. I have this really important errand, so, good night, Uncle! *(Starts to run offstage; thinks better of it; runs to Uncle Goldberg; hugs him quickly; speaks quickly.)* It's really really wonderful that you've moved back to the Soo, Uncle Goldberg. We'll spend some time together, talking…But, I'm really rushed now, so, good night.

(Stanley runs offstage. Uncle Goldberg doesn't notice. He stands a moment, looks about; speaks out loud.)

GOLDBERG: Pim, Pilgrim, Brock, Spring, March…then turn on Elgin… Bruce… Elgin…Bruce… *(Pauses.)* So what comes after Bruce? Stanley, what comes after Bruce?

(Uncle Goldberg looks for Stanley; shrugs. The lights cross fade to table in soda shoppe: Capy's. Fern sits facing Stanley, who sits facing Fern, moon struck; staring in lunatic fashion. He is in love. NOTE: Recommend that Stanley pushes Capy's set on stage and Fern is pre-set on her stool, set is on castered wagon.)

FERN: Happy birthday to you.

Happy birthday to you.

Happy birthday, dear Stanley,

Happy birthday to you.

(Fern waits for a response.) The song is over, Stanley. Stanley!

STANLEY: Huh?!

FERN: You just keep staring at me, Stanley. It's unnerving. Happy birthday.

STANLEY: *(Leans in toward Fern and whispers to her.)* I've never had a nicer birthday, Fern, I swear to you…

FERN: Oh, Stanley, that's really nice of you to say that…

STANLEY: Oh, no, no, it's true. Every year—all of them before this—me and my parents…Chinese food, aunts and uncles… *(Even more quietly.)* To be with you, on my own with you, in this restaurant, not eating, but instead watching you eat your French fries and cheeseburger…watching the red and green lights bounce from your hair…

FERN: *(Suddenly worried.)* My hair? *(She whips around.)* Is my hair too close to the lights?

STANLEY: *(Trying to recapture the quiet tones of thirty seconds ago.)* No, no, Fern. The light from the light…the beams of light…red and green.

FERN: Oh, you mean the light from the lights, not the lights themselves…I'm sorry, Irving…I interrupted you…

STANLEY: Stanley.

FERN: I said "Stanley"…

STANLEY: You said "Irving."

FERN: That's ridiculous. I said "Stanley." Why would I say "Irving?"

STANLEY: I don't know why you would say "Irving," but "Irving" is clearly what you said.

FERN: Let's not argue, Stanley. It's your birthday.

STANLEY: I'm sorry, I'm sorry…The pressure of the playoffs only eight weeks away.

FERN: What was that about the light on my hair? *(Smiles.)* The green and blue light?

STANLEY: Red and green.

FERN: Yes. *(She dips her potatoes into a circle of catsup on her plate and eats them.)*

STANLEY: May I tell you something wonderful about you, Fern?

FERN: Well, my, Stanley, sure…

STANLEY: All my life my parents have made me go out on dates with, well, a certain kind of girl…

FERN: Rosie Berkowitz?

STANLEY: How did you know that?

FERN: Rosie is my ultimate best friend, Stanley, so be careful…

STANLEY: Rosie Berkowitz is your *ultimate* best friend?

FERN: One of them. I happen to feel very sorry for her.

STANLEY: Because she's fat?

FERN: She's hefty, she's not fat.

STANLEY: *Hefty?* Like a rocky mountain is hefty! You wouldn't say "hefty" if you ever had to dance with Rosie Berkowitz.

FERN: I've danced with Rosie many times. Insensitive boys often leave her on the bench, so I've danced with her.

STANLEY: There. See? That's another wonderful thing about you, Fern.

FERN: What was the first wonderful thing?

STANLEY: Hmm?

FERN: The first wonderful thing about me? You never told me what it was.

STANLEY: Oh. The way you dip your French fries into the catsup one at a time, instead of making a big glob that you shove into your mouth and glom down, like a dinosaur…

FERN: Rosie does that?

STANLEY: Sure. Why do ya think she's so fat? Rosie Berkowitz would never make a circle like you do with catsup. She just pours the whole bottle out on her plate and jams the old fries right in, fistfuls at a time. It's really revolting.

(We hear: Chopin being played, lightly.)

FERN: Well. *(Smiles.)* Enough about Rosie, Stanley. *(Looks into his eyes.)* This is your birthday.

(She kisses Stanley. Chopin plays lightly. A tight spotlight fades up on the face of actor who plays Ardenshensky and Goldberg. In the following scene, he will play both characters, interacting with one another. He will accomplish this by changing hats and by his acting. When he plays Goldberg, he will don Goldberg's expensive derby…and, of course, Goldberg's "I'm not a poor man" manner. As he is playing two men on one park bench, he will face left when playing Goldberg and right when playing Ardenshensky. It is possible to widen the light ever so slightly, as the scene progresses—once the audience is comfortable with the style of the scene. It is night. There is a slight chill in the air.)

GOLDBERG: Is that you: Ardenshensky?

ARDENSHENSKY: What do you care, Goldberg?

GOLDBERG: I don't.

ARDENSHENSKY: So, don't ask.

GOLDBERG: I'm sorry I did. Pretend I didn't… *(He pauses.)* How old are you now, Ardenshensky?

ARDENSHENSKY: How old am I in what sense, Goldberg?

GOLDBERG: In how many senses can you count your age, Ardenshensky?

ARDENSHENSKY: In the Oriental sense, I'm eighty-four. In the cat-year sense, I'm one hundred seventy-eight…

GOLDBERG: In every sense, I'm older than you, Ardenshensky. I am, officially, the oldest living man in Sault Ste. Marie, Ontario, Dominion of Canada…

ARDENSHENSKY: I'm happy for you, Goldberg, believe me…I hated the title. I'm happy you took it back. I hated being old and being known for nothing else…I found it to be *pathetic*.

GOLDBERG: Very interesting, my dear young Ardenshensky. Very, very interesting…

(Both hats off. The actor rolls his eyes to heaven, in dismay. The lights cross fade to Irving and Fern, carrying bookbags, walking home from school.)

IRVING: My life is music, Fern, and that's what you are to me: I am Johann Sebastian Bach and you are my *Goldberg Variation*.

FERN: You mean music to your ears? That kind of thing?

IRVING: Roughly.

FERN: Let me just recap this. It's a little confusing. I am to you what *The Goldberg Variations* were to Bach, right? *(Giggles.)* I got a little confused, because Stanley's got an uncle named Goldberg...

IRVING: So what?

FERN: It's just a little confusing, that's all! No big deal, okay?

(There is a pause.)

IRVING: Fern, I would like to tell you something I have never dared tell another human being in the whole world.

FERN: Be careful, Irving, because Rosie Berkowitz—fat, or not—happens to be one of my very best friends...

IRVING: What are you *talking* about?

FERN: What are *you* talking about?

IRVING: My career.

FERN: Your career?

IRVING: My career. I hope I can trust you, Fern.

FERN: Of course you can trust me, Irving.

IRVING: I feel I can. I do...Fern?

FERN: What?

IRVING: I feel that I might be another Horowitz...

FERN: In what sense, Irving? You mean as good?

IRVING: Of *course,* I mean "as good!" You don't think I mean I think I'm gonna wake up one morning and actually *be* Vladimir Horowitz, do you?

FERN: Is that what you think I thought you thought? Because, if it is, Irving Yanover you are being *sooo insulting,*...

IRVING: No, Fern...Of *course* not!!! *(Pause, sigh.)* Sometimes, my genius frightens me, Fern.

FERN: You must never be frightened, Irving...at least not of something like genius.

IRVING: I know you're right! *(Pauses.)* I knew I could trust you. *(Pauses.)* I've chosen my piece for the playoffs, Fern...Chopin. *Waltz in C-Sharp Minor,* Opus 64 Number Two.

FERN: That's nice. I'm playing Debussy [Title of piece.]

IRVING: Oh, that's great...

FERN: Let me play my piece for you, Irving? Not the whole thing. Just a little...

IRVING: Oh, sure. I'd love it.

FERN: *(Taking a recorder from bookbag.)* I wish I could play like you...you really hate the recorder don't you.

IRVING: The soprano recorder is a fine instrument, Fern…ancient, primitive, almost…*tribal*…

FERN: Listen. *(Fern squeaks out a high-pitched half-minute of Debussy. When she is finished, she smiles at Irving.)*

(N. B. Music can be on sound tape.)

FERN: Did I make a fool of myself? Just tell me if I did, Irving, please?

IRVING: Not at all. Not in the least. You are a fine and sensitive player and…

FERN: I can tell you loathed it.

IRVING: It's not you. It's him.

FERN: *Who? (Looks about for Stanley; panicked.)*

IRVING: Debussy. It's Debussy I hate…

FERN: Irving Yanover! How can you possibly hate Debussy?

IRVING: Well, Fern, it's true. I just don't happen to like Debussy at all. He's sugary, syrupy. He's a minor, minor figure, in my humble opinion…

FERN: Calling your opinion "humble" is like calling Lake Michigan "damp," Irving Yanover! Debussy is a major figure and I happen to like him *enormously!* He happens to be my first choice!

IRVING: *(Deeply ashamed.)* Oh, God, Fern, I'm really sorry. Of course, you're right. You should play Debussy. He was a man and he lived and he wrote music the very best he could and he died and you should play his music and I'm really ashamed of myself for having said that…

FERN: *(After a pause; quietly.)* I understand, Irving. You needn't feel ashamed.

IRVING: Fern, I have spent many days of my life around many, many girls…

FERN: Rosie Berkowitz?

IRVING: Why do you keep bringing up Rosie Berkowitz?

FERN: She happens to be a friend.

IRVING: She's nice, Rosie Berkowitz. A nice girl. Sort of a tub, but very nice. Her cousin, Arnold, used to play first string on the James Street Aces with a friend of mine.

(Suddenly, Stanley Rosen screams angrily at Fern from Capy's, opposite side of stage. He stands next to table and ice-cream chairs.)

STANLEY: For God's sakes, Fern, I've been waiting here for nearly two hours. *(The scene has shifted once again to Capy's Bar and Grill. Stanley is, as they say, fit to be tied. The lights widen to include Stanley and Fern and Irving, who stands at the piano, watching Fern and Stanley. They will "act" that other students fill the imagined other tables and are overhearing Stanley's rage.)*

FERN: I…I'm sorry, Stanley, I got confused…I thought I made the date with Irving…

STANLEY: You told me Capy's at three, so, at three I was at Capy's. Now it's five and where am I? Still at Capy's but you're here, too, and with who?

IRVING: Whom...you said "who."

STANLEY: If you enjoy life, I wouldn't, Yanover, okay?

FERN: This is a nightmare!

STANLEY: You're telling *me?* You're not the one waiting here for two-and-a-half hours only to watch you walk in the place holding hands with this brain-damaged putz!

IRVING: *(Stepping in.)* This really *is* a nightmare!

STANLEY: You say something, Yanover?

IRVING: Yuh. I did, Rosen. I said that this is a nightmare.

STANLEY: You wanna step outside, Yanover?

FERN: Stanleyyy!

IRVING: Typical Rosen move: He waits for us for two hours and then right away he wants to step outside. *I* don't want to step outside. I've just been outside. But, listen, Rosen, you wanna step outside, be my guest: step.

STANLEY: Ho. Ho-ho. Ho-ho-ho. It's hard for me to sit still for your rapid-fire slashing wit, Yanover.

IRVING: You're not sitting, Rosen, you're standing. When your knees are stiff and your *tookis* is perpendicular to the floor, you are standing. When your knees are bent and your *tookis* is parallel to the floor, it is then you are sitting.

(Stanley will shove Irving.* N. B. Shove = *.)

STANLEY: Damn! I forgot...*tookis* up: stand*; *tookis* down: sit*...this man has a firm grip on the basics*...what a *thinker**...what a great goddamn *mind. Tookis* up: stand.* *Tookis* down: sit.* *Fabulous!**

FERN: I'm leaving before the fist fight starts again, thank you...

STANLEY: No, don't leave, Fern, please! I am not fighting! Please stay! This is my only afternoon off! I'm not clear again until Monday! *(To Irving; loud whisper.)* If she leaves,* Yanover, I will drop out of school* and dedicate my life to your death.*

IRVING: Any time,* any place,* any Army you wanna bring with you, pecker-face!*

FERN: You both promised me! *You promised me!*

STANLEY: *(Suddenly shift; to Fern.)* We're not fighting! *(To Irving.)* Are we fighting?

IRVING: Absolutely not.

FERN: Let's sit down, together, then, okay?

STANLEY: But, you're *my* date, Fern, dammit! *(Another fierce whisper, to Irving.)*

If that *tookis* of your goes down, this foot of mine goes up…if you get my point…and you *will*…

(Stanley twists Irving's flesh, unseen by Fern.)

IRVING: *(To Fern.)* I have to go home, now, really. I shouldn't stay. I've, uh, got to help my father with inventory…

STANLEY: You have a father? Gosh, I thought you were found under a rock, putzface!*

IRVING: At least I was *found,* shit for brains! You've yet to be discovered…like Pluto…and I don't mean the planet, Rosen. I mean Goofy's friend, the dog…

STANLEY: This is the goddamn limit! Turd-nose! My foot is heading for your anus and I don't mean the planet, either!*

FERN: *(Fern starts to sob. Her shoulders shake. She moans, rasps, shouts.)* Will you two *stop*…will you two please stop…will you two please please *please* stopppp? *Will you? Will yoooo?*

IRVING: We're not fighting, Fern…

STANLEY: Not at all…

FERN: That's not it! *(Moans; sobs.)* Oh, Goddd…

IRVING: We're really not fighting, Fern. Look at us…

STANLEY: There's no reason to cry…

IRVING: I apologize, Fern, I really do…Don't cry.

FERN: *(Crying openly.)* I'm not crying…

IRVING: We really weren't going to fight…not in front of you.

STANLEY: Honest to God…not in front of you…

FERN: *(Sobs.)* That's not it…That's not why I'm upset…

STANLEY: What's it, then?

IRVING: Why are you upset?

FERN: Because…*I can't…tell you apart!*

IRVING: You can't tell who apart?

FERN: You and Irving.

IRVING: I *am* Irving.

FERN: *(Sobs.)* You seeee?

(Stanley and Irving stare at each other a moment.)

STANLEY: You can't tell me apart from Irving Yanover?

FERN: No, I can't. I really can't. You both play piano, you both crack jokes, you're both depressed all the time, you're both Jewish, you're both skinny, you're both conceited…

IRVING: Rosen has dandruff.

FERN: Oh, my God! That was really *cruel!*

STANLEY: I'll kill you for that!

IRVING: Rosen is round-shouldered.

FERN: So are you. You're much more round-shouldered than he is.

IRVING: I am not!

STANLEY: You are, Yanover!

FERN: You are so!

STANLEY: Practically a hunchback…

IRVING: An hunchback…

STANLEY: How about *an* hit in the head, Yanover?

FERN: *No fighting!*

IRVING: Irving started it. I didn't. Don't blame me.

STANLEY: Don't blame me, either, Fern: Blame Rosen!

FERN: *Oh, my God…*I really can't tell you apart: It's true! *It's true!… (She sobs.)* Every night, before I go to sleep, the phone rings and it's one of you…as soon as I hang it up, I know the other one will get mad at me…because the other one has been calling and calling, waiting for the line to stop being busy… *(Pauses.)* Just the same, just exactly the same… *(She sobs, again.)* You dance the same, you kiss the same, you both like to hold the same hand, you like the same books, the same movies, the same records, you're both terrible athletes, A+ students, neither of you smokes, nor drinks, both of you crack bad jokes, endlessly…and you both talk about Chopin all the time…and…you both…upset me *so much!* Ooooo! *(She sobs, again.)*

STANLEY: Fern Fipps, this is really insulting. It's not insulting for Yanover to be mistaken for me, but, I am…insulted, deeply. Deeply!

FERN: I knew I made the date with you, Stanley, but I got confused and thought you, Irving, were Stanley…that's why I was late, Stanley.

IRVING: And our date was tomorrow, Fern…I was supposed to practice in Music Hall today, so I can cream Rosen come the Playoffs.

STANLEY: Come the Playoffs, dear boy, the cream will be Rosen. The *creamed* will be Yanover. *(Stanley threatens to hit Irving.)*

FERN: *No fighting! You promised! You promised me, both of you!*
(Stanley and Irving face each other, fists ready.)

IRVING AND STANLEY: We're not fighting!

FERN: I can't stand it! *I'm going to end up hating both of you!*

STANLEY: This is your goddamn fault, Yanover!

FERN: …I like being with both of you, but I can't be with both of you…and I can't choose one over the other because I can't tell you apart…

STANLEY: Loookkk, I have a simple solution, Fern…

FERN: *(Sobs again.)* What is it?

STANLEY: How about the concert? Maybe the better man should win you in the playoffs, Fern. Let the winner really *win.*

IRVING: Aren't you kinda making a mistake there, Rosen?

STANLEY: I hardly think so, Yanover…

IRVING: Oh, really?

STANLEY: Oh, really…

FERN: Oh, that's such a good idea, Irving.

STANLEY: Stanley…

FERN: *(To Irving.)* Stanley, I mean…

STANLEY: Me, Fern, me…

FERN: Ooooo my God! The playoffs aren't until the end of June. It's only May 10th! How will I ever *live* 'til the end of June?

IRVING: Until then, you go out with only me, and after that the winner… Irving.

FERN: Until then I'll go out with you, Irving, one week and you, Stanley, the next week, and then you, Irving, the next week, and so on… *(Seriously.)* Please, say "yes?" *Please!*

STANLEY: Yes, I say "yes"…

IRVING: I really hate this. I want you to know that I really and truly hate this…Yes, okay, yes.

FERN: *(Thrilled.)* I…am…sooo…*relieved!*

(We hear a loud oriental "gong" then oriental music. Lights up in The Ritz Cafe. Pearl and Barney Rosen sit around table with Esther and Moses Yanover. Mr. Wong, an old Chinese Waiter, played by same actor who plays Ardenshensky and Uncle Goldberg, serves them their meal.)

ESTHER: If only our sons could get along as well as their parents get along…

PEARL: *(Smiling.)* "With each *other*" you mean?

ESTHER: *(Smiling; laughing lightly.)* Well, of course I mean "with each other?" I don't mean "If only they could get along by *themselves*"…

PEARL: It would have been a little more clear if you had said "If only your son and my son could get along with each other, as well as you and I get along with each other…"

ESTHER: Thank you. I'll remember that.

MR. WONG: Who gets the egg foo yong?

BARNEY: There, there and there, Mr. Wong. Thank you.

MR. WONG: And the fish special? Who gets the spicy sole?

MOSES: Mr. Rosen is the spicy soul.

BARNEY: Here.

PEARL: *(Laughs.)* Barney is certainly not the spicy sole. Barney *ordered* the spicy sole!

MOSES: *(Laughs.)* Oh, no, Pearl, I said exactly what I meant. Barney is the spicy soul.

(Esther laughs.)

BARNEY: Oh, God, look at the spicy sole. I should have ordered the spicy *heel!*

MOSES: That was my joke, from last week's meal…

BARNEY: I think it's also your *fish* from last week's meal!

MOSES: That was also my joke. From the week before last…

ESTHER: *(Smoothing things.)* No, it wasn't. It was *my* joke.

BARNEY: I think she's right.

MOSES: I think you're right.

PEARL: *Bon appetit! Mangez bien, mes amis!*

(Pearl smiles brightly. Barney eats noisily. Esther looks at Moses and rolls her eyes to Heaven. Moses gives Esther his most subtle "Don't start trouble" look. They eat.)

PEARL: When's the last time you talked to Binky Berkowitz?

ESTHER: Not since Mah Johng, last Thursday. Why? She's not well?

PEARL: She's well. Rosie's driving her a little crazy…

BARNEY: Crazy, for Binky Berkowitz, is not a long drive…

ESTHER: What's with Rosie? Grades?

PEARL: Straight A's and A+'s, Rosie. Brilliant girl…

ESTHER: Handsome, too…

MOSES: She's nice, Rosie…

BARNEY: She's too fat. It's a shame, the way they shovel the food into her. Young girl. Fat as a horse…

ESTHER: How can you say that about a young girl?

BARNEY: She's a fat young girl, that's why…

(He laughs at his own joke. Everybody pauses and eats.)

ESTHER: So, what's with Binky?

PEARL: Binky thinks Rosie's seeing a boy on the side…

BARNEY: Which side? *(Laughs.)*

ESTHER: Barney!

PEARL: *(Confidentially.)* He's not Jewish…

BARNEY, ESTER, AND MOSES: *(Mumbled understanding.)* Mmmmm…

PEARL: From Cabbagetown…He's related to the girl who used to work for you…

MOSES: Annie Ilchak?

(Pearl nods.)

MOSES: They're a nice family... *(Smiles.)* These things happen in a small town like this. It doesn't mean much. The kids outgrow it...

ESTHER: These things do *not* happen...not with Jewish children...in *any* town!

PEARL: I totally agree, Esther.

(Barney and Moses exchange a knowing glance. There is a pause. Everyone eats again.)

PEARL: So? How's your Irving?

ESTHER: Exhausted. He practices day and night...

PEARL: Our Stanley, too...day and night.

BARNEY: We're sleepless.

MOSES: I wish Harry Truman never set foot in Canada. Competition is a waste of time, if you ask me...

PEARL: *That* you can say again, Mosie.

ESTHER: In what sense?

PEARL: Hmm?

ESTHER: In what sense do you mean we should say that again, Pearl?

BARNEY: What Pearl means is that our Stanley is...well...unbeatable.

MOSES: What?

ESTHER: Oh, really? Mosie happened to mean that Irving is wasting his time because he needn't practice to beat your Stanley. He can beat your Stanley without practice. Isn't that what you meant, Mosie?

BARNEY: I don't think that's what your Mosie meant, Essie...

ESTHER: I think a wife knows what a husband means...

MOSES: Just a minute! I don't like what I'm hearing here!

PEARL: And neither do I!

ESTHER: I'll tell you what I think: I think that if the children want to compete, let them...If Mackenzie King and Harry Truman are both in favor of competition, then I'm in favor of competition, too...

PEARL: I agree...

ESTHER: As for us we are all adults and we are very close friends...

PEARL: Don't be ridiculous!

ESTHER: In what sense am I being ridiculous, Mrs. Rosen?

PEARL: We're not close friends. We're neighbors and we're Jews. When you're a Jew in a town like Sault Ste. Marie, you take what other Jews are in the neighborhood. You're in the neighborhood, we're in the neighborhood...no more, no less...

ESTHER: That is possibly the most insulting thing I have ever heard in my life, Mrs. Rosen.

(All stop eating except for Pearl.)

MOSES: I have a feeling, Essie, that what you have heard, so far is nothing!...compared to what's coming when my temper goes. And my temper is going, Mr. Rosen...Mrs. Rosen...I warn you both!...

BARNEY: You see, Pearl? I told you it would come to this!

ESTHER: You told her what would come to this, Mr. Rosen? That you could meet with the poor schlepp Yanovers at Ritz Cafe and make insulting remarks? Hmmmm? I have a piece of bad news for you, Mr. Rosen... (or is it still Royal?...) My Irving Yanover could beat your Stanley in a Chopin playoff, with one hand tied behind his back...

PEARL: I've heard him play, your Irving, and that's precisely the way it sounds...

ESTHER: I will not have my son slurred like this, Mrs. Royal-Rosen.

PEARL: This is not a slur. This is a fact of life...it so happens that Chopin has some heart and some soul...when your Irving played at shull last year, it was completely mechanical...like a windup toy...no heart, no soul.

MOSES: I have heard enough...Esther, hand me my coat.

BARNEY: Oh, sure, run. A typical Yanover move: There's trouble; run. Run, go, run, run...

MOSES: You want heart and soul? Good, great! Here from the bottom of my heart is sole... (*Moses picks up Barney's fish and places it in Barney's hand.*) Here. Hand this to your wife. Wong! Our coats!

BARNEY: I am... (*Pounds fist on the table.*) ...pounding... (*Pounds table again.*)... pounding the table, Yanover (*Pounds table again.*) ...so that I don't... (*Pounds table again.*) ...pound... (*Pounds table again.*) ...you... (*Pounds table again.*)

(*Mr. Wong enters with coats.*)

MR. WONG: Excuse me, is everything all right here?

MOSES: Does everything *look* all right! Give me my coat! Thank you!

BARNEY: *"My coat"* is right! It happens that you still have my coat, Yanover!

(*Pearl, Moses, Esther, simultaneously.*)

PEARL: Tell them, Barney! They should hear it, clearly!

MOSES: What coat? I paid you cash money!

ESTHER: This is Mosie's coat!—

BARNEY: There was another coat: tweed, bluish grey Mackinaw!...you borrowed it and I like that Mackinaw, Yanover, I do, I really do. I will have that Mackinaw back, Yanover.

MOSES: You told me to *keep* that lousy Mackinaw! You told me it was a *gift!*

BARNEY: Like hell I did!

ESTHER: May I put in my two cents?

BARNEY: Oh, shut up!

MOSES: What?

ESTHER: I'll answer for myself, Mosie, thank you. *(To Barney.)* Until Mosie brings you your Mackinaw, Mr. Big-Mouth-Tell-A-Lady- (a mother yet) -To-Shut-Up…if you are cold…then…wear this!

(The war is on again. Esther mashes her egg foo yong on Barney's shoulder. Barney takes the egg foo yong and mashes it onto Moses' shoulder. Moses takes the egg foo yong and mashes it onto Pearl's shoulder. All of this must be silent, wordless. Pearl, ending the scene, takes the egg foo yong and mashes it onto Mr. Wong's shoulder.)

MR. WONG: Get out! Get out of here! *Get out!*

(Esther and Moses and Pearl and Barney all scream. We will hear the sons yell back in amazement, from their beds, offstage.)

PEARL AND BARNEY: *Stannnleyyy!*

ESTHER AND MOSES: *Irvvvinngggg!*

IRVING: *(Offstage; in a sudden; shocked.)* What?

STANLEY: *(Fearful symmetry.)* What?

ALL POSSIBLE PARENTS: *Get up and practice!*

(Blackout. Telephone light up, at once. At same time, light fades up in Fern's window. Stanley moves into telephone light and talks to Fern, as if on telephone. Fern holds actual telephone in hand as she talks.)

FERN: Did you hear what happened in the Ritz Cafe?

STANLEY: I heard, but, how the hell did *you* hear! Who told you?

FERN: My parents were there with the Fergussons…

STANLEY: Your parents *saw?*

FERN: Every bit of it. They couldn't wait to tell me. They practically *woke me up* when they got home!

STANLEY: I wonder if Yanover knows?

FERN: He knew already before I called, same as you…

STANLEY: You called Yanover *first?*

FERN: Don't, Stan, don't be jealous. I flipped a coin…ooooppp, my father's coming upstairs. Wanna meet me after church, tomorrow?

STANLEY: I have to work from eight to three in the store, to pay back for using the car…

FERN: I'll be waiting on the corner of Pim and Queen at five past three, precisely…How's that?

STANLEY: Great…

FERN: We'll talk, then. I've really gotta go… *(To her father.)* It's Tricia, again. I hung up, I hung up!

(Click of Fern hanging up telephone in a hurry. Stanley crosses to shop to Uncle Goldberg.)

STANLEY: Uncle Goldberg, listen to me! I'm not crazy and you're not crazy, but they are crazy! Two weeks ago, they chastised me for being too competitive about the playoffs; now, they *yell* at me to practice *more...* *(Imitates his father and mother.)* Win, Stanley, win! Win, win, Stanley, win. You'd think it was the goddamn Stanley cup!

GOLDBERG: It would kill you to win? You think your father doesn't deserve a victory from his son?

STANLEY: Et tu, Uncle Goldberg? Do you *really* know what's going on here?

GOLDBERG: The word is you're keeping time with a girl who isn't Jewish.

STANLEY: *(Shocked and amazed.)* I shall just simply pretend I didn't hear what I just heard, Uncle Goldberg. That subject is a closed door. I will now tell you what's really going on with my parents.

GOLDBERG: "A closed door?"

STANLEY: Don't interrupt me!?

GOLDBERG: Please, Stanley...You're talking to a man my age with such disrespect?

STANLEY: Please, Uncle Goldberg. Last night my father stood up in the middle of the Ritz Cafe in front of many, many people I know, and screamed at Mr. Yanover to return a mackinaw he borrowed...

GOLDBERG: *(Interrupting.)* A borrowed mackinaw shouldn't be returned?...

STANLEY: Mr. Yanover borrowed the mackinaw nineteen years ago!!!

GOLDBERG: In the Talmud...

STANLEY: *(Screams.)* Don't interrupt me!

(There is a small silence.)

GOLDBERG: If you're not careful, you'll grow up and scream just like your father...

STANLEY: *(Softly.)* That's just what I was thinking. I'll end up in the Ritz Cafe throwing egg foo yong at my closest friends.

GOLDBERG: He threw egg foo yong?

STANLEY: They *all* threw egg foo yong! Actually, Mr. Yanover threw spicy sole.

GOLDBERG: I didn't know that.

STANLEY: Did you know that they've been banned from the Ritz Cafe for six months?

GOLDBERG: This I knew.

STANLEY: It's all because of the piano contest, Uncle Goldberg. My parents have *cracked* under the pressure, that's what!

GOLDBERG: I'm going to tell you something, Stanley...

STANLEY: It's getting late, Uncle Goldberg, I...

GOLDBERG: *(With authority.)* Don't interrupt me!

STANLEY: Sorry.

GOLDBERG: When I was twelve years old, I was shipped across to this side, by boat, with an uncle. Ardenshensky was on the same boat. You know him?

STANLEY: The old, old guy?

GOLDBERG: He's not so old. Twelve, and my uncle leaves me with one of his wife's cousins, here in the Soo...a Mrs. Weinstein, who took me in mostly because my uncle gave her thirty dollars, and also because she needed somebody to sweep her shop for her. She sold chickens... *(Pauses.)* I stayed here 'til I was twenty, and then I went to Montreal, and I made my fortune, but, all the time I was here in the Soo, I don't think ten people knew my name: I was just the skinny, sad nobody, who swept up Mrs. Weinstein's chicken shop... *(Pauses.)* Your mother's been writing to me for years about your piano playing. You want the truth? I came back here to see one of my relatives make a name for himself, here... make a little bit of history for himself and for our family. *(Pauses.)* I have no sons, Stanley. I never married...

STANLEY: I'll do my best, Uncle, I... *(Sees Fern entering.)* Oh, my God, my God, it's way, way past three!

(Fern enters the store.)

FERN: It's twenty past three, Stanley. I waited and waited! What is *with* you?

GOLDBERG: Hello. Are you after menswear?

STANLEY: Fern Fipps, this is my uncle, Uncle Goldberg...Uncle Goldberg, this is my...friend, Fern Fipps. I'm Stanley. *(He rolls his eyes to heaven.)*

FERN: I'm very happy to meet you. Stanley's told me a lot about you.

GOLDBERG: *(To Fern.)* Are you Jewish?

FERN: Me?

GOLDBERG: I know the answer.

(Moses and Esther Yanover enter. Moses carries an old mackinaw: the borrowed item.)

MOSES: Hello, Stanley...

ESTHER: Hello, Stanley...

STANLEY: Oh, my God, *hellooo*, Mr. and Mrs. Yanover...

MOSES: You can tell your father I've brought the mackinaw.

ESTHER: No temper, Mosie...

MOSES: *(Yells a whispered yell.)* Esssieeee, stop! *(Smiles. Looks around.)* Where's your father, Stanley?

STANLEY: Do you know my Uncle Goldberg? This is Mr. Yanover and this is Mrs. Yanover. This is Uncle Goldberg…

MOSES: How've you been, Goldberg?

GOLDBERG: Peachy…How's by you?

MOSES: Also peachy…

GOLDBERG: How's by Mrs. Yanover?

ESTHER: Also peachy…

GOLDBERG: So, this is good: Everybody's peachy…

FERN: I'm Fern Fipps, and you must be Irving's parents. I've heard so many wonderful things about you…

(Pearl Rosen calls down from upstairs; she buzzes intercom. Stanley runs to speaker, talks.)

STANLEY: *What?*

PEARL: *(Over intercom.)* Are there customers in the store with you? Stanley? Stanley?

STANLEY: Oh, my God! *(Yells into phone; to Pearl.)* Nobody, mama. Just me and Uncle Goldberg!

PEARL: *(Into intercom.)* Really?

STANLEY: Really! *(Stanley faces the Yanovers.)* That wasn't my mother! My parents aren't home. They're on vacation… *(To Goldberg.)* Shut up, you! *(Stanley grabs a sportcoat from the rack, throws it at Fern, whispers to her, fiercely.)* Miss Fipps! Your father's suit coat! Take it and go home! My parents will come down here and see you…

FERN: What are you *doing*, Stanley? This isn't my father's!

STANLEY: Please, Fern, take this suit coat home to your father and wait for my call! Please, Fern, please! *Allez, allez, rapidment!*

FERN: What is this, Stanley?

STANLEY: Get out of here, Fern, *please!*

(Stanley shoves Fern out of the door. There is an embarrassed pause.)

ESTHER: You have a lovely girlfriend, Stanley.

STANLEY: Oh, Fern's not my girlfriend, Mrs. Yanover. She's Irving's girlfriend. *(We hear a prizefight bell. Stanley looks at Goldberg; shrugs. The Yanovers move toward Irving, in Yanover store.)*

IRVING: Not mine: *his!*

ESTHER AND MOSES: Whose?

IRVING: *His!*

ESTHER: You will *not* go out with a girl who isn't Jewish, and that is simply, utterly, absolutely *that!* Promise me, Irving Yanover!

IRVING: I can't, Mama. I can't promise you…

ESTHER: Oh, my God! What if my mother—*Alivoh Shalom*—could listen in from Heaven on such an answer, Mr.-Never-Heard-Of-Hitler-And-What-He-Did-To-The-Jews!

IRVING: My God, Mama. Are you comparing me to Adolph Hitler, if I go to a movie with a girl who isn't Jewish?

MOSES: *(Embarrassed, but loyal to Esther.)* Not exactly…

ESTHER: What "not exactly?" What? What? *(To Irving.)* That is exactly what I am comparing you to: Adolph Hitler, Mussolini, and Attilla the Hun…

MOSES: Esther!…

ESTHER: *(Angrily, to Moses.)* Do not "Esther" me on this subject, you! *Do not! (To both.)* I am not an outsider in the family. I *am* part of this family! This is not just a *man's* house: This is a house with a mother and a father and a child. I am sick of the men teaming up, sick, sick! This is a family—a Jewish family!—and this family has rules and *rulers!* I am the mother in this family, Irving Yanover, and I am telling you—*Telling you!—You will promise me you will not go out with this girl!*

IRVING: *(Sickly.)* Oh, my God…

(He stands, runs from the house. Moses has trouble looking at his wife. Esther pauses a moment; crosses to her table. Moses follows her.)

ESTHER: *(Heartbroken.)* I wanted more children, Mosie. I always said that, didn't I? I always said one child—an only child—is not *normal*… (Weeps once. Then she smiles. Then she acts as if angry, looks at Irving's place at table.) How could we have a son who's so skinny?*

(The lights cross fade to Rosen store, where Stanley stands facing his parents. They are united against him and they are enraged.)

STANLEY: His! I swear on the memory of Toronto, she is Irving Yanover's girlfriend. Not mine: his!

PEARL: So, why was she in our store?

STANLEY: She was not in our store!

PEARL: I *saw* her leaving our store young man, plain as day from the front window. She was running and she was carrying a suit coat!

STANLEY: That is simply not true!

BARNEY: So, where is Mr. Silverswieg's suit coat? His pants are still on the hanger, but his suit coat is definitely missing!

STANLEY: It's not missing!

BARNEY: Missing! It's missing!

PEARL: I saw the girl running with it!

STANLEY: That's just ridiculous!

BARNEY: Why would a young girl like that steal a men's suit coat?

PEARL: If you expect your parents to put food on your plate, young man, do not sneak girls who are not Jewish into your parents' store. A word to the wise is sufficient!

STANLEY: Oh, my God!

(And with that, Stanley, like Irving, takes off. He runs from the house. Lights shift to park. Irving runs in from one direction; Stanley from the other. They meet in the middle, stop, circle one another.)

IRVING: You…

STANLEY: You…

(They move at each other in slow motion. Stanley throws a roundhouse punch at Irving at precisely the same moment Irving throws a roundhouse punch at Stanley. At precisely the same moment, they connect their punches to each other's nose. They groan in slow motion. At precisely the same moment, they both grab at their identically wounded noses. The prizefight bell jangles, seven jangles.)

(Stanley runs home. Irving runs to park, both circling stage, twice. The lights shift to Irving sitting on park bench next to Ardenshensky. Irving's head is back as his bloody nose coagulates, heals.)

IRVING: *(Moans, quietly.)* Oh, Godddd…

ARDENSHENSKY: I assume you're not praying. Why the "Oh, God?"

IRVING: It's my parents…

ARDENSHENSKY: They're not well?

IRVING: They're not *kind*. They're not *fair*.

ARDENSHENSKY: Are you Yanover or Rosen?

IRVING: Yanover. Definitely Yanover.

ARDENSHENSKY: I thought so.

IRVING: Could I ask you an important question, Mr. Ardenshensky?

ARDENSHENSKY: If you have to.

IRVING: Mr. Ardenshensky, is Mrs. Ardenshensky, uh, Jewish?

ARDENSHENSKY: There is some aspect of Mrs. Ardenshensky that doesn't seem to you to be Jewish?

IRVING: Forget I asked, really…

ARDENSHENSKY: Which did you say you were? Yanover, or Rosen?…

IRVING: Rosen, Mr. Ardenshensky…Pearl and Barney's boy…Barney Rosen Menswear, Queen Street…

(Fern calls softly from edge of stage.)

FERN: Irving…

(Irving and Ardenshensky look up.)

IRVING: Will you excuse me, Mr. Ardenshensky. I have to go.

ARDENSHENSKY: No, stay! I'll go. It's crazy to waste a bench on an old man, alone. Stay... *(Ardenshensky stands, smiles at Irving.)* I saw nothing.

(He shuffles offstage. Fern enters, goes to Irving.)

FERN: Do you know how truly insulting this whole thing has been for me?

IRVING: I have an idea...

FERN: You *don't*, Irving! You weren't there! Stanley Rosen actually said to me "Get out of here before my parents see you!"...

IRVING: Oh, well, Rosen's an animal. We've established this as a fact of life...

FERN: It's all because I'm not Jewish, you know...

IRVING: Oh, God, well, why do you think that, Fern?

FERN: Oh, come on, Irving Yanover. You think I'm some kind of dumb dippy? I know about Jewish parents.

IRVING: How?

FERN: You forget who my ultimate best friend is.

IRVING: Rosie Berkowitz talks about it?

FERN: Constantly. I shouldn't be telling you this, but, Rosie has a crush on Andrej Ilchak...

IRVING: Yuh, so? The Ilchaks are wonderful, wonderful people...

FERN: Yuh, but Andrej's Ukrainian, and Rosie's mother and father hate Ukrainians...

IRVING: My parents don't. I mean, you can't lump everybody together, you know. All Jews aren't exactly like the Berkowitzes...

FERN: Be careful what you say, Irving...

IRVING: I know she's your ultimate best friend...

FERN: That's not what I was going to say.

IRVING: What were you going to say?

FERN: Mrs. Berkowitz and your mother had a long conversation about me, recently...

(A beat.)

IRVING: Let's just drop the whole subject, Fern. You're not going out with my parents. You're going out with me...

FERN: I don't want to drop the whole subject! My parents don't have a prejudiced bone in their bodies...

IRVING: Oh, yuh, well, how come you never tell them it's me who's calling, hmmm?

FERN: I do so!

IRVING: Come on, will you? You think I'm a dope? You think I can't tell?

FERN: It's my father. He really hates Jews...

IRVING: He does? Oh, God, that's terrible.

FERN: How about *your* father?

IRVING: My father's no problem. It's my mother. You're not the first non-Jewish girl I've loved, you know...

FERN: I know. You told me...

IRVING: My mother tried to get me to promise that I wouldn't go out with you...

FERN: Did you?

IRVING: Promise? Uh uh...

FERN: Did you stand up to her?

IRVING: Sort of. I stood up...

FERN: And?

IRVING: I, uh, ran out...

FERN: Oh, God, this is hard for me to admit out loud. You've got to take this in the right spirit, Irving...

IRVING: Of course I will...

FERN: My father said "There's never been a Jew in our family, not since the beginning of time..."

IRVING: *(After a long, long, long pause; clench-jawed.)* That is the worst thing I have ever heard in my entire life, and I have heard some horrible, horrible, *horrible* things...

FERN: Oh, yuh, well, how do you think I felt when Stanley Rosen shoved me out the door with a blue pinstripe suit coat saying "Get out of here before my parents see you!"

IRVING: Oh, yuh, well, *Rosen,* sure, he's brain damaged!

FERN: Stanley Rosen is not brain damaged, Irving Yanover! He is my *friend!* It's not him, it's his *parents,* and *my* parents and *your* parents...

IRVING: I guess.

FERN: I *know...*

IRVING: You've talked to Rosen.

FERN: He feels awful...

IRVING: He smells pretty bad, too...

FERN: What?

IRVING: Just kidding...

FERN: You're *always* kidding!

IRVING: Our parents are wrong. You are a wonderful, wonderful person, Fern, and I care for you...

FERN: You are, too, Irving, and I care for you, too...

IRVING: There is absolutely nothing wrong with our going out, together!

FERN: Absolutely nothing…

IRVING: Our parents are acting unreasonably…

FERN: Totally…All we're doing is *going out together, right?*

IRVING: And they're all acting completely insane! Imagine if we got *married?*

FERN: My father would kill me!

IRVING: My mother would kill herself!

FERN: Do you ever really think about us…in the future…together… *married?*

IRVING: Us? I do, Fern. I think about it a lot…

FERN: I just got goose bumps.

IRVING: Me, too…

FERN: I want to be kissed.

IRVING: Yes.

FERN: No arms, no hands…

IRVING: What about lips?

FERN: Lips are fine.

IRVING: Fern. Fernnnn…oh, Fern…

FERN: Irving. Irving…oh, Irvinggggg…

> *(Irving and Fern kiss a long, passionate kiss—no hands, no arms, of course. We hear: Chopin, being played by a piano, on tape. And then a great symphony orchestra joins in. There are many stringed instruments, many human voices singing. The lights fade slowly to black. The music continues to play. The lights fade up again. Irving is gone. Stanley is in his place, precisely. At first, we do not realize that it is Stanley that Fern is now kissing—no hands, no arms, only lips. They break from the kiss and the music stops. Now, we know.)*

STANLEY: Fern. Fernnnn…oh, Fern…

FERN: Stanley, oh, Stanley, ohhh, oh, Stanleyyyyy…

STANLEY: You're wonderful to forgive me, Fern.

FERN: I know it's not you, personally, Stanley, I know it's your parents.

STANLEY: Sometimes I wonder if I were adopted.

FERN: You don't look like your parents?

STANLEY: Oh, no, I look exactly like them. It's just that we don't *think* the same.

FERN: Same exact thing as my parents. *(Hands suit coat to Stanley.)* Here's the suit coat back.

STANLEY: Oh, see! You not only forgive me, you also return the goddamn suit coat! *(Stanley sighs three times.)* It's funny…we've known each other since first grade—I mean who would've ever guessed that you and I would end up…you know…

FERN: In love?

STANLEY: Are you?

FERN: Are *you* in love with *me?*

STANLEY: It's hard to be the one who answers first.

FERN: Let's answer at exactly the same time, Stanley. I'll count backwards from five…Ask the question out loud…*now!*

FERN AND STANLEY: *(Overlapping.)* Are you in love with me, (Fern?) (Stanley?)

FERN: Five…four…three…two…one…

(Simultaneously.)

STANLEY: Yes, oh, yes!

FERN: I just don't know, Stanley! *I just don't know!*

STANLEY: *(Truly upset.) You just don't know?* My God. Fern, that was really shitty!

FERN: Well, I'm just being truthful…

STANLEY: Yuh, well, I never would have said what I said if I knew you were going to say what you said. I mean, I was pretty *positive* you loved me, ya know what I mean?

FERN: I *do* love you, Stanley!

STANLEY: You do?

FERN: Of course, I do…

STANLEY: Oh, God, that's *great!* I'm in love with you, too, Fern.

FERN: I didn't say I was *in love* with you, Stanley Rosen! I said I *love you.*

STANLEY: What the hell is the difference?

FERN: Oh, God, Stanley, please, don't be upset! Please, don't spoil a beautiful, beautiful evening… *(Pauses.)* I know that I love you. But, I don't think I can technically be *in love* with two people at the same time…

STANLEY: Oh, my Godddd!

FERN: Stanley Rosen, please, don't! We have a sacred pact.

STANLEY: I'm sorry, Fern. I apologize…

FERN: I know you do, Stan, and I accept…What I mean, Stan, is this: When people are *in love,* they marry, right?

STANLEY: They certainly should.

FERN: It shouldn't matter if one's Jewish and the other's Presbyterian, right?

STANLEY: Not if they hide out in Saskatchewan, for the rest of their lives!

FERN: We're not marrying each other's *parents,* Stanley. We're marrying each *other*…

STANLEY: *(Stunned; thrilled.) Us?* Each *other?* Getting *married?* God, Fern, I'm getting goose bumps! *(Moonstruck.)* Are you really thinking about us getting married, Fern? You and me? Stanley and Fern?

FERN: You and me or Irving and me. It depends on how things, I dunno... *progress.*

STANLEY: How could you just say that *out loud,* right to my goddamn *face?* How could you?

FERN: Don't ruin our night, Stanley Rosen! You absolutely promised me you wouldn't talk jealously!

STANLEY: *(Furiously.)* I am hardly talking jealously, Fern! I'm just...very... pissed off...

FERN: Please, don't use bad language around me, Stanley! It's so...*disrespectful!*

STANLEY: Rough words are only words, Fern. Sometimes, speaking words that are rough help me stop myself from, I dunno, *being* rough...

FERN: You mean like *saying* you hate Irving helps you stop yourself from starting a *fight* with him? That sort of thing?

STANLEY: Exactly my point.

FERN: Well, I suppose if nobody overhears...I suppose if it really helps the situation...Just go easy, Stanley, because I never ever hear bad words...

STANLEY: *(After a long pause.)* Yanover is a turd-faced, brain-damaged, no-balled putz!

FERN: *(Covers ears.)* Oh, Stanleyyy...don't... *(She uncovers her ears and listens intently.)* What else?

(Stanley looks at Fern, amazed. The lights cross fade to Barney and Stanley in Barney's store, stocking the shelves.)

BARNEY: I'm really glad you found Mr. Silversweig's suit coat, Stanley. He was really furious.

STANLEY: Everything evens out, Poppy. I've got to use the car again, tonight...

BARNEY: Out of the question. The Yanovers have driven two times straight. It's definitely our turn to drive tonight...

STANLEY: I thought you were fighting with the Yanovers...

BARNEY: We are.

STANLEY: And you're going out to dinner with them?

BARNEY: Of course. We always do.

STANLEY: I don't get it.

BARNEY: What's not to get? If Mosie Yanover shot me in the leg on Tuesday, I'd still have to eat supper with him on Wednesday.

STANLEY: *Why?*

BARNEY: Because we *always* eat supper with the Yanovers on Wednesday. We used to eat Thursdays, but it collided with the girls' Mah-Jong games... *(Laughs.)* Friends fight, sometimes, Stanley. It's a small town, Sault Ste. Marie. You see your friends a little too often...

STANLEY: Did you ever go out with a girl who wasn't Jewish, Poppy?

BARNEY: Where did *that* come from?

STANLEY: Did you?

BARNEY: I did, yes. Why? Did somebody say something to you?

STANLEY: No. Why?

BARNEY: I went out with a girl named Jeanie Shlopac...from my school. She was Russian Orthodox. Beautiful girl, good grades...very nice.

STANLEY: Did you ever think about marrying her, Poppy?

BARNEY: Jews marry Jews, Stanley...

STANLEY: Poppy, *please.* I need you to talk to me...

BARNEY: Not on this subject, Stanley...

STANLEY: Do you love mama, Poppy?

BARNEY: What kind of a question is *that?*

STANLEY: I need to know.

BARNEY: *(After a long, long pause.)* Yes, Stanley, I do: I love your mother very, very much. Your mother is my partner. She's my wife...

STANLEY: Did you love Jeanie Shlopac?

BARNEY: Honestly?

STANLEY: Please, Poppy...

BARNEY: If this ever gets back to me, Stanley Rosen, you will never borrow the car for the rest of your life. Even after I'm dead, you won't borrow the car...

STANLEY: You loved her?

BARNEY: *(Covers intercom speaker, just in case.)* A lot.

STANLEY: So, why didn't you marry her?

BARNEY: Because, Stanley, people should marry their own...

STANLEY: Maybe things are changing, Poppy...

BARNEY: Sure. Things are worse then ever! *(Confronts his son, seriously.)* After what's just happened in the world, Stanley, it's more important than ever for Jews to marry Jews. Six million babies times six million babies times six million babies. It's going to take a long time to catch up for what's been lost...

STANLEY: Oh, God, Poppy, I know what you're saying. I really do. But, people aren't *statistics.* People have *feelings.* Don't you ever regret not marrying Jeanie Shlopac? I know I never would have gotten born, I know what I am asking. But answer me honestly, Poppy, *please?* Don't you ever regret it? Don't you?

BARNEY: *(Quietly.)* I'm done with this conversation, Stanley. This is silliness. I'm done with this conversation...

(Barney turns his back on Stanley. Stanley pauses a moment and then runs from the store. There is a moment's pause. Barney bows his head, sadly. Stanley moves downstage; talks as if on telephone.)

STANLEY: Yanover? I'm coming over.

(Lights fade up on an amazed Irving Yanover, in Yanover living room.)

IRVING: Who's this?

STANLEY: Stanley Rosen.

(The fight bell sounds, as Stanley crosses into Yanover house.)

STANLEY: She's nuts, you know. We don't look anything alike.

IRVING: Of course, she's nuts. Nuts is the Human Condition. Have you read Camus?

STANLEY: *(Lying through his teeth.)* Most of Camus. But, it's been a long time.

IRVING: Uh hahhh! A blind spot in your intellectual growth, Rosen! Now that I know your weakness, I shall leap in and triumph…

STANLEY: I never saw two men look less alike!

IRVING: I agree.

(Stanley crosses to table.)

STANLEY: Do you think Fern's father is really a Nazi?

IRVING: Naw, I don't think he's so much a Nazi as he is a Nazi-supporter.

STANLEY: Mmm. *(Nods in agreement.)*

IRVING: It's exactly like you not being so much an athlete as an athletic supporter…

STANLEY: *(They both squeeze invisible horns and make "nahn-nah" sound.)* Ho, ho! *That* was rich. *(Pauses.)* Could we leap over the small talk, up to some medium talk, Yanover?

IRVING: Be my guest: leap.

STANLEY: How'd you get your parents around the idea of Fern Fipps being somebody you date?

IRVING: Parents, my dear Rosen, have a strong tendency to see life *as they want it to be* rather than life as it most obviously *is*…until, of course, a Stanley Rosen comes along and takes the truth and tries to *rub it in parents' eyes!*

STANLEY: A basic survival technique, my dear Yanover. Blind the enemy's parents with the truth and your own parents will never see the *truth.*

IRVING: If I were you, I wouldn't go into Philosophy for a living.

STANLEY: You know what Plato said?

IRVING: Remind me.

STANLEY: Plato said, "Never wear argyle socks with a glen-plaid suit."

IRVING: Plato was in the menswear business?

STANLEY: "Morris Plato's Togary."

IRVING: Is it true what my father said? That you wrote a song called "Prelude to the Sale of a Pair of Pants?" That's what your father told *my* father, anyway...

STANLEY: I did. I did that.

IRVING: I composed a tune called "Fanfare for Five Flannel Sheets and a Pillowcase."

STANLEY: You ever play four-handed Gershwin?

IRVING: Is that like doubles pinochle?

STANLEY: Aha! A major blind spot! Do you know Oscar Levant?

IRVING: Didn't he live over on Pim Street?

STANLEY: Get serious, Yanover! Oscar Levant is just about the greatest mind in the twentieth century, that's all...He wrote a book called *A Smattering of Ignorance,* about how he and Gershwin fought all the time.

IRVING: They fought too, huh?

STANLEY: Oil and water...I'll loan you the book. It's just probably the greatest book ever written in English, that's all.

IRVING: No kidding?

(Stanley produces a dog-eared copy of a book by Levant.)

STANLEY: *A Smattering of Ignorance.* Be my guest, Yanover. Just read the opening paragraph.

(Stanley tosses book across store to Irving, who catches it.)

STANLEY: My life was changed by Oscar Levant. There's more to life than Frederic Chopin, m'boy.

(Irving is reading; pretends to be engrossed totally.)

IRVING: Shhh. I'm reading...

STANLEY: Some middlebrow would-be pseudo-intellectuals claim Camus has a brain, but history will prove that the greatest thinker of the twentieth century was, unquestionably, Oscar Levant.

IRVING: *(Looks up. Playacts exasperation.)* Will you *please?* I am reading. If you think this is a good book, Rosen, you're out of your mind! This is a *great* book, Rosen! A *great* book!

STANLEY: I gave this book to my father to read.

IRVING: What did he say?

STANLEY: Obvious line: "I used to think you were a lunatic. Now, I'm *convinced!*"

IRVING: Lunacy is a son's birthright...

STANLEY: It's in the Talmud. Page eight...

IRVING: Page *nine.*

STANLEY: You know your Talmud…

IRVING: Back to front…

STANLEY: *(Masturbation joke.)* Like the front of your hand…

IRVING: That was funny. Maybe I was Levant in an earlier life?

STANLEY: This is true, you were Levant and I was Gershwin. You see, my dear Yanover, the subtle difference between Levant and Gershwin is the subtle difference between talent and genius…

YANOVER: Really?

STANLEY: Really.

IRVING: You wanna try to back up your fancy talk with some fancy action?

STANLEY: Okay, palley-pal. You see these mitts? *(Makes two fists.)*

IRVING: Yuh, so?

STANLEY: Watch 'em and weep. *(Stanley walks to Irving's piano and plays Gershwin's* Rhapsody in Blue.*)*

IRVING: That is just great, Rosen. Just goddamn *great!*
(We hear: Esther's voice over funnel-tube intercom, from store below. We don't see her, just hear her.)

ESTHER: *(Offstage.)* Irving! What are you playing?

STANLEY: *(Startled.)* What?

IRVING: It's my mother…over the tube-and-funnel intercom… *(Yells into funnel.)* What, Mama?

ESTHER: *(Offstage.)* Irvinnnggggg! How can you be standing at the intercom and still playing the piano at the same time?

IRVING: My arms reach. I'm a growing boy. I grew! Don't be a pest, Mama! Don't make me stuff fruit in the intercom again!

ESTHER: *(Offstage.)* Who's playing the piano, Irving? Answer me!

IRVING: Pearl and Barney's boy: Stanley.

ESTHER: *(Yells into intercom.)* We're coming up!
(Lights cross fade to dining table. Irving and Stanley sit; Moses and Esther join them. A meal has just been eaten. Esther offers a second helping of dessert to Stanley.)

STANLEY: It was a lovely meal, Mrs. Yanover. I'm really stuffed…

ESTHER: Another drop?

STANLEY: No other drops, thank you very much.

ESTHER: It's so good to see you in our house, again, Stanley. It's been such a long time…

STANLEY: Oh, yes, long time, Mrs. Yanover…

ESTHER: Months.

STANLEY: *Years.*

ESTHER: Oh, not *years!*

STANLEY: The last time I was here I was eleven. Now, I'm seventeen.

MOSES: How can this be? Your parents are here at least once every other week...

STANLEY: The last time I was here, there was a war on...

IRVING: In my bedroom and on the back staircase...

(Stanley and Irving laugh.)

IRVING: Rosen and I had a three-and-a-half-hour fist fight while you and the Rosens played Contract Bridge...

MOSES: Who could forget?

ESTHER: In this *house?* This is *impossible!* You're just saying this.

MOSES: Well, it's wonderful that you two have worked out your disagreements...

STANLEY: A great deal more will be determined in a week's time, Mr. Yanover...

YANOVER: Young Mr. Rosen is preparing you for a Yanover triumph, Poppy...

STANLEY: We shall see what we shall see, young Mr. Yanover...

MOSES: Still and all, it does my heart good to know that in all of Sault Ste. Marie, the best and next-to-best pianists are a Yanover and a Rosen...

IRVING: ...in that order...

MOSES: In *any* order! It does my heart good. And the difference between the best and next-to-best man is hardly noticeable.

STANLEY: So they tell us.

IRVING: So they tell us.

ESTHER: *(Out of nowhere; smiling.)* So, tell me, Stanley: Are you still going steadily with Margaret Fipps's daughter, what's her name?

STANLEY: In what *sense,* Mrs. Yanover?

IRVING: *(Chokes on water.)* Choking! Choking!

MOSES: *(Leaps up, on automatic pilot, and pounds son's back, as he has for many years prior.)* Hands over the head! Hands over the head!
(Irving raises his hands over his head. Esther will join in and Irving will make a command to Stanley, all in the same muddle.)

ESTHER: Hands over the head! Hands over the head!

IRVING: *(To Stanley.)* You, go home!
(Irving and Stanley both run: Stanley exits; Irving goes to park, to Fern. Lights cross fade.)

FERN: I got my notification today from North Bay Normal School...for elementary school teaching...

IRVING: You got in?

FERN: I did.

IRVING: Heyyyy…Fernnnn…That's great.

(Fern weeps.)

IRVING: What is it? Fern? What is it?

FERN: *(Through her tears.)* I don't want to study elementary school teaching, Irving…I really don't. *(Quietly.)* You and Stanley are off and doing exactly what you want: music. I…well…I'm doing what I think people expect of me: studying to become a third- or fourth-grade teacher. My father never actually asked me what I want to do with my life…

IRVING: It's *your* life, Fern. People have got to live up to what they expect of *themselves*…

FERN: I told my father that I want to study engineering and he said "That's not for a girl…" He says teaching's *perfect*. I mean, he doesn't *ask*. He just decides.

IRVING: I think you should study to be an engineer. Hell, you get the best math grades in the whole school. If not for you, Rosen and I would have flunked math *cold*…speaking of which, I am… *(He hugs Fern more closely.)* Nothing like a warm woman for a cool night.

(They kiss again.)

IRVING: You'll be a *great* engineer, Fern…and that's a fact!

FERN: It's an awful thing to say out loud, but, when we kiss like this, Irving, I really hope it's you who wins the playoffs tomorrow night…

(They kiss, passionately. We hear: Chopin played on dueling pianos, with great gusto. The lights fade out. The lights fade in. Stanley Rosen is standing on Fern's gutter-pipe, under Fern's window. He calls inside.)

STANLEY: Fern? Fern?

(Fern comes to window and is amazed to find Stanley standing on shaky old gutter-pipe.)

FERN: What are you doing?

STANLEY: I wanted a kiss before I went to sleep…not for luck (I don't need luck), but for inspiration. You're my inspiration, Fern…

FERN: What are you standing on?

STANLEY: The gutter-pipe…

FERN: Is it safe?

STANLEY: Oh, God, I hope so! Maybe we should hurry?

FERN: You walked all the way over here just for a kiss, Stan?

STANLEY: Peddled—then I climbed.

FERN: Oh, Stan. You're so romantic.

STANLEY: You *are* Romance, Fern.

FERN: Oh, God, Stan. I felt all funny when you just said that.

STANLEY: Me, too.

FERN: *(Kisses him quickly.)* You'd better go…before my parents hear.

STANLEY: I only want to win the playoffs because I want to win *you*, Fern. I want you to know that.

(The telephone rings.)

FERN: The phone.

(Fern looks away to grab phone. Porkchop growls under Stanley, who moans. The gutter-pipe buckles, collapses. Stanley crashes to ground. Porkchop chases him instantly away.)

FERN: *(Into telephone.)* Just a sec… *(Looks at Stanley.)* Stan, I… *(But he is gone.)* Stan? Stan?

(We hear: The sound of Porkchop, in distance, eating something. The lights cross fade to Yanover home. Esther stands at swinging door, calling offstage to Irving.)

ESTHER: What are you doing? You've been in there for an hour!

IRVING: *(Offstage.)* I'm soaking my hands in tea!

ESTHER: You're soaking your hands in *what?*

IRVING: *(Offstage.) Tea!* It strengthens the skin!

ESTHER: It also stains your hands, doesn't it?

IRVING: *(Offstage.)* Oh, my Goddd!

ESTHER: Are they stained?

IRVING: *(Offstage.)* Not at all! No stain!

ESTHER: *(Sniffs.)* Do I smell bleach water?

IRVING: *(Offstage.)* No!

ESTHER: You have your hands in bleach water!

IRVING: *(Offstage.)* I don't!

ESTHER: You do! I know you!

IRVING: *(Offstage.)* I do not have my hands in bleach water, mama! Go away!

ESTHER: Mosieeee!

(Moses walks to door.)

MOSES: Open this door! Show me.

IRVING: *(Door opens. Irving's hands appear onstage like puppets.)* Are they still brown?

MOSES: Yes.

IRVING: *(Offstage.)* You call this brown?

MOSES: Dark brown, yes.

IRVING: *(Offstage.)* Give me ten more minutes… *(Pulls hands offstage. The door closes, again.)*

MOSES: It smells like World War I in this house! My eyes are tearing! You will destroy your hands if you leave them in bleach, Irving! What are you trying to do?

IRVING: *(Door reopens. Hands reappear.)* Now *this* you wouldn't call brown, would you?

MOSES: Brown. It's brown…

(Lights cross fade to Stanley, standing facing his parents. He holds his hand in front of him in his other hand. He is in pain.)

PEARL: You broke your hand?

BARNEY: You broke your hand?

STANLEY: I broke my hand. I think so. It feels it…

PEARL: How?

BARNEY: How?

STANLEY: Exercise. Exercise…

BARNEY: Exercise?

PEARL: Exercise?

STANLEY: Squeezing a rubber ball. I read that squeezing a rubber ball was the difference between good players and great players…so, I squeezed.

BARNEY: For how long, Stanley?

STANLEY: I had a little trouble sleeping, so I exercised a little extra…About five-and-a-half hours. *(Moans.)* It's really killing me.

PEARL: Between now and the contest tonight, young man…no more exercise and no more reading. Barney, get Epsom Salts and he'll soak. Trust me. Don't I know?

STANLEY: *(Confidentially.)* Mama, I know this sounds silly, but, you'll love me still if something goes wrong, if I don't, you know, win?

PEARL: Stanley David Rosen, what kind of a question is that?

STANLEY: What kind of an *answer* is that?

PEARL: Of course, I'll love you! If you robbed a bank, I'd still love you…

STANLEY: Really?

PEARL: No ideas, you! Stanley, you have a talent and you have training. You will sit at the piano, you will relax, you will let your talent and your training control your playing, and you will win. This family has achieved something and the Yanovers must be stopped…

STANLEY: It's important to you that I win, isn't it?

PEARL: Very.

STANLEY: No matter what?

PEARL: No matter what.

(Barney reenters with Epsom salts.)

BARNEY: An hour's soak in this stuff should do the trick…

STANLEY: Poppy, you want me to win, don't you?

BARNEY: Does a bear pee in the woods, Stanley?

STANLEY: *(Laughs. Groucho imitation.)* He soitenly does!

BARNEY: I soitenly want you to win. Not for me, Stanley. For your mother…
(They all laugh. Pearl looks up to Heaven; talks to God.)

PEARL: All night? You let him squeeze a rubber ball five-and-a-half hours???
What's the matter with you???
(The lights cross fade to Irving with Esther and Moses, near the Yanover piano, opposite side of stage. Irving is trying to tie his necktie, but the pain is too intense.)

IRVING: Could you tie it for me, Poppy? When I try to bend my fingers, the skin cracks. I can't make the knot…

MOSES: I'll tie the tie, but, I can't play the piano…

IRVING: Can I ask you a question, Poppy? Fella to fella?

MOSES: If you're asking me if you have to win the contest, Irving, the answer is "No, you do not have to be a contest winner in this life."

IRVING: You don't think it's important to win?

MOSES: I think it's important to love life…

IRVING: I think you're right.

MOSES: There's no right or wrong about it. You're a wonderful son, Irving. I wish your hands weren't brown and cracked, but, you're a wonderful son…nevertheless… *(Moses beams at his son.)*

IRVING: That wasn't my question, Poppy?

MOSES: What wasn't your question?

IRVING: The whole speech you made about contest winning. My question was different.

MOSES: What's your question?

IRVING: It's just between us, okay?

MOSES: Could there be any doubt?

IRVING: Poppy, what if, just before you and Mama were married—say, fifteen minutes before the wedding ceremony—you found out Mama wasn't Jewish? Would you have married her anyway?

MOSES: What a question!

IRVING: Would you have?

MOSES: Your mother, she could have turned purple fifteen minutes before the wedding and I would have married her…

IRVING: *(Relieved; big smile.)* I *knew* it!

MOSES: But, that's not my whole answer, Irving…

(Irving looks at his father.)

MOSES: It takes two people saying "I do" to make a marriage. You might want to ask your mother what she would have done fifteen minutes before the wedding if she found out I was really Michael Sean O'Yanover...

IRVING: I wouldn't dare ask her!

MOSES: What do you think she would have done?...

IRVING: She would have walked away...

MOSES: That's one of the things I love most about your mother, Irving. She has rules... *(Smiles.)* We're different, your mother and I... *(Pauses; Smiles.)* It's important for Jews to marry Jews...but, it's also important that the love be there in abundance... *(Pauses.)* We happen to have a great abundance in this family... *(Pauses.)* I saw her in Rosen's store. She seems like a nice girl.

IRVING: Thanks, Poppy.

(There is a pause as Moses holds Irving's face in his hands. Esther enters carrying long white gloves and cold cream.)

ESTHER: Give me your hands. This will work...

IRVING: What are you doing?

ESTHER: Cold cream on your hands, first, and then my white cotton gloves...filled with cold cream. The cold cream will fill in the cracks from the tea...

IRVING: By tonight?

ESTHER: If God is kind... *(Looks up.)* ...for a change! Mosie, start the car...

MOSES: *(Nods.)* I'll start the car. *(Moses exits.)*

IRVING: I can't do this. I'd rather not compete!

ESTHER: You will compete and you will win...

IRVING: Do you really think winning is that important, Mama?

ESTHER: Winning, in general, no. Winning, specifically, tonight, absolutely *yes*...

IRVING: No matter what the prize turns out to be?

ESTHER: This is bigger than a prize, Irving...

IRVING: It certainly is, Mama...

ESTHER: Our next door neighbor, when I was growing up, had a cousin who sang in the opera...a baritone. I can remember hearing the story over and over again, when I was a girl. The singer came out on stage at the Metropolitan Opera House in New York City, New York, and he had put his mother in a seat in the front row. When he came out on stage, just before he sang, he waved to his mother. Not a big wave. Just a wave. And then he sang. And all the people sitting around his mother kept asking her over and over again who she was, why did he wave? *(Pauses; smiles to Irving.)* Ever since you started taking lessons, I've known what it was I wanted, Irving. To sit in the front row at Carnegie Hall in New York City, New York, and to have you come out on stage, sit at the piano, look at me, wave. *(Smiles.)* ...Tonight, is the first step on the road to Carnegie Hall, Irving. I know it is...

IRVING: I thought you were set on my going to law school.

ESTHER: Now there's something the matter with law school?

IRVING: Law schools don't prepare people for playing pianos at Carnegie Hall, Mama...

ESTHER: And lawyers can't also play pianos?

IRVING: I'll do my best, tonight, Mama. I promise.

ESTHER: *(Holds Irving's face a moment; then, simply.)* You're Irving Yanover. *(Kisses him.)* Now... *(Opens cold cream jar.)* Cold cream on the hands and hands into the gloves.

IRVING: Mama, I absolutely won't wear gloves. I absolutely refuse...

(Mother stares at son. Irving jams his hands into the gloves. Stanley calls across to Irving. The lights cross fade, as Irving moves to Stanley and the park.)

STANLEY: Yanover.

IRVING: Rosen.

STANLEY: Cold night.

IRVING: Cold night. What's with your hand?

STANLEY: *My* hand? What's with your gloves?

IRVING: Gloves?

FERN: Nobody must ever know of our plan...of the way we worked it out. Whichever of you who loses must never ever tell anyone ever...

(Stanley and Irving nod. Fern smiles and then becomes stern.)

FERN: Whichever of you who loses must accept the loss for what it is. You must promise to never call me again and if we meet in school or in the movies or on the street or something by accident, just nod.

(Irving and Stanley nod.)

FERN: I make my pledge now... *(She looks at both of them.)* I pledge to never talk to the loser again, except by accident... *(She averts her eyes from them.)* I pledge to love, honor, and obey the winner...I pledge to write a letter every day, without fail, at the very least for the next two years...I pledge to marry and dedicate my life to the winner, the summer after next. *(She looks at both, solemnly. Her face is tearstained as she weeps, openly.)* There is no way I can lose. I love both of you.

(Irving and Stanley giggle.)

FERN: *(Pauses: then soberly.)* Do we all agree?

IRVING: I…yes.

STANLEY: I…me, too.

FERN: There were times in the past few days when I've had great doubts…do I want to be married to *any*one…*ever?* But, standing here now, looking at both of you…knowing that promises and plans *must be kept*…knowing that my love for both of you is true…*really and truly true*…well… *(She kisses Stanley.)* Good luck, Stanley. *(She kisses Irving.)* Good luck, Irving.

(The lights widen to full stage, as the pianos now roll forward. The Rosens and the Yanovers and Uncle Goldberg now sit in chairs facing the dueling pianos. Emcee's voice booms out.)

EMCEE: *(Over loudspeaker.)* Hullo? Is this on? Ladies and Gentlemen, applause, please, for the finalists in the First Annual Cyrus Drinkwater Music Competition…Stanley Rosen and Irving Yanover, both from Sault Ste. Marie, Ontario!

(The Yanovers, Rosens, Fern, and Uncle Goldberg all applaud. Taped applause supports over loudspeaker system, lightly. N. B. The sound of sixty people, no more. Stanley and Irving walk to their pianos, bow to the front, embarrassedly. Irving waves to Esther: a small, hep wave [of the period]: a circular motion. They sit.)

PEARL: Why did your Irving wave to me?

ESTHER: Oh, my God! He was certainly not waving to *you!* He was waving to his *mother!*

PEARL: Oh.

(Fern enters; sits. The mothers spot her.)

ESTHER: *(To Moses.)* There she is…

PEARL: *(To Barney.)* There she is…

EMCEE: Both contestants will be playing Chopin: *Waltz in C'-Minor*, Opus 64, #2; with separate judges watching each finalist. But first, they will play *Fantasie Impromptu* in C-Minor, Opus 66 for two hands, for precision scoring…

(Irving and Stanley play sweetly, under the following scene.)

ESTHER: There's Stanley's girlfriend, Pearl…

PEARL: I beg your pardon, but that is Irving's girlfriend. Irving's *steady* girlfriend…

ESTHER: Right girl, wrong boy. I think you've been lied to…

PEARL: Would you like to place a bet as to who's been lied to, Mrs. Yanover?

ESTHER: Name the stakes…

PEARL: I think that the stakes are quite evident… *(Taps Fern's shoulder.)* Excuse me, Fern, but, there's a small disagreement—a misunderstanding, really, that wants to be settled…

FERN: Hello, Mrs. Rosen… *(Smiles to Esther.)* Hello, Mrs. Yanover.

ESTHER: Hello, Fern. How's your mother?

FERN: She's fine, thank you…

ESTHER: And your dad?

FERN: My dad is fine, too, thank you…

ESTHER: Who's girlfriend are you, Fern? Tell her, please. She's confused…

FERN: I'm sorry, Mrs. Yanover…Mrs. Rosen…but, I'm really sworn to secrecy. Irving and Stanley and I all have a sacred pledge to one another…

PEARL: About going steady?

FERN: Oh. no. It's much, much bigger than that. It's about marriage. Please, ask me no questions and I'll tell you no lies. Okay?

(There is a moment's pause. Esther whispers to Moses. Pearl whispers to Barney. Barney whispers to Uncle Goldberg. A single word travels down the row and then back again.)

MOSES: Marriage?

BARNEY: Marriage?

PEARL: Marriage.

ESTHER: Marriage.

BARNEY: Marriage?

MOSES: Marriage?

PEARL: Marriage.

ESTHER: Marriage.

(And then, at precisely the same instant, like Semitic Rockettes [of sorts], they all slap their own foreheads with the palms of their hands. The lights cross fade from the parents to the pianos. One spot on each piano. An emcee calls over loudspeaker, into auditorium.)

EMCEE: Applause, once again for our two talented young finalists, Irving Yanover and Stanley Rosen…

(We hear: light applause.)

EMCEE: We now come to the actual competition…Are the judges ready? Gentlemen, are you ready?

(Stanley nods. Irving nods. The emcee calls out front a final time.)

EMCEE: I can't understand where Mr. Drinkwater is…Does anyone here know Mr. Drinkwater, personally?

UNCLE GOLDBERG: I do.

EMCEE: Where is Mr. Drinkwater, sir?

(All parents stare at Uncle Goldberg, amazed.)

UNCLE GOLDBERG: Mr. Drinkwater is unavoidably detained. He told me that he'll be talking to the winner at a later time. Mr. Drinkwater would like everybody to know that this whole thing is his fault and that he feels ashamed.

(Uncle Goldberg goes to chair far side of stage, sits alone. Stanley stares at him, amazed, as do the others.)

EMCEE: *(Over loudspeaker.)* Okayyy...Then, we'll begin the competition. The format is unique: both competitors will play the same piece—Chopin [Opus 64, #2]—at precisely the same time. But, separate judges will watch each finalist, scoring one to ten points in three categories: technique, interpretation and feeling. Gentlemen, on three...one, two...three.

(Irving and Stanley begin to play Chopin piece, in unison, sweetly. Fern, Uncle Goldberg and all parents will now pray. And we will hear their prayers.)

UNCLE GOLDBERG: *(To Heaven.)* Dear Lord, I have made a terrible, terrible mistake. I am totally to blame. Please, send us a miracle...

PEARL: *(To Heaven.)* How could you let me do this? I've pushed my son into marriage with *her!* How could you let me do this?

ESTHER: *(To Heaven.)* This is my fault. How can this be my fault? You're God! Why did you make me do this?

FERN: *(Head down, praying.)* Dear Lord, I have made a terrible, terrible, terrible mistake. Please forgive me, but I don't want to marry *anybody.* I love Irving and Stanley but I definitely want to break my promise. I want to get out of this, Lord...Please, send us a miracle!

ESTHER: *(Turns, faces Fern; speaks to her.)* There's no way out. Not with Irving...

PEARL: *(The same; to Fern.)* There's no way out. Not with Stanley...

ESTHER: I know my son...

PEARL: I know my son...

ESTHER: Once his mind is made up...

PEARL: *(Completes the thought.)* ...he's like a Great Lake. He'll never change his mind.

ESTHER: Never.

(Irving and Stanley continue to play the Chopin piece for another fifteen or twenty seconds, sweetly, perfectly; and then Stanley switches from Chopin to Gershwin. Irving is startled.)

IRVING: What the hell are you doing?

STANLEY: I'm making a winner out of you, Yanover!

IRVING: Like hell you are! I'M NOT GETTING MARRIED!

> *(Irving hits a series of clinkers that would curdle new milk on contact. Stanley tries to out-clinker Irving's clinkers. What was, in the beginning, sweet and slightly romantic music is now a cacophony of dissonant sound. Now discord. The boys slam away at their pianos.)*

IRVING: You're winning, Rosen, you're winning!

STANLEY: Like hell I am! I'm not getting married! You win!

IRVING: Me, neither, Rosen, me, neither! I'm not getting married, either! You win!

STANLEY: You're winning, Yanover!

IRVING: I am like hell!

BARNEY: Your son is winning, Yanover!

MOSES: Like hell he is, Rosen! Come on, Stanley, win!

ESTHER: Come on, Stanley, you can do it! Win!

PEARL: Come on, Irving, win, win, win!

> *(They play even worse. Lights cross fade to audience. The "music" continues, on tape. Esther and Moses hug each other. Barney and Pearl hug each other. Uncle Goldberg runs over and hugs Fern. The music is now sweet Chopin, played by the boys, on tape. The lights cross fade to soft moonlight lighting on park bench. Actor who plays Ardenshensky sits on park bench, holding two hats: Ardenshensky's rumpled grey hat, and Goldberg's dapper black derby. He will again play a scene in which the two old men are in confrontation (and conversation), by dint of his changing personalities and hats with each change of character, instantly, magically.)*

ARDENSHENSKY: You made a mess, Goldberg. Are you ashamed of yourself?

> *(Goldberg shrugs; wordlessly.)*

GOLDBERG: The children didn't want to compete, after all. It was the parents. What the parents say at home, the children tell on the street.

ARDENSHENSKY: I know the book. *(Smiles.)*

GOLDBERG: I'm going back to Montreal, first thing in the morning.

ARDENSHENSKY: Good.

GOLDBERG: You get the title. You…win.

ARDENSHENSKY: Makes no difference to me.

GOLDBERG: We'll never see each other again.

ARDENSHENSKY: This is true.

GOLDBERG: I wish you well, Jacob.

ARDENSHENSKY: I wish you well, too, Goldberg.

GOLDBERG: *(Smiles.)* So?

ARDENSHENSKY: So?

> *(Actor takes off hat, looks front, smiles. He clasps and shakes his own hands. both men saying good-bye. He wraps his arms around himself, hugs himself: both men, embracing. They "link arms." Exit. The lights cross fade to Fern, Stanley, and Irving standing together, in the park. The music continues: Chopin being played sweetly by two children. N. B. The playing should be clearly the playing of young people, not yet accomplished.)*

FERN: Of *course,* I forgive you!

STANLEY: You do?

IRVING: You do?

FERN: As long as you forgive me.

STANLEY: For what?

FERN: For not being honest. I don't want to get married. I love you both. I really do, but, I don't want to be bound to marry either one of you. I wasn't honest. I hope you can forgive me...I love you both. I really do.

STANLEY: We love you, too, Fern...

IRVING: Speak for yourself, turd-face! *(To Fern; suddenly.)* I love you, Fern. I really do...

STANLEY: I love you, Fern.

> *(Fern kisses Stanley. She starts to kiss Irving, who pulls back.)*

IRVING: Not with Rosen-breath.

> *(He wipes Fern's lips with his cuff. Fern and Irving kiss. Fern looks at them both.)*

FERN: So?

> *(They look at each other a moment. Fern turns, exits. Stanley and Irving walk in the moonlight together.)*

STANLEY: So, Oscar?

IRVING: So, Gershwin?

STANLEY: I think we made trouble.

IRVING: I think we made trouble. Why'd you do it?

STANLEY: Blow the Drinkwater money?

IRVING: Yuh.

STANLEY: For you, boychik: I wanted you to win... *(Pauses.)* You? What was in your sick mind?

IRVING: Same thing: abject generosity: I wanted you to win.

STANLEY: Uncle Goldberg wants to give us both equal amounts.

IRVING: I heard. Nice of him. How'd he make so much money?

STANLEY: Seltzer. Thirty-five years of selling seltzer, in Montreal…seltzer… Drinkwater…You get it?

IRVING: *(Playacting.)* Too deep for meee…There's that much money in seltzer?

STANLEY: Apparently.

IRVING: Maybe I should go into seltzer.

STANLEY: Just don't go over your head…

IRVING: I always thought it was a tad strange that the Cyrus Drinkwater Prize was first announced in the Jewish *Forward*, in Hebrew.

STANLEY: That is probably because Uncle Goldberg does not, as they say, read a great English…

IRVING: So?

STANLEY: So?

IRVING: Would the co-loser of the Chopin playoffs like to sit?

STANLEY: He wouldn't mind.

(They sit.)

STANLEY: I heard you might study law.

IRVING: Why? Lawyers can't also play pianos?

STANLEY: Just in case, huh?

IRVING: Just in case. And you? I heard medicine.

STANLEY: I would prefer to lose a leg. Buttt…just in case.

IRVING: We could live our whole lives doing things just in case, if we're not careful.

STANLEY: Precisely why we have to be careful, my dear Yanover…just in case!

IRVING: My father told me once that the way to choose a good enemy is to pick a friend. He'll know exactly where to strike.

STANLEY: My father said the same thing.

(Stanley and Irving do secret handshake of cow being milked. Both say "Moo.")

STANLEY: How come your hands are brown, my boy?

IRVING: What's with the ace bandage, Ace?

STANLEY: Long story.

IRVING: Long story.

STANLEY: Life, my dear Yanover, is full of mystery…Look at the lights of our town…fireflies…We shall name the streets between here and Algoma Steel: Lake Street, Churchill, Elizabeth…I helped Uncle Goldberg relearn them.

IRVING: Make a right on Pine and a left on?…

STANLEY: …Wellington Street East.

IRVING: *(W.C. Fields's voice.)* Ah, yes, Wellington was a great man and a good street to boot.

STANLEY: Pim…

IRVING: Pilgrim…

STANLEY: East…

IRVING: Brock…

STANLEY: Spring…

IRVING: March…

STANLEY: Elgin…

IRVING: Bruce…

STANLEY: Dennis…

IRVING: Tancred…

STANLEY: Gore…

IRVING: Andrew…

STANLEY: Huron…

IRVING: And a left on Patrick to Algoma Steel!

STANLEY: It'll be a cold day in hell when we forget the names of these mighty streets!

IRVING: And I'll tell it to the world! *(Irving stands, moves to imagined cliff; yells out, singing to tune of "Sweet Sue.")* Sweet Soooo.

STANLEY: *(Does the same.)* Sweet Sooo…

IRVING: It's a nice place to come from.

STANLEY: A *nice* place. Can you imagine what it's gonna be like for our parents, after we leave?

IRVING: I can't imagine.

STANLEY: Try.

> *(Irving squeezes out a conjured look into the future, seeing his parents.)*

IRVING: Not a pretty picture.

STANLEY: *(Conjures up the same image.)* Not a pretty picture. *(Calls out to parents, asking them to enter, for the sake of the audience.)* Show them…

> *(The parents enter the Ritz Cafe. We hear the sound of an Oriental gong. Oriental screens fall into place and Oriental music plays. The parents sit in their chairs. They are grumpy, depressed. Mr. Wong enters carrying a huge tray with their food upon it. He refuses to serve them until they keep their promise.)*

MR. WONG: Let's see the hugs, please…

BARNEY: That's just silly, Wong. Can't you see how nicely we're getting along?

MR. WONG: No hugs: No eating in Ritz Cafe, no egg foo yong, no spicy sea bass, no egg drop soups, no chicken chow mein…

MOSES: *(Interrupts.)* Mr. Wong, really, there's no need…

ESTHER: No need at all, Mr. Wong…

PEARL: Mr. Wong, *really*…

BARNEY: This is just *crazy!* Mr. Wong, please…

MR. WONG: Ancient Chinese saying: "You can whitewash a crow, but it won't last." Hug, please, food getting icy.

PEARL: Really, Mr. Wong, we're getting along just fine. Can't you tell?

MR. WONG: Hugs, please, by time I count three, or "Bye bye, bass. Hello, trashy-can…"

MOSES: No! I'm famished. I'll hug. Come here, Barney, sing for your supper…

(Moses and Barney embrace. They are both instantly friends again.)

MOSES: Ah, Barney, you're my pal…really.

BARNEY: Who else do we have to argue with, Mosie, huh?

PEARL: *(Arms extended to Esther.)* Essie?

ESTHER: Oh, Pearlie…

(The women embrace.)

ESTHER: Oh, Pearlie, Pearlie, who wants to grow old?

(The women choke back their sadness. Esther looks at Mr. Wong, smiles.)

ESTHER: You're very clever, Mr. Wong. No wonder we eat here three nights a week, lately.

MR. WONG: Nobody in my family was ever clever, Mrs. Yanover, so, we had to listen to clever people and we tried to remember some of the clever things they said…Who gets the spicy sea bass?

BARNEY: My pal Mosie.

(Mr. Wong serves and talks.)

MR. WONG: "Before you beat a dog, find out whose dog he is…" Egg foo yong?

ESTHER: My friend Pearl.

MR. WONG: "Eggs, if they're wise, don't fight with stones…" Chicken chow mein?

MOSES: My pal Barney.

MR. WONG: "If you can't smile, don't open a shop." *(Pauses.)* "Don't judge a man till his coffin is closed…" *(Pauses.)* "Enough mosquitoes sound like thunder…" *(Pauses.)* "When the heart dies, you can't even grieve…" *(Pauses.)* "Nobody believes the old." *(Mr. Wong has served dinner to all.)* "If the rich could hire other people to die for them, the poor would make a wonderful living." *(Shrugs.)* If we didn't *have* competition, my dear Yanovers and Rosens, we couldn't aspire to live without it…Enjoy your meal.

(The gong sounds, again, a final time. The lights cross to Stanley and Irving, center.)

IRVING: So, Gershwin, when we leave this town, once and for all, how are we going?

STANLEY: I say we take a right when we leave Pine…and between Elizabeth and Churchill, we pick up the Trans-Canada…

IRVING: Then 17E to Sudbury…

STANLEY: North Bay…

IRVING: Ottawa…

STANLEY: Montreal…

IRVING: Toronto…

STANLEY: North America…

IRVING: The Western Hemisphere…

STANLEY: The planet Earth…

IRVING: The Universe!

IRVING: Quite a road, the Trans-Canada. It'll get you anywhere

STANLEY: Absolutely *any*where!

IRVING: From genius to talent…

STANLEY: From talent to reality…

IRVING: So?

STANLEY: So?

(Both boys shrug, look at one another. Wordlessly, they embrace, center. After a moment, they separate. Stanley exits off, right; Irving exits off left. The lights fade out. The lights then snap on, as if for curtain call. Mr. Wong re-enters, still in costume. He raises his hands and stops the applause. He removes his ancient Chinese cap, smiles, reveals himself as Ardenshensky, speaks to audience.)

ARDENSHENSKY: It's me: Ardenshensky. You thought maybe I was Wong from the Ritz Cafe? I'm an actor! I'm working! *(Smiles.)* So that's it. Three plays are finished: *Today, I Am A Fountain Pen, A Rosen By Any Other Name* and, finally, *The Chopin Playoffs.* These plays will never replace night baseball, or cure cancer, but, they might give you some small idea about what it was like to be alive…in our time…on our tiny dot on the planet Earth… *(Smiles.)* Do you know about the merger of the Israeli airline, El Al, with the Italian airline, Alitalia? They called the new one "Vell, I'll tell ya"…You wonder what became of us all? Vell, I'll tell ya… *(Smiles.)* The schmendrick Goldberg moved back to Montreal, two days after nobody won his piano contest, not only making me happy, but also making me once again the oldest living man in the Soo…as if I care… *(Smiles.)* Fern became an engineer and designed many big bridges, one of which leads in and out of Sault Ste. Marie. She married and had three children—all girls—and they all accomplished big things. *(Smiles.)* Stanley Rosen moved back to the Soo and married Rosie Berkowitz. They have two grown children and an excellent retail business. *(Smiles.)* Irving Yanover is a lawyer in Toronto. In his spare time, he writes stories about growing up Jewish in Sault Ste. Marie, some of which got turned into stage plays, but, this you know, already… *(Smiles.)* As for the parents, they're all dead, of course, except for Essie Yanover, who is over ninety now and lives not far from Irving, who she claims is, as a son, "Not bad"… *(Smiles.)* As for me, Jacob Ardenshensky, I never lived, so I never died. I'm just twenty-one characters in three plays: no more, no less… *(Smiles.)* After all, this wasn't real. These were just plays. None of it happened this way…not at alll…welllllllll…not exacttttlyyy…

(The lights widen to include entire cast. The actors bow. The lights and music fade out.)

The play is over.

THE ALFRED TRILOGY

INTRODUCTION

"THE ALFRED TRILOGY"

Alfred the Great, Our Father's Failing, Alfred Dies

"The Alfred Trilogy" is the centerpiece of "The Wakefield Plays," a seven-play cycle, including *Alfred the Great, Our Father's Failing, Alfred Dies;* plus four interrelated one-act plays that compose "The Quannapowitt Quartet." Those plays are *Hopscotch, The 75th, Stage Directions,* and *Spared.* (These four one-act plays can be found in the Smith & Kraus edition of some of my shorter plays, *Israel Horovitz Collected Works Volume One: Sixteen Short Plays.)*

I wrote "The Alfred Trilogy" and "The Quannapowitt Quartet" during the decade of the 1970s, which was neither an easy time for America, nor for me. I had just regathered some strength, after the dizzying success of plays of mine such as *The Indian Wants the Bronx, Line, Rats, It's Called The Sugar Plum, The Honest-To-God Schnozzola*…which won prize after prize—the NY Drama Desk Award, two OBIES, a Pulitzer nomination—plus, the Jury Prize at Cannes went to my first film, *The Strawberry Statement,* and a dozen screen-offers followed. I'd gone from being totally, utterly unknown to being, well, if not exactly a household word, like *Kleenex* or *DeNiro,* certainly, within theatre and movie circles, famous enough to feel totally, utterly terrified. And for reasons still too complicated to understand or explain, I decided that I would only allow my plays to be performed in NYC, if critics were forbidden to attend and review. I stuck to that death-wish/promise for some five years. Thus, the entire seven-play cycle of my "Wakefield Plays" were produced in NYC, quite handsomely—the four short plays of "The Quannapowitt Quartet" were mounted at the Public Theatre by Joseph Papp, with star-studded casts including John Heard, Mary-Beth Hurt, Ellen Greene, Patti LuPone, John Glover, Elizabeth Wilson…and "The Alfred Trilogy" was mounted at The Actors Studio, featuring many of our greats and near-greats, such as John Cazale, Michael Moriarty, Jill O'Hara—and not a single review was written. It's a pity. I made a mistake. The plays and the actors were worthy of kind words, and a larger, more public arena.

Rereading the plays, as I have just recently done, I am struck by their complexity and darkness…especially in contrast to the most-bearable lightness of "The Growing-Up-Jewish Trilogy," collected in this very volume. A flood of memories washes over me. One of the funniest, darkest, is a memory of the brilliant Michael Moriarty. During rehearsals of *Alfred Dies,* Moriarty had hit an understandable bottom. Playing the role of Alfred in *Alfred the Great* and *Our Father's Failing* is enough to depress the most resilient of people. Michael was hardly that to begin with. What attracted him to the role and to the plays was his own not-insignificant darkness. Rehearsals for *Alfred Dies* were too much to bear…for all of us, really. Ben Levit, who directed the plays at the Actors Studio, was patience personified. But, even Ben was feeling the strain. These plays are *dark*…like pitch.

On this particular day, we were rehearsing the scene in *Alfred Dies* in which Emily forces Alfred to confront his knowledge of their incestuous relationship. The web of dark complication for Alfred L. Webber is tugging at his throat. He is choking in guilt. At some point in the scene, Alfred/Michael is meant to shave. During one rehearsal, Michael dropped his razor and shaving brush possibly ten times, causing Ben to scream out to the props-lady in frustration "Get Alfred a Dopp Kit!" The props-lady was occupied, elsewhere, and called back… "Excuse me, what?"…to which Ben replied "Alfred…A Dopp Kit."

Michael had been lost in darkest thought, and only half-heard Ben, who screamed, once again, "Alfred…A Dopp Kit!"…Michael came out of his waking nightmare, his eyes widened into a kind of mad confusion, as he called out to Ben and me, "Are you saying that Alfred is *adopted*?"

I am terribly proud of "The Wakefield Plays." For me, these plays represent a solid life-accomplishment. I had had eight one-acts in a row produced in NYC, during the nineteen months prior to writing "The Alfred Trilogy." I wanted to put forward a larger work. I'd made quite of lot of money from writing films. I bought a house, bought time in graduate school, educating myself, finally… and, ultimately, lived on my movie-earnings, while doing something I felt to be holy and pure: writing plays. I didn't want the critics looking over my shoulder, writing praise or worse, I didn't want the hype…I simply wanted to do my work as a playwright-artist. "The Wakefield Plays"—notably "The Alfred Trilogy"—is the result of that work.

I am thrilled to offer them, again, in this new Smith and Kraus edition.

What follows is not at all a planned essay on "The Alfred Trilogy," so much as a collection of bits and scraps of information that I jotted down in notebooks during the 1970s, about the plays and their early productions. Somehow, scattered as it may be, these bits and scraps seem appropriate to include in this new edition. The final entry is a piece I wrote and published in the *Village Voice*, some years ago, eulogizing John Cazale, immediately after his death. Much that I wrote about John applies to my other dear friend Lenny Baker, as well. It's been twenty years, since John and Lenny died, and I still seem to think of them, both, every day. Jamie Hammerstein said to me, recently, "Even though twenty years have passed, I still have John and Lenny on almost every casting list I put together." I do, too.

THE CYCLE

If the seven plays are to be produced as a cycle, they should occupy five theater evenings, in the order that follows:

Evening #1: *Hopscotch* and *The 75th*
Evening #2: *Alfred the Great*
Evening #3: *Our Father's Failing*
Evening #4: *Alfred Dies*
Evening #5: *Stage Directions* and *Spared*

Under certain circumstances, it might be possible to spread the plays over seven nights, separating the paired plays from their mates, presenting them independently, on their own evenings.

CASTING AN ACTING COMPANY

It is my hope that a small acting company might service the entire cycle, with performers changing roles skillfully from play to play.

"The Quannapowitt Quartet" works well with five actors; "The Alfred Trilogy" might require seven. I should think that eight performers could perform the entire cycle, given an extraordinary director and a long rehearsal period.

"The Wakefield Plays" is a cycle comprised of "The Quannapowitt Quartet" and "The Alfred Trilogy."

"The Quannapowitt Quartet" includes four interrelated short plays, *Hopscotch, The 75th, Stage Directions,* and *Spared;* "The Alfred Trilogy" includes *Alfred the Great, Our Father's Failing,* and *Alfred Dies.*

ALFRED THE GREAT

The first draft of *Alfred the Great* was given an invitational reading at the American Center for Students and Artists, Boulevard Raspail, Paris, on January 11, 1972, under the direction of Henry Pillsbury.

During July and August 1972, the second draft of the play was revised and the third draft was given a public staged reading at the Eugene O'Neill Theatre Center, Waterford, Connecticut, under the auspices of the National Playwrights' Conference. It was designed by Fred Voelpel and directed by James Hammerstein, with the following cast:

MARGARET	Peggy Pope
ALFRED	Lenny Baker
WILL	Kevin O'Conner
EMILY	Geraldine Sherman

A fourth draft was written after the O'Neill Center reading, which was revised into a fifth draft, presented for public performance at the Pittsburgh Playhouse, Pittsburgh, Pennsylvania (first night: March 17, 1973), designed by Robert Frederico and directed by James Hammerstein. The cast was as follows:

MARGARET	Nancy Chesney
ALFRED	Harry Cauley
WILL	John Cazale
EMILY	Carol McGroder

After the Pittsburgh Playhouse production, a sixth and final draft was completed for reading at the 1973 National Playwrights' Conference, O'Neill Theatre Center, Waterford, Connecticut, July 15–August 12, 1973. There, *Alfred the Great* was performed for the first time in conjunction with *Our Father's Failing,* Part II of the trilogy then called "The Wakefield Plays." (Now that the Wakefield cycle is complete, *Our Father's Failing* is Part II of The Alfred Trilogy, Part IV of The Wakefield Plays.)

The first public performance of the final draft of *Alfred the Great* was given on November 28, 1973, at the Trinity Square Theater, Providence, Rhode Island. The production was designed by Robert Soule and directed by James Hammerstein. The cast was as follows:

MARGARET	Nancy Chesney
ALFRED	Richard Kneeland
WILL	George Martin
EMILY	Naomi Thornton

The play toured to the Walnut Street Theatre, Philadelphia, and the Wilbur Theatre, Boston, still under the auspices of the Trinity Square Repertory Company, but with a changed cast. The Trinity Square Repertory Company's text was allowed production in December, 1974, at the University of Saskatchewan, Saskatoon. The author was not present.

Alfred the Great was then set aside for about three years, to allow for work on the other plays of the Wakefield cycle, but for interim readings at the Manhattan Theatre Club (with Michael Moriarty insinuated into the cast, for the first time, as Alfred, and Diane Keaton as Margaret, and John Cazale as Will), and at the New Dramatists Committee, in 1976, when all three plays of the trilogy were read in repertory, with a cast featuring Joanna Miles, Michael Moriarty, Nancy Chesney, John Cazale, Dominic Chianese, and Madeleine Thornton-Sherwood, under the direction of John Dillon.

After the New Dramatists Committee readings, it was decided to put full effort into the completion of *Alfred Dies,* and, once again, *Alfred the Great* was set aside, and the acting company moved, by invitation, to The Actors Studio, West 44th Street, New York City, where *Alfred Dies* was rehearsed and performed. There was also, in January 1977, a production at Colby College, Waterville, Maine. The author was not present.

At the conclusion of performances of *Alfred Dies,* there was a reading at The Actors Studio of *Alfred the Great,* and an agreement to produce both *Alfred the Great* and *Our Father's Failing* at the studio in the coming season was made with Carl Shaefer, executive director of the studio.

It was at this juncture that John Dillon left the company, because of his own father's failing health, and ultimately because of his accepting a job with the Milwaukee Repertory Company as artistic director. John Cazale also left the acting company at this time, for reasons of ill health. He died of lung cancer within the year.

During December 1977–February 1978, *Alfred the Great* underwent minor changes to adjust the text to changes made in other plays of the cycle. The final version then was rehearsed and performed, in repertory with *Our Father's Failing,* at The Actors Studio, New York City. Ben Levit was the director, Paul Eads was the scenic designer, and Jennifer von Mayrhauser was the costume designer, with the following cast:

MARGARET	Jill O'Hara
ALFRED	Michael Moriarty
WILL	Paul Gleason
EMILY	Lois Markle

REAL AND INVENTED BACKGROUND FOR *ALFRED THE GREAT*

The Quannapowitt Indians once inhabited the town of Wakefield, Massachusetts. They are all presumed to be dead now, as there appear to be no known descendants, no traces, but for bogus Indians: the Wakefield Tribe of Red Men, a men's social club.

The Wakefield Red Men costume themselves as Quannapowitt Indians and march each Fourth of July in the Independence Day Parade, sponsored by Wakefield's popular West Side Social Club. Wakefield's yearly parade, during the 1950s–1970s, was reckoned to be the largest of its kind in the Commonwealth of Massachusetts.

The majority of marching Red Men played musical instruments and populated the Red Men's Band, creating music and spectacle that was clearly a favorite of Wakefield's children and a high point of the Independence Day fete.

Between the years 1956 and 1966, the population of Wakefield, Massachusetts, allegedly diminished by several thousand people. During precisely that decade, the pregnancy dropout rate among Wakefield Memorial High School's female seniors was alleged to be the lowest in the history of the Town: less than two percent.

The Marching Red Men's band was traditionally led by Wakefield Memorial High School's drum majorettes. Red Men drummers were positioned at the rear of the band, with clarinets in the penultimate slot.

During the 1975 Independence Day Parade, the West Side Social Club itself created a parade float displaying the legend "200 YEARS AGO TODAY— THAT'S THE WAY IT WAS." A burning house was set upon the float, atop a long-bedded trailer truck. A family of Caucasian pioneers, portrayed by West Side Social Club actors, costumed for the occasion in pioneer dress, was set inside the house, play-acting life's final moments. Surrounding the trailer truck and float, on the street, were several other West Side Social Club members, costumed as Indians, armed with bows, arrows, knives, guns, and torches, play-acting the slaughter of the pioneer family and the destruction of their home.

Attendance at the 1975 Independence Day Parade was, allegedly, the highest in the history of Wakefield's annual celebrations.

The Wakefield Memorial High School's drum majorettes also costumed themselves as Quannapowitt Indians. Traditionally, they performed at high school athletic events wearing red suede dresses, beads, and feathered headdresses. Their legs and arms were stained reddish-brown with makeup. Their shoes were of the black-and-white saddle-shoe style. Wakefield Memorial High School's drum majorettes were traditionally Caucasian with traditionally Caucasoid features. One rare exception was noted in the 1950s, when a full-blooded Indian was elected to the drum majorettes' corps. She was alleged to be the stepdaughter of a local family who had been adopted from a Canadian Indian tribe. She allegedly colored her hair blond during her high school years and was not then known to be a non-Caucasian. Her Indian birth was revealed by her, later in life, when she achieved international recognition as a songwriter and performer and had, by then, allegedly, stopped coloring her hair.

Notes written in Paris, France, December, 1971.
Revised, Gloucester, Massachusetts, August, 1976.

OUR FATHER'S FAILING

Our Father's Failing had its initial exposure in staged readings at the Eugene O'Neill Memorial Centre, Waterford, Connecticut, at the National Playwrights' Conference, 1973. The readings were directed by Larry Arrick, with the following cast:

SAM	Jay Garner
PA	James Noble
ALFRED	Lenny Baker
EMILY	Carolyn Coates

Subsequently, *Our Father's Failing* had its world premiere production in March–May 1976 at the Goodman Theatre, Chicago. The director was John Dillon and the designer Stuart Wertzel, with the following cast:

SAM	Dominic Chianese
PA	Joseph Leon
ALFRED	Lawrence Pressman
EMILY	Lanna Saunders

In the next season, the play was revised and presented in readings at the New Dramatists Committee (insinuating Michael Moriarty into the cast as Alfred and John Cazale as Pa), and at The Actors Studio. There were several offers by commercial producers to present the play, isolated from "The Alfred

Trilogy," but it was agreed by the author and the acting company that a full effort would be given to the completion of the text to *Alfred Dies,* in a rehearsal and production period, by invitation of The Actors Studio, New York.

Our Father's Failing was thus set aside until December 1977–February 1978, when the play was presented at The Actors Studio, in repertory with *Alfred the Great.* The director was Ben Levit, the scenic designer was Paul Eads, and the costume designer was Jennifer von Mayrhauser. The cast was as follows:

SAM . . . . Dominic Chianese
PA . . . . Sully Boyar
ALFRED . . . . Michael Moriarty
EMILY . . . . Lois Markle

Jules Irving asked to present "The Alfred Trilogy" during his final season as producer at Lincoln Center's Repertory Theatre, but died before the plays were produced.

REAL AND INVENTED BACKGROUND FOR *OUR FATHER'S FAILING*

During the years 1964–1974, there were more two dozen major fires that destroyed buildings in Wakefield, including Castle Clare, in 1974.

In 1930, at age fifty-three, Clarence Hoag began building a castle on the topmost hill on Oak Street, Wakefield. Hoag, a printer with a small shop in Boston's Grain Exchange Building, worked on his castle, Castle Clare, nights, carrying construction materials to his site by hand, by wheelbarrow.

Castle Clare was completed in 1949, although neighborhood people had scoffed at Hoag and his project, labeling Hoag an eccentric, claiming he would never live long enough to fully complete or inhabit his castle. By 1956, it became clear that Hoag would indeed be a long liver.

According to his daughter, Jennie, "…he lived so much longer than even *he* expected. All that hard work seemed to extend his life, not shorten it…He put a new roof on the castle when he was eighty, crawling all over the top of the thing."

On October 5, 1974, Castle Clare was razed by fire. Only stone stairs remained. Wakefield's Fire Chief, Walter Maloney, said, "…the fire that destroyed Castle Clare was…deliberately set."

Notes written in Gloucester, Massachusetts, August, 1975.

ALFRED DIES

Alfred Dies was initially introduced in a reading at the New Dramatists Committee, New York, during the winter of 1976–77, directed by John Dillon, with the following cast:

ALFRED . . . . Michael Moriarty
LYNCH . . . . Dominic Chianese
EMILY . . . . Joanna Miles
ROXY . . . . Peg Murray

Ellen Chenoweth, administrative director of The Actors Studio, New York, initiated an invitation by Carl Shaeffer, executive director, and Lee Strasberg, artistic director, for the play to be rehearsed and presented at The Actors Studio, during the same season. It was agreed that the play would be presented as an open rehearsal of a work-in-progress and was so presented during January 1977.

Ben Levit replaced John Dillon as director; Madeleine Thornton-Sherwood replaced Peg Murray as Roxy; Paul Eads designed the scenery; Susan Tsu designed the costumes.

Subsequently, there were two productions in the same season, both billed as world premiere.

The first world premiere was presented at the Magic Theatre, San Francisco, March–June 1977. The director was John Lion, with the following cast:

ALFRED . . . . D.J. Buckles
LYNCH . . . . Irving Israel
EMILY . . . . Jane Bolton
ROXY . . . . Linda Hoy

The next world premiere was given in the summer repertory season, 1977, of the American Stage Festival, Milford, New Hampshire. The director was Ben Levit, the scenic designer was Christopher Nowak, and the costume designer was Jennifer von Mayrhauser. The cast was as follows:

ALFRED . . . . William Meisle
LYNCH . . . . Patrick McNamara
EMILY . . . . Etain O'Malley
ROXY . . . . Ann Patomiac

Finally, a reading of *Alfred Dies* was given at The Actors Studio, New York, in repertory with *Alfred the Great* and *Our Father's Failing,* in February 1978. The text was completed by the author in June–August 1978.

REAL AND INVENTED BACKGROUND FOR *ALFRED DIES*

The Catholic population of Wakefield, is predominantly of Irish and Italian descent. The Italian community is located southeast of Main Street, near the border of Wakefield and Saugus, and is popularly known as Guinea Gulch.

Wakefield's Irish population is dispersed throughout the town, joining near the railroad station at St. Joseph's Church, Sundays. Italians have their own churches, all found in their particular community. Wakefield's Irish-Catholic youth is educated, primarily through eighth grade, at St. Joseph's School (founded 1924), commonly known as St. Joe's. For secondary school education, young Irish-Catholic men seem to choose either Malden Catholic High School or Wakefield Memorial High School (nonsectarian). However, in 1961, Austin Preparatory School for Catholic Boys opened its doors in Reading, Massachusetts, cutting severely into Malden Catholic's enrollment from Wakefield and neighboring towns. Austin Prep is staffed by monks of the Augustinian order, who also staff Merrimack College in nearby North Andover, Massachusetts.

Wakefield's young Irish-Catholic women are usually insinuated into the Nazareth Academy (founded 1947), a Catholic secondary school located on the hill above Wakefield's exclusive Park Section, near the Stoneham town line.

The nuns who teach the young women belong to an obscure order called the Sisters of Charity. Locally, they, as well as the young women themselves, are known as Nazarites. The Nazarites are in fact an ascetic Hebrew sect, worldwide; excluding, of course, Wakefield, Massachusetts, where they are instead middle-class Irish-Catholic girls.

An emergency fund-raising campaign was held during 1973, to raise several thousand dollars with which to keep the Nazareth Academy in operation during what the Wakefield *Daily Item's* editor called "these troubled times."

The money was raised and the Nazareth Academy continued operation and does as of this writing.

Little is known about Nazareth graduates.

Notes written by I.H., Gloucester, Massachusetts, July 1975.

THE WEBBER-LYNCH FAMILY LINES:

The interrelationships of the two families, as given below, were sorted out by Mary Winn, who was Assistant Director during the New Dramatists Committee readings and the Actors Studio productions of "The Alfred Trilogy."

ALFRED

> Emily's husband
> Emily's brother
> Pa's son
> Father of Margaret's child

WILL

> Margaret's husband
> Margaret's brother
> Willie-Boy's son
> Sam's nephew
> B.J. Lynch's brother
> Roxy's son(?)

SAM

> Margaret's stepfather (and uncle)
> Pa's best friend
> Willie-Boy's brother
> Will's uncle
> B.J.'s uncle
> Roxy's lover
> No children

ROXY

> Emily's mother
> Margaret's stepmother
> Pa's lover
> Two children with Willie-Boy
> Will's mother

WILLIE-BOY

> Will's, B.J.'s and Margaret's father
> Sam's twin brother
> Roxy's lover (two children)
> Sophie's (Alfred's mother) lover

EMILY
Alfred's wife
Alfred's sister
Pa's daughter
Roxy's daughter

MARGARET
Will's sister
Willie-Boy's daughter
Roxy's daughter
Mother of Alfred's child
Sam's stepdaughter

PA (TOMMY)
Alfred's father
Emily's father
Roxy's lover (fathered Emily by Roxy)

B.J. LYNCH
Margaret's brother
Will's brother
Willie-Boy's son
Sam's nephew

SOPHIE
Alfred's mother
Pa's wife
Willie-Boy's lover
Bruce's mother

BRUCE
Alfred's brother
Emily's stepbrother

John Cazale played in most of my plays, from 1967–1977, including Alfred the Great *and* Our Father's Failing. *What follows is a eulogy written by me, published in the United States by* The Village Voice, *March 27, 1978, at the time of Cazale's death.*

A EULOGY:
JOHN CAZALE (1936–1978)

Great actors give reason to the art of dramatic Writing. They change the awful velocity that is life passing. They offer a play's audience spots of perfect time, a life made heroic, and, finally, a system of how to live: a trail guide toward a higher quality of life.

The great actors possess a great patience: to endure great pain or provocation. They possess a great forbearance. They possess a great calm for quiet waiting, for perseverance. They possess a great view of life: to select the moments from a text that are high, out of the ordinary, away from the sour and the soiled. They delicately string these gemlike moments, one after the other, into a gift to the audience, the visible, wearable system of life that is the reason of art. And all of this the great actors must fashion from the dramatist's hopelessly self-centered and imperfect text.

To extract universal truths from the clack and self-pity that is the playwright's private ravings—the play—this is the art of the great actors. To hop from a play's moment of truth, to another, to another, dancing upon each moment lightly, as though they were stepping-stones across a magical pool (ever so careful to miss the stones that are broken and untrue)—this, too, is the art of the great actors.

To perform a laugh, when life dictates a smile, or less; to perform a scream when life dictates a complaint, or less; to perform an action, when life dictates a worry, or less; to perform a dance, when life dictates a stall, or less; to perform a question, when life dictates an answer, or less; this is the art of the great actors.

They make vellum of paper pages.

They make light.

John Cazale was such an actor. His greatness was unquestioned by all who touched him, and by all who were touched by him. Unquestioned. He would laugh at the pretensions of this earnest eulogistic tribute; he would weep for its concern. Such was Cazale's vision: through eyes that always saw the book through its cover.

John Cazale was the perfect blend of Ariel and Bartleby: a sudden laugh stopped by a sudden silence; a perfect silliness that broke dreaded dead-walled reveilles. Such was the range of Cazale's perceptions. Such was the delicacy of his St. Francis of Assisi face: to make visible the subtleties of grim and grin, and all between.

Some images from the private life that was the work he shared: Sal, eyes unmoving, fixed, as though they fell from a high place into those unfathomably deep sockets, dotting that unforgivably sweet face; Gupta, the Indian, moving through the jabs and poisoned epithets, to smile with understanding, to touch with love and purpose; Fredo, the perfection of a lounge player, ever hopeful, ever ashamed of his longings, his eyes flickering from down to even lower down; those same eyes now on Angelo's best face, a gaze across to Meryl Streep's supreme Isabella, pulling her around, around, and they would build a love for the rest of his life, and beyond, and we the audience, would notice, we would smile, we would try to learn; Dolan, dangerous, ridiculous, as silly a man as ever drew a sword, now alternatively much more dangerous, much more silly than ever imagined: a fabulous fool; Ui's lieutenant, gimped and sallow, Sal's fixed eye even less moving here, even deeper, a Bartleby *risus puris,* a miracle. Brecht, Coppola, Gorky, Hansberry, Shakespeare—all the lucky writers played by Cazale, improved by Cazale, touched by Cazale. All the lucky writers…

John Cazale happens once in a lifetime. He was an invention, a small perfection. It is no wonder his friends felt such anger upon waking from their sleep to discover that Cazale sleeps on with kings and counselors, with Booth and Kean, with Jimmy Dean, with Bernhardt, Guitry, and Duse, with Stanislavsky, with Groucho, Benny, and Allen. He will make fast friends in his new place. He is easy to love.

John Cazale's body betrayed him. His spirit will not. His whole life plays and replays as film, in our picture houses, in our dreams. He leaves us, his loving audience, a memory of his great calm, his quiet waiting, his love of high music, his love of low jokes, the absurd edge of the forest that was his hairline, the slice of watermelon that was his smile.

He is unforgettable.

Alfred The Great

MARTIN ESSLIN
ON *ALFRED THE GREAT*

Editor's Note: Martin Esslin is perhaps best known for his highly literate and intelligent study, The Theatre of the Absurd, *a casebook analysis and comparison of some of the world's most adventurous and significant contemporary playwrights. Esslin has also served as head of radio drama for the British Broadcasting Corporation, and has authored numerous books, critical articles, and essays. His book publications include* Reflections: Essays on Modern Theatre, Brecht: The Man and His Work, *and* The Peopled Wound: The Work of Harold Pinter.

I had the great privilege of being, in a small way, associated with the genesis of *Alfred the Great:* I was assigned to work with Israel Horovitz and James Hammerstein, the director, on the preparation of its first public rehearsed reading at the O'Neill Theater Center at Waterford, Connecticut, in the summer of 1972. The National Playwrights' Conference is a unique experiment: By confronting an author with a critic and a director and enabling him to see the painful and usually irreversible process of production compressed into a relatively short span of time—and made reversible in the sense that the performance that results is not a once-and-for-all opening with all the fire consequences of an unfavorable press reaction, it can give the playwright valuable insights into the workings of his own creative process and thus make it possible for him to perfect his creative methods. That, at least is the theory behind it. It can happen that it does not work out that way. Some playwrights are too vulnerable, too insecure, to be capable of gaining any advantage from critical comments during the process of rehearsal; and some of the critics and directors involved may be out of sympathy with the workings of the minds of some of the writers; so their comments may be misguided or just plain wrong.

My collaboration with Israel Horovitz was among the happier instances: Not being a raw recruit, but an established and highly regarded playwright who took his play to the O'Neill in the full knowledge of what he was doing and why he was doing it, he was not only capable but eager to submit his work to the acid test of reactions from other, critical professional minds. Suggestions were flying to and fro and one idea sparked off another. Israel would retire for the night and reemerge the next morning with a new scene, even a whole new act, which, after further discussion, he would equally cheerfully rewrite or consign to the wastepaper basket.

Now I must hasten to add that I don't think that all plays, all kinds of plays, would benefit by such a process of continuous redrafting. In the case of *Alfred the Great,* however, Israel Horovitz knew that he was embarking on a major undertaking, an exploration of his own mind that was so ambitious and far-reaching that he himself might not be quite aware of where he, or rather his subconscious, was heading. So the true shape of the images that were there, powerful but still submerged, their full meaning and import, could only gradually be brought to the surface and once there, had to be examined, weighed up, and polished over and over again.

When I read the first draft of the play, my first impression was of a black farce, funny but somewhat puzzling. Gradually I became aware that there was more behind it: that here was the first of a trilogy of plays that dealt with some kind of personal, or regional, perhaps even national myth; a trilogy which could be an American, mid-twentieth century, equivalent to a major national myth like the Oresteia. Of course, a mid-twentieth century Oresteia can never be tragedy in the grand classical manner. Our times are tragi-comic rather than truly tragic: hence the admixture of farce which, however, cannot hide the profound and vital problems that form the basic theme. *Alfred the Great* is the first of three plays that will form a "Wakefield Cycle"; there is, of course, one "Wakefield Cycle" already in existence—a series of medieval mystery plays about the creation of the world, and its redemption, which were performed at Wakefield, Yorkshire. Wakefield, Massachusetts, in the nineteen seventies is a very different place: But there too man's guilt and weakness and his possible redemption are the issue.

There are many layers to Israel Horovitz's complex and profound dramatic structure: There is the first layer of farce, there is a second layer of the psychoanalysis of a family situation: the relationships of sons to fathers, brothers to sisters, husbands to wives. If one wanted to find an easy label to sum it all up, one could say that the *leitmotif* of it all is sexual greed, sexual guilt, sexual impotence. In a nation so dedicated to virility that the worship of *machismo* has almost become a national religion, the emergence of this impotence theme seems to be highly significant of the mood of our time. It has certainly struck me, an outsider who has become a very frequent visitor to the United States and who follows the trends of the literature and arts, very forcibly indeed that the country seems to be developing an anxiety neurosis about impotence. And anyone who knows anything about impotence will be aware how dangerous such a neurosis must be with its tendency towards establishing a vicious circle of feedback from which it will be increasingly difficult to escape.

That is, I feel, the point at which the family situation becomes a national myth: Impotence, after all, is the nightmare of the potent; national impotence must be the nightmare of all-powerful nations; particularly in situations where the cycle of eternal success, eternal victory, has been broken by a misfired war, like the one in Vietnam.

Wakefield, Massachusetts, is Israel Horovitz's hometown. He depicts it in its decline, its population diminishing, decaying, polluted, doomed—and the people in it guilt-ridden and grotesquely pursued by nightmares of violence, incredible feats of sexual prowess, yet basically impotent and sterile.

I am convinced that a nation's poets are the ones who diagnose its state of mind with the deepest insight, long before it becomes widely apparent; and in doing so they often also predict a nation's fate, become its true prophets. The deep purpose of such prophecy is not a fatalistic acceptance of doom, but to serve as a warning, a tool of self-examination and thus to become the starting point of corrective action. I am equally convinced that Israel Horovitz is such a poet, and such a prophet. Hence my conviction that the "Wakefield Cycle," of which *Alfred the Great* is the opening chapter, will prove to be a work of major import and impact.

Martin Esslin

For Samuel Beckett

THE PEOPLE OF THE PLAY

MARGARET: Forty, small, pretty, Irish.
ALFRED: Forty, handsome, tends to the elegant.
WILL: Forty, wholesome good looks, tough, not muscular.
EMILY: Forty, handsome, tends to the elegant.

THE PLACE OF THE PLAY

Living room of early-nineteenth-century New England home; owned by Will and Margaret, Wakefield, Massachusetts.

THE TIME OF THE PLAY

Start of fall.

…but when I think of all the books that I have read and of the wise words I have heard spoken, and of the anxiety I have given to parents and grandparents, and of the hopes that I have had, all life weighed in the scales of my own life seems to me a preparation for something that never happens.

—William Butler Yeats
The Autobiography of William Butler Yeats,
"Reveries over Childhood and Youth" (1914)

Alfred The Great

ACT I
SCENE I

Living room. Saturday, mid-afternoon. Stage in darkness. Three sharp knocks are heard. Same sound will precede each scene of play. First words of play—Alfred's—are heard.

ALFRED: So. We begin?

(Lights to full, suddenly. Margaret stands in living room, facing Alfred, who has just arrived in room. Room is of classically New England architectural lines and furnishing, except surprisingly sparse, nearly without furniture or decoration. An essential stuffed sofa set center stage; heavily stuffed armchair set downstage right, thronelike. Coffee table is used in front of sofa; cigarettes, ashtray, and cigarette box, on top. Pedestal ashtray is set stage right of chair. A hooked rug may be used, but no other stage dressing wanted. No windows but for stained-glass panes in staircase wall and smoked-glass panel in front door, perhaps surrounded by small stained-glass panes. Kitchen door on swing hinge, stage-left wall; front door set opposite, stage-right wall. Cellar door nonfunctional, but visible, under staircase balcony. Upstage wall over-sized, passes offstage, either side, into infinity. Infinite height as well. Alfred faces downstage, head bowed; he is nervous. He wears suede shirt jacket, buff-colored trousers, loafers, deep-colored shirt, open at neck. Margaret, equally nervous, fidgets, faces him. She wears pastel peignoir, puff slippers, a smile.)

ALFRED: Shall we, Margaret? Shall we begin?

MARGARET: Yes, I suppose. *(Pauses.)* It's not that I'm not delighted to see you. It's just that I'm really...well...surprised. There are knocks...I go to the door...and it's you: Alfred! What are you doing here?

ALFRED: *(Angry at first.)* I don't know. (Pauses; quietly.) I don't know. I wanted to see you...to see my old house...see the town...see Wakefield...I wanted to see you.

MARGARET: *(Embarrassed.)* I'm happy to see you, too. It's been ten years...

ALFRED: *(Correcting her.)* Fifteen.

MARGARET: Really?

ALFRED: *(Smugly.)* Fifteen.

MARGARET: It's been fifteen years. That's a long time. I'm happy to see you again. You're cute, Alfred…cute. You never were. If you were, I didn't notice. But you certainly are now. Cute.

ALFRED: *(He turns away from her.)* Don't play with me, Margaret. Really. I know what I look like. Okay?

MARGARET: Alfred…

ALFRED: Please.

MARGARET: *(Suddenly. Her scream will not be acknowledged by Alfred.)* Will you, for Jesus Christ's sake, sit down? *(Silence.)* Fifteen years? Really?

ALFRED: *(Smiling.)* You were twenty-five. Just. Me too. You were heavier. Not heavy. Heavier.

MARGARET: *(As an apology.)* That's a long time.
(He looks at her. They smile. They kiss.)

MARGARET: *(Making conversation.)* How's Emily?

ALFRED: Oh, fine. Same as ever. Will? How's Will?

MARGARET: Will's become a model father. I know it's hard to believe, but it's true. Will's become a model father.

ALFRED: *(Surprised.)* You've had children?

MARGARET: Well, no. There was Will, Jr.…and the little girl…

ALFRED: Oh, yes, the little girl. Forgive me. I'm sorry. For a moment, I forgot…Will, *Jr.?*

MARGARET: Yes. Remember Will and Ruby had…well, Alfred…trouble?

ALFRED: Trouble?

MARGARET: Trouble. Senior year.

ALFRED: I'm afraid I don't follow…

MARGARET: Do you remember Ruby? She was F, junior year…

ALFRED: "F" in what sense, Margaret?

MARGARET: Cheerleader lineup.

ALFRED: Oh. "F"! I see… *(Thinks.)* W…A…K…E…Ah, yes, Ruby. Skinny, wrenlike, sad-eyed…?

MARGARET: Will got her in trouble.

ALFRED: You don't say? Trouble? Family-way sort of thing?

MARGARET: Will, Jr.

ALFRED: Of course. I must have known that and forgotten… *(He walks from Margaret; changes the subject.)* Nice room. Good-size room. Nice dimensions, nice proportions. Just right. Nice. Nice. Nice room. I always liked this room…

MARGARET: *(Quickly.)* Damn it, Alfred, I know you're rich. I've read the papers.

ALFRED: It's…uh…nothing.

MARGARET: Will works a twelve-hour day. Eight to eight. Hasn't had a raise in seven years now.

ALFRED: It's nothing. I was lucky.

MARGARET: Will and I are very happy, Alfred. I warn you. We are very happy. Happier than I ever thought I could ever be.

ALFRED: I'm happy to hear that.

MARGARET: Will's become quite a gentleman. Quite a gentleman. No more of the rough stuff you remember.

ALFRED: I don't remember any rough stuff.

MARGARET: The school psychiatrist said he was angry because he was a foundling. Those foundling days were the seeds of the rough stuff. All passed now. Night school. Eight-to-eight and then night school. Quite a gentleman, Will is. Very hardworking and *very* well liked around these parts now, I can tell you *that*.

ALFRED: Margaret, this may shock and amaze you, but…I don't really remember Will well…

MARGARET: Stoneham High…played left end…also ran the hundred…ten-two-and-a-half… fast, wiry, quite cute…?

ALFRED: Oh…*Stoneham* High…Perhaps I didn't really know Will at all. It's hard for me to separate what I've forgotten from what I never knew: very little difference as the years fly by. He's how old now: Will?

MARGARET: Forty.

ALFRED: He's forty, and he still goes to school?

MARGARET: After work, in the evenings. Self-help is Will's middle name.

ALFRED: You must be proud…

MARGARET: I certainly am…

ALFRED: I can understand…

MARGARET: Will and I have a great deal in common…

ALFRED: Really?

MARGARET: My not knowing exactly who my father was, and Will's being a foundling…

ALFRED: Oh, in *that* sense…

MARGARET: Those are the ties that truly bind.

ALFRED: What are?

MARGARET: I beg your pardon?

ALFRED: The ties?

MARGARET: That bind? Family. Origins…

ALFRED: Oh. Right.

MARGARET: Let's take you, for example. After all these years and all that success, look at you.

ALFRED: How so?

MARGARET: Right back here: in your old town, in your old house.

ALFRED: Everybody I've got's buried here…in this town. By the lake. Quannapowitt. Ever see the cement bench?

MARGARET: The what?

ALFRED: The cement bench on my family plot. It's got my name stamped right on the back of it. Ever see it?

MARGARET: We're in the other cemetery.

ALFRED: I know that! Christ, I know that! I just thought you might have taken a walk through and seen the bench.

MARGARET: No, I haven't. Not yet, anyway. I might, though: someday… Cement?

ALFRED: It's a white cement bench. It's got my name—our family name— etched right into the back of it. *(Pauses.)* Who sits on it?

MARGARET: That's true enough.

ALFRED: *(Quickly, clearly.)* Everybody I ever had is lying right there: foot of the bench. Right in the dirt. Excuse me. The soil. I should have said "the soil." Fresh soil. And fresh roses. On the soil, not in it. Somebody has been putting cut roses on my brother's grave. I wish I hadn't stopped smoking. I haven't thought about a cigarette for two years.

MARGARET: You want a cigarette?

ALFRED: Nope. Quit.

MARGARET: Mind if I smoke?

ALFRED: Nope. Smoke.

MARGARET: I won't. If you don't want me to, I won't.

ALFRED: Smoke.

MARGARET: You're right. It'll kill me.

ALFRED: Smoke. Don't worry about me. Really. I'm okay.

MARGARET: I really shouldn't… *(Lights a cigarette.)* That's better.

ALFRED: *(Clipped; a command.)* Put it out.

MARGARET: What?

ALFRED: Put it out. If Will wants you to die, that's his business. I don't want you to die. Put it out.

MARGARET: Will wants me to stop smoking.

ALFRED: I don't care. Put it out.

(She does.)

ALFRED: Good. Did that hurt? I mean, did that kill you not to have the cigarette??? It's a piggy habit. Really piggy.

MARGARET: Did Emily quit?

ALFRED: In what sense, Margaret?

MARGARET: *(Smiling.)* Your own wife? You couldn't stop her?

ALFRED: Stop her?

MARGARET: From smoking.

ALFRED: Emily's a big girl. If she wants to kill herself, that's her concern, not
mine.

MARGARET: Piggy.

ALFRED: Hmmm?

MARGARET: Piggy. You said, "It's a *piggy* habit."

ALFRED: I did?

MARGARET: Always. Always did. That's one of your very favorite words.

ALFRED: Piggy? I suppose.

MARGARET: God.

ALFRED: *(Overlapping.)* Piggy?

MARGARET: God.

ALFRED: *(Overlapping.)* You shouldn't smoke.

MARGARET: God.

ALFRED: *(Overlapping.)* It's really dumb.

MARGARET: God.

ALFRED: *(Overlapping.) I* think it's dumb.

MARGARET: No wonder Emily hates you.

ALFRED: Emily doesn't hate me.

MARGARET: Of course she does.

ALFRED: She *does?*

MARGARET: She always *did.* I know. I've read the papers. I think Emily's very
sophisticated.

ALFRED: When did you meet Emily?

MARGARET: Meet who?

ALFRED: Emily.

MARGARET: Well, never.

    (Silence.)

ALFRED: Why did you say, "she did"?

MARGARET: Did what?

ALFRED: Hate me.

MARGARET: She did. She went three years without talking to me.

ALFRED: Three years?

MARGARET: Three years and three months. She talked to everyone else, of course, but to me she said nothing. I know. I saw it in the papers.

ALFRED: Then it *must* be true!

MARGARET: That's very difficult.

ALFRED: What's very difficult?

MARGARET: *(With deliberation.)* To say nothing: It's very difficult to say nothing. At least, I *think* it would be difficult to say nothing. I've never said nothing. *(Smiles timidly.)* I've never said nothing.
(Alfred walks to Margaret, stares straight at her face, then drops his eyes down the front of her body. When his eyes return to her eyes, Margaret pulls away, back from him, smiling bravely.)

MARGARET: I often wonder, don't you?

ALFRED: Course I do. *(Pauses, smiles.)* I'm surprised that you and Will never had any children together. Didn't Will want any?

MARGARET: It's not Will. It's me. I can't…have any.

ALFRED: Well, that doesn't sound right. Have you seen a good doctor?

MARGARET: Just the locals…you know…Flynn and his son…

ALFRED: There. You see. Inconclusive. You need to see Mass. General men. Top specialists. You should assume *nothing*. For all you know, Will might have had it once and lost it.

MARGARET: Lost it?

ALFRED: It happens. *(Pauses; embarrassed.)* Happened to me. I went impotent once. Twice, really.

MARGARET: Impotent is different.

ALFRED: I know, but it frightened me all the same.

MARGARET: Don't most men go…impotent?

ALFRED: How do you mean?

MARGARET: Well, impotent.

ALFRED: But how, exactly?

MARGARET: *(Nervously.)* Impotent. Impotent. Can't get it up.

ALFRED: I don't know.

MARGARET: I'm sure they do. Are you worried?

ALFRED: I'm terrified.

MARGARET: Are you still?

ALFRED: Terrified?

MARGARET: Impotent.

ALFRED: I don't know.

MARGARET: When was the last time you…tried?

ALFRED: Last night.

MARGARET: And you couldn't?

ALFRED: I could. I did.

MARGARET: Oh. And before that?

ALFRED: Before *what?*

MARGARET: God, Alfred. When did you try before that?

ALFRED: Before last night? *(Pauses.)* Yesterday morning. *(Pauses.)* And I succeeded. *(Pauses.)* But you never know when it's going to hit again. *(There
is a long pause.)* How do you know expressions like "get it up"?

MARGARET: I don't know. I heard it.

ALFRED: *(Controlled anger.)* Does Will say things like "get it up"?

MARGARET: *(She probably giggles.)* I don't know. He might have. I've heard it
in jokes. Old men can't "get it up."

ALFRED: I was thirty-two when it happened.

MARGARET: That was eight years ago.

ALFRED: That's not old, thirty-two. *(Pauses.)* How would I know about "most
men"? I don't sleep with men.

MARGARET: God.

ALFRED: I would be frightened with you in bed right now. Frightened it
would hit.

MARGARET: No wonder Emily hates you.

ALFRED: She'll never let me forget it.

MARGARET: You couldn't get it up for Emily? *(She enjoys her question.)*

ALFRED: Twice. She only knew about the first time.

MARGARET: That doesn't make sense.

ALFRED: She was asleep the second time. I waited until she was asleep. I figured that if it hit, she wouldn't know. *(Pauses.)* It hit. *(Pauses.)* She didn't
know. I don't sleep well, Margaret. It's difficult.

MARGARET: For you.

ALFRED: To sleep.

MARGARET: I'm sure.

ALFRED: I can't close my eyes.

MARGARET: I'm sure. *(Pauses.)* You can't what?

ALFRED: Close my eyes. I never blink. Didn't you notice? I can force a blink.
Watch. *(He blinks.)* I just did. *(He blinks again.)* See? It's really no problem, if I *force* them down. But the natural normal state of my eyes is…

MARGARET: Wide open…

ALFRED: …wide open.

MARGARET: It must be difficult.

ALFRED: It was hell for the first nine or ten years.

MARGARET: Now?

ALFRED: Now? Oh it's much better. I have to force things a bit, but it's much better. You have to work at getting what you really want. I've actually been quite successful.

MARGARET: I know. I've read the papers.

ALFRED: I've had my picture in the papers.

MARGARET: I've seen them.

ALFRED: I was in bed with Emily.

MARGARET: In the paper?

ALFRED: When it hit. *(Too quickly at first.)* I kept thinking that the door was going to open. I couldn't put it out of my mind. I kept thinking that the door was going to open and everybody I knew was going to burst into the room. They were at the door. I couldn't stop thinking that.

MARGARET: Was I there?

ALFRED: Were you *where?*

MARGARET: At the door?

ALFRED: Oh. Yuh. I suppose.

MARGARET: I wasn't, was I? I wasn't there.

ALFRED: My God! That's a very complicated idea.

MARGARET: Who was at the door?

ALFRED: *(Angrily.)* Just people from the city. Nobody from here…

MARGARET: *(Correcting him.)* From *home.*

ALFRED: From home. Nobody from home. Just city people.

MARGARET: Sophisticated.

ALFRED: Huh?

MARGARET: The group. Probably a very sophisticated group.

ALFRED: It was just a daydream.

MARGARET: A daydream?

ALFRED: It wasn't real.

MARGARET: It happened in the daytime?

ALFRED: In the morning.

MARGARET: You and Emily?

ALFRED: When we woke up…I *think* it was morning!!!…It doesn't matter. *(Pause.)* I can't remember.

MARGARET: Did it begin then?

ALFRED: The terror?

MARGARET: The three years of no-talking?

ALFRED: *(Softly.)* No.
    (Silence.)

MARGARET: "Never let it get into your mind."

ALFRED: I beg your pardon?

MARGARET: That's what Will says: "Never let it get into your mind."

ALFRED: Has Will ever gone…you know…

MARGARET: Well…Alfred! That's really *personal!*

ALFRED: I'm really terrified. I mean, it would help to know. Has he?

MARGARET: No. No, he hasn't.

ALFRED: God damn!…

MARGARET: Will is an unusual man.

ALFRED: God damn!…

MARGARET: Stop it. Don't be ridiculous. We don't do it every five minutes.

ALFRED: God damn!…

MARGARET: Sometimes we don't do it for weeks. Once we went four months without doing it. One whole summer.

ALFRED: No wonder your marriage is shaky.

MARGARET: My marriage isn't shaky.

ALFRED: It isn't perfect.

MARGARET: It's close.

ALFRED: It's shaky.

MARGARET: You can't come back here after all these years and…and pass judgments like that. Everybody isn't rich, you know. There are certain privileges you have that everybody doesn't have. God knows how you got them. I mean, it certainly is ironic that out of all the kids in our class, you, Alfred L. Webber, the very *least* likely to succeed, succeeded. *(Pause.)* I happen to be very happy.
(Silence. Alfred walks to her. They kiss. They break apart from each other. Each looks down, avoiding eye contact.)

MARGARET: Why did you think otherwise?

ALFRED: My mother and my father were born in this town. Their mothers and fathers, too. Imagine that.

MARGARET: The same for all of us…mostly.

ALFRED: They're buried, side by side, every one of them, down at Lakeside. My father hated the lake. He never let me swim in it. Said it was full of dangerous weeds. Pull you down and hold you under. Every summer, we packed up the whole house—everything we owned, on the back of his truck—and went twenty miles down the road, to Hamilton, our summer house. A place for the winter, a place for the summer. A place to be poor, a place to be poorer. *(Pauses.)* Oh, Margaret…seeing you now.

Standing here in the house in which I grew up...seeing you now...still so pretty...so pretty...

(They smile at each other. They do not touch, do not kiss, but stand frozen instead, each watching the other's eyes. Will enters. He is ill-clad in sport jacket or gabardine suit. He carries two bags of groceries. Margaret and Alfred pull away from each other, violently.)

WILL: *(Very, very hostile.)* Company?

MARGARET: This is Alfred.

WILL: *(Still hostile.)* Honest to God???

ALFRED: Honest to God.

MARGARET: I've told Will a lot about you, Alfred. *(Pauses.)* This is Will.

(The men shake hands.)

WILL: *(Dryly.)* Pleasure.

ALFRED: Pleasure.

WILL: Mag's told me all about you.

ALFRED: Don't believe it.

WILL: *(Suppressing anger.)* Seen all your clippings. Mag's got a scrapbook full of your clippings. You get a lot of media. She's filled up a good couple of scrapbooks over the years. Used to get me jealous. Not so much as the letters: They used to drive me *crazy*, first nine or ten years, watching Mag sit down to write you a letter every night. She hardly ever mentioned my name in them. Like I didn't exist.

MARGARET: He used to read them.

WILL: Hell of a thing, at the end of the day, when you need company most, and your wife's got her *work* to do. *(Laughs.)* That's what she used to call it: her work. Honest to God. She'd say, "I got to get a little work done now, Will." Then she'd sit down for a sonofabitchen *hour*, puffing on her cigarettes, writing to good old Alfred L. Webber, boy wonder. Used to get me jealous. Not anymore.

ALFRED: You've kept a scrapbook?

MARGARET: Sure. Why not? How many famous people do I know?

WILL: When are you leaving?

ALFRED: Huh?

WILL: You're living down in the city. Just home for the day?

ALFRED: Oh. I don't know. I'm just looking around. You know.

WILL: *(Smiling.)* Funny to see you in the flesh. I think of you as a little picture. You know, it always galls me that somebody like you gets his picture

in the paper every five minutes…for *what?* Makin' money? Takes no
brains ta make money, right?

ALFRED: *(Moves to his suitcase and picks it up. Stands near door.)* Well, I guess
I should be going.

MARGARET: Stop it. Will, Alfred's going to stay with us for a while.

ALFRED: Stay? Me?

MARGARET: *(Quickly.)* You're not going to the Lord Wakefield! Will?

ALFRED: I really should go.

WILL: No, you don't. Stay.

ALFRED: But I want to go, really.

WILL: *(Really arch, tough, hostile.)* No, you don't. Stay. You stay here, like Mag
wants. What the hell, you two were sweethearts long before I came into
the picture. You're all Mag ever talks about, Alfred. You're her ideal man.
I know you better than I know the President. Day doesn't seem to pass
without your name comin' up. Alfred this or Alfred that. You're always
in the paper. You stay, Alfred. You stay as my guest right here in my
house…long as you want. Hell, how many celebrities do I get to talk to?
None. You're the first. I'm enjoying this already.

MARGARET: *(Chatty; takes Alfred's suitcase.)* We have a nice quiet room
upstairs…Or you could have Will, Jr.'s room. *(Realizes.)* It's your old
room! Use that one! That's not as quiet, but it's bright. And it's on the
front. There's a lot of traffic… *(She laughs. Goes upstairs.)* …not a lot of
traffic by *your* standards. Five or six cars a day. You remember. You could
stay way upstairs and have two rooms adjoining: It's like a private apartment…

WILL: *(Cuts in, abruptly.)* Will you for Chrissakes shut your mouth? You're makin'
a goddamn fool of yourself! (To Alfred, coolly; calmly.) Alfred, you'll stay in
your old room. It's my boy's room now. He's away at college. You can
have the whole room to yourself. It'll be good for you…to be back in
there. It'll help you to remember what things were like around
here…The good old days, right? *(Smiles.)* I know the room's not big. I
mean, I know it's not what you're accustomed to, but it's the best I've
got. You know what I mean? *(He starts to exit the room, thinks better of it,
stops, returns to Alfred.)* Oh, yuh. Only thing I ask is that you not make
too much noise after ten. I work long days. *(Starts to exit room again,
thinks better of it again, stops again, returns to Alfred again.)* Oh, yuh.
Alfred? One other thing. You touch my wife, I'll break your head. I don't
care who you are. Okay? Night. *(Will exits.)*

(Alfred is blank-faced. He opens cigarette box on coffee table, extracts cigarette,

which he places in his mouth. He extracts matches from the same box, lights cigarette, drags deeply, coughs deeply, coughs again.)

ALFRED: *(Brightly.)* He's very nice: Will. I like him.
(The lights black out.)

SCENE II

Later. Stage in darkness. Three sharp knocks are heard. First words of scene—Will's—are heard.

WILL: You ashamed of your ears?
(Lights to full, suddenly. Alfred, on sofa, newspaper section on lap. He faces front. Will, in chair, remainder of newspaper in his hands. He is staring across at Alfred. Alfred has been doing crossword puzzle. He wears a silk paisley robe; pencil is between his teeth. Will wears white cotton undershirt; has small terry-cloth towel over his neck as scarf. Will's section of newspaper is open to television page.)

ALFRED: *(Face turns slowly to Will. He removes pencil from mouth; smiles directly to Will.)* Hmmm?

WILL: Are you ashamed of your ears?

ALFRED: *(Sustaining the smile.)* I don't understand?

WILL: Your hair…

ALFRED: *(Pretending to "just get it".)* Oh, my hair! Over my ears…I didn't get it. That's pretty good. "Are you ashamed of your ears?"…

WILL: *(Angrily.)* Don't bullshit me. It's not that funny. I saw it on television. We watch a lot of television around here. I don't suppose you do. I read in the paper that you think television is the wasteland. 'Sthat true?

ALFRED: Huh?

WILL: *(Prophetically.)* …Television is the wasteland.

ALFRED: *(Matching Will's tone, mimicry.)* April is the cruelest month.

WILL: Huh?

ALFRED: Sometimes things get into newspapers that aren't exactly true.

WILL: Yuh. You said *that* in the same interview. Where do *you* get off being interviewed? Is that what papers have come to? Coverin' any bullshit that comes down the pike?

ALFRED: I think it's funny.

WILL: Oh, really?

ALFRED: Oh, really.

WILL: *(Quickly, he yells.)* Too bad you don't have a wife who cuts out every goddamn word I say and pastes it into a goddamn scrapbook. Too bad. Then you'd see how *oh-really-funny* you really are. *(Silence.)* What did you do today?

(Silence.)

ALFRED: Mrs. Fuller's dead.

WILL: Dead?

ALFRED: *(Displays newspaper to Will.)* It's in the *Item*…

WILL: Couldn't say "dead." *Item* hasn't printed the word "dead" in thirty years…

ALFRED: *(Looks at newspaper.)* Does so. Right here. Look: The headline. "Francine Fuller Passes On."

WILL: Oh, well, right: *passes on.* "Passes on" is a hell of a lot different from "dead."

(Alfred looks at Will, silently. Will laughs. A moment passes.)

(Note: Following section through the silence should play rapidly, reflexively.)

ALFRED: Sold her store quick enough…

WILL: *(Overlapping.)* No point in waiting…

ALFRED: *(Quickly.)* Who bought?

WILL: Dunno…

ALFRED: Nice old lady…

WILL: She was all right…

ALFRED: *Very nice*, I'd say…

WILL: She was all right…

ALFRED: Never had children…

WILL: Never wanted any…

ALFRED: Nice old lady…

WILL: She was all right…

ALFRED: Ninety-one, they say…

WILL: Nice old lady…

ALFRED: *(Smiles.)* She was all right.

(A short silence. Alfred smiles at Will.)

WILL: *(Without looking up from his newspaper.)* It's all changed. Kids don't have to study Latin anymore.

ALFRED: I beg your pardon?

WILL: *(Looks up at Alfred now.)* Saw the coach. Said kids don't have to study Latin anymore. I took Latin all four years. Flunked it twice. Flunked it cold. *Omnia Gallia est divisit in tres partes. [sic]* I'll never forget that. Never forget that till the day I die. *Omnia Gallia est divisit in tres partes. [sic]*

Oh, yeah. Course, I don't go dropping knowledge like that around, like some people I know...

ALFRED: Sorry, Will...

WILL: *(Redux.)* Now...Well, now it's all changed. Kids ain't gonna get the education. It's all modern. Nobody has to know nothing anymore. Kids are so stupid I wanna puke.

ALFRED: What year were you?

WILL: Same as you.

ALFRED: Same year? Well...I'm surprised.

WILL: Why? You think you're younger? I got bad news for you: I'm four months younger than you. I checked it against the newspaper this morning. You know you're in the newspaper?

ALFRED: Really?

WILL: Oh, you didn't know?

ALFRED: No, I didn't.

WILL: Really?

ALFRED: Really. Will, I don't understand why you're so...

WILL: That's funny...

ALFRED: What's funny?

WILL: Funny you didn't know you were in the paper.

ALFRED: Well, I fail to see where that's so unusual...

WILL: Oh, but it is...

ALFRED: Oh, but it isn't! I'm in the news a lot, dammit! It's no big deal in my life, believe-you-me...

WILL: Then how come you called the paper?

ALFRED: Huh?

WILL: "Huh? Huh?" How come you called the paper? I heard you on the phone last night. Called the paper from right here. Couldn't even wait till the paper opened.

ALFRED: I don't...

WILL: *Come off the bullshit!* I listened in from my room. *(Pause.)* I thought it was funny. *(Pause.)* I don't blame you, Alfred. Hell, if I could get *me* in the paper...what the hell?...If you don't push yourself, who's gonna? I don't blame you, Alfred.

ALFRED: The editor of the *Item's* an old friend.

WILL: I said, "I don't blame you."

ALFRED: She's an old friend.

WILL: That's rich.

ALFRED: That happens to be the truth!

WILL: Suit yourself.

ALFRED: I don't like the implications…

WILL: *Neither do I!*

ALFRED: She is an old friend.

WILL: And you're news, Alfred. You're news.

ALFRED: *(Stands, moves to stairs.)* Terrific! Look, I'll pack my stuff and clear out…

WILL: *(Yells.)* Alfred! You stay, goddammit! Goddammit! *(Pauses; Alfred stops, looks at Will, who speaks softly now.)*

WILL: I work hard, Alfred. Goddamn hard. Eight-to-eight's when I'm there. Got to get there. Up at six. Maggie's always sleeping. Doctor said it was nerves. I used to worry about it, but lately…well, I don't much care whether she gets up or whether she sleeps. Barren women get boring after a while. Don't much care if she sleeps or if she gets up: don't seem much different. *(Silence.)* How are *you* doing?

ALFRED: *(A reasonable attempt at contact.)* Oh, okay. Okay. I'm a little tired, Will. Can't seem to get my eyes closed…at night…sleeping. Difficult. Can't seem to get my eyes closed.

WILL: Force them.

ALFRED: I do. I will. It's odd.

WILL: Must be.

ALFRED: The town, I mean. I keep seeing fat grown-ups with little kids trapped inside. You know what I mean?

WILL: *(Staring at Alfred.)* No.

ALFRED: All the kids I knew became their parents. Like us, I suppose.

WILL: Us? Like our parents? Really? What is that: a joke?

ALFRED: There's a French joke that always makes me smile: *Je pense, donc je fuis.* You ever hear that one, Will?

WILL: *(Humiliated; angrily.)* Great. I love jokes.

ALFRED: Sorry, Will. *(Pauses.)* Will?

   (Will looks at Alfred.)

ALFRED: I know exactly why I've come back, Will. I know exactly why I'm in this house, in this town. I know exactly why.

   (There is a short silence. Will stares at Alfred. They hold eye contact. Will breaks the silence.)

WILL: It's not the same, is it? You come back to a place after years and years of bein' away, and it's smaller, dirtier, it's not so friendly as you remember…

ALFRED: Oh, I don't know about that…

WILL: I went back, too. To Stoneham.

ALFRED: *(Laughs.)* To Stoneham?

WILL: Som'pin' funny? What's funny?

ALFRED: Stoneham's only two miles away. Right up the top of Prospect Street…

WILL: Still my home, isn't it? I've got some real memories goin' there. Nothin' like this garbage heap…

ALFRED: *(Overlapping.)* Stoneham's a pretty town. One of the prettiest…

WILL: *Was* a pretty town. Now it's all hot-dog stands…

ALFRED: How many hot-dog stands?

WILL: *(Straight to Alfred, without a pause.)* Fifty, sixty…

ALFRED: What?

WILL: *(Exploding.)* You really think you're something special, don't you? I listen to you spouting off some foreign goddamn words and now I'm supposed to shut up…I'm supposed to tell you how many hot-dog stands got put up in Stoneham???…You really think you're something…

ALFRED: I'm sorry, Will…

WILL: *(Furiously.)* I know *who* you are and *what* you are and what you come from, Alfred. I know *plenty, plenty!* You can't pull your highfalutin goddamn hoity-toity goddamn *airs* around *me,* ya know! So just don't you try, *okay?*

ALFRED: I'm…uh…I'm sorry, Will.

WILL: *(Imitates Alfred's apology.)* You're…uh…you're what, Alfred?

ALFRED: I'm sorry, Will. That's what I said: I'm sorry. I apologize…

WILL: Just 'cause I was brought from a foundling home makes me no less of a native son.

ALFRED: It certainly doesn't.

WILL: They put a hot-dog stand where my house used to be. Take-out crap. That's enough, huh? I mean when that happens, it's as though the whole goddamn world just became a goddam…well…you know…a goddam… well…uh…

ALFRED: Hot-dog stand?

WILL: Hot-dog stand.

ALFRED: They tore your house down?

WILL: *(Embarrassed.)* It fell down.

ALFRED: Really?

WILL: It wasn't much of a house. You may recall that it wasn't much to speak about.

ALFRED: I never saw your house.

(Silence. Will smiles at Alfred.)

WILL: I like having you here. I even hurried home from work tonight. Can't remember hurrying back to this garbage dump in fifteen years. I even told my boss you were staying with me. Showed him the paper. He was very impressed. We don't get much in the way of celebrities around here. You read it yourself in the paper: "luminary." That's what you are in this town, pal. A goddamn luminary. *(Will slaps Alfred's back and laughs.)* Just like our parents, huh? When are you planning on seeing your father? You better get in a good night's sleep before *that* little *tête-en-tête [sic]*, huh?

ALFRED: *(Quietly.)* He's dead, Will.

WILL: Who's "dead, Will"?

ALFRED: My father. He's dead.

WILL: Oh, well, your way's fine with me, Alfred: Mr. Luminary. Just fine. Any way you want to play it.

(Silence.)

ALFRED: Kinda quiet around here.

WILL: Your father hated livin' down here, Mr. Luminary. Hated every minute. Hated the town, hated the people…hated the church, hated the steeple. *(He laughs.)*

ALFRED: He loved it. Told me Wakefield, Massachusetts, was the best place on the face of the earth. The very best place. Wakefield…Massachusetts… U.S.A.…North America…Western Hemisphere…Earth…Universe… Infinity… *(Alfred smiles.)* …New England.

WILL: Musta been drunk…

ALFRED: I believe him, now…

WILL: …or crazy?

ALFRED: Watch it, Will.

WILL: Okay. Okay. Fine. Any way you want. *(He points to coffee table.)* The cigarettes are in the box. That one. Right.

ALFRED: I don't smoke.

WILL: Bring me one.

ALFRED: Huh?

WILL: The matches are in the box, too. Never used to be. *Mahhh*-gret thinks it's classy. Goddamn cigarettes and matches together in a goddamn wood box on the goddamn wood coffee table…gettin' stale together. Hurry up.

ALFRED: *(Rather surprised and amused.)* You want me to light it?

WILL: Why? You got a cold?

ALFRED: Cold? Oh. No. No, it's just that I don't smoke.

WILL: Light it.

(Alfred takes a cigarette, a match, lights it, hands it to Will, who leans back in his chair, drags deeply, smiles.)

WILL: *Omnia Gallia est divisit in tres partes. [sic]* That's a pretty sound, isn't it? I dunno. Things just always *sound* better in Latin. I'll never forget it, as long as I live. Ah, some things can't be talked about: They just are.

(Margaret enters down stairs, smiling until she hears Will's next line. She winces. Glances disapprovingly at Will as she passes him.)

WILL: Kids make me want to puke.

(Margaret to sofa. Smiles at Alfred, deeply. She wears a lacy nightgown and a capelike robe. She smiles. Alfred stands. She sits on the sofa. Alfred sits opposite Will.)

MARGARET: Cigarette?

WILL: *(Quickly.)* He don't.

ALFRED: *(As quickly.)* I stopped.

MARGARET: *(As quickly.)* I forgot. *(Silence.)* I read the article in the paper today. It was lovely. Did you see it?

ALFRED: No.

(Will laughs.)

ALFRED: I think I'll go to bed. I have to be up early… *(Stands, starts an exit.)*

MARGARET: Couldn't we all talk awhile?

WILL: Sit.

ALFRED: I'm a bit sleepy.

WILL: You can sleep late.

ALFRED: I have an early appointment.

WILL: Bullshit.

MARGARET: *(Embarrassed.)* Will!

WILL: Just saw it in the paper: in Alfred's *Item* interview. Here… *(Reads from newspaper.)* "The Twentieth-Century concept of raised consciousness is all bullshit."

MARGARET: Will!

WILL: He doesn't like TV, either. Says that's bullshit, too.

MARGARET: Will!

WILL: Maggie doesn't like me to say "bullshit."

MARGARET: It's true. I really don't.

ALFRED: It's just a word.

WILL: Bullshit.

ALFRED: Doesn't mean anything.

WILL: Bullshit.

ALFRED: You're acting childish, Will.

WILL: *I* am?

ALFRED: I do remember your being obstreperous…your throat…infected…I think you had them out…

(*Will is angry; returns to reading his newspaper. Alfred returns to reading his newspaper, as well. Margaret waits a moment in silence, then looks from Will to Alfred, settles a smile on him; speaks.*)

MARGARET: I always look forward to a talk in the evening.

(*Alfred looks up from his newspaper. He and Margaret smile at each other. Will looks up from his newspaper, sees them smiling, watches awhile; speaks.*)

WILL: I would like to see an entrance exam for junior high school. We pay a lot of tax to support a school that doesn't teach nothing anymore. There should be a stiff exam. If a kid flunks, no junior high school. Let 'em work. Like me and Alfred. We worked for what we got. A stiff exam. That's what.

(*Silence.*)

MARGARET: It's very nice.

ALFRED: Huh?

MARGARET: Your robe.

ALFRED: It's Italian.

MARGARET: It's *still* very nice.

ALFRED: Yours is very nice, too.

WILL: For Jesus Christ's sakes…I could just leave the room!

MARGARET: I just told him his robe was pretty. It is. *You* wouldn't wear a robe like that. I bought you a robe in Filene's that was *gorgeous:* absolutely gorgeous. He wouldn't wear it, Alfred. It was much nicer than yours. Yours is lovely, but his was *gorgeous.* Never said "Thank you." Never even acted like I bought him a gift. I think men look just wonderful in evening robes.

WILL: Her *stepfather* wore a bathrobe.

MARGARET: My stepfather wore a *robe.*

WILL: Day and night. You'd think you were in a goddamn hospital!

MARGARET: He had a day robe and a night robe. He was a very elegant man.

ALFRED: I remember your stepfather. Sam. Right. I remember him…

WILL: What's to forget? He was here every goddamn day! He practically *lived* here for ten years. He no sooner went through the front door of the asylum when he snuck right out the back—right back down here again. Like I said: day and night.

ALFRED: (*Quietly.*) When did you…lose him?

MARGARET: Lose him?

WILL: Lose him?

ALFRED: Lose him? When did you?

MARGARET: It's complicated.

WILL: He ran away.

ALFRED: He *what?*

WILL: Ran away.

ALFRED: From here?

WILL: Yup. One day he packed up his *day* goddamn robe and his *night* goddamn robe and he was gone. He didn't even leave a note.

MARGARET: It was awful. His mind weakened.

WILL: Bullshit.

MARGARET: It did. I could see it coming.

WILL: He hooked himself up with Anderson's widow.

MARGARET: His mind was slipping. It was an awful thing to watch. Awful thing to watch...

WILL: Seventy-three and he could still get it up like a kid.

MARGARET: It was an awful thing to watch.

WILL: *(Laughs.)* Isn't that somepin'? Robe or no robe, I gotta hand it to the old son of a bitch: He could still get it up like a kid. The old widow Anderson didn't know what hit her. *(Leans in now; loudly.)* Sam and Andy's widow were carryin' on like two cocker goddamn spaniels. It was *un-be-lievable!* The speed with which that man could operate! I think he nailed her first right down at Pottle's Funeral Parlor! It's true! It wasn't six days after the burial before she was hanging around here every night. I caught 'em right where you sit: She was leanin' over and he was taking her from behind. I couldn't believe my goddamn eyes. It was unbelievable. I hadda ask 'em to leave the house. It's degenerate. You can't come home to a show like that every night.

MARGARET: His mind snapped. It was an awful thing to watch.

WILL: I'm gonna take a shower. You two...talk. *(He stands and walks up staircase. Exits.)*

ALFRED: I don't really remember your stepfather well.

MARGARET: He was not terribly tall, muscular, with reddish hair?

ALFRED: Vaguely.

MARGARET: Very short, thin, with brownish-reddish hair.

ALFRED: I think so.

MARGARET: A tiny, little man. Wiry, with thick glasses. Bald with a scraggly fringe...

ALFRED: Oh, yes. I remember him and I do think that I remember your stepmother…Roxy, right? Woman of wonderful spirit. Wonderful zest for life. If I remember correctly, she loved a good laugh.

MARGARET: Oh, she did love a laugh. She never had many good ones herself, poor thing, what with her life riddled by scandal and all…But, listen, health is the important thing, really. Don't you think?

ALFRED: Is she still…?

MARGARET: Oh, very much, very much. She's right up there in the home… with all of them…all of her friends. Nazareth Academy's a home now… *(Smiles.)* Why am I telling *you* this? You certainly know about it…

ALFRED: No, I don't know. And how about Sam? Is he there as well?

MARGARET: *(Totally changed attitude here; suddenly.)* I don't understand what the hell you're doing, Alfred!

ALFRED: I'm sorry?

MARGARET: You know he is!

(Pauses; they hold a stare between them.)

ALFRED: Who puts the flowers on my brother's grave, Margaret? Quite an extravagant gesture after fifteen years, I should say…

MARGARET: *(Turns away; pauses. Turns back; smiles.)* I could see his mind sliding. Every day he grew worse and worse…

ALFRED: Every day…worse and worse?…

MARGARET: I hope it never happens to you, Alfred…I hope you're spared.

ALFRED: Spared?

MARGARET: No, Alfred, not me. I've never even *seen* your brother's grave. Not me.

ALFRED: I'm sorry it's so difficult, Margaret, but it is. I'd like nothing more than to be here…home…with you, relaxed, in my old house, with you, alone, making love…

MARGARET: *(Shocked, somehow.)* Alfred L. Webber!

ALFRED: I don't seem to be able to relax anymore. Never…Not even while I was kissing you…

MARGARET: How did it feel?

ALFRED: Huh?

MARGARET: To kiss me: How did it feel?

ALFRED: How did it feel to kiss you?

MARGARET: After all these years: How did it?

ALFRED: Oh…well…exciting. Kissing you excited me. Stimulating…sexually. *(He laughs. Imitates child performing "Ali Baba.")* Made me feel open, sexually. Open…sexually!

(Alfred laughs; Margaret suddenly slaps his face.)

MARGARET: You haven't changed a bit. Dirty mind. Always a dirty mind.

ALFRED: *(Throwing her on the sofa; roughly.)* You're forty! We're forty! What can be dirty when you're forty?

MARGARET: I'm frightened of you.

(All in one supremely graceful move, Alfred to Margaret: They kiss. Will reenters and sees. Emily, Alfred's wife, enters through the front door. It all must occur in one move. Alfred is the first to sense what's happened.)

ALFRED: Will, this is my wife, Emily. Emily, this is Margaret's husband, Will. Margaret, this is my wife, Emily. I'm Alfred.

WILL: *(Angrily; incredulously.)* What the hell is going on?

ALFRED: Will, calm down. Calm down, Will. This is really quite funny, if you think about it: comic.

(Will circles the room.)

WILL: What the hell is going on?

ALFRED: *(His composure cracking.)* Will you calm down?? Margaret and I were kissing. Just kidding around! Two grade-school sweethearts reminiscing and kissing. There is absolutely nothing to worry about. Absolutely nothing. Emily, take your coat off and sit down.

(Emily doesn't move.)

WILL: What the hell is going on?

ALFRED: *(Waxing hysterical.)* Will, you're hysterical. Nothing is going on. Emily, take your coat off and sit down. You're staring.

(Emily doesn't move.)

WILL: Margaret. Say something.

MARGARET: *(Catatonic, near-arrest.)* I...I...

ALFRED: Will, there is absolutely nothing to be concerned about.

WILL: I heard every word.

MARGARET: *(Simply, an explanation.)* He does that a lot. He listens in on the telephone.

ALFRED: I know.

MARGARET: He heard me talking to my mother.

ALFRED: He heard me talking to the paper.

MARGARET: Who???

ALFRED: The paper! The paper!

WILL: I heard every word. You gonna marry her?

ALFRED: *(Shaken.)* Are you crazy?

WILL: Sounded pretty much like that to me. Course, maybe you were both just kidding. Maybe you knew I was listening in from the kitchen and you wanted to give me a good laugh.

MARGARET: I want to go to bed. This is dis*gust*ing!

(Will walks to her and slaps her face.)

WILL: *(After a pause, dryly.)* That's because you said "disgusting." You wanna hear *disgusting?* I'll give you *disgusting! (To Alfred.)* I almost killed a man because of her.

MARGARET: *Will, for God's sakes!*

WILL: It's true, Alfred. He was from Woburn. The paper man's helper. The paper man buys our paper. Still does. Old newspapers, tied in bundles. Fifteen cents a hundred pounds. Ain't much, but we don't have much. Maybe you noticed, huh?

ALFRED: I…uh…I didn't notice anything out of the ordinary, Will.

MARGARET: *Will, please…*

WILL: Can't take it, huh? Why didn'tcha think of that before, huh? All's I'm doin' is playing back what's true, ya know, *Maahhr*garet. She has no shame. No shame!

MARGARET: Stop, Will…

WILL: Yuh, sure I'll stop, sister. Same as you! *(To Alfred.)* I go over her house for an afternoon visit, you know. I was just a kid. I'm having wet dreams in the afternoon…hoping *Maahhr*garet here'll let me have a feel, maybe. *(Pauses.)* I go into the house and it seems like no one's home, you know? I listen for noises. I'm just about ready to call out her name and I hear 'em…down below. In the cellar. I go over to the stairs and look down. There they are. Honest ta Christ! No shame! She's right the Christ outa her blouse and brassiere and then the skirt and the underpants and there they are…doin' it. *Doin' it!*

MARGARET: Oh, my dear sweet God… *(She moans.)*

WILL: *(He moves to the weeping Margaret.)* Lucky I happened in, huh? Big guy. A real lummox…from Woburn. A big jamoca. A lummox. *(To Alfred.)* You get the picture?

MARGARET: Please…

WILL: No shame. No shame. I coulda killed him easy. I didn't. What the hell? He had kids. No reason they should carry the burden, right? It wouldn'ta taken much for me to kill him…if I had gone on. You follow my message?

ALFRED: You…uh…think about it much?

WILL: No. I don't…*uh*…think about it much.

ALFRED: Well, that's quite a story to swallow, Will…Really gets the imagination cooking…

WILL: I'll cook your ass.

ALFRED: I beg your pardon, Will.

WILL: Shut up.

ALFRED: Will?

WILL: Shut up!

ALFRED: Calm down, now, Will…

WILL: *(A command.) Shut the fuck up!!*

MARGARET: *(Sobbing.)* Please…

WILL: The light down there's dim…dark…but I could see them. Still can. I swear to God, I still can. *(Pauses.)* We weren't married, then. We were falling in love.

(Margaret runs from the room; exits up staircase.)

WILL: *(Softly, almost weeping.)* Nice to meet you, Emily. Heard a lot about you from Alfred here. He's a regular blabbermouth when it comes to his wife. *(Will walks to the door. He yells upstairs.)* I'm takin' a walk round the lake! *(Will opens door. Exits.)*

(Emily has been staring silently throughout scene. Alfred crosses and sits in Will's chair. He holds his back to Emily; does not face her as he speaks.)

ALFRED: I told you not to follow me here.

(The lights fade to black.)

End of Act I.

ACT II
SCENE I

Later. Stage in darkness. Three sharp knocks are heard. Church bells in distance, two chimes. The first word of the act—Alfred's—is heard.

ALFRED: Don't.

> *(Lights to full, suddenly. Emily lays on sofa, under oversized patchwork quilt. She wears a long night-robe. Emily faces into back of sofa, upstage. There is a small paring knife in her hand, unseen by audience. Alfred stands downstage of her. He speaks to her again, loudly.)*

ALFRED: I said *don't!* *(Pauses.)* Give it to me. *(No result.)* Hand it over. *(No result.)* I'll just have to take it, then... *(He walks to sofa, in silence, his hand extended. Forces knife away from her.)* That's better. *(He carries an apple, which he cuts into with knife. Eats a slice. Moves to chair. Sits.)* It's a pretty town, isn't it? You'd never guess. Never. I remember when we were little, bunch of us tied a kid named Georgie Landry to a big elm tree. Set a fire. Burned his legs. Crippled him. We were playing cowboys and Indians. You'd never guess, would you? *(Pauses.)* Pretty town, isn't it? Try to get some rest.

> *(Emily sobs.)*

ALFRED: Don't.

MARGARET: *(From top of stairs.)* Is she sleeping?

ALFRED: No.

MARGARET: *(Downstairs.)* Poor child.

ALFRED: She'll be fine.

MARGARET: *(In room now.)* Poor child.

ALFRED: She's fine. Really. Really, she's fine.

MARGARET: *(Very hostile.)* Poor child.

ALFRED: Stop it.

MARGARET: Hmmm?

ALFRED: What do you want?

MARGARET: Here?

ALFRED: Here.

MARGARET: Here? In this room?

ALFRED: Here. In this room.

MARGARET: *(Aggressively.)* That's a funny question coming from you.

ALFRED: We'll leave as soon as Emily can travel. She's... overwrought.

MARGARET: There's no need to leave, Alfred. It's quite nice having you here.

Both of you. Will is enjoying himself. He told me this morning. He told me he was enjoying himself. *(Pauses.)* Will hasn't enjoyed himself in fifteen years.

ALFRED: Was that true…what Will said? Did he really nearly kill someone… like he said? Was that true?

MARGARET: That was the last real pleasure Will had. *(Silence.)* How was your day?

ALFRED: Pleasant enough. Poked around the house a bit with Emily… Showed her all my old hiding places…

MARGARET: Yes. I saw you.

ALFRED: We took a walk…down by the lake…A bit of shopping on Albion Street…Pleasant enough.

MARGARET: How's your father? Been up there yet?

ALFRED: My father?

MARGARET: Your father. How is he?

ALFRED: Dead.

MARGARET: Still?

ALFRED: Is he still dead? Is that what you're asking me? Is my father still dead?

MARGARET: Why are you still pretending, Alfred? What are you trying to prove? Can't you see it's difficult enough for me having you back here… having you in the house with Will and all…without your acting weird like this…without this little charade?

ALFRED: Margaret, please believe me, but I really don't know what you're talking about. My father's dead. My father, my mother, my brother…they're all gone: all dead. There's just me now.

MARGARET: I don't know why you're acting this way…like you forget…I don't know why on earth you're doing what you're doing. I agree that most things are best left swept under the rug; but…Oh, God, Alfred, *what do you want from us??*

ALFRED: I don't like jokes like this, Margaret. I suppose it's funny…to Wakefield people…to play spooky little jokes…but my father, Tommy Webber, is dead. Margaret. Dead. I've been in the cemetery and I've seen the headstone…

MARGARET: Your father, Tommy Webber, is in the asylum on the hill…just where you put him. I'm sure you have your reasons. *(Exits into kitchen.)*

ALFRED: Margaret?… *(Calls to Emily.)* Sit up. *(He calls to Emily again.)* Sit up. *(She doesn't move.)* Sit up. *(No response; he crosses to her.)* Sit up!! *(He pulls her arm, hoisting her into a sitting position, just as Will enters from kitchen.)*

WILL: You lovebirds at it again?

(Emily drops back to the flat of the sofa. Alfred drops Emily's arm, turns away from her.)

WILL: Hey, listen, you wanna kill her, kill her. It's a free country. *(Will takes a baseball cap out of his pocket. He places it on his head.)*
(Alfred stares at it; really quite startled.)

WILL: *(Strutting.)* Like it?

ALFRED: *(Shocked; stunned.)* Where did you…Where?…Where did…

WILL: You're stuttering.

ALFRED: That cap is…

WILL: Vet's Field…church league…

ALFRED: My…

WILL: Very racy. Like it.

ALFRED: His…

WILL: Cost me an arm and a leg.

ALFRED: *(Laughs nervously.)* That's my father's cap.

WILL: Couldn't be. It's mine.

ALFRED: That's my father's. I know that cap. My father's…Hey, Will?
(Alfred stands and walks up to Will. He reaches for the cap, but Will pulls it back from him. The action should much resemble a child's prank.)

ALFRED: Hey, let's see it, Will?

WILL: How could it be your father's cap, Alfred? I thought your father was dead? Isn't he, Alfred?

ALFRED: That's true. It couldn't be. Couldn't be his. *(Alfred sits, smiling at Will.)* Seen today's paper?

WILL: Nope.
(Alfred pretends to get interested in newspaper. Will struts in front of Alfred now, cap on his head. Will laughs.)

WILL: Don't know what you're talking about. *(He laughs again.)* Alfred? *(Pauses.)* Don't you know, Alfred? You act like you don't know… *(Pauses.)* Look at me, Alfred.

ALFRED: Give me the cap, Will.

WILL: *(To Emily.)* He's crazy, your Alfred. I heard that all celebrities were crazy. Always heard that. Now I know for sure.

ALFRED: Give it to me, Will.

WILL: Don't think so. Not until you open your eyes.

ALFRED: You're going to pay for this.

WILL: Already did. Six bucks.

ALFRED: Okay, Will. We'll play it your way.

WILL: *(Flips cap back onto his head. He walks to the door, laughing.)* You know something, Alfred? I'm glad you came home. I figured it would get piggy, you know. Lot of screaming and yelling. Really obstreperous bull-shit. Ya know what I mean? But you've got real style, Alfred. Real style. *(Smiles.)* You really spruce up the old place. You add a little spice. *(Will opens the door.)* I do, however, think it's kinda weird...the way you're tryin' ta kinda remain...well...*blind* to certain matters, huh? You really ought to open your eyes. *(Exits.)*

ALFRED: *(Sits in chair. He seems stricken.)* Emily? *(No reply.)* Fine. Don't look at me. *(Pauses.)* Emily, I'm...very frightened. *(Pauses.)* I'm...I'm sorry I left the way I did. I don't pretend to understand why I did, I just did. I...I felt I had to. I was frightened... *(Pauses.)* Emily? *(Pauses.)* There's something wrong with my mind, Emily. My memory...My mind. I seem to have forgotten...things. *(Pauses.)* My knees are wet. My entire body is perspiring. This is simply atrocious. Look at me...No. Don't... *(Pauses.)* Emily, I need your help. I believe that my brother was murdered and that Will...well...did it. *(Pauses.)* I'm going to need your help. I know it's odd for me to be asking...asking you...for help...but I must. I must push on through this...be certain...what happened. *(Pauses.)* They're listening in, Emily, so I'm going to have to yell now. *(Pauses; then he yells loudly, sobbing.)* Em-i-leeee!
(Alfred places his head on his knees. Emily sits up, faces forward; smiles. Tableau. The lights fade to black.)

SCENE II

Later. Stage in darkness. Three sharp knocks are heard. First words of scene—Emily's—are heard.

EMILY: It's just an old thing I picked up, somewhere.
(Lights to full, suddenly. Will, in chair, staring at Emily, who sits center-stage, on sofa. Emily wears long, straight-lined dress, no shoes. Quilt is gone. Note: Emily should sit in precise position, smiling, as end of prior scene; as though freeze frame in which only dress and companion have changed. All else the same.)
EMILY: It's really old. Fifteen years. It's really old.
WILL: I think it's...sophisticated. That's what it is: sophisticated. You look very sophisticated in that dress, Emily.
EMILY: Thank you, Will. You're kind to say that.

WILL: It's true. You must have been quite a looker in your day…

EMILY: Mmmm. You're kind to say that, too.

WILL: Not that you're not okay now. You are: okay now. But I can tell that you really must have been something. Something special, I mean. Margaret and I never have talks like this, ya know that? We almost never talk at all. *(Pauses; shrugs.)* Oh, sure…in the beginning, we musta… Maybe not. In the beginning, there's plenty a other things occupying your mind, right? *(Smiles.)* I'm really enjoying this. You?

EMILY: Yes.

WILL: Where did you first hook up with Alfred?

EMILY: I believe that Alfred and I first hooked together in Magnolia. At a weekend at Magnolia Manor. We spent our first date watching the Greasy Pole Contest in Gloucester. *(She smiles at Will.)* Have you ever seen it?

WILL: Yuh, seems to me I did. I forget.

EMILY: A long hard stiff pole sticks straight out from a wharf. Men walk it. I found the contest to be quite stimulating.

WILL: Sounds great.

EMILY: Alfred never had a girl before me. I was his first. Can you imagine?

WILL: Now I gotcha…

EMILY: Sorry?

WILL: *(Thinks he's back in a world of reason.)* Margaret.

EMILY: Margaret?

WILL: He had Margaret. Had her in the eleventh grade.

EMILY: *(She laughs.)* Nooooo.

WILL: He did so.

(Emily laughs again.)

WILL: Alfred got Margaret in trouble, during the summer of the eleventh grade.

EMILY: Trouble?

WILL: Family way. She was in it.

EMILY: I see.

WILL: Little girl. They gave it away.

EMILY: They gave it away? Like a gift? That sort of thing?

WILL: To a home, up over the line in New Hampshire. They do those sort of things up there.

EMILY: I don't follow.

WILL: Alfred and Margaret had a little girl together and they gave it away…to some home…for adoption…in New Hampshire. What's so hard to follow?

EMILY: *(Quietly.)* It's not hard to follow. It's hard to…accept.

WILL: Alfred was the father all right. He ruined her. Margaret: ruined. Did something to her mind. Made her barren. Alfred ruined her.

EMILY: Are you certain, Will?

WILL: I saw it with my own eyes…Margaret…Saw her stomach. Everybody in town saw it, too. I myself had my own trouble…

EMILY: In what way?

WILL: Family, same as Margaret. I got a Wakefield cheerleader in trouble. F…

EMILY: F?

WILL: F.

EMILY: And you gave the child away?

WILL: *Are you crazy??*

EMILY: What is this? A pop quiz, Will?

WILL: I would *never* do a thing like that!

EMILY: Nor would I.

WILL: I would cut off a finger before I would give a baby up for adoption…

EMILY: As would I.

WILL: It isn't manly.

EMILY: That's not *my* reason, exactly, Will, but I do understand.

WILL: My son, Will, Jr.…I made sure he was born and I made sure he was raised with the best money could buy…

EMILY: Your *son?* Where is he?

WILL: My son. Beautiful kid. He's off in college now. Imagine that? I'm forty and I've got a kid twenty-one…

EMILY: You must be proud?

WILL: Proud? Proud? I'm *more* than proud! Best thing I ever did was to insist that Will, Jr., be brought up right.

EMILY: And you never wanted more?

WILL: Kids? Sure I did.

EMILY: But you didn't?

WILL: It wasn't me: It's her. Barren. I told you. Alfred saw to that. Why do you think I hate him so much?

EMILY: I'd wondered why.

WILL: Now you know.

EMILY: Margaret's been tested?

WILL: A million times. There's no doubt…

(Emily just stares at Will silently.)

WILL: What're you starin' at? There's no doubt. I talked to the doctor myself. Psychological barrenness…

EMILY: Really?

WILL: What are you getting at?

EMILY: Margaret's clever.

WILL: What are you?…Kidding me?…Or what? Margaret? Clever?

EMILY: I could have saved myself a lot of, well, trouble, Will…if I had known what Margaret learned in high school…

WILL: And what's that?

EMILY: To stop trying.

WILL: I don't follow.

EMILY: No, you don't. You certainly don't.

(Silence. Will doesn't move.)

WILL: I guess you couldn't get interested in a townie like me. Ah, I know. Alfred's got all those city ways down pat. That kind of round-shouldered bullshit. *(Pauses, changes tone.)* I got dirt under my fingernails. Alfred probably bites his. I used to know a joke about fingernails…I forgot it.

EMILY: He *did*.

WILL: Huh?

EMILY: He quit. He quit biting his fingernails when he quit smoking. He gave up all forms of sucking.

WILL: *(Honestly embarrassed.)* Heyyy, watch your talk, okay?

EMILY: You're sweet, Will. *(She smiles at Will.)* You're living in another century.

(Will moves to Emily; stops. Momentarily loses courage.)

EMILY: I do find you attractive, Will. I really do. Kiss me.

(As they kiss, Alfred enters.)

ALFRED: Nice. Really nice.

(They pull apart.)

ALFRED: Sorry. I'm not being discreet. I should have knocked.

WILL: There's nothing going on, Alfred—really.

ALFRED: Oh. I thought you two were…you know.

WILL: Naw…

EMILY: Alfred?

ALFRED: Forget it. Forget it. Sorry I asked. *(He exits.)*

WILL: Hey! Alfred!!! Where the hell's he going??? He just left us alone.

EMILY: *(Quietly.)* Balls!

WILL: What?

EMILY: Balls?

WILL: *(Disgusted.)* That's what I thought you said. Goddam! *(Clenches eyes closed, three times. Sits.)* I'm getting a headache.

(Three knocks at the door.)

WILL: Yeah?

    (Alfred enters.)

ALFRED: It's lonely in the kitchen. Mind if I sit in here with you?

WILL: *(A gentleman.)* Come in. Sit down. I don't mind. It's fine with me.

    (Alfred sits.)

WILL: Cigarette?

ALFRED: *(Smiling.)* Quit.

EMILY: Fingernail?

ALFRED: *(Without changing his smile.)* Why don't you try stuffing it where the sun never shines?

WILL: Jesus. Nice talk. Really piggy. You know what I mean? *(Squints.)* My head feels like a broken arm.

EMILY: I was just telling Will about Magnolia.

ALFRED: I know. I heard. You only watched Margaret get *laid,* Wilbur. I had the pleasure of watching *Emily* get beaten up.

WILL: Hmmm?

ALFRED: The Magnolia locals didn't take really well to Emily's…to Emily's kind. *(Smiles.)* The word is that they chased Emily's…How would you say it?…They chased Emily's *party* right out of town. On *foot,* too. Straight up the old route one-twenty-seven into Manchester Center, and then on through to Gloucester Harbor. It must have been a hell of a run for an old man… *(Pauses.)* The Greasy Pole Contest was on that day and their departure caused quite a sensation, I'm sure. A youngish woman, naked, a craggy old man, also naked, and a gaggle of locals chasing after.

WILL: *(To Emily, who is looking away.)* What's he talking about?

ALFRED: They say the Greasy Pole contender…a B.J. something…was so disconcerted, he walked right off the end of the pole, forgetting to lift the red flag…

WILL: *(To Alfred.)* What craggy old man?

ALFRED: *(Smiles.)* Oh, *that!* Emily's always had a certain active curiosity about craggy old men…At the time Emily and I first hooked up together, she was seeing a very wealthy, very craggy, very old fellow—from Yugoslavia, I believe.

WILL: Yugoslavia?

ALFRED: Silk robes are nothing, Will. Nothing. Emily's Slav wore the real stuff.

    (Emily slaps Alfred's face. A clean, loud single slap, with her left hand. Alfred stands firm; continues, apparently unbothered.)

ALFRED: …garter belts…

(Emily slaps him again: right-handed.)

ALFRED: ...dark-seamed tinted nylons...

(Emily slaps him again: left-handed.)

ALFRED: ...fake-fun-fur coats...

(Emily slaps him again: right-handed. He stops talking, smiles. He walks to the door: stops. He walks to Emily.)

ALFRED: That was unpleasant. Not unattractive. But unpleasant. *(Pauses. He then returns to the door.)* Night. *(Alfred exits.)*

(Will stares wide-eyed, disbelieving. There is a pause. Will exhales a great deal of breath: sits.)

WILL: I don't understand.

EMILY: *(To Will; cruelly direct.)* No, you don't! You certainly don't! *(Pauses; inhales, exhales.)* My mother was a virgin when she married him. *(Pauses.)* She was a virgin when she died. *(Pauses.)* My father was a sainted man. *(She lights a cigarette.)* I wish I'd met him. *(She coughs.)* Alfred's right. I really must quit. *(Pauses.)* Just shut up, Will. *(Pauses.)* I LOATHE NOISE! I CAN'T THINK!

WILL: Are you all right?

EMILY: I'm all right.

WILL: You sure?

EMILY: I have never in my entire life met another woman who was even one half as unhappy as I am.

WILL: What are you looking for here, Emily?

EMILY: *(After a pause.)* There are times I look in the mirror and there's no one there.

WILL: I'll bet you look great in the mirror.

EMILY: Sometimes, instead of me, it's Alfred in there...in the space reserved for my reflection.

WILL: Sneaking up? That kind of thing?

EMILY: Yuh.

WILL: Sometimes, a man just sneaks. He doesn't want to. He just does.

EMILY: I spent my first ten years in an orphanage. The next ten in California, in a boarding school for the very gifted. I was very gifted, Will.

WILL: Not me. Not even at Christmastime. *(He laughs.)* That was a good one. *(Smiles.)* The best ones just sneak out, don't they?

EMILY: Is Alfred's father still alive, Will?

WILL: Course he is.

EMILY: Where?

WILL: Up on the hill. Nuthouse, with all the rest of 'em....How come he's pretending his father's dead, huh? What's all that about, anyway?

EMILY: I don't know. I *will* know. I just don't...yet. *(Smiles.)* We do have a lot in common, Will.

WILL: Now that you mention it, I guess we do. Yuh...Hey, listen, I gotta tell you, Emily: Around these parts, growin' up 'n' all, Alfred was known as a real jerk, ya know? Eighteen years old and he makes a clear million sellin' a swamp. Who woulda guessed, huh? I mean, who the Christ woulda ever guessed? But, so far as *I'm* concerned, million or not, interviews or not, boy wonder or not, Alfred L. Webber was, is, and will be a first-class jerk. I gotta tell ya that.

EMILY: Thanks Will. That certainly clears things up.

WILL: You're playin' with me. I don't like it, okay?

EMILY: Can you prove that Alfred's father's alive, Will?

WILL: Easy. Have a look? *(He takes a baseball cap from his pocket and places it on his head.)*

EMILY: Is that Alfred's father's cap?

WILL: Yup. You like it? His father just gave it to me.

EMILY: Alfred told me his father died...fifteen years ago...Alfred came up here for the funeral. I remember consoling him.

WILL: That was his brother.

EMILY: His what?

WILL: His brother. Alfred had a crazy brother...Bruce...A real jerk. It's all through Alfred's family. Bruce, his name was. Big. He grew up in Woburn.

EMILY: But Alfred grew up *here*...in Wakefield.

WILL: Half brother. Different mothers. Alfred's father moved around a lot. You get what I mean?

EMILY: Not exactly.

WILL: This is a small town, Emily. Things maybe...well...*pass* in a town like this that might not pass elsewhere.

EMILY: I don't understand.

WILL: *(Suddenly turns to Emily, cap on head. He mimics her cruel epithet, precisely.)* No, you don't. You certainly don't. *(He smiles. He settles back into chair. A pause.)* They built a hot-dog stand where my house used to be, Margaret. They really did.

EMILY: Margaret. You called me "Margaret."

WILL: I'll tell you somepin': If I had the courage, I would run myself a nice hot tub, climb in, close my eyes, and slide.

EMILY: *(Pauses, then softly.)* You called me "Margaret." Will? *(Pauses.)* Will?

WILL: *(A forlorn statement; a fact.)* She's the only woman I'll ever love.

EMILY: Margaret?

WILL: Margaret.

EMILY: Perfect

WILL: She is the only woman I have ever met who really pays attention.

EMILY: Have you ever told her this? Margaret.

WILL: She wouldn't listen.

EMILY: You ever try?

WILL: She doesn't listen.

EMILY: I'm confused.

WILL: I had a chance…

EMILY: To what?

WILL: …get out of here. I had a chance to get out of here. Fifteen years ago. Her boyfriend…I should have left then.

EMILY: Her *what?*

WILL: Boyfriend. The guy in the cellar. From Woburn. That was her boyfriend…

EMILY: The one you strangled?…

WILL: The one I *what?*

EMILY: Strangled. You said you strangled the man from Woburn.

WILL: *(Stares absently at the sofa.)* Re-covered.

EMILY: Who?

WILL: The sofa. *(He pauses; speaks softly now.)* Used to be a nice dark blue. She changed it to that stuff that's on there now…I liked the dark blue better…

EMILY: How do you feel about red, Will?

WILL: Red?

EMILY: Red roses, specifically?

WILL: I like them. I like them very much, but I don't like your questions. *(Silence.)* Alfred's come a long way.

EMILY: He works hard…

WILL: I work hard…

EMILY: *(Sits on the arm of Will's chair.)* Not the same.

WILL: *(Jumps up and moves away.)* Another article in the paper today. About a scholarship. Is that true?

EMILY: Didn't see it.

WILL: Alfred's set up a big scholarship in the old man's name.

EMILY: Will, I…yes. Yes, he did.

WILL: *(Counts to himself, in whispers.)* Nine, carry two…

EMILY: What are you counting, Will?

WILL: I'll *never* see that much money, ya know…Not in my life…not in one lump sum. *(Looks up.)* Betcha wonderin' how I came to own this house, huh? Betcha wonderin' where I got the money…His old house, too.

EMILY: How?

WILL: Back taxes. Ten thousand dollars…a thousand down, nine ta carry… fifteen years. Almost *free,* as house prices go, and I could barely swing it. I had ta work weekends first five years or so…just ta make ends meet… And that jerk gives a goddamn scholarship at the high school that'd buy ten of these rattraps! Ten of 'em! Ain't that just the last laugh on all of us, huh? On *me,* especially! He grows up right here, goes away at eighteen—a millionaire—comes back a trillionaire, probably—and here's good old Wilbur M. Lynch, pushing the truck every mornin', trying to pay off the taxes he left behind. Livin' in the *box* Alfred's champagne bottle came in.

EMILY: It's only money. Alfred is unhappy.

WILL: What am I: a laugh a minute?

EMILY: *(Crosses to Will's chair and leans over him.)* Alfred's impotent.

WILL: In what way?

EMILY: Alfred's impotent…He can't…

WILL: Get it up?

EMILY: Get it up.

WILL: *(Amazed and delighted.)* You're crazy.

EMILY: That may be, but it does not in any way alter the fact that Alfred cannot…

WILL: *(Laughing.)* Get it up?

EMILY: Get it up.

WILL: He got it up, last night.

EMILY: What?

WILL: He got it up, last night. I saw them.

EMILY: Margaret…

WILL: …and Alfred.

EMILY: You saw Margaret and Alfred…

WILL: …doing it.

EMILY: Will you FOR CHRISSAKES let me finish a sentence??

WILL: Sorry.

EMILY: Where?

WILL: Same as always. In the living room…here…

EMILY: …On the sofa?

WILL: Same as always…

EMILY: You watched?

WILL: Well…yuh…yuh…I did…I watched.

EMILY: For how long?

WILL: Thirty-five minutes.

EMILY: What? You watched for thirty-five minutes?

WILL: That's *nothing*. I can go an hour.

EMILY: Say that again.

WILL: I can go an hour.

EMILY: You want to prove it?

WILL: I wouldn't…I wouldn't mind. We have to find a place…

EMILY: Sofa's fine with me…

WILL: They're in the house.

EMILY: So?

WILL: So I think we should find a place.

EMILY: You care if they catch us?

WILL: No. You're right.

> *(Pause. Emily turns off light and begins unbuttoning Will's shirt. She stands behind chair, leaning over him. Both face front.)*

EMILY: You think about it much?

WILL: No.

EMILY: What do you think of, when you see them?

WILL: See them?

EMILY: In your mind?

WILL: How pretty they are.

EMILY: Really?

WILL: Maggie's pink, the slipcover was a nice deep dark blue. Like deep water. He was all suntanned from being outside. She was pink. Pushing and pulling at each other. I thought he was killing her…with all the pushing and pulling and the noises she was making…She never made those kind of noises for me. *(Pause.)* Then I saw her face. *(Pause.)* He wasn't killing her. *(Pause.)* Around here, people understand.

EMILY: You've still got a pretty good figure…physique. *(Moving in now.)* …Very nice to the touch.

WILL: *(Seriously considers what Emily has said.)* Naw, I'm way outa shape. Soft. You shoulda looked me up twenty years ago…Used to be really something. Something special. *(Pauses.)* Too much drink, too much TV, too much sittin' around… *(Pauses.)* Course, I could join the Y an' work out a little. Maybe get some development back, huh? *(Pauses.)* Would you like that?

EMILY: That's a terribly exciting idea, Will.

WILL: You gonna keep your things on?

EMILY: No. Uh uh… *(She unbuttons front of dress.)*

WILL: You're really beautiful.

(Will stands and moves to Emily, who moves back from him. She is against the sofa. He follows: hugs her.)

WILL: We never get women like you around here, Emily, not even in the summertime. Never…Tell me what to do…

EMILY: Will, listen…

WILL: What?

(Emily is bent backwards against the arm of the sofa. Will, in front, trying to press her down.)

EMILY: The man on the sofa was Alfred's brother, right? You killed Alfred's brother, right, Will???

WILL: What are you talking about???

EMILY: That *was* his brother, right? Will, I've got to know. Please, Will. The man from Woburn…in the cellar…and the man on the sofa? That was the same man: Alfred's brother. Right, Will? Will, please?…

WILL: You must think I'm stupid. You must think I'm a dope!

(Will rises with clothes and moves to stairs, trips. Alfred appears at top of stairs.)

ALFRED: You okay?

EMILY: Nothing is certain.

ALFRED: What did he tell you?

EMILY: Nothing is certain.

ALFRED: *What did he tell you???*

WILL: What the hell gives here?

ALFRED: Strip him.

EMILY: Alfred, don't be ridiculous…

ALFRED: I'm tired of waiting. *Strip…him?. (Yells.) Move!*

(Will has fallen on the stairs and has, until this point, remained frozen in one spot, listening. He now crawls up the staircase, two steps. Stops. Alfred moves down the staircase, two steps. Stops. Emily moves across room to bottom stair. Stops. Will raises his head and stares wordlessly, first to Emily, then to Alfred. They each move one additional step toward Will, as the lights fade to black.)

End of Act II.

ACT III

Later. Stage in darkness. Three sharp knocks are heard. Church bells in distance, two chimes. First words of the act—Alfred's—are heard.

ALFRED: How do you like it, so far?

(Lights to full, suddenly. Alfred stands on landing on top of staircase behind Will, who is stripped to his underpants and socks, bound, and gagged. Will's legs and arms are poked through staircase railing and tied around spindles. The gag in his mouth is his white cotton undershirt. Emily and Margaret sit on sofa, as far apart as possible.)

ALFRED: I think that Will looks rather well in rope, don't you? *(Alfred leans down into room, smiling.)* Don't you think he does, Margaret?

MARGARET: Please, Alfred?

ALFRED: Please, *what,* Margaret?

MARGARET: Let me take the gag out of his mouth.

ALFRED: But if I were to do that, Will could talk…I prefer holding the old status quo, for a while… *(To Will.)* You don't mind holding the old status quo, do you, Will?

WILL: *(Struggling.)* Argghh…

ALFRED: Right! Will has a great affinity for things Latin. Status quo is Latin, Will: the tongue of the Church…

WILL: Ughhh…

ALFRED: I would have to say that Will actually has a proclivity for things Latin.

WILL: Uggghhhhhhhh!

ALFRED: Now you've gone too far, Will. I'm afraid I'll have to put my finger to your proclivity, so to speak. *(Twists gag tighter.)*

WILL: Arggghhhh!

(Alfred twists gag considerably tighter. Will winces.)

ALFRED: I should have said so not to speak. *(Pauses.)* Better. Much better.

MARGARET: I think the gag may be hurting his mouth.

ALFRED: Yes. I think so. Emily, I want a cold drink. Ginger ale.

(Emily stands and exits. All watch.)

ALFRED: *Emily's been a good wife.*

MARGARET: You must be very happy. You two seem like you were made for each other.

ALFRED: She should not have followed me here. She was told to stay home. Not like Emily at all. Not at all…

MARGARET: What do you want?

ALFRED: Want?

MARGARET: Want.

ALFRED: Now?

MARGARET: Now.

ALFRED: Ginger ale.

(Emily enters, gives Alfred a glass of ginger ale.)

ALFRED: Thank you. *(Pause.)* Here's to you. *(Tips his glass to Will.)* Nice. Really nice. *(Pauses.)* Emily?

(Emily smiles, stands, walks to Will.)

EMILY: The thing is, Will, we think you murdered Alfred's brother.

MARGARET: What?

ALFRED: Shhh. This is the good part.

EMILY: When you walked in that day, Will…when Margaret here was being indiscreet…that's when you strangled him, right?

MARGARET: What is she talking about?

EMILY: The man in the cellar and/or on the sofa: the man who was monkeying with you in the cellar and/or on the sofa. That was Alfred's brother… Right?

MARGARET: I'm leaving the room. I see no reason why I should be made to sit through such a disgusting display of…of…

EMILY: Of what?

MARGARET: In my own home.

EMILY: *(Smiles.)* I appreciate your obligatory false exit, Margaret. Sit down.

(Margaret does.)

EMILY: Better. If there is one thing on the face of this earth I understand, I understand the reason a woman—any woman—moves from point A to point B. Any woman. Even a Wakefield woman. Alfred?

ALFRED: Huh?

EMILY: It's your ball game.

ALFRED: Right. Now then, Will…Margaret…when I first came back to town…to Wakefield…to the old *turf,* I didn't actually have an inkling why. I've had increased difficulty…with my memory. I don't remember easily…

WILL: *(Yells through his gag.)* Yoooaww rememmmm…

ALFRED: Was that a low-flying plane? *(Smiles.)* Well, now. Almost as soon as my foot touched down in Wakefield, on Albion Street, precisely…I knew why…why I'd come back…what I had to do. Will? Margaret?

MARGARET: What?

ALFRED: My brother was murdered. I'd tried for years to put it out of my mind…not get involved. But now I'm home. The murder of my brother needs avenging. His murderer must confess and…well…be punished.

WILL: *(Trying to yell through gag.)* Yooo awrrr craazzzziii…!

ALFRED: I beg your pardon?

MARGARET: How dare you…of *all* people…carry on like this?

ALFRED: Me, of all people?

EMILY: Him, of all people?

MARGARET: Yuh. *Him* of all people. Yuh.

EMILY: What exactly do you mean, Margaret? I'd like to know.

ALFRED: I wouldn't mind knowing myself, Margaret.

MARGARET: Alfred, for the love of God! *(Sudden anger.)* Not in front of *her,* Alfred!

EMILY: Me?

MARGARET: You! Right, you! There are certain matters that don't concern outsiders like you… *(Pauses.)* Just what I said: not in front of you.

EMILY: I'll turn my back…

MARGARET: *(Yells; suddenly.)* We…don't…talk…about it!

ALFRED: About what? *(Pauses.)* About what?

EMILY: About what?

ALFRED: About what?

MARGARET: I'm sure you have your reasons, Alfred. I'm sure you do.

ALFRED: Rest assured. Rest assured. I talked to a lot of people downtown, before I came here to the house. Wakefield people love to talk, don't they? *(Smiles.)* It seems that quite a lot of people knew that you and my brother were quite close…

MARGARET: We were…

ALFRED: Lovers.

MARGARET: That's not true!

ALFRED: Do you solemnly swear?

MARGARET: I've never had a lover!

WILL: Arggghhh!

MARGARET: Never!

WILL: ARGGGHHHH!

ALFRED: Just one. My brother.

MARGARET: That's not true.

ALFRED: Seems my brother used to come here just about every day…while Will was working.

MARGARET: Who told you that?

ALFRED: Will.

MARGARET: Will?

WILL: Argggghhhh!

ALFRED: See?

MARGARET: Why would Will say anything like that?

EMILY: Will's an unusual man.

ALFRED: We'll see. *(Alfred runs upstairs to Will.)* Okay, Will. *(Alfred removes Will's gag.)* Shut up, Will. Margaret?

MARGARET: What?

ALFRED: Don't you miss him?

MARGARET: Not in front of Will…

ALFRED: Don't you?

MARGARET: No.

ALFRED: He loved you.

MARGARET: I know.

ALFRED: He used to write to me about you.

MARGARET: He did?

WILL: He didn't, ya dumb bitch! *(Yells down to Alfred now.)* Knock it off, Alfred! You're really wearing out your welcome, you know that, pal?
(They are, all three, sitting now on the sofa: Alfred and Emily on the ends, Margaret sandwiched in the middle. Will breaks the silence.)

WILL: I never did. I couldn't…This is really crazy!

EMILY: Why is Alfred's concern for his brother crazy, Will? *(No reply. Emily yells.)* Why?

WILL: Alfred's brother, Bruce B. Webber, was a prime, first-class *jerk,* that's why! You know what we use'ta call him? I'll tell you what: *Cootie!* That's what Bruce B. Webber was known as in this town: Cootie Webber…

MARGARET: Wilbur Lynch, that is not true!

WILL: May God strike me down deader than a doornail if it's not true!

MARGARET: In fifth grade! In fifth grade, yes…Cootie…

WILL: On accounta his monkey…

EMILY: I beg your pardon?

WILL: On account of his monkey. That's why we called him Cootie…because all the kids figured he caught cooties…from his pet monkey. Bruce B. Webber had a pet monkey…on his *shoulder!* Some normal fella, huh?

MARGARET: In fifth grade, for God's sakes! Bruce B. Webber had a pet monkey in fifth grade!

WILL: That doesn't make him any less of a joke around here. That's exactly what your brother was, Alfred, and you know it: the town joke. You were so ashamed of him, you didn't hardly acknowledge he was even alive. Everybody knew that to be true. *Everybody!*

ALFRED: My brother was valedictorian of his class here, Emily…voted the most likely to succeed…

WILL: Cooties…all over his shoulders…

ALFRED: Right. You got it, Will…Now I see why you had to murder him: A man with cooties can't be allowed to walk a Wakefield street. The town's just not big enough…

MARGARET: Why the good Lord ever *ever* stuck me in a house for all these years with Wilbur Lynch is something I will never understand…if I live to be a hundred and eighty! *What…did…I…do???*

WILL: You want me to answer that question, sister? Want me to?

(Margaret looks away from Will's stare. Will laughs.)

WILL: All right. Suurrrrre… *(Will looks at Emily.)* I've got plenty to say about Mr. Bruce B. Webber. Plenty!

EMILY: I'm all ears, Will.

WILL: Straight A's at Wakefield High and where did it get him? Think about *that,* huh? He goes off to college, starts drinkin' and highfalutin politics and bullshit…next thing we know he's back here in town, a layabout, a good-for-nothin', a Guinea-wino…

MARGARET: Wilbur Lynch!

WILL: Wilbur Lynch my ass! Bruce B. Webber was a falling-down wino and that's a *fact. A fact!*

MARGARET: Bruce B. Webber was a fine, understanding man who made me feel clean and beautiful and, for once in my life, not dumb…and that's a fact. *That* is a fact… *(Quickly, to Alfred.)* He was never as special as you, Alfred…never as exciting to me…never as funny or clever as you…But he was fine, Alfred…Emily…it's true. Bruce B. Webber—drinker, or not; skinny, or not; oddball, or not—was a fine, understanding man, who made me feel clean and made me feel beautiful and let me be what I am.

WILL: And what's that?

MARGARET: What's what?

WILL: What you are? What's that?

MARGARET: Not dumb.

WILL: You were dumb enough to fall for Bruce B. Webber's bullshit…and Alfred L. Webber's bullshit…and Tommy Webber's bullshit…and if there had been a Webber dog, you woulda fallen for Doggy Webber's bullshit, too!

EMILY: Tommy?

ALFRED: You're stooping, Will...

EMILY: Will?

MARGARET: Stop it!

WILL: Bullshit, I'll stop it. Everybody's looking at me here, like I'm the crazy
one, right? Well, I've got a real piece of craziness to straighten out here:
Tommy Webber is alive. Alive. Alive and the same sex maniac he was,
sixty years ago. And that's a fact. They use ta say if somebody would hold
a rattlesnake's mouth open long enough, Tommy Webber would—

ALFRED: God damn it, this is really enough! I will not have my father's memory dragged through this mudwrestle of yours, Will—

WILL: Memory?

MARGARET: Memory?

ALFRED: Memory. My father's life was hardly perfect, but it was hardly what
Wilbur Lynch's filthy little mind would have it be. Now Goddamn it.
Goddamn it! *(Pauses.)* My brother was murdered and I will have a con-
fession now, please. Now, please! *(Pauses.)* I feel cold!

MARGARET: Will...please don't... *(She sobs.)*

WILL: Cry your ass off! See if I care. I've played dumb long enough...
(Alfred places his head in his lap and sobs.)

WILL: Great. Two of you cryers...perfect, huh? You wouldn't catch me crying.
It ain't manly.
(Emily walks to Alfred and strokes his cheek. Will watches a moment.)

ALFRED: Enough!
*(Alfred stands, eyes clenched closed. He crosses to the chair; feeling his way as
a blind man. He knocks against the chair, causing the pedestal ashtray to fall
over. He sits, smiling into the others astonished silence. Alfred faces forward,
smiling broadly now.)*

EMILY: What are you doing?

ALFRED: That's better. It's okay now, Will...I'm okay. Talk, Will. I'm still listening.

EMILY: You closed your eyes. What are you doing?

MARGARET: You've closed your eyes. *(To Will.)* Alfred's closed his eyes.

ALFRED: Talk, Will. Will? Will? *Will!*

MARGARET: Alfred; please...

WILL: It's been fifteen years...

MARGARET: Alfred...

WILL: C'mon. Alfred...what's the point?

ALFRED: My brother...that's the point. My brother.

MARGARET: Stop acting like this, Alfred. Emily, make him stop…Please, Emily…

ALFRED: Yes, Emily, make me stop.

EMILY: That's enough, Alfred.

ALFRED: What's enough?

EMILY: Open your eyes.

ALFRED: And why?

EMILY: I said, "Open your eyes."

ALFRED: And if I don't?

EMILY: Think.

ALFRED: About what?

EMILY: Think.

ALFRED: Don't try to run me, Emily! I won't have it!

EMILY: *THINK!!!*

ALFRED: Don't talk to me like that.

EMILY: Like what?

ALFRED: Like I'm a fool.

EMILY: But you are.

ALFRED: I despise you.

EMILY: I own you.

ALFRED: Stop it.

EMILY: Say it!

ALFRED: I despise you.

EMILY: Say it.

ALFRED: *(Quietly.)* You own me.

EMILY: Much better.

    (Alfred has shrunk in the chair. He is very frightened indeed.)

EMILY: Sit up now, Alfred. Don't embarrass me. *(Pause.)* I said, "Sit up!"

    (He does.)

EMILY: Better. Now open your eyes.

ALFRED: *(He slumps back down in chair.)* Nope.

MARGARET: Why are you acting this way?

ALFRED: *(Slowly at first; then with moderate speed.)* Why am I acting this way? Why am I acting this way? *(Pauses.)* I had one brother, just one. He was very special to me. I don't have to explain to anyone why he was: He just was. I come home. I discover that what I've thought to be true was: was true. That my brother was murdered…by him: Will. A man who claims my brother had, of all things, a monkey; and my brother was with you at the time of his death, Margaret. That you were hanky and he was panky. *All that! All that!* I am slightly more than forty years of age. That's not a toddler, forty. I'm sure you'll agree. And here I am, sitting in a room with my dead brother's mistress, her husband the killer, my wife Emily, who has been unfaithful to me in ways known only to scholars of ancient tribal unfaithfulness. I am told that my late, great, dead father is not only alive, but is, by reputation, the most promising pervert of this town. And I, his only remaining son, like most middle-aged men of my height, have but one father: him. I am sleepy. I am confused. I am frightened. I am unhappy. And last but not least, I am impotent. Why am I acting *which* way, Margaret? I don't know what you mean.

MARGARET: *(After a long pause.)* Like you hate me.

ALFRED: Oh, my Margaret. You *have* grown dumb.

MARGARET: *(Head bows; sobs.)* Oh, Alfred…

ALFRED: I am a very successful young man, I really am, Will. Spent my life…watching: eyes wide open. *(Pauses: hears Margaret's sobs.)* Why is she crying?

EMILY: I think the word you used was "dumb."

ALFRED: I used a dumb word, or the word "dumb." That was a syntactically ambiguous sentence, Emily. I'm surprised.

MARGARET: *Dumb.* You called me *dumb*.

ALFRED: Sorry. Come here, Margaret, we'll kiss and make up.

WILL: Go on. Couldn't care less.

ALFRED: *(To Margaret.)* Well? Well? Will you?

MARGARET: Doesn't frighten me, not at all.

ALFRED: *(A sudden pause.)* Oh…yes.

EMILY: Oh…yes, what?

ALFRED: My mind… *(Pauses.)* My late brother, he did have a monkey. I'd forgotten…

WILL: See? Some normal fella, huh? A monkey.

EMILY: He really owned a monkey? I loathe monkeys… They pick salt from their hairy little bodies and they masturbate.

WILL: Nice talk.

ALFRED: My brother Bruce did in fact have a monkey. He was, as Will said, a very quirky fellow—not the monkey: Bruce. The monkey was, as monkeys go, quite average… *(Pauses.)* I believe his name was either Peru or Argentina…

MARGARET: Peru.

ALFRED: Peru…right. Peru used to pee on our rug. Sad, but true. Peru'd just walk straight into the living room here and pee on the rug. Bruce used to slap the monkey's behind three times and then take him to the window out there in the front hall and throw him out the window. Not to hurt him. It's only four feet down to the ground. Bruce used to throw Peru out the window to train him…so he wouldn't continue to come in here and pee on the rug. Well…after about three months of such goings-on, the monkey still used to pee on the rug, but after he finished, he'd whack his own ass three times, run out into the front hall, and jump out the window.

WILL: I never liked monkeys, either. They make me nervous.

MARGARET: I like monkeys. I think they're cute.

(Alfred smiles into space, in Emily's direction. Margaret is pleased by what she imagines to be forgiveness in the air.)

MARGARET: I think it's good that we can all sit down and talk this way. It isn't everyone that can be…you know…*friendly,* the way we are.

ALFRED: I beg your pardon?

MARGARET: Don't you think?

ALFRED: *(Fiercely; abrupt change in tone.)* Don't I *think?* Is that the question? Don't I *think?*

MARGARET: *(She is angry now, too.)* Don't you think that it's wonderful that we're so friendly? Under the circumstances.

EMILY: *(Crosses to Alfred and begins rubbing his shoulders.)* Margaret thinks it's wonderful that we're so friendly. Do you ever wish you'd married Margaret instead of me? Do you, Alfred?

ALFRED: Margaret? Margaret *who?*

EMILY: You've forgotten so quickly! I thought you'd remember…everything. *(She laughs, looks at Will.)*

MARGARET: I remember everything, Alfred. *My* mind's just fine.

ALFRED: Then what went on in the cellar, Margaret? I know that "cellar" and "door" combine to form the finest sound the English language can produce, "cellar door," but what's the truth of it, eh? You and Bruce? Was it you and my brother Bruce? Bollicky? Bare-assed? Starkers? Will caught you, doing it? Didn't he?

MARGARET: It was Will and me. Our first time.

WILL: Margaret!

MARGARET: I never wanted to. He forced me. In the cellar. On the old tied-up papers. He thought I did it too easily. We waited nearly two-and-a-half years. He pawed me for two-and-a-half years, but it was still too soon…

WILL: She *enjoyed* it, for Christ's sakes! You ever hear of a woman, first time, who enjoyed it?

WILL: *(To Emily, who is smiling.)* You should have seen her, after that. Couldn't get it enough. Scared me. She did. Scared the hell out of me. One day she was perfectly normal, the next day: like an animal. I couldn't believe it. I think she's a nympho.

(Alfred laughs. Will yells to Alfred.)

WILL: She is! You think it's a picnic living with one of them? You try it, pal. Every time you walk through the door, she's wearing another silk god-damn bathrobe. The place stank of perfume all the time. The French perfumes weren't good enough. Not for *her* kind.

EMILY: Indian, right?

WILL: *(Looking down to Emily.)* Huh?

EMILY: Indian.

WILL: Right, she moved on to them Indian smells: patchouli. You can die from that stuff there. Couldn't get her to get dressed for more'n three years. She just kept changing from one bathrobe to another. On and off, on and off. It was embarrassing. Think about it, Alfred. Nice little house…looks normal enough, right. But right behind the door, in a bathrobe, there's a *machine* waiting! She's never had it enough. Never satisfied. It was wicked awful. Can you imagine working twelve hours, then coming home to *that?*

(Alfred laughs. Emily laughs as well. Alfred raises his hand and shushes Emily. Will looks to him again.)

WILL: You think it's funny, huh? I shoulda left the rotten two of you on the sofa. Maybe you don't believe it, Emily, but I saw 'em with my own eyes. Your wonderful Alfred was in the house no more'n a half hour and they were *right there*…right on the sofa.

MARGARET: That is a terrible lie.

WILL: Same place. I bought that sofa with the first money I ever earned after I married the bitch.

MARGARET: That is a terrible lie, Wilbur Lynch. That is a terrible lie.

WILL: I saw you. That sofa means nothing to her. The rotten bitch! It means nothin' to her. That sofa has been *sacred* to me. That's right: sacred! Means nothin' to either one of them. She would flop every man in Wakefield on my sofa if I didn't stop her.

ALFRED: You're really something, Will. *(Laughing again.)* Will was…watching. Will's a watcher, Emily. A keyholer.

MARGARET: I never know what he's talking about. I never do. The man has the most unthinkable, most unspeakable ideas…Dirty mind, Alfred. Filthy, dirty mind…

WILL: I got eyes, sister! I know what I saw!

MARGARET: It was fifteen years ago. He had no business sneaking in like that after all that time gone. He didn't come home to sleep for nearly six months. I didn't have any married life with Will at all. You know what I mean? None. I wasn't married to you, Will. Not now, not then. It's all in your mind.

EMILY: I haven't heard anybody say "married life" for years.

MARGARET: It's true!

EMILY: I'd certainly like to think you've cured him, Margaret. I hate to think of taking him home…not cured.

MARGARET: Taking *who* home?

EMILY: Alfred. He's been suffering for years now. Alfred isn't excitable. He doesn't…get excited. That's why he had to see you, Margaret: You're Alfred's stiffest memory.

ALFRED: I think that'll be about enough.

EMILY: He's been successful in every other way.

ALFRED: I said that's enough!

EMILY: It never seemed to worry Alfred as much as it worried me. *(Pauses.)* I felt…guilty. Alfred has a special talent for that: making other people feel guilty. *(Pauses.)* It's quite a treat for me to see you this way, Alfred. Eyes closed, huddled, small. I wonder what it was I thought you were.

ALFRED: Emily had a virgin birth. *(Pauses.)* The day she was born she was a virgin. *(Pauses.)* That was it for Emily. One day. *(Pauses.)* Emily thinks a chaste woman is a moving target. *(Pauses.)* Emily was a child molester.

EMILY: Too bad you grew up.

WILL: We had one of them right here in Wakefield.

ALFRED: A virgin or a grown-up?

WILL: A child molester. Looked a lot like you, Alfred…Same slanty eyes, same hunched back.

ALFRED: It's hard for me to sit still for your rapid-fire slashing wit, Will.

MARGARET: Little girl. Gave her away at birth. Up in New Hampshire. Gave her away. Probably better. *(Pauses.)* She doesn't have to grow up with the shame. *(Pauses.)* That's the worst, don't you think? *(Pauses.)* The shame.

EMILY: *Your* daughter, right, Alfred? Had to be, right. Your…little girl.

ALFRED: I was just a kid. High school. Will and Margaret had broken up. Will was off with my friend Richard's sister, Ruby…She was a cheerleader, Emily.

EMILY: F.

ALFRED: By God, Emily, you are really something.

EMILY: Jeez!

ALFRED: Margaret got pregnant. Mine. I got frightened. I ran. *(Pauses.)* I heard they'd married…these two…Will and Margaret. They were married by the time the little girl was born. I heard they put the child up for adoption…in New Hampshire. *(Pauses: to Margaret.)* Did he know? Did you tell him she was mine?

MARGARET: *He knew! He knew!* He couldn't *stand* it. *Couldn't stand it!* He promised it would be all right…when I married him. He promised me!… *(To Will.) You promised me, Will. You did! (To Alfred.)* He couldn't stand knowing she wasn't his…his own. He made me give her away, up in New Hampshire, near Keene…there's a home up there for that sorta thing…I didn't want to. He made me…

WILL: I thought…with my own son living with his mother and all…never seeing me…I thought I could… *(Sobs.)* I couldn't. I couldn't stand having her in the same house with me…

MARGARET: I always forgave you, Alfred, for running…away…from me and all. You had your right to try to become somebody and you did and I'm proud of you.…I understood…

WILL: *(Sobbing.)* Oh, God help me…

ALFRED: You open your mouth, Will! You open your mouth and you tell me the words that make this all straight and make this all clear, once and for all…*Will!*

WILL: *(Monotone; absolutely clear.)* I…am…so…unhappy.

EMILY: What was the little girl's name, Margaret? *(No response.)* Margaret? *(No response.)* Margaret?

MARGARET: I named her Elsa, but I called her Lorali. I wanted to keep her, but he wouldn't let me…

WILL: *(Whispered.)* Margaret…

MARGARET: He didn't think it was manly to raise somebody else's child. He wanted his own…wanted me to give him his own children. We tried…

WILL: *(Weeping.)* Margaret…

MARGARET: We couldn't. We tried, but we couldn't…His own son, Will, Jr., he never ever came around…visited…He hated Will. We kept a room for him, but he never slept in it. Not one night. Never…

WILL: *(Whispers.)* Margaret…

MARGARET: I never thought in my entire life I would ever speak about this again… *(Pauses.)* Will and I have blood between us…Brother and sister, husband and wife. We didn't find out for sure until after we were married…after we tried… *(Pauses.)* Blood tests, specialists, Mass. General

Hospital, the best, spared no expense, the best money could buy, but it didn't matter... *(Pauses.)* Brother and sister, husband and wife... Everybody in town's known for years. I don't know why you're pretending not to, Alfred. I'm sure you have your reasons... *(Pauses.)* Alfred's little girl, Elsa...I called her Lorali because I think a special little girl should have a special-sounding name, don't you? We gave her away... up the Newburyport Turnpike, up in New Hampshire... Probably better. She doesn't have to grow up with the shame. *(Pauses.)* That's the worst. Don't you think? The shame. *(Pauses.)* Lucky.

(Silence Alfred's head is bowed now. He may be weeping. Will's head bows during Margaret's small litany. Emily moves to Margaret and touches her shoulders. Margaret pulls back from her.)

MARGARET: Don't. *(Pauses; straight at Emily.)* I don't need that...Not now. *(Pauses.)* Not anymore. *(Moves to sofa: sits.)* Tell them, Will. *(No response.)* Will?

WILL: I didn't, goddammit, I didn't! *(Pauses.)* I swear to you. *(Pauses.)* I didn't. *(Head drops.)* I did. I killed your brother.

EMILY: Finally... *(Pauses.)* Alfred?

ALFRED: Yes.

WILL: I had to. You would have done the same thing, Alfred. Anyone would have. I had to. I did it. I killed your brother. I, Wilbur M. Lynch, strangled and killed Bruce B. Webber. Right there where you're sitting. By the sofa. I didn't mean to...I mean, I didn't plan it or nothin'. It just happened. I started screaming and so did he and Margaret started pissing and moaning and I put my hands on his throat and started squeezing. *(Pauses.)* It happened so *fast!* His eyes rolled up into his head and he started pullin' at his own chest and gasping and all. He had a heart attack, Alfred. It was some scene. I pull my hands away...he falls on his back, chest up in the air. No noise either. He's dead and it's all my fault...My fault. It wasn't that she didn't tell me. We talked about it. I promised I wouldn't butt in...I just couldn't help myself...I promised her that she could have somebody. I mean, deep down, I never ever really thought that she should have to live like some kind of nun or something...I did promise...but when I actually, in the flesh, saw her...doin' it...I got real crazy, Alfred. I never wanted to love her as much as I did...as much as I do. I do. I do.

EMILY: Love in Wakefield is truly wonderful. Quaint. New Englandy. Makes me want to eat a lobster.

MARGARET: You shut up! You shut your mouth! You don't belong here! You don't belong here! *You don't belong here! (Margaret is weeping.)*

EMILY: Alfred was quite successful once. Came back here…to Wakefield…for truth and beauty. You're the beauty, Will's the truth. *(Pauses.)* You two certainly cured his old problem: never saw his lids so low, so long. *(Pauses.)* Well…there it is, Alfred: the confession. I've kept my end of the bargain…Alfred: I've helped. Now all we have to do is punish the criminal and we can go home. Not that I haven't learned to love it here. I— *(Sees Alfred.)* What is it, Alfred? Alfred?

ALFRED: My father? He's really alive, isn't he? He's really not dead, is he?

MARGARET: We tried to tell you. We didn't know you didn't know…I mean, we thought you were kidding us. How could you not remember?

ALFRED: Is he in pain? *(Rubs his eyes again; squints.)*

MARGARET: Worse. The worst: He's silly. How could you not remember? He's been up there for years…Him, all of them…Your father is old, Alfred. He's failing.

ALFRED: Yes. *(Pauses.)* Silly. Perfect. I put him there, Emily. I did that… *(Pauses; stands. He looks at Will.)* I managed to forget…somehow. I did. *(Pauses. Rising; to Will.)* Will? Can't seem to get it up, eh, Will? Just don't seem to have the courage, eh, Will?

WILL: Don't know why. There's nothing to just staying alive like this. Nothing! I've been waiting for you, Alfred. Waiting a long time. Waiting for you to come home, Alfred…punish me. I tried myself…to kill myself. I've kept a gun in the night table…ever since…I…can't do it… I'm…afraid.

ALFRED: I'm home, Will. I've come home.

WILL: When?

EMILY: When what, Will?

WILL: I've got to be punished. Alfred's got to punish me…

EMILY: Oh, right. It's untidy, eh, Will? We've got to tidy things up… *(Sees Alfred, whose head is bowed again.)* Alfred? Will's waiting.

MARGARET: Alfred, please! It's got to stop…

EMILY: Are you protecting Will, Margaret? Why? What the hell do you want with him? You hate Will. Now, please think, Margaret. There has been a crime and there has to be a punishment. That's the way things are. Somebody's got to feel responsible here. This man wants to die. This man *deserves* to die!

WILL: It's true. I do. I really do.

EMILY: I think the decision should be yours, really, Margaret. After all, Alfred and I are…outsiders…this thing between you and Will is a family matter…

MARGARET: Please…

EMILY: Should Alfred punish Will?

WILL: Yes.

MARGARET: I don't know.

EMILY: Think…

MARGARET: Please…

EMILY: Think…

MARGARET: DO IT! Just leave me alone! Leave me out of it!

ALFRED: *(Looking up, staring at Margaret.)* Perfect.

MARGARET: Please, Alfred…

EMILY: You make a statement, Margaret. You can't be left out of it. You're in it!

MARGARET: I can't.

ALFRED: YOU OPEN YOUR MOUTH AND YOU TALK, YOU DUMB COW!!!

MARGARET: *(Stops; turns.)* ALL RIGHT!

ALFRED: What, Margaret?

MARGARET: I want Will to die.

(Will laughs.)

MARGARET: I do. I really do. *(To Will, with deep hatred; yells.) It's what you said you wanted, Will! (To Alfred.)* I do. I really do. *(To Will, with deep love; softly.)* I believe you now, Will. I do. I really do. *(She stops beside Will: Margaret on the floor below; her face next to Will, who is tied above, on the landing.)* I really do.

ALFRED: *(Rubbing his eyes against the sting of the brightly lit room.)* Yes. I thought so. *(Looks at Will.)* Been waiting a long time, haven't you, Will? I should have come home years ago…settled all this.

WILL: When?

ALFRED: When what, Will?

WILL: You've got to kill me, Alfred. You promised.

ALFRED: I what?

WILL: Promised. You said you'd punish the killer.

ALFRED: I said that? I said I'd "punish the killer"? I doubt it, Will. That doesn't sound like me at all. Not my style…

WILL: I have to be punished, Alfred. You have to kill me.

EMILY: But you just were, Will. Margaret just killed you.

MARGARET: What are you saying?

EMILY: It was a stunning show of grace, Margaret. Of strength and grace... and of love.

WILL: I have to be punished, Alfred...

ALFRED: Punishing you would be like taking a book from a blind man. You, Wilbur Lynch, are not only a blind man, you're also a dead horse, and never let it be said that I, Alfred L. Webber, ever beat such a beast as you.

WILL: When, Alfred?

ALFRED: My mind. Guess I'll have to visit my pa now. It's time for that. Better late than never.

WILL: When, Alfred?

ALFRED: When *what*, Will? You just won't *quit*, will you?

WILL: I have to be punished, Alfred.

MARGARET: Will?

(Will stares at Margaret a moment. She takes his face in her hands.)

MARGARET: I forgive you, Will. I do. I believe you, now. I believe you and I forgive you. I do.

(She kisses Will on the lips and runs up the staircase past him, into the bedroom, exiting the room. Will looks after her a moment, faces front, bows his head.)

ALFRED: It's Pa's turn now, Emily. My pa... *(Pauses.)* I'm going to have to visit him... *(Pauses.)* He's failing. My father's failing. He's an old man, Emily: mine.

(A gunshot sounds offstage, upstairs. Will is dead. Margaret's scream, offstage. There is a silence. A second gunshot. The sound of Margaret's body on the floor, offstage. Margaret is dead.)

EMILY: Oh...my...God...

ALFRED: Oh...my...dear...sweet...God. My God...

(Emily's and Alfred's eyes meet.)

ALFRED: *(He walks backwards to wall; back against it, he speaks.)* My...fault.

(He is silent. Tableau. The lights fade to black.)

The play is over.

Paris, Waterford, Providence, Pittsburgh, New York City, Gloucester—
1971–1978

Our Father's Failing

For Jean-Paul Delamotte.

THE PEOPLE OF THE PLAY

SAM: Ancient, white-haired, thin.
PA: Ancient, white-haired, thin.
ALFRED: Forties, thin, receding elegance.
EMILY: Forties, thin, receding elegance.

THE PLACE OF THE PLAY

Alternating between the porch and backyard of the asylum, and the living room of the Wakefield, Massachusetts, house.

THE TIME OF THE PLAY

End of fall.

Our jealousy on seeing children appear and enjoy life, when we are about to part with life, makes us all the more grudging and strict with them. We resent their stepping on our heels as if to urge us to be gone. And if we are made afraid because, truthfully, it is in the order of things that children can exist and can live, only at the expending of our existences and our lives, then we really should not get mixed up in this business of being fathers.

—Montaigne

Our Father's Failing

ACT I
SCENE I

Asylum. Sunday, dawn. Stage in darkness. Three sharp knocks are heard. Same sound will precede each scene of play. First words of play—Sam's—are heard.

SAM: Relax! It's not like you're starting fresh. Just pickin' up where you left off. Relax!

(Lights to full, suddenly. Two ancient men, Pa and Sam, seated on asylum porch, on rocking chairs. Screen door visible behind them, also partly boarded window. Possible to see figures hiding behind screen or window. Building oversized. Top and side edge not visible on stage. But for essential shrubs, porch, chairs and broken-off flagpole, sense of infinite space all around. Sam and Pa dressed in woolen robes against chill.)

SAM: Are you relaxed?

PA: Your tellin' me to relax is gettin' me nervous, Sam. We've gotta find out why Alfred's coming here, Sam. We've gotta have a plan.

SAM: Dangerous for a man your years to get excited. Think about pulmonary strangulation, heart attack, and stroke. Think about spontaneous pneumothorax.

PA: Well, now…that calms me right down. Thinking about pulmonary strangulation is the most calmin' thing I've thought about all day! I've gotta admit that now that I'm thinkin' about heart attack and stroke, I'm…well…almost tranquil. *(Pauses.)* You're so dumb, you don't know how stupid you are! Sometimes your ignorance astounds me!

SAM: Nothin' astounds *me* anymore. I've seen it all. *(Pauses; looks around.)* Where's the crow? Where's the goddamn crow???

PA: Where's the what?

SAM: The crow! The crow! *(Looks around for crow and then to Pa.)* Sure didn't take your Alfred long ta cause trouble, huh? Haven't heard buzzin' around Wakefield like this since the time the hornets got into the mollusk conch.

PA: What mollusk conch?

SAM: The one I use'ta hold up ta my ear ta hear the ocean.

PA: Buzzing?

SAM: Hornets.

PA: Hornets don't buzz. Bees buzz.

SAM: Hornets buzz. Believe you me, hornets buzz. *(Pauses.)* You see the *Item*?

PA: What for?

SAM: *(Reading.)* Says here "Alfred L. Webber"—your son—is givin' out "…a yearly scholarship to the top graduating Wakefield High senior—male or female—who intends to enter the field of real estate." *(Pauses.)* A thousand a year. Imagine that.

(Note: From time to time, it will be possible to see Alfred behind either the screen of the screen door or the glass of the window, peering out from the inside, eavesdropping on Pa and Sam. This might be a possible point in the play to introduce the image. Caution must be employed. The image must be extremely subtle. In this first instance, the audience should not be able to discern who it is they are seeing, just that someone is present in the house and is spying.)

PA: Male or female?

SAM: It's gotta be one or the other, right?

PA: That a statement or a question?

SAM: I'll let that one slide, too. *(Reads.)* "This year's prize was awarded to Arthur Goldberg." Goldberg? Must be newcomers.

PA: Enter the field of real estate?

SAM: That's what it says here.

PA: Lemme see that! *(Grabs paper; reads date.)* This paper's three weeks old!

SAM: *(Takes paper again; reads.)* News is news.

PA: A field of real estate. I get it. A humorous coded message.

SAM: He personally bestowed the award to Goldberg. Wellll, look at that: The award's in your name.

PA: I can read.

SAM: But you're not dead yet.

PA: Huh?

SAM: Awards have to be named for dead people. Like the Nobel, or the Pulitzer, or the Oscar, or the Emmy…

PA: Emmy who?

SAM: *Nobel* who? *Pulitzer* who? *Oscar* who? Who really knows? They were people…they had major money…and they passed on.

PA: "Field of real estate" is a joke. Can't you see? Alfred planted a joke in the *Item* to let us know he's finally comin' up here…that he's in touch. That's a joke, ya jerk!

SAM: What's a joke?

PA: Field of real estate.

SAM: That's a joke?

PA: Like a jam of raspberries. A drawing of curtains.

SAM: Those are jokes?

PA: If he's planning to open up that certain can of beans, we're screwed. Sam, we need a plan.

SAM: Peas.

PA: Huh?

SAM: Can of peas. You said beans.

PA: And if I wanted to say "peas," I woulda *said* "peas"! You've got the brains of a peanut butter and marshmallow fluff sandwich. *(Pauses.)* I'm hungry. What time is it?

SAM: I was just pointing out that Alfred's causing quite a commotion for a boy his age.

PA: He's no boy anymore.

SAM: He have an operation you didn't mention?

PA: Ho, ho, ho. Ho, ho, ha, ha, ho.

SAM: You know what they say: "Lightning never strikes once, but it strikes again."

PA: Who says that?

SAM: Protestants! Protestants say that all the time! If you'd only pay attention sometimes to what people are sayin', you'd hear! You would, ya know!

PA: Why don't you go somewhere?

SAM: Like where?

PA: Like away.

SAM: I will, I certainly will. And when I go, I know how I'm goin', too. Wanna try listening? Out route one-twenty-eight, Lynnfield way…

PA: When I grow a head under my arm is when I'll listen to that one again! Been listenin' to that one sixty-one years now…

SAM: But I never finished!

PA: 'Cause you *can't* finish! 'Cause you ain't got the stuff to finish *with!* You'll *never* finish!

SAM: I think I'll take a little walk…a stroll…a little promenade…a sashay… *(Pauses.)* Alone. *(Pauses.)* Some people are unable to do any or all of the above-mentioned.

PA: Ho ho. Some rapid-fire slashing wit. Ho ho ho.

SAM: Anything you might want from me before I shoot on up ahead?

PA: Yuh. There is. One thing.

SAM: What?

PA: A question.

SAM: Fire away. *(Smiles.)* This'll be rich. *(Pauses.)* I'm ready.

PA: What crow?

SAM: Hmmm?

PA: What crow?

SAM: The crow. The crow.

PA: I don't remember any crow around here.

SAM: He crows every mornin'…

PA: You're outa your mind…

SAM: That's beside the point.

PA: There ain't no crow.

SAM: He gets woken up by a crow every mornin' and he don't know it. And he's callin' *me* dumb and stupid.

PA: A crow?

SAM: A crow.

PA: What's he sound like?

SAM: You're askin' me what a crow sounds like? That's a question that needs to be answered? *(Pauses.)* Like a crow. Cock-a-doodle-doo.

PA: Cock-a-doodle-doo, huh?

SAM: *(Realizes.)* Awww!

PA: Cock-a-goddam-doodle-doo, eh, Sammy?

SAM: Awwwwwwww!

PA: Goddam-cock-a-goddam-doodle-cock-a-doo, eh, Sammy-boy?

SAM: Stop your gloatin'!

PA: I ain't gloatin'. Your memory loss ain't ever my victory.

SAM: No laughin', either.

PA: I ain't laughin'. Nothing funny about the aged, the miserable, or the pathetic.

SAM: No wonder my mind is crackin'. Trapped in an insane asylum, day in, day out, with a nut like you. *(Pauses.)* You are the worst. The absolute worst.

PA: I know the worst. The absolute worst. He's still blamin' me for his mother, that's what. Still holding it against me.

SAM: He ain't still blamin' you.

PA: He'll remember every detail.

SAM: Not *me*. I don't remember *any* detail.

PA: He'll probably have the police crawling around here…probably have us right into court.

SAM: My mind's been foggy for about thirty years now.

PA: That's exactly how long it's been: thirty years.

SAM: Yuh, I must be blockin' it out.

PA: We need an ace of a plan if Alfred's gonna admit why he's here…what he's really looking for.

SAM: An ace?

PA: An ace. You got a pencil?

SAM: What for?

PA: Our ace. You'll forget without a pencil. A man your age forgets. You're a hundred.

SAM: I am like hell! I'm only ninety-three.

PA: Get a pencil.

SAM: *(Produces pencil and pad.)* Okay, shoot.

PA: First, you be me. That'll shake him up. Destroy his guard. Make him speak what's really on his mind without a cover-up. You pretend to be me. Okay?

SAM: You mean, "Hiya, Alfred, I'm your pa"? That kind of you-be-me? Yuh. That'll probably work.

PA: That'll never work. I'll go deaf right after that.

SAM: Deaf?

PA: Deaf. Stone deaf.

SAM: Deaf?

PA: *(Feigning deafness.)* Eh?

SAM: That's older than Kelsey's nuts. That'll never work. Deaf is a deuce. We need an ace. We need something else.

PA: Then we might hit him with an elm tree. He always loved elm trees.

SAM: We hit him with a *what?*

PA: That's a manner of speaking. The elm trees are dead.

SAM: You know, sometimes I think you're less coherent than I am.

PA: I know. It worries me.

SAM: How about my "Way outa town" puzzle?

PA: Your "Way outa town" puzzle is way out of the question, Sam…

SAM: Give me a break.

PA: Not *that* one. No way.

SAM: The Widow O'Brien Scandal.

PA: The what scandal?

SAM: You tell him you lived with the Widow O'Brien. That you squired her daughter.

PA: You mean "sired," not "squired."

SAM: Whatever. Just tell him.

PA: *Tell* him? That'll work. There's our wild card. Even better than an ace!

SAM: I have my moments. They don't call me "Old Sam the Fox" for nothing.

PA: You mean "Old Sam the Limp" don'tcha?

SAM: Thanks a lot.

PA: You forget that, too?

SAM: Thanks. Really. Thanks.

PA: Crane's Beach. I love a dune.

SAM: Unlimited cruelty… *(Pauses.)* Tom? It's been so many years now, I'm not sure I remember—I'm not really sure what really happened. Or even when…

PA: Her name was Susan. She was a Congregationalist. Dark eyes. You were on the dunes. Crane's Beach.

SAM: I was in the truck…

PA: *(Suddenly angry.)* Don't open the door I think you're opening, Sam.

SAM: I never actually saw…

PA: That is a door in history that's long since closed and locked, Sam.

SAM: Well, I gotta crack it open for a peek, Tom. Before Alfred does.

PA: Alfred is never *ever ever* to know for sure, right, Sam? I've got your sacred word, right, Sam?—no talk to Alfred or Emily.

SAM: You've got my sacred word.

PA: Okay I'll help you remember. You begin. You tell me what you recall.

SAM: Okay. Here's what I remember. I'm in the truck nibbling my cruller. You go into the house to see if the brisket's ready or whether we should hit a couple of more stops first. I'm sittin', kind of in a daydream, when I hear an awful commotion. You run out, white-faced, and you tell me that you found Sophie and Willie-Boy sacked up together in your big bed and that you lost your marbles and went into a terrible crime-of-passion state and that you…well…used a knife.

PA: Alfred's Boy Scout knife. I killed them.

SAM: Dead.

PA: Dead.

SAM: Jesus! *Then,* what'd we do? I hate age. I really do. I used to be able to lie with complete ease. Now look at me. I'm a wreck!

PA: Alfred came in and we gave him the stuff to bury and then we sent him off to play with your nephew…Lynchie.

SAM: What stuff?

PA: The knife…Alfred's Boy Scout knife.

SAM: Oh, right. The Boy Scout knife…

PA: And his baseball cap and the bedsheets, all stained from the crime and the wiping up…

SAM: *(Weeping.)* What a thing.

PA: If you start your weeping again, Sam, I swear to God I will make your life miserable…

SAM: *(Looks up; amazed.)* That's painting both the pot and the kettle black, ain't it?

PA: I'm tired of talkin' on this subject, Sam: Pay attention.

SAM: I am.

PA: We burned out the room; and the police and the paper agreed with us that it'd just be better to cover up the clandestine and filthy part of it and let life go on. They all let it pass as though it was the fire that did it… punishment was given out all around: They were…well…dead…and we agreed to live up here…And that's it. The facts have been stated, Sam. You remember any of it, or is your brain too eaten away by disease?

SAM: If you were the Liberty Bell and I was Philadelphia, I still wouldn't dignify a crack like that! *I* remember! *I* remember! I only needed refreshing.

PA: Oh, really?

SAM: Oh, really! I remember each and every detail like it was the back of my hand. First the firemen came…Lazzaro's oversexed son, Alan…and then the new motorcycle cop—what's his name?

PA: Swede MacShane.

SAM: Swede MacShane.

PA: He pitched a great game against Melrose—

SAM: He sure did. Didn't give up a single hit till the top of the eighth…

PA: There's nothing to worry about, Sam. What was done was fair and forgotten. And forgiven. Everybody understood. *(Pauses.)* Sam?

SAM: What?

PA: Imagine if we'd just let them go on with their clandestine and filthy meetings and sex…This isn't Boston, ya know. This is Wakefield.

SAM: I'm just tryin' to get the story straight. No more, no less.

PA: They say Swede's brother, Mouse, used to sleep with his sister?

SAM: Mouse slept with Swede's sister?

PA: With Mouse's sister.

SAM: Are you kidding me? Mouse slept with his own sister?

PA: She was good lookin'…

SAM: Mouse slept with his own sister? Jesus God! If these old lips could ever talk… *(Pauses.)* Wait a minute! Mouse never had any sister! He was adopted. He was an Indian! He never had any sister.

PA: *(After a long pause.)* I think you're right. *(Pauses.)* Old age is no picnic, Sam.

SAM: Picnic? You hungry?

PA: I said that aloud, if you'd only listen.

SAM: Fluffernutter?

PA: I *asked* ya for one maybe ten minutes ago!

SAM: *(Starts to exit. Stops. Turns to Pa.)* On pumpernickel?

PA: If you'd unwax your ears, you'd understand!

SAM: I hope *you* understand *this:* If I had my choice, I would never live with you...waxy ears or not!

PA: If I had my choice of living with a toad or living with you, I would definitely hop for the toad. *(He laughs.)* Hop for the toad! *(He laughs again.)*

SAM: How do I endure your rudeness? *(Exits.)*

PA: Because you're waiting to cash in on my money.

SAM: *(Reenters immediately.)* Me? Money? Me? Ah, well now, sure—there it is—the lurking truth. *(Pauses.)* Alfred, yes. Me, nuts. Alfred is coming for the money. I didn't want to leap to that before, champ, but that is certainly what's been right up there in the back of my mind, Alfredwise! And I'm glad it's out in the open now, too. I really am!

PA: Money is the *last* thing he'd want.

SAM: Course he wants our money. Why else the hell do you think he'd take to troublin' himself to climb up here? To drink a whiskey with us? We don't drink. To smoke a cigar with us? We don't smoke.

PA: Maybe he's lookin' to triple-date.

SAM: Sometimes you ain't funny at all.

PA: First off, it ain't *our* money. It's my money.

SAM: I didn't say anything different.

PA: Oh yes ya did...

SAM: Oh no I didn't...

PA: *(Yells.)* Ya did!

SAM: *(Yells.)* I didn't!

PA: *(Screams.)* Did!

SAM: *(Screams.)* Didn't!

> *(Sam exits into house, slamming door. Pa sits alone. Sam reenters with fluffernutter sandwich, which Pa eats in one chomping move. Sam sits in rocking chair, silently, as does Pa, in opposite chair. They stare straight out, rocking back and forth. Each man is furious with the other. Pa finally breaks the silence after he first stops rocking.)*

PA: Ain't a one of my so-called friends hanging around for anything but my kickin' off, is there? Well, I can promise you one thing, Sam: You ain't seein' a penny of *my* money, so you might as well just knock me down and take whatever coins there are in these old pockets of mine.

SAM: Ain't no coins in your pockets…

PA: That's all you got to say?

SAM: I might add how I feel about that filthy rotten mouth of yours: I don't like it much, I might add that. I might just add how you sometimes break my old heart…

PA: Only thing even come close to breaking *my* heart was your grotesquely ugly brother.

SAM: Which brother?

PA: Willie-Boy.

SAM: We were twins.

PA: You walked right into that one, Sam.

SAM: That supposed to be a joke?

PA: You walked right into it!

SAM: You think that's a joke?

PA: Walked into it, hook, line, and sinker.

SAM: A joke is a sacred thing to me. I have lived my life lookin' for the perfect joke. A joke, for me, is an ideal, a way of life, a religion, a great blind date: a sacred thing. What you just mouthed ain't nothin' *like* a joke. The midget and the monkey: *That's* a joke…

PA: I heard it.

SAM: The raccoon and the chicken farmer's niece: That's a joke.

PA: I heard it, and I didn't get it.

SAM: The mongoose and the Mexican chef's boa constrictor… *(Sam is giddy with laughter.)*

PA: I heard it, I got it, I hated it.

SAM: *(Angrily.)* The Polish dancer and the pink whale.

PA: Nothin'.

SAM: The Italian priest and the ice-cream freezer…

PA: Pure smut.

SAM: The swimmer and the loan shark…

PA: C'mon, will ya?

SAM: The molester and the stunted linebacker…

PA: Sad to see…

SAM: The groundhog and the skinny man…

PA: *(He quietly chortles.)* Yuh…
      (Sam waits, watches, gurgles laughter. Pa laughing.)

PA: That was a good one.

(Silence. They rock in their chairs awhile.)

SAM: You're gonna love Alfred, all right. I can hardly wait to see your face all lit with lovelight.

PA: Save it for a song, will ya?

SAM: Oh, sure, for you it'll be just like lookin' in an old mirror. After all, an apple tree can't fall far from the ground.

PA: That's the truth.

SAM: What's the truth?

PA: Alfred's the only one loves me for what I am.

SAM: And what would that be?

PA: Huh?

SAM: And what would that be that he loves you for? Your warm and friendly smiles? Ain't ever seen one. Your happy, chatty conversations in the mornings? Can't say I seen one of them, either. Your fancy clothes? Would he be lovin' you for your fancy clothes? Maybe it's your breath?…

PA: Don't be bitter, Sam.

SAM: *(Building to screams.)* Bitter? Bitter? Me, bitter? Not on your rotten life am I bitter! I don't care if you get yourself conned out of your life savin's by your Alfred. I really don't!

PA: He don't want the money, Sam.

SAM: *(Yells.) I'll prove to you he does!*

PA: *(Yells.) I'll prove to you he don't!*

SAM: *(Screams.) You're on!*

PA: *(Screams.) You're on!*

    (They sit. Rock awhile.)

SAM: *(After a silence.)* Sorry I yelled. It's just that I hate to see you, you know…*do it.*

PA: Hate to see me do what? This'll be rich. Hate to see me do *what,* Sammy?

SAM: Hate to see you make such a raccoon's ass of yourself.

PA: I ain't gonna get myself engaged in this bickerin'. Not over money. And certainly not over a raccoon.

SAM: In the bushes.

PA: Huh? Animals?

SAM: Don't look now! Wait a minute! Now look. See him? Alfred! *(To Pa.)* You just shut up, now.

PA: What for?

SAM: Ace number one is about to be dealt! Where's your memory? We have a plan! *(Calls.)* Alfred! Over here!

(Alfred enters.)

SAM: Hiya, Alfred.

(Alfred looks from one old man to the other, staring at them, silently smiling.)

SAM: Yup, it's me, your old pa. *(Moving to Alfred.)* Don't you recognize me, Alfred? It's me. It's really me. *(To Alfred.)* You haven't changed a bit, Alfred. Twenty—thirty years older, but that's all. *(Pause.)* How do I look? *(Alfred stands staring.)*

SAM: Don't say much, do ya, Alfred?

(Alfred turns his back to men.)

ALFRED: *(Without turning to face Pa.)* Hello, Pa. You look great.

SAM: Musta been a hard climb up. Up the hill, huh?

ALFRED: You're a sight for sore eyes...

SAM: Wicked awful climb, huh? *(Smiles.)* How come it took you thirty years?... *(Pauses.)* Good thing we didn't plan supper.

ALFRED: You haven't changed a bit, Sam...still full of spunk. *(Faces Sam; smiles.)* How's Roxy?

SAM: You knew it was me all along, didn'tcha?

ALFRED: I never forget a mouth, Sam. *(Smiles.)*

SAM: I ain't closin' it just yet, sonnyboy. I got more aces to play. Crap! What's next?

ALFRED: Hello, Pa. You look great. You're a sight for sore eyes. You haven't changed a bit.

PA: *(Pawing the air.)* Who's there?

ALFRED: *(To Pa.)* What're you doin'?

PA: What say?

ALFRED: *(To Sam.)* What's the matter with him?

SAM: Deaf.

ALFRED: Deaf?

SAM: Deaf.

PA: Deaf.

SAM: Went deaf just a short time ago. If you had been here earlier, he mighta heard you. *(Pauses.)* It's a pity you're late, Alfred.

ALFRED: How late?

SAM: Thirty years. How's that for late?

ALFRED: *(As if deaf.)* What's that?

SAM: *(Loudly.)* How's that for late?

ALFRED: You walked right into that one.

PA: *(Laughs.)* You haven't changed *too* much, son.

ALFRED: Not too much, I guess...Been down by the old Elm Street house.

SAM: Seen the… *(Loudly.)* ELM TREES?

ALFRED: Elm trees are gone. Front of the house. Beetles, prob'ly, huh? Musta finally killed 'em.

SAM: Just as well. Elm trees give off poison gas. Just as well they're gone. You live around elm trees long enough, you die.

(Pa and Sam laugh.)

SAM: Four aces.

ALFRED: Does he mean the singing group?

SAM: I wish you'd seen the beetles, Alfred. Seen 'em at work…

ALFRED: Does he mean John, Paul, George, and Ringo?

SAM: You're in a pickle, Alfred. And I know a way out.

PA: Exactly what card are you playing, Sam?

SAM: I repeat: You're in a pickle, Alfred. And I know a way out.

PA: Uh-uh, Sam.

SAM: C'mon…

PA: He's been tryin' this one-liner on me for sixty-one years now, Alfred. It's the lowest.

SAM: I am not talkin' ta you, ya know. I am talkin' to your son! *(To Alfred.)* If you wanted to end it…elsewhere, Alfred, I do happen to know a way out of this pickle… *(Pauses.)* If and when I go, it's the way I want to go… *(Pauses.)* You know what I mean, Alfred? *(Pauses.)* First I'm going to head out one-twenty-eight, Lynnfield way, then up the Newburyport Turnpike: route one. Then straight up to New Hampshire. *(Pauses.)* You know where to go after that, Alfred?

PA: Close it down, Sam.

SAM: I didn't finish.

PA: Sam…

SAM: I almost finished.

PA: Belt it up, Sam. I'm talkin' over the deal.

SAM: God damn. *(Pauses.)* God damn…

PA: *(To Alfred.)* How old are you now?

SAM: Ninety-three.

PA: *(To Sam.)* Not you. *(Points to Alfred.)* Him. *(To Alfred.)* You. How old?

ALFRED: Forty…ish.

SAM: His money ain't gone, ya know. He ain't spent a penny of it. It's all here somewhere.

PA: Sam!

SAM: Whoopsie!

PA: Goddamn you, Sam Lynch!

ALFRED: Fascinating.

SAM: Huh?

ALFRED: I think it's fascinating. This place. You two…The way you quibble. Like an old couple. Like a husband and wife.

SAM: What's he sayin'?

PA: What're you sayin'?

ALFRED: Quibble. Quibbling. You two. Like a couple: a husband and wife.

SAM: What the *hell's* he saying?

PA: What the *hell* are you saying?

ALFRED: I do believe our respective needles are stuck in our respective grooves… *(Smiles.)* A husband and wife…a couple…usually sexually opposed, which is to say a man and a woman…married…joined… hitched…one might even say *flying united*… *(His attitude suddenly changes.)* I think you two should know that I've forgotten nothing. Every fact, every detail, every shred of the past is at my disposal…*Laissez-moi dire tout d'abord que je ne pardonne à personne…personne! (Smiles.)* That's French. It means I don't forgive you…

PA: You're not speaking English, Alfred…

SAM: You don't forgive us for not gettin' married? Is that what you're sayin'? *(To Pa.)* Is *that* what he's sayin'? *(To Alfred.)* Is that it? *(To Pa.)* Jesus! That's it! *(To Alfred.)* Pardon *my* French, but as far as I'm concerned, I hope the Boston and Maine Railroad runs over your legs. And that's the truth.

ALFRED: I don't forgive and I don't forget. There is a very large debt owed to me…There is a very large amount that wants to be collected…

SAM: What's this now? Money, is it?

ALFRED: I don't forgive and I don't forget. You two will pay…like a husband and wife…a joint return.

PA: If that ain't the most disgusting thing I've ever heard! If you think that's a way to talk to a father, you've got rocks in your head! Play a card, Sam!

SAM: *(Stands: a proclamation.)* The Widow O'Brien Scandal!
(Sam exits into house. Alfred doesn't seem to notice that Sam has yelled what he has yelled. Instead of becoming anxious, Alfred seems calmed by Sam's exit.)

ALFRED: How ya feeling, Pa?

PA: Huh?
(Alfred goes to screen door, looks in.)

PA: What're you looking for?

ALFRED: Are we really alone?

PA: Looks that way.

ALFRED: *(Closes the solid door behind the screen door.)* How ya feeling?

PA: You closed the door.

ALFRED: I thought Sam might…ya know…be listening in. I'd like to talk.

PA: Did you hear Sam, Alfred? He screamed, "The Widow O'Brien Scandal," and then he made a sudden exit.

ALFRED: Oh, yes. I noticed that.

PA: The Widow O'Brien Scandal, Alfred. That's supposed to throw you for a loop. A major ace was played there. Think about it, Alfred. *The Widow O'Brien Scandal.*

ALFRED: Ahhh, yes. I think I remember. Wasn't she the Polish dancer with the pink whale? Or was she the swimmer who got involved with the loan shark?

(Silence.)

PA: What the hell did you come back here for?

ALFRED: An old debt, Pa. I told you.

PA: An old what?

ALFRED: *(Pauses; then quietly.)* I have to clear up an old debt.

PA: You need money?

ALFRED: *(Laughs.)* Money? Not me. Don't touch the filthy stuff.

PA: Heard you set up a scholarship in my name.

ALFRED: That's a fact.

PA: "Enter the field of real estate."

ALFRED: *(Smiles.)* Yes.

PA: That a city joke, Alfred?

ALFRED: Sir?

PA: I'm too old for this. I'll have to play another ace now…

ALFRED: I beg your pardon.

PA: How's what's'ername?

ALFRED: Who?

PA: What's'ername.

ALFRED: I don't know…

PA: How she is?

ALFRED: *Who* she is?

PA: What the hell is her name? She's medium height…

ALFRED: You're gonna have to give me a better clue.

PA: She's your wife.

ALFRED: Emily? Why did you bring her up?

PA: Yuh. That's her: Emily. Emily O'Brien, isn't it? How is she?

ALFRED: She's gone.

PA: Gone?

ALFRED: Gone.

PA: How come?

ALFRED: She threw a clock radio at me.

PA: She did?

ALFRED: Didn't reach me. *(Pauses.)* It was plugged in.

PA: Good thing it wasn't a portable.

ALFRED: That was incisive. *(Pauses.)* She must have tiptoed…into the room. *(Pauses.)* I have trouble sleeping. I don't blink.

PA: O'Brien is an ace of a name. You don't what?

ALFRED: Didn't you notice? I don't even blink.

PA: No wonder you have trouble sleeping. Isn't there risk of your eyes drying out or something?

ALFRED: I use drops.

PA: I would try to blink, if I were you. I really would.

ALFRED: I haven't blinked in thirty years. Not since my mother…passed away. Doctors say I must have been traumatized.

PA: It was rough on all of us.

ALFRED: Yuh. Rough.

PA: I heard you're stayin' back down at the old house. 'Sthat so?

ALFRED: Yuh. I'm sleeping in the upstairs room. Same as ever.

PA: I haven't been down there, even for a visit. Not since your brother Bruce…passed away. Musta traumatized me, too. Huh?

ALFRED: Musta. It was rough on all of us.

PA: Sam's family…what's'isname and his wife what's'ername…they still livin' down there?

ALFRED: Will and Margaret? They…moved.

PA: I'd love ta have a look at the old place…Wonderful memories.

ALFRED: Pretty weird.

PA: Who?

ALFRED: Bein' in my old room. I should feel bigger in it, now that I'm…you know…grown. But I don't. Opposite.

PA: I'm shrinkin' myself: 'bout four inches shorter already. Age. Hope I don't grow much shorter. Hate to end up…you know…*tiny.*

ALFRED: If that's your idea of small talk, let's drop it, okay?

PA: But I didn't start it. You started it. Lemme just ask you straight, Alfred: Why'd you come back up here, really?

ALFRED: I don't forgive you. That's exactly why I'm back here right now… 'cause I don't forgive you.

PA: *You* forgive *me?* That's a switch, ain't it?

ALFRED: How so?

PA: Don't you kinda have it switched around? Aren't *I* the one who's s'pose'ta be forgiving *you?*

ALFRED: For what?

PA: Are you kidding me? What the hell are you playing here?

ALFRED: I'm not playing anything.

PA: Wait a minute! Just wait a minute. Are you trying to tell me you're not grateful?

ALFRED: For what?

PA: *For goddamn protecting you!* That's what!

ALFRED: You're not making a lot of sense, Pa.

PA: Your mother.

ALFRED: My mother's dead, Pa. She's still dead.

PA: You don't remember, do you? Is that how you're playing it? *(Pauses; yells.)* Look at me!

ALFRED: *(Screams.) I'm looking at you!*
    (Silence.)

PA: You really don't remember, do you?

ALFRED: Remember what? Remember what?

PA: *(Calls to screen door.)* Sam!
    (Sam enters through door.)

PA: We're done with our personal family talk now, Sam.

ALFRED: Remember what?

SAM: *(Hands Pa a plate and a glass.)* Fried chicken and a beer.
    (Sam offers a pencil and a pad of paper to Alfred.)

SAM: You oughtta write this down. A man your age forgets. *(Pauses.)* Fried chicken and a beer. Twice a day. Never misses. *(Pauses.)* Keeps him fit.
    (Alfred doesn't accept paper. Sam shrugs. Smiles.)

SAM: How's what's'ername? *(To Pa.)* Her name? What's her name? Irish, isn't it?

ALFRED: Emily? What's Emily's name? You want to know what Emily's name is?

PA: That's sort of a city way of bein' angry, huh, Alfred?

SAM: Alfred's picked up a lot of city ways. *(Pauses.)* No dirt under his nails. *(Pauses.)* Probably bites 'em. *(Pauses.)* Probably files 'em. *(Pauses.)* I don't file mine. I just throw 'em away. *(Laughs.)* You picked up a lot of city ways, Alfred.

ALFRED: Remember what, Pa? Remember what?
    (Sam exits into house. Sam reenters through screen door, carrying food tray. Hands bowl to Pa.)

SAM: Here's dessert. *(To Alfred.)* One scoop vanilla, one scoop strawberry, one tablespoon hot Indian pudding, and thick hot fudge over the whole heap. *(Pauses.)* Twice a day, also. *(To Alfred.)* Keeps him fit.
(Sam pauses. Offers paper and pencil. Alfred refuses them.)

SAM: Well, Jesus, Alfred, if you're gonna be takin' care of him 'stead of me, you gotta learn the ins and the outs. *(Pauses; angrily.)* Well, who the hell did ya think's been gettin' the food in 'im all these years? Greta Garbo? Mary Pickford? Eric von Stroheim?

PA: Is she pretty?

ALFRED: Who?

SAM: What's'ername?

PA: Does she…satisfy you? Was it a…smart move…to marry her?

SAM: You can speak your piece here, Alfred. *(Pauses.)* We're…family.

PA: Did ya hear that, Alfred? *(To Sam.)* Jesus, Sam, if you're not the pathetic one. *(Pauses.)* You ain't family, Sam. Just get that crazy thought out of your head. Alfred's family, I'm family: You ain't family.

SAM: I crouch like a toad inside there for ten minutes waiting for an ace to work, and now I have to listen to this? The two of you make me sick. *(Pauses.)* The *three* of you make me sick…

PA: Shut up, Sam.

ALFRED: What three?

PA: Sam! God damn you…

ALFRED: What three, Sam?

SAM: You, your old man, your nervous wife: all in it together. Three thumbs in the pudding, three short-order cooks in the broth, three coins in the fountain…

PA: You're dealing too many cards, Sam!

ALFRED: She's been here all along, huh, Pop?

PA: Sam, I never shoulda started with the likes a you. I shoulda seen your colors sixty-one years ago! No more cards! This is a mixed deal!

ALFRED: I want an answer!

SAM: You try hanging around with the likes of yourself for sixty-one years. See how you like those particular colors! *(To Alfred.)* It's been hell, Alfred…

ALFRED: *(Sits; folded arms.)* I'm sitting and I'm waiting…Sam…Pa… *(Stares at them.)* I said I'm sitting and I'm waiting. Let's hear it…
(Pa looks at Sam; Sam looks at Pa; speaks.)

SAM: *(To Alfred.)* Oh, I'd love to tell you. Oversexed and foul-mouthed: Those are your father's main qualities. I hate to be the one to tell you, Alfred. I really do. But it's the God's honest truth. Foul-mouthed and oversexed.

He doesn't just *think* he's had 'em all; he's actually had 'em all. I know. Believe me, I know. Who do you think they run to—poor old things—after he's…used them? To me. To Sam. Safe Old Sam: That's what they call me. *(Pauses.)* Now, I'll bet you're wondering why they would call me such a thing. Why they would ever come running to old Sam. You deserve an explanation. I'm gonna tell you why. *(Pauses.)* I'm impotent, Alfred. Been impotent for sixty-one years now. *(Pauses.)* I can still actually remember the moment it hit…Laying on the beach in Ipswich. Crane's Beach.

ALFRED: When? How long has she been here?

PA: Sam? Answer Alfred.

ALFRED: *(To Sam.)* When?

SAM: Around midnight on a Tuesday. Susan…

ALFRED: *(To Sam.)* The subject is Emily.

SAM: I said "Susan." Her name was Susan. Little dark-and-darting-eyed Congregationalist. Slim and very wealthy. Just got ourselves ready…Just mounted her…when the biggest fuckin' wave you ever seen…washed right over us…

ALFRED: I said the subject was Emily! Where's Emily? Now you open your mouth and speak, Pa.

SAM: …like a ton of wet bricks…

PA: Don't worry yourself about it, Alfred…

SAM: …Drug me right off of her. You might even say that it washed us asunder…

ALFRED: *Don't worry about it?* My wife moves in with my father and I'm not supposed to worry about it?

SAM: Hoisted me up and catapulted me more'n a hundred yards. Slammed me right down on the beach, like a clean but crazed human bomb, bare-assed, right beside a nun…She was, at that point, just minding her own business, cooking weenies on an open fire….

PA: You've got to learn to face things, Alfred…Open your eyes.

SAM: Landed almost on top of her. Knocked the poor sonofabitchin' nun face down in the sand…Goddam full moon, too…

PA: It's going to be painful, Son.

SAM: Painful? I haven't had a hard-on in sixty-one years.

ALFRED: *(To Sam.)* I really think you should stop. Emily's here, right? How long? When? Answer me, goddammit!

SAM: June it was. Black June. *(Stepping in between Pa and Alfred.)* Gonna be sixty-one years this spring. *(Pauses.)* I must hold some kind of Guinness record. *(Pauses; smiles.)* Maybe I should have a party and celebrate.

ALFRED: I have never actually punched a hundred-year-old man before…

SAM: I'm ninety-three…

PA: *(Calls offstage.)* Okay, Emily, c'mon out!

SAM: Are you crazy? He's going to get violent. He threatened me. Didn't you hear him?

PA: *(Calling again.)* Emily!

SAM: Pay no attention to your father, Alfred. The man's mind is gone. Been gone for years. Now, then: She started throwing weenies at me. Flinging them wildly, out of control. There wasn't much I could do but run.

PA: Emily?

SAM: The Fourteenth Annual Sacred Blood Beach Party was a mere ten yards away. They must have thought I was just someone come to help with the weenies. Until the moon broke through the clouds. Pay attention, Alfred.

PA: Emily! Get out here!

SAM: Sixty nuns, thirty priests and two hundred deeply religious children. *(Pauses.)* Doubt if I'll ever actually have a hard-on again.
(Emily enters from inside the house. She wears an old woolen winter coat, collar up, unbuttoned. She hugs the coat closed. Alfred stares at her, backing away as she continues forward.)

SAM: Saw dozens of doctors. Even some specialists. But there's nothing you can do once it's planted in your mind. *(Pauses.)* Every time I see a decent-looking woman, I…well…feel a little urge, you might say…But then…right away…I feel the thud of weenies against my chest… *(Pauses.)* Ten or twelve thuds and I'm finished. *(Pauses.)* Might as well kill all the women, far as I'm concerned. *(Pauses; sees Emily.)* Hi, Emily. How's it going? *(Crosses to door; pauses.)* That's how it happened.
(Sam exits. Emily stands facing Alfred.)

EMILY: Hello, Alfred. *(No response.)* Aren't you going to talk to me? *(No response.)* It's not what you're thinking. Don't look so wounded. *(Pauses.)* I haven't betrayed you.
(Alfred looks down.)

EMILY: Alfred?

PA: Look at her, Alfred.
(Alfred turns away.)

PA: You cryin', Alfred? *(Pa tries to stand; cannot. Calls to screen door.)* Sam!

SAM: *(Enters immediately.)* What's the matter?

PA: Is he crying?

SAM: *(Crosses to Alfred and looks.)* Looks that way.

PA: God damn it.

> *(Alfred bolts from the stage. Silence. Pa looks after Alfred. Emily bows head. Pa looks at Emily. Sam looks at Emily. Pa and Sam turn their faces to each other. Tableau. The lights fade to black.)*

End of Act I.

ACT II
SCENE I

Asylum. Night, later. Stage in darkness. Three sharp knocks are heard. First words of the scene—Emily's—are heard.

EMILY: Open your mouth, *God damn it!* You can't just sit there, staring! Say something!

(Lights to full, suddenly. Two chairs—one a wheelchair; table with plate of cookies upon it. Emily, on pathway at trellis. Wheelchair has been turned upstage, so occupant of wheelchair faces Emily, back of chair to audience. Man in wheelchair's identity disguised from audience at this point.)

EMILY: You can't just smile and stare. Who the hell do you think you are? Buddha? *(Pauses.)*

(There is no reply. Emily walks downstage. As she does, chair swivels with her. Man in wheelchair is now revealed as Sam.)

EMILY: *(Sits on other chair.)* Nothing drives me bananas faster than smiling, staring, and silence. Will you *for Christ's sake* say something?

SAM: *(Looks up, quietly.)* Did I tell you the one about the elephant who became an Iowa University co-ed and the field of corn?

EMILY: *(After a long pause.)* The hell of it is that I actually *asked* you to speak.

SAM: You heard it?

EMILY: Yuh.

SAM: How about the Canadian pole-vaulter and the nymphomaniac?

EMILY: Heard it. Hated it.

SAM: How about the fast turtle and the slow Arab?

EMILY: Adolescent ravings.

SAM: I told you already?

EMILY: Mmmm. You did. Sorry.

SAM: How about the six Polacks and their American light bulb joke?

EMILY: *(Mimes changing an electric light bulb, one hand.)* You mean "Only one American is used to change a bulb: like this?" *(Looks at her own hand.)* Oh, my God! Now you've got *me* doing it! I think you should stop all jokes, Sam, before some people get their feelings hurt.

SAM: How about the Polish war bride and the exploding python?

EMILY: Vile. And please skip the ten-foot Pole, okay?

SAM: How about the bald soprano and the Polish Mime Opera?

EMILY: My grandmother was Polish.

SAM: You should never wait to tell a man like me a fact like that. I could've said something embarrassing.

EMILY: *(She offers Sam a cookie.)* What do you really want, Sam?

SAM: *(Eats cookie.)* Outta this mess. And I know how I'm gettin' out, too… *(Pauses; slyly.)* First I'm heading out route one-twenty-eight, Lynnfield way, and then up the Newburyport Turnpike into New Hampshire…

EMILY: *(Screams.) Sam!!!*

SAM: I've got to find out why Alfred came back…what he wants from us.

EMILY: I'd be the last one to know what he wants from anyone.

SAM: You're his wife.

EMILY: That's what I said: I'd be the last to know.

SAM: He's planning to take him back, isn't he?

EMILY: Who's planning to take whom back?

SAM: Alfred. Tommy: his father. Alfred's gonna take him back with him, isn't he? To the city. That's Alfred's plan, isn't it?

EMILY: Oh, I don't think you have to worry about *that,* Sam. *(She offers him another cookie.)*

SAM: Pardon my French, but the way I see it, *merde* has to be the word that springs to mind. *(He eats cookie in a gulp.)*

EMILY: Let me slip a fact your way, Sam. Alfred is definitely not planning to take his father away from Wakefield…not to the city, nor any place else. That's a fact.

SAM: Take him! Couldn't care less, believe you me! He don't represent nothin' more ta me than sixty-one years of hard luck and bad times. No more, no less.

EMILY: I don't know…from where I'm standing, it seems to me you two get on real well…a kind of *team*…

SAM: Sure, from where you're standin'! *(Ironic laugh.)* Don't you believe it, dolly! That's only the top layer you're lookin' at! Underneath all those smiles and backpats, there's an *iceberg* lurking! And you know what they all say: Underneath that iceberg, there's *fire!*

EMILY: I never looked at it quite that way.

SAM: Well, I'm sorry ta haveta be the one ta open your eyes, but there it is.

EMILY: Uhh, there *what* is?

SAM: The sorry truth. I wouldn't spend five minutes more in this rattrap, if I didn't gotta.

EMILY: You don't "gotta," nobody's "gotta"…

SAM: Oh, no. I'm not here for my health! Of course I gotta!

EMILY: Why? How come? How come you gotta, Sam? How come you gotta stay here…in Wakefield…cooped up with Pa? It's like you're in prison, together, isn't it?

SAM: That's about it. Yuh. You sure love snoopin', don'tcha?

EMILY: Are you?

SAM: Am I what?

EMILY: In prison?

SAM: That's for me to know and you to find out, cookie…

EMILY: Are you waiting to inherit some money? Is that it?

SAM: What money? I don't think I like your insinuendos, sweetheart!

EMILY: Ah, that's it, huh? Cash.

SAM: I wouldn't touch his rotten money, if I were on my hands and knees in the Sahara, and he had the only spare change for a Coke in the whole desert…I'd rather parch and pass out…maybe even away.

EMILY: Your just *saying* it doesn't make it so. Not enough for me.

SAM: There's *more* than enough, cupcake!

EMILY: Money?

SAM: Money.

EMILY: To go around?

SAM: You bet your sweet little derrière-ie.

EMILY: It amazes me that in practically no time I've learned to follow your thoughts. You've brought out a talent in me I didn't even know I had…

SAM: That's what they all say.

EMILY: You're quite a guy, cookie-pally-sweetheart-dolly-baby-cupcake…

SAM: So they tell me.

EMILY: You make an offer, Sam?

SAM: Sex?

EMILY: Money.

SAM: Sex for money or money for sex?

EMILY: What's the difference?

SAM: *What's the difference?* You've got to be kidding! One way, you pay me: the other…

EMILY: …You pay me. *(Smiles.)* What I had in mind was neither. I meant an offer of money for me to…well…leave.

SAM: The yard?

EMILY: The town. To stop my snooping. *(Smiles.)* What's your offer? *(There's a long pause.)* Sam?

SAM: No deals.

EMILY: Really?

SAM: No deals.

EMILY: It seems to me that something terrible is going to happen here.

SAM: I know. No deals.

EMILY: I'm sorry you're caught up in it. You're a charming fellow.

SAM: Yuh. Charm is my secret. Got me where I am today. No deals.

EMILY: *(Change of attitude.)* Okay, Sam. Let me just get right down to it. What's keeping you here? *(No reply.)* Answer me!

SAM: *(Matches her attitude.)* How about you answerin' me, Suzie! What's keepin' *you* here? Yankee hospitality? Cheap lobsters? How about you answerin' *me* for a change, huh? I wouldn't mind a fact or two.

EMILY: Want to trade off?

SAM: How so?

EMILY: Fact for fact.

SAM: I don't follow.

EMILY: We trade facts. I give you a fact...a nice big juicy one. Then you pay me back: fact for fact. Seems fair, doesn't it?

SAM: Depend on your nice big juicy one.

EMILY: Okay, let's see... *(Suddenly angry.)* Pay attention!

(Sam stares at her.)

EMILY: Once upon a time, there was a very young and very beautiful young woman of Irish persuasion, named Emily Marie O'Brien, who shall remain nameless. She was born to unknown parents; reared, as they say, in a foundling home in Boston; sent to California, for ten years, to a very special boarding school for very special *gifted* children. There, she was first told her full name by a visiting Eastern nun, who claimed to know young Miss O'Brien's natural mother, who was said to have been a nun as well. *(Pauses.)* Mine was a deeply religious family: *all nuns,* it seems. In my mind's eye, I see them all lined up for a family portrait: two hundred penguins at a buck a head...The scene is a banquet...cafeteria style. *(Smiles.)* I have just winked the lid over my mind's eye.

(Sam looks up.)

EMILY: Just shut up, Sam.

SAM: I didn't say a word.

EMILY: Now then. In Magnolia, Massachusetts, just up route one-twenty-eight, out Lynnfield way...

SAM: You think I don't know that?

EMILY: I said "Shut up," Sam...

(Sam sneers.)

EMILY: In Magnolia, Massachusetts, Miss E. M. O'Brien, the very special and very beautiful young woman, was vacationing for the summer...also working as a chambermaid. At the hotel, she met one Alfred L. Webber, Boy Wonder. Young Mister Webber was called "Boy Wonder" because he had made his first million by the age of eighteen. He sold a swamp in Wakefield, Massachusetts, due south of Magnolia, just down route one-twenty-eight… *(Puts her finger to her lips; looks at Sam.)* Shhh… *(Smiles.)* At the age of eighteen, Alfred L. Webber, buyer and seller of vast parcels of land, was already outstanding in his field…real estate.

SAM: Yuh. Sure. Out, standing in his field of real estate. Heard it. Hated it.

EMILY: *Pay attention!*

SAM: Okay.

EMILY: They met and married. They honeymooned at the very hotel at which they met. He bought it for their honeymoon: all cash. He sold it just after their honeymoon, realizing a considerable profit: all cash. *(Pauses.)* The next twenty years passed quietly, without incident. There were four children, all born dead.

SAM: I'm sorry.

EMILY: *You're* sorry? *You're* sorry? How the hell do you think *she* felt???

SAM: Wicked awful.

EMILY: Ah, Bartleby! *(She looks up at Sam and smiles.)* One day the husband, who was to that instant the hardest working and most energetic man the wife had ever even *heard* of, he…the husband…woke up and turned to her…the wife…and you know what he said to her?

SAM: How many guesses?

EMILY: "I'm giving it away."

SAM: He…the husband…said, "I'm giving it away"?

EMILY: Precisely.

SAM: Sounds like the start of an off-color joke to me.

EMILY: I loathe jokes, Sam. A joke to me is the lowest thing I know. I rate joking right down at the bottom of the list with pushing and shoving.

SAM: You musta been a great date in your day, Emily.

EMILY: He, the husband, gave it all away. Every penny they had. *(Pauses.)* Can you imagine?

SAM: Certainly, I can imagine.

EMILY: Their car, their other car, their house, their other house, their boat, their other boat, even his, umm…autographed baseball cards and pictures from show-business personalities: all of it. *(Pauses.)* Lucky thing they were spared having children.

SAM: Me, too.

EMILY: Four stillbirths. They all died in their seventh month, but she carried them…the whole route. Four of the great mystifying freaks of medical history, those four kiddoes. Every specialist was called in, but nothing could be done. Baby after baby, born dead. Can you imagine?

SAM: I can imagine.

EMILY: Just about everyone and everything near them suffered. Even their flowering rhododendron bush…it withered and wilted and…well… passed on. *(Pauses.)* What a depressing couple they were, those two.

SAM: Four.

EMILY: Huh?

SAM: I thought you said *four*. Kids.

EMILY: The mother and the father. She is speaking now of the mother and the father: Emily and Alfred.

SAM: Oh.

EMILY: The father gave up hope, finally. He never again put himself in a position in which he might again be…disappointed. They had an unwritten agreement… *(Pauses.)* He stopped touching her and she stopped talking to him. They stayed together in that state…for years. Very crazy, huh? Can you imagine?

SAM: How come you keep asking me that, over and over?

EMILY: Asking you what?

SAM: If I can imagine. Of course, I can imagine. I've been livin' right beside the real source of crazy, sixty-one years now. You don't own suffering, you know.

EMILY: It's Alfred I own.

SAM: Huh?

EMILY: I own him, Sam. Where my life began is a mystery…and where it ends…that's a mystery, too. But right now, in the middle of it all…I intend for day after day of perfect clarity. Alfred L. Webber, Boy Wonder, tied himself up with me and I intend to keep the knot just where it is. And if anybody interferes, Sam…you or anybody else… *(Pauses.)* …they have me to contend with. We have a lot in common, Sam…

SAM: I know.…

EMILY: I should think you do… *(Pauses.)* I have no more intention of giving Alfred up than you have of giving Tommy up.

SAM: The money? Is that it?

EMILY: Money is simply a detail that will have to be dealt with, no more, no less. Such is life. Although money is, however, one of the buttons that I push to get Alfred's dander, as they say, up. Whenever you hear me mention money, Sam, you'll know that I am pushing Alfred's button. It's way beyond money, Sam. Way beyond. It's his soul. Just now I don't seem to have one of my own. Until I do, Alfred is not free. He's owned. *(She stands, walks behind chair; lights cigarette, sits; exhales.)* I have never in my entire life met another woman who was even one half as unhappy as I am…

(Sam offers her a cookie. There is silence.)

EMILY: Here we go, Sam. I intend to keep my promise to Alfred. I've promised him that I would help uncover certain information—juicy facts. Alfred has a memory problem…a serious memory problem. There's a great deal I have to help him remember. And when he does, we go home. Life passes "go," collects two hundred dollars, and goes home. *(She produces a baseball cap, which she shows to Sam.)* This is a baseball cap that is supposed to shock and amaze you. Fami*liar* or fami*lial?*

SAM: Where…where…where'd you get that?

EMILY: Whose is this?

SAM: Where'd you get that? Who gave you that cap? Where'd you get that? *Answer me!*

EMILY: Why are you so upset?

SAM: Did Alfred give you that? *(Quietly.)* You better tell me.

EMILY: It's just something I…well…something I dug up. To show you. Talk, Sam.

SAM: About what?

EMILY: Sam?

SAM: We used to wear hats like that. Years ago.

EMILY: And?

SAM: *(After a long pause.)* It's just a cap.

EMILY: Whose?

SAM: Ours. We used to wear 'em, years ago, when we were together.

EMILY: We? You and Alfred?

SAM: Me and Tommy.

EMILY: Did you play on a team?

SAM: When we were in business together: the paper business.

EMILY: Manufacturing?

SAM: Delivering. We had the biggest route on the North Shore. Covered maybe ten or twelve towns…

(Sam reaches for the cap, when Emily withdraws. There is a pause. They look at each other silently.)

SAM: It's true!

EMILY: *(Suddenly.)* Don't you fucking tell me what's true and what isn't!

SAM: *(Whistles.)* Boy, what a mouth on you...

EMILY: Why are there so many old people in Wakefield, Sam? I've never in my life *seen* so many people so incredibly old! Do they move here? Were they born here? Who are they all? *(Pauses.)* What the hell did you *do???*

SAM: *(Stands.)* I can't talk anymore.

EMILY: You're gonna have to!

SAM: I'm...going in the house. Tommy must be hungry now. *(Moves to door.)* Sorry ta haveta just run like this...

EMILY: What is going on in this town, Sam? What are you hiding? What terrible thing have you all done??? *Talk! TALK!!!!*

SAM: Back off, tootsie...

EMILY: *(Moves between Sam and door.)* I spent a week watching Alfred badger a man into confessing to a murder. You know what? I don't believe that man committed that murder at all. You know who I'm talking about, Sam Lynch...your niece and nephew, Sam Lynch: Will and Margaret. I watched Alfred settle in at the home of his old high school girlfriend, Margaret, and her husband, Will. I discovered that Alfred's brother was murdered. That Alfred's one tiny shred of sanity focused itself on finding his brother's killer... *(Pauses.)* Lo and behold...Lo and behold... *(Pauses.)*

SAM: You're snooping way outa line! Now, *back off!*

EMILY: I don't think Alfred's brother was killed by Will. I think Alfred killed his own brother. I think Alfred killed his own brother and you're all hiding it...protecting him.

SAM: *Back off!*

EMILY: I've got a right to know the truth, Sam. Is that what Alfred's unable to remember? Is that the crime here? Is that what Alfred's unable to remember? Is that the crime that drew him back to this horrid little scene? He did, didn't he? Alfred killed his brother, didn't he? *Didn't he???* See? I know who dunnit! Alfred dunnit. But, *what,* God damn it! *Alfred dun what???*

SAM: *(Summoning his strength, he pushes Emily.)* Back...the fuck...off!

EMILY: It's really anxiety-producing, isn't it, Sam? Whatever it is you're all hiding—you're all protecting Alfred from—it's really quite anxiety-producing. It makes you all quite nervous, doesn't it, Sam? *(Quietly.)* Sam?

SAM: *(Composure reasonably regained, but winded.)* I'm really sorry I hit you, Emily. I try never to hit women and I hate like hell to make an exception out of a girl like you. You gotta understand something: I've made promises here. When you've made a promise and kept it for thirty years…well…it ain't too easily breakable, is it? *(Pauses.)* I'm sorry I struck you…physically and all…but you're milking some very sacred cows around here. I can't be party to such goin's-on. My advice to you is simple: Get out while you still can. All this mess is strictly family: his, not yours. *(Reaches out.)* Gimme the cap. I'll take it in to Tommy. It's his.

EMILY: Does Alfred know about it?

SAM: About *what?*

EMILY: Okay. The cap. Does Alfred know about the cap?

SAM: Course he does. He buried them, didn't he? Didn't Alfred give that cap to you?

EMILY: Alfred buried *who*, Sam?

SAM: *Who?* Alfred buried the caps…the stuff. I've said too much. I'm goin' in! *(Moves again to door to leave.)*

EMILY: Sam, this is an awful thing to say to a man of your good looks and pride, but here it comes…Sam, I'm a lot stronger than you are and, if it comes to it, I could hurt you…I wouldn't want to…but I see what's needed here.

(The back door suddenly swings open. Alfred enters. He smiles to Emily.)

ALFRED: Very kinky goin's-on…

SAM: He musta heard everything! What a goddamn family!

ALFRED: Excuse me for not knocking. I was listening in from behind the door. *(Nods to Sam.)*

(He smiles to Emily; sits. Emily hides the cap.)

ALFRED: Do you really, Emily? *(Pauses.)* Do you really *see what's needed here?!!* *(Pauses.)* That's quite a prospect: your really seeing what's needed *here.* *(Smiles, to Sam.)* Get inside, Sam.

SAM: It's nothin' like you think! Nothin' went on between us. I swear to God, Alfred, we were just talking. *(Pauses; frantically, to Emily.)* Tell him, Emily.

ALFRED: Out!

EMILY: Alfred?

(Alfred smiles.)

EMILY: I'll destroy you, Alfred.

(Alfred laughs.)

EMILY: Alfred? *(No response.)* Answer me, Alfred.

SAM: I'm gonna leave you two lovebugs alone, okay?

(Alfred now stands directly in front of Sam.)

SAM: I'm goin' in… *(Pauses.)* I'm gonna tell him what I've seen, Alfred. How weird you're behavin'. *(Pauses.)* He ain't gonna be too proud.

ALFRED: Good night, Sam…

SAM: I'm goin' in, don'tcha worry about *that*… *(Pauses; looks at Emily.)* I'm goin' in now. *(Smiles.)* Good seein' ya again, Emily. *(Nods.)* Nice little wife ya got here, Alfred. *(Door opens.)* 'Night all! *(Exits.)*

ALFRED: *(After a pause.)* I'm really shocked and amazed that you've missed what you've missed. All this time in town and you don't know. *(Shakes his head.)* You're slowing down, Emmy. *(Smiles.)* All those golden old-timers are Wakefieldians. *(Pauses.)* That's what they like to call themselves: Wakefieldians. *(Pauses.)* Status quo set in. About thirty years ago. Around the time my mother passed away… *(Pauses.)* "Passed away" is a euphemism. "Status quo" is, of course, Latin: the tongue of the church. *(Pauses.)* You might say that Wakefield is the ultimate town experience: No one's been born and no one's died in thirty years now. Everyone here's stayed put…so to speak. It's been a real curse. *(Pauses.)* I'd forgotten. My father *had* to be alive, didn't he? They all are. It's a Wakefield tradition: a real status quo.

(Alfred, sitting in rocking chair smiling across to Emily. Emily, sitting on porch railing. She bows her head. Tableau. The lights fade to black.)

SCENE II

Asylum. Dawn. Stage in darkness. Three sharp knocks are heard. Church bells in distance, four chimes. Repeat. Rooster crows twice. Silence. First words of scene—Sam's—are heard in darkness.

SAM: How about the Englishman and the trained kipper? How about the pig with the poker game? How about the Czechoslovakian whore with the French tennis racquet? *(Pauses.)* How *about* the Czechoslovakian whore with the French tennis racquet?

(Lights to full, suddenly. Pa, on porch alone, in rocker. He is silently staring at Sam, who stands hiding from Pa, head bowed, at corner of house. Sam raises his head a bit; nearly weeping. He is frightened.)

SAM: How about the magician's trained snake and the Scotch brand Magic tape?

PA: You come out here on a high-level mission and I don't even get a report? What kinda joke is this?

SAM: There was a two-horned toad and a unicorn…

PA: Nobody ever comes out here to *fail*, Sam!

SAM: Maybe it wasn't a unicorn?…

PA: Where the hell have you *been?*

SAM: Maybe it wasn't even a two-horned toad!…

PA: You're not gonna even try, huh? No explanations: just babble? Just more goddamn *babble?*

SAM: Maybe it was the sailor and the trained cod…They all start to blend together at my age…Poor old me.

PA: Did you tell her? *(Pauses.)* Sam? *(Pauses; no reply.)* I'm talkin' to you, Sam… *(No reply.)* Did you tell Emily? *(No reply.)* Sam? *(No reply.)* Did you…betray me? *(No reply. Pa screams.)* SAM!

SAM: *(Quickly.)* No, dammit! Course not! *(Pauses; turns, looks at Pa.)* I…

PA: Easy enough to find out, ya know. *(Points his finger at Sam.)* You got your last chance right now. *(No reply.)* She's still here, ya know.
   (Sam looks up, surprised.)

PA: Emily!
   (Emily enters through screen door. She carries tray, laden with food. Walks to Pa.)

EMILY: Here. The usual.

PA: You know my friend Sam, don't you, Emily? Sam, this is my friend Emily. Emily, this is my friend Sam. *(Pauses.)* Always pleases me when I can get friends together: When I can get worlds to, you know, collide.

EMILY: *(Smiles to Sam; turns to Pa, smiles.)* BLT on toast and a mocha frappe. Hope you like it. *(Looks at Sam; smiles sweetly.)* Hello, Sam.

PA: Aren't you ever gonna say hello, Sam? *(After a pause; to Emily.)* He's kinda rude for his years. Grew that way. Didn't used to be. *(To Sam.)* You didn't used ta be rude, did you?
   (Emily exits through screen door, with tray. Men are suddenly animated; rapid-fire exchange.)

SAM: You are the looney-bird of all time! What the hell did you tell her?

PA: *Me? Me? You're* asking *me?*

SAM: Well, *I* certainly didn't tell her anything!

PA: You think *I* did? You're a major-league dodo, Sam!

SAM: And you're a gorilla's ass!

PA: What'd you call me?

SAM: Looney-bird?

PA: Gorilla's ass.

SAM: That's right…

PA: *I'm* not the one's be'n spillin' the wax beans…

SAM: Well, it ain't me, pally-pal. Not a bean—not a *pea*—has slipped through these sealed lips…I am a bank vault.

PA: You better be tellin' the truth!

SAM: *You* better be tellin' the truth!

PA: Why don't I believe you somehow?…

SAM: Because you've been senile for sixty-one years!

PA: You've been *impotent* for sixty-one years!

SAM: Impotence has no effect on decisions and thinking the way senility does! Impotence attacks the *body*, not the mind!

PA: If I could walk, I'd chase you!

SAM: I'll let ya walk: c'mon, walk! Chase me!

(Pa strains to stand. Cannot.)

SAM: *Hah! hah! hah! HAH!* If you aren't the most foolish lookin' turd I've ever seen!

(Sam now fakes deep laughter, as Pa strains again to stand.)

SAM: Whew! Lookit you! If you aren't the most ridiculous-lookin' dung ever dumped around here! Whew! I'm gonna split open from this uproar of laughter!

(Pa stands.)

SAM: Whew! *(Sam sees Pa standing.)* You're standing.

PA: That's right.

SAM: But, you can't.

PA: That's right.

SAM: I take it all back. *(Sam rushes to Pa. Stops. Backs up.)* Sit down. *(Sam takes a rational tone.)* Sit down.

(Pa stares at Sam.)

SAM: Tommy?

EMILY: *(Calling from behind screen door.)* Ready or not, here I come.

(Pa sits. Emily enters. Sam stares. Emily is wearing cap.)

EMILY: Like it?

PA: *(To Sam. Pa beams at Emily.)* It's nice to have the touch of a young woman again. *(Pauses.)* Such a touch has been missing around here for quite a while.

SAM: She has the cap. *(Pauses.)* It's on her head.

PA: *(Looks at Emily.)* I think you're looking prettier every day, Emily.

SAM: Oh my God. If I drank, I would drink now. If I smoked I would smoke now. If I used drugs, I would drug now. *(Pauses; walks to rail, sits on it.)* I am one shocked and amazed old duffer, that's what I am. *(Feels his chest. Stops; looks up walks to Pa and places Pa's ear to his chest as best he can.)* Listen to my heart!

PA: Put it in a song and sing it.

SAM: *(Raises a clenched fist to Pa.)* I'll put this in a song, ya jerk! You see what's on her head?

PA: *(Looks at Emily. Sees hat.)* Where'd you get that? From Alfred?

EMILY: Warm.

PA: Huh?

EMILY: You're getting warm. *(Smiles.)* Want another try?

PA: *(Motions to Sam; speaks to Emily.)* Him?

EMILY: Closer.

PA: Gimme a hint: familiar or familial?

EMILY: I'm going to find out sooner or later, you know…

PA: Sam?

SAM: What?

PA: Buy us some time.

SAM: *What?*

PA: I need to think.

SAM: Huh?

EMILY: Sam?

SAM: What?

EMILY: Aren't you ashamed?

SAM: Did you ever hear the one about the bloodsucker and the scarecrow?

EMILY: *(To Pa.)* Aren't you ashamed?

SAM: How about the Hollywood starlet and the Santa Monica starfish?

EMILY: *(To Pa.)* Aren't you humiliated?

SAM: How about the agony and the ecstasy?

EMILY: *(To Pa.)* It's pathetic to watch…

SAM: How about the old man and the sea?

EMILY: It shames me just to look at the two of you…

SAM: The greatest story ever told?

EMILY: …to feel…connected…to feel connected to you. It shames me.

SAM: The butcher, the baker, the candlestick maker… *(Pauses.)* Christ! *(Panicked.)* I'm running dry! *(To Pa.)* Will you *for crying out loud* do something!?!

PA: Go on!

SAM: *(Panicked.)* Where? *(Pauses; then slyly.)* I know where. *(Smiles.)* Out route one-twenty-eight, Lynnfield way…

PA: *(Screams.)* Sam!!! *(After a long pause; quietly.)* Alfred's mother.

EMILY: Alfred's mother?

PA: Alfred's mother.

EMILY: What about her?

PA: How she...died.

SAM: Here we go...

PA: Nobody even thinks about it anymore...It's a small town, Emily. People understand.

SAM: It was terrible on the boy.

PA: She was all charred.

SAM: Burned to a crisp. Most horrible thing you'd ever want to see.

PA: Just her room...

SAM: Only hers...

PA: Can you imagine?

SAM: Can you imagine?

PA: Whole house left untouched...

SAM: Just her room...

PA: Hardly a trace of smoke in the air...

SAM: No smell...

PA: Just her room...

SAM: Awful thing...

PA: She certainly was...

SAM: Shocked us all...

PA: Years to come...

SAM: Quite a blow...

PA: Dead.

SAM: Burned.

PA: Goddamned cigarettes!

SAM: Filthy habit.

PA: Begged her to quit.

SAM: Couldn't quit.

PA: Hardly even tried.

SAM: He begged her to.

PA: I begged her to.

SAM: Did no good.

PA: Not a bit...

SAM: Once habit takes hold...

PA: You're a goner...

SAM: Goner.

PA: Done for.

SAM: Absolutely.

PA: Absolutely.

SAM: Alfred!

PA: Huh?

SAM: There! Alfred.

(In silence, Alfred enters, walks to porch, sits. Silence. Alfred stands. Walks downstage toward rose trellis, in silence. Stops near Emily, turns to men.)

SAM: We were just tellin' Emily about the wicked awful fire.

ALFRED: I came home from school and there was a wicked awful commotion at the house. *(Pauses; smiles.)* That's the right word, isn't it, Pa? Commotion? Isn't that what we called it?

(Pa nods.)

SAM: Alfred.

ALFRED: What?

SAM: She...uh...she don't...uh...she don't exactly...*comprendez.*

ALFRED: Well, let's just straighten her right out then, Sam. *(To Emily.)* *Preparez* to *comprendez!* *(Pauses.)* Lynchie and I were playing together. Lynchie was a neighborhood kid. Very *close,* eh, Pop? Lynchie was Sam's nephew...Lynchie was also Margaret's brother and, as it turns out, her husband-and-brother Will's half brother. *(Smiles.)* Family ties are some little buggers to bind, huh, Em? Don't even bother trying. Hardly worth the effort...and not central to my tale of woe. *(Pounds his chest with his fist, acting tragedy. He smiles.)* Oh, woe. Oh, woe. *(To Emily.)* Lynchie was beating me up. That's what we did after school most days, Lynchie and me. He'd beat me up. We'd wrestle. He'd win and I'd...well...lose... *(Smiles.)* There was a fire engine. Red and loud. Rushing up North Avenue, crossing the tracks down at the bottom, near Prospect. We were playing in the patch of grass at the intersection. *(Pauses.)* That is to say, that's where Lynchie was holding me down and choking me. *(Pauses.)* We chased the engine to the house...my house. Right to it. *(Pauses.)* They'd brought a resuscitator to try to bring them around. Too late. Both gone.

SAM: Awful thing.

ALFRED: Huh?

SAM: I was just commenting that it was an awful thing.

(Alfred stares at Sam.)

SAM: Sorry.

ALFRED: Sam was there first. Pa'd come home early with Sam. Sam found them together in the big bed. *(Pauses.)* Sam was there, first. Weren't ya, pally? First to see the dirty deed.

SAM: *(To Pa.)* What the hell did you tell him? What's goin' on here?

ALFRED: *(To Emily.)* Pa usually brought his business associates home for lunch.

SAM: I demand an explanation!

ALFRED: *(Cutting him off.)* Try not to interrupt.

SAM: I was in the truck, waiting. I never saw…

PA: Sam!

ALFRED: Ah, yes, the truck. Pa and Sam and Willie-Boy had a purple Chevy. Very pale, pouf-purple quite an advanced color for Wakefield, now that I think of it. They were in the paper business, together. *(Smiles.)* I'm surprised Sam didn't tell you.

EMILY: He did.

ALFRED: I'm not surprised.

EMILY: They delivered.

ALFRED: Wrong.

SAM: I smell a double-cross.

PA: Shut up, Sam.

EMILY: That's what Sam said: delivering.

ALFRED: Nope. Collecting. Door-to-door buying. They bought bundles of old newspaper from people—baled them in sixteen-hundred-pound bales and sold them to the mills up in Bedford and Fitchburg. *(Pauses.)* The West Side Waste Paper Company. *(Smiles.)* Ten. I was ten years old, Emily and they never even thought to ask me how I felt about it: about my…mother. *(To Pa.)* S'pose you had a lot on your mind then, huh, champ?

EMILY: Who set the fire?

ALFRED: The fire was after the fact, Emily. More of a cremation than a death. The fire just…well…destroyed the evidence. The evidence being one mother and one mother's friend.

EMILY: Mother's friend?

SAM: I've been lied to for thirty years. Thirty miserable years. *(To Pa.)* You broke your word. You broke your word. God damn you…

ALFRED: Don't bother, Sam. Let's face the facts, okay? Let's remember together… *(To Emily.)* My mother had a boyfriend. Not really the man of *your* dreams, her boyfriend. He drove a bread truck. Bond Bread, to be specific. He brought my folks their morning crullers. They found my mother and her boyfriend together and they…did…what they did. *(Walks to porch and sits; looks at Sam.)* You see, I really do remember.

SAM: Me too. I remember, too. *(To Pa.)* You hear me? *(Yells.)* You hear me!?

PA: *Who invited you? (Pauses.)* He talked me into it, Emily. I was a worker back then. I wanted to work. *(Pauses.)* It wasn't even eleven, it was ha'-pahst ten. Who the hell wants lunch at ha'-pahst ten? *(Pauses.)* Insatiable Sam, that's who. Badgered me into it. He did, Emily. He worked me up into it.

SAM: It was done before I ever got into the house, Emily—that's the truth of it. I just helped with the fire.

PA: She hated my guts. I knew she did. For years I did. *(Pauses.)* Did nothin' about it, though. *(Pauses.)* I was a gentleman. *(Pauses.)* Never knew a woman to carry on in her own house, though. Never did. He was there every *day*, Emily. I swear to God, I never knew when to come home… never knew when he would be there with her. *(Pauses.)* Finally, I got them to meet in his truck, first thing in the morning. He'd drop off the crullers and she'd go out the back and into his truck and then they'd drive out God knows where together for the rest of the morning. I'd have my coffee and, well, cruller, you know, alone…and then I'd go off into a hard day's work. Straight through—nonstop—till dinnertime: noon. *(Pauses.)* Arm in arm in my own room in my own house in my own bed.

EMILY: Is that why there's only one grave? Are they buried together?

PA: Huh?

SAM: The bodies. Only one grave. How come. Tell her how come. *(Screams.)* *Tell her!* She wants to know where my brother's grave is and I'm just gettin' a fuckin' good hunch! *Tell us both!*

PA: There's just one: hers. I wouldn't bury him. I wouldn't have him—you know—near her no more. I had him cremated.

SAM: You lied to me! You said he didn't want burial! You said it would've gone against his will. You said he *wanted* cremation. Wanted his ashes strewn over the lake. Asked for it in his will. I shoulda known you were lying. He always hated the lake. I scattered them: me. From over near the Yacht Club. Some of them blew back on me. His ashes. They got in my eyes, on my sport coat, and even into my T-shirt. *(Pauses; near tears.)* He was my brother.

PA: Willie-Boy. That was his name: Willie-Boy. Sam's ugly twin. He was supposed to be my friend…partner and friend. Can you imagine?

SAM: He wasn't a bad guy, Emily

PA: *(Screams.)* Don't you defend him!

SAM: I didn't. I stuck by you, didn't I? *Didn't I?*

PA: *(Screams.)* If I had that son of a bitch here right now, I'd kill him. I would. I really would. You did exactly the right thing, Alfred.

EMILY: What right thing? *(No reply.)* What right thing?

ALFRED: I am a man. I am forty. I am standing in an insane asylum with my mother's killers; my old pa and his best friend, Sam, two major-league lunatics. I see that my charming and pythonlike wife, Emily, is here, too: Emily: a devoted wife. *(Smiles.)* Devoted to exactly *what,* God only knows. *(Smiles again; moves to side.)* I could kill you all, now, to avenge my mother. It wouldn't make any difference to me. I can only be punished once. *(Sternly.)* The murder of my mother will be revenged: absolutely and completely. I stake my life on that fact. My brother couldn't do it, but I can. I will. I stake my life on that fact... *(Pauses, smiles.)* I'm going back down below now...to the house. Join me, if you want to, Emily. Or don't. Either way, I actually couldn't care less. *(Nods to Pa and Sam.)* Pa. Sam... *(Smiles.)* Be seein' ya. *(Alfred exits.)*
(There is a long pause. Emily speaks, coldly.)

EMILY: Pa, what right thing?

SAM: For the love of Christ, what right thing? What the hell's goin' on here?

PA: I'm through talkin' on this subject now. *(To Sam.)* Get her out of here. *(To Emily.)* I'm through talkin' on this subject now.

SAM: I can't believe my own ears anymore... *(Pauses.)* I never thought I'd live to see the day... *(Pauses.)* I'm goin' inside. *(To Pa.)* You're comin' with me. We're going to talk: just you and me. You stand, and you walk and you follow me. Now. *(Pauses.)* I know you can. Remember? *(To Emily.)* He can.

EMILY: Sam?

SAM: What?

EMILY: A simple yes or no will do... *(Pauses; then matter-of-factly.)* Did Alfred kill his mother?

PA: Sam!

EMILY: Answer me. Sam. Am I right, Sam? Is that what you're all hiding? Did Alfred kill his mother? Sam? Sam? Am I right? Sam?

SAM: I hope you're wrong, girlie. For the sake of somebody's goddamn so-called best friend. I hope you're wrong.

PA: *God damn it! (Punches arm of chair.) God damn it! (Turns to Emily.)* Just what the hell are you lookin for, huh? HUH?

SAM: What the hell is going on here? *(Screams.)* WHAT THE HELL IS GOING ON HERE?

PA: Sam. Go inside! *Go inside!!!* I'll be right in. Go, Sam Goddammit, go!

SAM: Thirty years, you two-faced lying coot! *(To Emily.)* Thirty years, I've been protecting him. *(To Pa.)* Guilt! *Guilt!* I didn't throw Willie-Boy and Sophie into the sack together, ya know! I didn't ask for him to be my twin, either! Both of those things just happened. *(To Emily.)* He's kept me guilty—kept me protecting him—more'n thirty years now. *(To Pa.)* Something's fishy here, pally. Something's as fishy as a trout. I've been lied to, right? *RIGHT! (To Emily.)* I know I'm crazy. I've never doubted it. First one of my brothers hangs one of his own sons and now look what's happened to my only *other* brother. *All my brothers, for Christ's sake!* Course I'm crazy! Who the hell wouldn't be? *(To Pa.)* But I'm no dummy, pal! I'm no dope! That's where you made your big mistake. *(He turns away and faces Emily. He will check Pa's reactions, defiantly, as he speaks to Emily.)* You asked me why I've been stayin' here, Emily…Now you're gonna know: because I figured I'd get the electric chair if I didn't… Because I was an accomplice to a murder…Because I was an accomplice to the murder of his wife, Sophie, and my brother, Willie-Boy Lynch… *(To Pa.)* Here we go, pal. *(Pauses.) Here…we…go!* I was in the truck, waiting. Tommy here ran out of the house and told me he'd killed 'em— told me that as straight as a man talking to God. Asked me to help with the fire. It all happened fast. He killed Sophie and Willie-Boy and I helped light the fire to burn up the evidence—to make it look like an accident. *(Screams; to Pa.) That's all I did in this:* help. I think they were dead before this one—Tommy Webber—ever got into the house! I think I've been lied to. I think I was an accomplice to nothing more than a lie. I think the best years of my life have been shot protecting a lie. I'll get you for this. I'll get even. I curse you! *(To Emily.)* I think it's time for certain nonfamily members to join together against certain family members, if you get what I'm driving my point at, so to speak. *(Pauses.)* I think that you and I have more in common than just good looks, Emily. First I want to talk to him and then you. *(To Pa.)* I'll be waitin' inside, pally. *(Pauses.)* I've got a whole new ace ta deal. A whole new ace. *(Sam exits into house, slamming door behind him.)*

(After a long pause, Emily speaks.)

EMILY: He killed her, didn't he?

(Pa looks up at Emily.)

EMILY: Alfred killed his mother, didn't he?

PA: *I* killed her. She wasn't just his mother, she was also my wife. A husband has certain rights, when a wife is out of line. *(Pauses.)* And a father has certain obligations...to a son. A father has an obligation to protect his son. No matter what. *No matter what.*

(Silence. Pa stares at Emily. Emily bows her head. Tableau. The lights fade out.)

End of Act II.

ACT III
SCENE I

Living room, as in Alfred The Great. Midnight. Stage in darkness. Three sharp knocks are heard. Church bells commence sounding their midnight: twelve chimes. First words of the scene—Sam's—heard in darkness.

SAM: *(Offstage.)* I'm hiding you in the kitchen, Tommy Webber. You're gonna have to know the truth!
    (Bells complete twelve chimes.)
SAM: Now, you keep your ears open and listen! You hear me?
PA: *(Offstage.)* What?
    (Lights to full, suddenly. Stage is empty. Alfred appears on the top of the staircase. He is wearing robe and slippers. He leans over railing, looking into room. He leans back, looking up to foyer on second floor, not visible to audience. He leans into room again, calling quietly.)
ALFRED: Who's down there?
SAM: *(Calling from kitchen.)* It's me: Sam…your father's friend from the hill.
    (Alfred moves down staircase to center section of stairs. He waits and watches. A moment passes. Sam enters from kitchen, carrying a glass of water. He looks around living room; seems confused.)
SAM: Alfred?
    (No response. Alfred is leaning against wall on staircase, into shadows.)
SAM: Hello? *(No response.)* Alfred?
    (Sam moves into room, looking around. He carries water carefully. Sam gives a cursory, desultory look to staircase area, but turns instead suddenly to look at area near kitchen door, believing someone is waiting on living-room side. Sam's back is now fully turned to Alfred, who leans into room and speaks quietly.)
ALFRED: What's in the kitchen?
SAM: *(Whirling around to face Alfred.) There* you are!
ALFRED: Why were you in the kitchen?
    (Alfred sits on landing, allowing his legs and feet to fit between spindles in staircase railing. He smiles. Sam drinks the glass of water, slowly and deliberately.)
ALFRED: You drank a glass of something.
SAM: Wakefield water. Nothin' like a glass of Wakefield water when you're feelin' outa sorts. *(Toasts Alfred, raising glass to him, and then smiles.)* Here's lookin' atcha… *(Drinks remaining drops of water.)* Mmmm-good.

(Sets glass on table.) I might as well get right to the point. *(Looks around room again and then speaks in loud, stagy voice.)* I kinda got some bad news...

ALFRED: Why are you yelling?

SAM: *(As loud as before.)* I said, "I kinda got some bad news."

ALFRED: She can hear you perfectly well if you use your normal voice.

SAM: Who?

ALFRED: Can't you, Emmy? *(No response.)* You're gonna have to take my word for it, Sam...

SAM: Who? Her? *(Laughs.)* That's rich.

ALFRED: What's your news?

SAM: *Bad* news...

ALFRED: What's your *bad* news?

SAM: Your father.

ALFRED: My father?

SAM: *(Stagy too-loud voice again.)* He's been threatening it for sixty-one years... *(Pauses.)* Guess he meant it.

ALFRED: Guess he meant *what?*

SAM: He ran away.

ALFRED: *(Smiling; amused.)* He what?

SAM: *(Annoyed.)* It's no goddamn laughing matter. He ran away. They were beating him, ya know. He was hurt, ya know. *(Pauses.)* He broke free and scooted.

ALFRED: I don't think my father is much of a scooter, Sam....

SAM: There's a lot you don't know about him. *(Looks around the room.)* Where is she?

ALFRED: Emily? *(Pauses.)*

SAM: *(Suddenly worried.)* Oh, crap.

(Sam turns and runs into kitchen. Alfred stands and walks down staircase slowly, entering room. He goes to sofa, sits; waits. Sam reenters room and goes to staircase.)

SAM: She ain't in *there*... *(No response.)* Hello?

ALFRED: *(Quietly.)* Hello.

SAM: *(Whirls about.)* That supposed ta be cute?

EMILY: *(Quietly, from top of staircase.)* Hello, Sam.

ALFRED: Why, look! It's Emily... *(He has imitated Sam's stagy voice.)*

SAM: Coupla goddamn hot spooks...Wicked funny, you two—wicked funny.

EMILY: What's the matter, Sam?

SAM: I got some really bad news. *(Pauses.)* The old folks, they came around and beat up Tommy: Alfred's father. *(Pauses.)* While they were hitting him he broke loose and ran away. Sorta fired off, loping, into the fields…

EMILY: What about the money, Sam?

ALFRED: *(To Emily.)* What did you ask him, you?

EMILY: Did he take it with him, Sam?

ALFRED: I find it slightly monstrous…

EMILY: Answer me, Sam?

SAM: One at a time!

ALFRED: I find it slightly monstrous of you, Emily, to be mentioning money at this particular time…Please, don't.

EMILY: Okay, *you* ask him.

ALFRED: Not yet.

EMILY: Sam?

SAM: *(Wide-eyed; astonished.)* What?

EMILY: Did he take it with him?

SAM: Definitely not. He took nothing with him. *(Shrugs.)* You…uh…*can't* take it with you.

EMILY: How do you know?

SAM: How do I know *what?*

EMILY: That he didn't.

SAM: I just do. *(Pauses.)* I was there. *(Pauses.)* I…uh…held his arms.

ALFRED: That certainly fits the category of surprising retorts, Sam. You say you held his what? His arms?

SAM: It was right that it be me who did it. Who held him. *(Pauses.)* It was more like a hug than anything else. I wouldn't have hurt him knowingly. *(Pauses.)* Not physically.

ALFRED: *(Smiling.)* What the hell are you talking about?

EMILY: I think you should pay attention, Alfred. You have something to tell Sam and Sam has something to tell *you.*

SAM: I tried to stop it, Alfred! I really did…The old people. They came from all over town. They hated him. Roxy…the hag…she's hated him for about seventy years now. Hates you, too, Alfred. She figures you're the reason this town's cursed the way it is. Old folks livin' way past their prime, the way we do. Your fault…

ALFRED: Roxy? Your Roxy?

SAM: Yuh, my Roxy. My ex. His ex…everybody's ex. *(Smiles.)* She's never been one to forgive or forget. She's been especially hateful since she heard what went on with Margaret and Will down below…And when I told her you were takin' all his money…well…*wellll*…that just kinda drove her off her nut, altogether. *(To Emily.)* Roxy was the one who actually broke his arm. She hit him with a shovel. *(Pauses; to Alfred.)* I was just holding.

ALFRED: Is this somebody's idea of a joke?

SAM: Worst thing I ever saw: All the old folks—they got like beetles in for a feast: swarming all over him. Their minds were poisoned. They were scared…scared he was gonna die finally…without, you know…sharing. *(Pauses.)* He broke loose, twistin' and snakin' through the rotten pack of them. He slithered right and left until he saw the clear of the field over Winn Street way, near the Boston and Maine bridge…Then he pranced and galloped… *(Pauses.)* Ya really gotta hand it to 'im, Alfred. For a fella his age, he's still quite a spunky broken-field runner…

EMILY: Where are they now?

SAM: Who?

EMILY: Where are they? The old people…everybody?

SAM: Still looking. Still out there…hunting.

ALFRED: For my father?

SAM: For the money.

ALFRED: But…we've got to…we should…

EMILY: Go out?

ALFRED: We should. We have to find…

EMILY: Your father?

ALFRED: Emily, for God's sakes…you've got to let up on me…

EMILY: Say it, Alfred!

ALFRED: Is any of this true, Sam?

EMILY: Finish your sentence, Alfred… *(Screams.)* Alfred!

ALFRED: Will you please just pull back from me?

EMILY: *(Pauses; then angrily.)* Alfred, will you for Christ's sakes finish *some-thing???*

ALFRED: Sure.

EMILY: *(Falsely composed.)* Fine. Fine. Now, Alfred, we have to find *what?* *(Composure ended.)* Sam's waiting! *I'm* waiting!

ALFRED: Really smug, aren't you? *(Pauses; to Emily.)* Really getting pleasure from this, aren't you? *(Pauses; to Sam.)* I want the money, Sam. I have a large debt to pay. *(To Emily.)* You're going to get every speck of what's coming to you, Emily. Every crumb. Okay?

SAM: *(Loud stagy voice.)* Is that the reason you came back here? *(Even louder; more slowly as well.)* To…get…your…father's…money?

ALFRED: *(To Emily.)* What's the matter with him? *(To Sam.)* What's the matter with you?

SAM: *(Still loud and stagy; projecting his voice into the kitchen, over his shoulder.)* I said, *"Did you come back here to get your father's money?"*

ALFRED: Sam, we're right here in the room with you, remember? What is this?

SAM: *(Not stagy at all now, but fiercely angry.)* I wanna hear it from you once and for all, ya little bastard! *(Moves to Alfred.)* You go off for years...*years!*...and you never make any real contact with us...We never know what the hell you're doin'...what you're sayin'...*nothing!* *(Close to Alfred now and even more fiercely and seriously spoken.)* Now you're here...suddenly...unannounced and uninvited, too. *(Pauses.)* You really threw my schedule off. *(Suddenly yells.)* What the hell do you want from us? *(Pauses; tone changes.)* If it's his money, just tell me, loud and clear.

ALFRED: I hardly think it's the money, Sam. I hardly think that fits.

EMILY: Alfred!

ALFRED: Money is actually Emily's level of need just now. Money's exactly what it will goddamn take to goddamn get her goddamn once and for all off my goddamn aching back!

EMILY: It's not that simple, Sam...

ALFRED: I believe the legendary character is Simple *Simon*, Emily.

SAM: You always got time ta make light of things, don'tcha? Ya always got time for makin' laughin' matters...makin' jokes outa serious things...

EMILY: Like lovemaking.

SAM: Huh?

ALFRED: I think that'll be just about enough, please...

EMILY: Making a joke out of making love... *(Pauses; to Sam.)* Alfred...When I first met him, he was a laugh a minute...

ALFRED: I said that'll be enough!

EMILY: Things have slowed down some. *(Pauses.)* Alfred hasn't given me so much as a chuckle in years... *(Pauses.)* Hardly a smile. *(Pauses.)* I think he's lost his sense of humor, altogether.

ALFRED: *(Fiercely.)* Shut it, Emily!

EMILY: You're goin' to say it now...loud and clear. *(To Sam.)* You're going to get your reason, now: Why Alfred's here...why he came back to Wakefield... what he wants. What he *really* wants, beyond the money, Sam. *Way* beyond! *(To Alfred; yells.)* Now! Finish *some*thing, Alfred! You're going to have to finish *some*thing! We have made an agreement, remember: a contract!

ALFRED: I wish you wouldn't...

EMILY: There is a great deal you would like to remember...a great deal that you have forgotten that you would like to remember. You would like. Sam's got some things that he would like, too. Sam would like to know what exactly it is you want, Alfred... *(To Alfred.)* Let's give Sam something he needs, Alfred: The real reason—why you came back here—what you want. What you would like.

ALFRED: Please, Emily.

EMILY: I would like, Alfred. *(Screams.)* Begin your sentence with "I would like." *(Screams.)* Alfred!!!

ALFRED: I would like...

EMILY: Go on...*Finish!!!*

ALFRED: I would like...

EMILY: My father...

ALFRED: My father...

EMILY: *All of it!*

ALFRED: I would like...my father...to die. *(Bows head.)*

SAM: *(After a pause.)* That's it? That's why he came back?

EMILY: Perfect.

SAM: You ungrateful little twat... *(Pauses.)* You Pillsbury-pancakey little tit... *(Pauses.)* You only get one father, pansy. Just one: him.

EMILY: Now, Sam. I have your sacred word. *(Pauses.)* Go bring it in here, Sam.

SAM: I hate doin' this. I really do. I've done some wicked things in my day, but I really hate this one.

EMILY: Bring it in here, Sam. Now!

ALFRED: It's here? *(Pauses.)* Sam? Money? For Emily?

SAM: Huh?

ALFRED: Where?

SAM: In the kitchen. All the time.

ALFRED: The money?

SAM: No. *(Pauses.)* Your father. *(After a pause.)* He's been in the kitchen the whole time. Heard every word. *(Pauses.)* I never liked you, Alfred.
(Alfred walks to kitchen door. He opens door, looks inside kitchen. Emily laughs. Alfred returns to Emily, faces her.)

ALFRED: Whose idea was this? Whose splendid idea was this?
(He moves to chair; sits. Emily moves behind chair; strokes Alfred's hair. She walks to side of chair; stares at Alfred, who is staring straight out front.)

EMILY: This is the first time, in all the years I've known you...you've actually looked...your age.
(Sam has been standing, watching them. Alfred in chair. Emily behind chair, touching Alfred's hair. Sam at sofa, standing. Tableau.)

SAM: *(Moves to kitchen door. He knocks on door—a signal: three knocks.)* Saddest thing I ever seen.

(Sam opens door. Pa standing there. Pa enters room. Wears greatcoat. Holds arms inside. Tableau. Sam leads Pa to sofa.)

SAM: He heard every word. *(Sam pauses. Stations Pa at corner of sofa.)* You better hurry, Alfred. Ain't got much time left. *(Pauses.)* You can't look at me accusingly. The whole thing's your fault. *(Pauses.)* He's failing. Hmmm. That's right.

EMILY: *(Pauses.)* This is the worst I've ever done to you, isn't it?

ALFRED: No. *(Pauses; looks at her.)* Not the worst. *(Head down now.)* No.

PA: Look at me, Alfred. Pick up your head and look at me.

SAM: Look at your father, sonny.

(Sam pauses. No response. Alfred continues to look at his shoes.)

SAM: You hear me, sonnyboy? I told you to look at your father!

PA: You're going to have to face it, son. *(No response.)* I'm sorry, Alfred, but I'm going to have to make you remember exactly what it was you did. *(Pauses.)* I'm sorry. I really am.

SAM: I can vouch for that, Alfred. There isn't a sorrier son of a bitch in the whole Commonwealth of Massachusetts.

(Sam pauses; no response from Alfred.)

SAM: You gotta pick up your head and look at your father, Alfred. You're gonna haveta face both him and the facts. Ain't much of a list ta choose from, but there it is… *(Pauses.)* Alfred?

PA: Alfred?

EMILY: Alfred?

SAM: Alfred?

PA: *(Angrily.)* Alfred!

(Alfred, in chair, head down, slowly lifts his face and looks into Pa's eyes. Sam watches and then bows head. Emily watches and then bows head. Tableau. The lights fade to black.)

SCENE II

Living room. Later, just before dawn. Three sharp knocks are heard. Stage remains in darkness. First words of scene—Pa's—are heard.

PA: My days of protecting you are comin' to a close.

(Lights to full, suddenly. Alfred in chair, head bowed. Pa sits on end of sofa,

back against arm, nearly reclining. Faces Alfred. He holds one arm with his other arm, both inside ill-fitting greatcoat.)

ALFRED: *(Slowly looking up. Their eyes meet.)* I want you to know why. I didn't mean it.

PA: Mean what?

ALFRED: What I said. What you heard. I was tricked into it. I was tricked.

PA: Makes no difference.

ALFRED: It does to *me*. It really does. I want you to understand.

PA: But it makes no difference to me, Alfred. And what makes no difference to me…well…makes no difference. *(Pauses.)* I want *you* to understand.

ALFRED: Oh, I do. I really do.

PA: Oh, you *don't*. You really *don't*. *(Pauses.)* There's no *time* left for what makes a difference to *you*. I'm through taking the blame. I'm through lying.

ALFRED: She was my mother.

PA: She was what?

ALFRED: My mother.

PA: *SHE WAS MY WIFE!*

(Alfred turns his back to Pa, who is outraged by the move. Yells suddenly.)

PA: *Do you goddammit! understand me???*

ALFRED: Yes, Sir. I'm…sorry.

(Alfred and Pa look at each other.)

PA: I never ever heard you say things like "Yes, sir," or "I'm sorry"…not when you had some *position*.

ALFRED: No, sir…I mean…I'm sorry, sir…

PA: When I was your age, I could… *(Pauses.)* When I was forty, I was… *(Pauses.)* Hope you've learned something, Alfred. When I choose to go… when I die…and you get your power back…*real* power, I mean…hide it. *(Pauses.)* Never let it be counted. *(Pauses.)* Never let them know the limits. *(Pauses.)* I never did. *(Pauses.)* That was my secret. *(Pauses.)* You know how old I really am? *(No response.)* Take a guess.

(Pa laughs, softly. After a moment's silence, Alfred speaks.)

ALFRED: When you were sixty-three, I was just getting myself born. You'd been away four months already. *(Pauses.)* Can you *imagine*? *(Pauses.)* By the time my ship, as they say, sailed into port, you were four months gone *(Pauses.)* My mother said you'd run away…run away from home. *(Pauses.)* A man your age. *(Pauses.)* You missed my most important birthday, Pa. I've often wondered exactly what it was I'd done that offended you…that drove you away…

PA: I can explain that…

ALFRED: *(Explosively.)* Don't you *goddammit* interrupt me! I loathe being interrupted by you! *(Pauses.)* Apologize!

PA: *(Quietly.)* I'm sorry.

ALFRED: I said *apologize!*

PA: I'm…I'm sorry.

ALFRED: You never let me finish.

PA: I'm sorry. I'm sorry I took the blame for you, son. I'm sorry I lied. I was wrong. Dead wrong.

ALFRED: I don't understand.

PA: Open your eyes, Alfred.

ALFRED: What the hell are you talking about?

PA: My wife…your mother.

ALFRED: Oh, really? You think about her much? You miss her? Do you see her in your dreams?

PA: Wouldn't be much point in it, Alfred. She's dead.

ALFRED: What goes through your mind when you do think about her?

PA: But I *don't*. I said I don't.

ALFRED: But when you *do*…

PA: But I *don't!*

ALFRED: *(Screams.) I want an answer! (No response.)* Okay, Pa. Stay crazy. *(Pauses.)* I think about the box we put her in and whether or not it was really airtight, like they promised us…like it said in the brochure. *(Pauses.)* I kept the brochure for years… *(Pauses.)* How much flesh is left now? That's quite another question high on the list of things I think about. *(Pauses.)* What color is it? Are the maggots still nibbling away and, if so, what specific kind of maggot is attracted to my ma: grub or larva; blue-bottle maggot or cheese-fly maggot? *(Pauses.)* I've done quite an exhaustive study. I've become quite an expert in the long overlooked field of body rot. *(Pauses.)* No one really knows how the maggot gets in: how it penetrates the sealed box. Nobody knows where the maggot comes from, period. Nobody even knows where the word "maggot" comes from. Etymologically speaking, the maggot is a mystery. *(Pauses.)* So's my mother, thanks to you. *(Pauses.)* It's as though I never had one…as though she never, well, existed. *(Pauses.)* I'm bringing her back. Sorry.

PA: Sorry? Why?

ALFRED: Everything born dies. Once you've seen the thing itself, you can't pretend. Can you? *(Yells.) Can you?*

PA: No, you can't pretend.

ALFRED: Let me get to my essential question, please. Cremation or burled walnut, Pa? Which do you prefer?

PA: Is that a question that needs to be answered?

ALFRED: Cremation certainly has its good points. It's maggot-proof and quite tidy. We should be realistic in these matters... *(Pauses.)* And I could scatter your ashes, if you'd like. I'd do that for you. *(Pauses.)* I could maybe hurl them into the wind and scatter them over Quannapowitt. Or Good Harbor Beach down in Gloucester...Maybe even Gloucester harbor during the Greasy Pole Contest. Or maybe Magnolia? Or Wingaersheek Beach? Or Crane's, down in Ipswich? *(Pauses.)* Course, I'd be running the risk that the wind would turn against me...that your ashes might blow back into my face...into my eyes...cause me to blink and maybe miss something that was really *considerable. (Suddenly.)* I could promise you *anything*, couldn't I? Just the way you promised *her? (Softly.)* I just don't understand how you can feel nothing.

PA: You don't believe it, do you, son? You really can't open your eyes to it, can you?

ALFRED: I was there, Pa. I have eyes. I have a memory.

PA: Look at the cap, Alfred. Try it on. It was yours, Alfred, remember?

(Alfred holds cap—does not place it on his head.)

PA: No? You will. Sooner or later you will. You'll have to.

(Sam and Emily enter together. Alfred looks at Emily, angrily.)

ALFRED: You!

EMILY: *(To Alfred.)* Is it over?

ALFRED: I feel cold.

EMILY: Pa?

SAM: He looks pretty bad...Nearly finished. *(Pauses.)* Crow's *already* dead. Just saw him layin', feet curled under, West Ward path. All buggy already, too. *(Pauses.)* Old people layin' down sick, all over town. Looks as if everybody's gettin' set for the big change. *(Pauses.)* Guess we'll all go now. *(Pauses.)* Course, when I go, I do have a plan. Wanna hear it?

PA: No.

SAM: No?

PA: No.

SAM: It's wrong. It ain't fair. It's wicked. It angers me somethin' awful. I know the man's a liar, a cheater, and a fornicator, but this is too much...*too much! (Pauses.)* What did he ever do, really, ta deserve this kinda pain and punishment? A ton of horrible lies does *not,* in *my* book, add up ta this horrible ending. Not for such a man. *(Pauses.)* Your father was a good man, Alfred. He lived a good, clean-and-moral, hard-working life. Lies, cheating, and fornication to the wind… *(Pauses.)* It simply ain't fair.

PA: What ain't fair, Sam?

SAM: The life.

PA: The life?

SAM: The life.

PA: Shut up, Sam.

SAM: About what happened…I couldn't stop it…

PA: I saw that okay. But why'd you have to start it?

SAM: Been with this man nearly all my life. I know he's a liar, but all the same… *(Pauses.)* I've never known a man with his qualities. *(Pauses.)* I'd be…nothing…without him. *(Pauses.)* Everything I got, I owe to him. Even though he's a liar… *(Pauses.)* He…well…taught me everything I know. *(Pauses.)* Liar or not, this man's a saint. *(Pauses.)* He's the one I'd burn for. *(Pauses.)* I never married because of him… *(Pauses.)* He…satisfied…me.

(Sam's hand is on Pa's cheek, his thumb near Pa's mouth. Pa bites Sam's thumb. Sam squeals and yips.)

SAM: The filthy bitch just bit me!

PA: And I'll do it again.

SAM: *(Mortified; outraged.)* That bite might have just cost you the best friend a man ever had.

PA: Who? You? Man's best friend?

SAM: I hated that crack. *(Pauses.)* That crack did it. *(Pauses.)* I'm gettin' outa here. I've had enough. *(Pauses.)* Sixty-one years. Sixty-one miserable years. *(Sam moves to Pa; points his finger at Pa.)* You lied to me, Tommy. You goddamn lied.

(Pa bites Sam's finger. Sam squeals and yips.)

SAM: Doggone! This bullshit artist drew blood! *(Pauses.)* Doggone. *(Pauses.)* This is curtains, partner. *(Pauses; looks at his finger.)* Doggone.

PA: *(Laughing.)* Get outa here, Sam. *(Pauses; smiles.)* I've had enough.

SAM: Sure. *(Pauses; to Pa.)* I'll go. *(Pauses.)* I'm on my way. *(No response.)* I'm blowin' this town. *(Takes five steps in silence.)* Doesn't bother me a bit. *(Five more steps. At door now.)* I ain't usually a quitter, but sixty years is where I draw the line. *(Pauses.)* Tom?

PA: Yuh, Sam?

SAM: God bless. *(Pauses.)* Tommy?

PA: Yuh, Sam?

SAM: It kinda annoys me that you're…well…but, long as you are, well…

PA: What, Sam?

SAM: You gonna let me?

PA: Let you what?

SAM: Finish?

PA: Can you?

SAM: It came to me just after noon. After all these years of work I have it. I swear to God: the greatest story ever told!

PA: Go on, Sam…

SAM: Oh, God… *(Pauses; grinning now.)* When you take an idea like this, as I have, and work on it and work on it and work on it, as I have, it just gets better and better. *(Pauses.)* A small perfection is what's comin'…

PA: Go on, Sam…

SAM: Okay, okay. *(Pauses. Poses.)* I've always felt that the best way out of this wicked awful mess called the life was out route one-twenty-eight, Lynnfield way and right up the Newburyport Turnpike…that's route one…straight up into New Hampshire… *(Pauses.)* You wanna know where ta go from there?

PA: Where, Sam?

SAM: *(To Alfred.) You* wanna know?

ALFRED: Where, Sam?

SAM: *(To Emily.) You* wanna know?

EMILY: Where, Sam?

SAM: *(Taking stage fully now.)* Here it comes…"The Way Outa Wakefield!"…the greatest story is finally gettin' told. The ending…the punch…the capper…the over-the-top…the *risus puris! (To Pa.)* Ask me again, Tom.

PA: Where, Sam? Did you forget the ending, Sam? The punch? The capper? The *risus puris?* He forgot!

(There is a long, painful pause, in which it becomes quite obvious that Sam has forgotten the ending to his joke.)

PA: He forgot.

SAM: *(Shocked and dejected.)* Oh, my dear God. Oh, my dear sweet God… *(Pauses; moves to side of stage in false exit. He stops. He returns again to the center of the stage.)* If I ever *EVER!* try that one again, I'm gonna take a little more time settin' it up! *(Pauses; moves to side of stage. Stops. He turns to Pa.)* You'll see. *(Sam exits the play.)*

PA: *(After a pause.)* Used to keep disbelieving that Sam's really crazy…

(Pauses.) Lately, it's been harder than ever to disbelieve... *(Pauses.)* Alfred?

ALFRED: Right here.

PA: Sam left, huh?

ALFRED: Sam left.

PA: He's gone, huh?

ALFRED: He's gone.

PA: He lied, ya know. He's really a hundred. I'm a hundred and three.

EMILY: Sam's gone.

PA: Man's been tryin' ta kill me for years now. Sixty, maybe sixty-one... *(Pauses.)* Accomplished th' opposite. Kept me alive. Kept me alive and then some. *(Pauses.)* Every day, day after day, he put six drops of poison...strychnine...in my mornin' glass of Wakefield water. *(Pauses.)* Caused me some pain at first, but with some interestin' side effects. Strychnine was the ticket. Doctors were amazed. *(Pauses.)* Made me potent. Able and anxious ta please...every woman in town. Stoneham and Reading, as well. *(Pauses.)* Made a real lover of me. *(Pauses.)* To make a lover of a man who's so full of hate is quite a thing. *(Pauses.)* Sam did that for me. *(Pauses.)* Sixty-one years, six drops a day, never missed a mornin'... *(Pauses.)* That's friendship. *(Pauses.)* Gone now, I guess. *(Pauses.)* Is he outa sight?

EMILY: Sam's gone.

ALFRED: He's gone, Pa.

PA: Emily?

EMILY: Open your eyes, Pa...

PA: Can't...Don't want to...Not now...

EMILY: You've got to...tell me. Now. Did Alfred kill his mother?

ALFRED: Stop it...

EMILY: You promised me...to tell me...out loud...*NOW!*

ALFRED: *(Softly intensely.)* Back off from him...

EMILY: Nobody knows but you...Alfred can't remember. Will you for *Christ's* sake open your eyes!

ALFRED: You stay away from him! *(Moves to her.)* Do you hear me?
      (She turns.)

ALFRED: Step back.

EMILY: Please, Pa, answer me.

ALFRED: Hey!

EMILY: Answer me!

ALFRED: Hey!

PA: Okay, what's your question?

EMILY: Did Alfred kill his mother?

ALFRED: Hey!

PA: *(To Alfred.)* Stop making noises!… *(Pauses.)* Yes. *(Pauses.)* Yes, he did.

ALFRED: *(Quietly.)* That's not true. *(Bows his head.)*

PA: He thought he was doin' me a favor, I guess. *(Pauses.)* He was just a kid.

ALFRED: That's not true.

PA: He killed 'em both. Stabbed them with his Scout knife while they were in bed together. *(Pauses.)* My bed. He musta thought I wanted that: Wanted them punished. *(Pauses.)* He was protecting me from knowing.

ALFRED: That's…not…true.

PA: Sam and me, we took the blame for it. I told Sam I'd done it. Sam never knew the real truth. I spared him from that. *(Pauses.)* If Sam'd known, he never woulda stayed with me. I had to hide it from him. *(Pauses.)* Sam trusted me. He always did. Gone now… *(Pauses.)* Alfred was only ten then, that's all. No point in making a boy ten suffer. I wanted to protect him: the boy: Alfred. *(Pauses; screams.) I made a mistake!!! (Pauses; quietly again.)* Alfred did the murders. I took the blame, but he's got the guilt. And that's the truth. *(To Alfred.)* There it is, Alfred. In the open now. The cap probably still fits. Try it. *(To Emily.)* His cap. He wrapped his Scout knife and best baseball cards in it. Put it all in a cigar box…

EMILY: Dutch Masters.

PA: Yuh. Dutch Masters. How'd you find it?

EMILY: I was persistent, Pa. That's my nature.

ALFRED: *(To Emily; deliberately.)* I want you…out of my life. *(Pauses.)* Good-bye, Emily.

EMILY: Alfred, I…

ALFRED: *(Cutting her off.)* I said *good-bye.*

PA: You'd better go…If you want to punish Alfred for what I told you, that's *your* business. My business is ending now. I want to be with Alfred for a bit. *(Pauses.)* I'm sorry to have to give you such…bad news… *(Pauses.)* A father should die with his son nearby. You're not my son. Alfred's my son. You'd better go. I'm gettin' close now

ALFRED: I…want…you…out…of…here… *(Pauses; turns to Pa.)* Okay, Pa? Did you hear me? *(To Emily again.)* I want you out of my life. *(Yells.) Do you hear me?*

EMILY: *(After a long pause.)* Fine, Alfred, fine. *(Smiles.)* Perfect. *(Pauses.)* I know it all, Alfred. All the pieces have finally fit together. I know all about the Widow O'Brien Scandal, Alfred. I know it's true. *Did you hear me, Alfred?* I said that I know. I do…I know why you had to marry me, why you forced me, why you held me down. I even know why my babies died. I know it all.

ALFRED: *(A circus barker's voice.)* Good-bye, Emily!

PA: Emily?

EMILY: What?

PA: What is it you want, Emily? What is it you *really* want?

EMILY: Pa… *(Moves to side of stage.)* I never thought you'd ask. *(Turns to Alfred.)* I shall destroy you, Alfred. I swear it. It's going to take time and money, but I've got both…lots…I'm going to destroy you, Alfred. I really shall. *(Pauses.)* No one will be able to stop me Alfred. Not you. Not me. No one. *(Pauses.)* I swear it. *(To Pa.)* Pa? You asked and now you know: Alfred dies. I swear it.

(Emily goes to Pa. She kisses him. Emily goes to Alfred. She kisses him. Emily exits the play.)

ALFRED: *(After a long pause.)* She's gone, Pa. Emily's gone. *(Pauses.)* It's just us now. Just family.

PA: Tell me what to do, Alfred. It's just us now. Family: father and son. No one's tricking you now. It's just us. Tell me straight. I want to leave it to you.

ALFRED: I don't understand. Leave *what* to me?

PA: The decision. Live or die. Which?

ALFRED: *What the hell are you talking about?*

PA: Me…

ALFRED: What?

PA: No one here now…just you and me…Tell me!

ALFRED: Pa, please don't…Just be quiet now…Shhhh.

PA: Quick Alfred! Live or die! *(Gasps for breath.)* Put it simply…Tell me simply. I want to hear it from your lips…your mouth…Your mind…

ALFRED: *I don't know!*

PA: Think!

ALFRED: I don't know!

PA: Hurry!

ALFRED: Don't, Pa!

PA: I have to!

ALFRED: You don't…!

PA: I *want* to!

ALFRED: We never talked!

PA: Don't be stupid! *(Pauses.)* Do you hear me???*

(There is a long pause; Alfred places cap on head.)

ALFRED: Yes. *(Pauses; realizes.)* They were all together: buried. In a Dutch Masters Cigar box. Sealed. Wood. I remember now, the cap, the knife, my best baseball cards. I must have figured they'd punish me—catch me—The cards were there, Pa—I'd forgotten—All signed and wrapped in alphabetical order. I was neat—ordered. Joe Cronin, Dom DiMaggio, Bobby Doerr, Bob Ferris, Mickey Harris, Higgins, Wally Moses, Johnny Peskey, Wagner, Ted Williams, Rudy York. *(Pauses.)* It's true, Pa, isn't it? *I* was the one who did it. I did. *(Pauses.)* I'd forgotten. I killed your wife…my mother…You've been protecting me, haven't you? *(Pauses.)* Pa? It still fits, Pa. *(Pauses; waits.)* Pa? Look, Pa. *(Softly.)* Pa? Get up. Don't die. *(Suddenly angry.)* You've got no right to do this! *What I did I did for you!* I thought you were…a great man. *(Changed tone.)* Get up, Pa. I don't want to stay alone with this. Pa? *(Pauses.)* Pa? I don't. I really don't. *(Pauses; smiles.)* I'm very successful, Pa…I've been very lucky. I am quite a successful young…man. *(Pauses; softly.)* Pa? I've gotta be punished, Pa… *(Pauses.)* Pa? I've gotta… *(Softly.)* Pa, it's me: Alfred.

(Silence. Pa, on sofa, absolutely still. Alfred, on sofa, unmovingly. A moment passes. Alfred stands, moves to chair, sits, removes cap. He moves his face toward the auditorium, stops, stares straight out front. He bows his head. Tableau. The lights fade to black.)

The play is over.

Paris, Chicago, New York City, Gloucester—1971–1978.

Alfred Dies

For Martin Esslin.

THE PEOPLE OF THE PLAY

ALFRED: Forties, thin, once elegant.
LYNCH: Forties, thick, tough.
ROXY: Ancient.
EMILY: Forties, thin, once elegant.

THE PLACE OF THE PLAY

A makeshift prison room; set in the storage room under the lanternlike cupola bandstand, the Common, Wakefield, Massachusetts.

THE TIME OF THE PLAY

End of June, start of July.

An aged man is but a paltry thing,
A tattered coat upon a stick, unless
Soul clap its hands and sing, and louder sing
For ever tatter in its mortal dress,
Nor is there singing school but studying
Monuments of its own magnificence:
And therefore I have sailed the seas and come
To the holy city of Byzantium.

—Yeats

Alfred Dies

ACT I
SCENE I

Prison room. Dawn. Stage in darkness. Three sharp knocks are heard. Same sound will precede each scene of play. Church bells in distance, four chimes. First words of play—Alfred's—are heard in darkness.

ALFRED: *(Yells.) Anybody out there? (Pauses.) Hello!*

(Lights to full, suddenly. Storage room for park benches, under the bandstand, under the Common, Wakefield, Massachusetts. The room is circular, stone-walled.

A makeshift prison has been constructed in the room of equidistant metal bars. The floor space of the prison cell occupies one half of the entire floor space of the room. There are two doors in the room, no windows. One door is upstage right, connecting the room to a staircase leading to the outside. The second door is on the upstage left, in the cell, leading to an unlit back room. There is a door to the cell, downstage center, constructed of equidistant bars, held closed with lock and key, plus a padlocked heavy chain.

Park benches are stacked along the walls outside the cell. Three benches are lined one in front of the other, downstage left, for use by those outside the cell. There is no furniture in the cell.

A small table is set, downstage left, upon which a telephone sits. Opposite, a small court stenography machine is set on a proper table, with a stenographer's chair set under. Both table and chairs are castered.

Crates are stacked along the wall between the door to the room and the stenography table. One of the crates is a portable refrigerator for food storage. A long pole, padded at one end, leans against the stageright wall.

There are three overhead light sources visible: one lamp, exceedingly bright, hangs center of cell; a second, downstage right, over benches (it is not on at start of play): and a third light hangs over stenography table. Cell light and stenography table light are lit.

A ventilation duct is seen overhead, near where pole is leaned. Possible to open duct for fresh air by poking same with pole. Also possible to poke caged person in cell with pole.

Weather in room cool and damp: unusual in contrast to July's heat in world above ground. Sense of absolute silence wanted, when no one creates sound in room. No sounds from outside world above evident during play until its conclusion.)

ALFRED: *(Calling from offstage, behind door.)* Anybody out there?

(Three sharp knocks again. Source revealed now as Alfred knocking on back of door, which suddenly flies open. Alfred hurtles out onstage, self-propelled, stopping at downstage bars of cell. The lights hurt his eyes. He shields them, not blinking. He is shocked and amazed to discover that he has been caged. He moves about the inside circumference of the cell, feeling the bars as he goes. His eyes adjust to the new lighting. He studies the room outside of the cell. He calls again.)

ALFRED: *Hello?*

(There is no reply. Pause. He moves to the open door on upstage wall of cell. He peeks outside, calling, with head offstage, poked into darkened room above cell.)

ALFRED: *Anybody out here, either?*

(There is no reply. Alfred exits into upstage darkened room. For a moment, there is no one onstage. Alfred's voice, heard calling in darkened room.)

ALFRED: *Anybody hear me?*

(No reply. Silence. The downstage left door opens quietly. Lynch enters.)

LYNCH: Hello?

ALFRED: *(His voice from back room. He thinks he has been answered.)* Hello!

(Lynch looks around room and into cage. Alfred runs onto stage.)

LYNCH: Alfred!

ALFRED: *(Delighted to see another person in room.)* Hello!

LYNCH: Hey, Alfred. It's me! *(Moves to bars of cell.)* Don't you recognize me?

ALFRED: *(Confused.)* I beg your pardon…

LYNCH: It's me: Lynchie…

ALFRED: Lynchie?

LYNCH: Lynchie. Lynchie. From West Ward School…

ALFRED: I didn't go to West Ward School. I went to Warren School…

LYNCH: *(Takes bulb from paper bag, exchanges same in downstage-left light. He stands on chair.)* Lynch, for Christ's sakes! From church league basket-ball…Saint Joe's!

ALFRED: I certainly didn't play for Saint Joe's!

LYNCH: Lynch, Alfred, Lynch! From B.C.!

ALFRED: B.C.? *(Pauses.)* I never went to B.C. *(Pauses.)* I've parked at

B.C.…nights…on dates…But that was a long time ago. *(Pauses; smiles.)* I think there's been a tremendous mistake here.

LYNCH: I know you know me. Look at me. Look at me. *(He stands in front of cell now, smiling.)*

ALFRED: Well, there is a look of the familiar about you.

LYNCH: I'm Margaret's brother.

ALFRED: Excuse me, but did you say you were Margaret's brother?

LYNCH: *(Laughing now.)* You remember, now, huh? Lynchie. We use'ta have terrific fistfights, you and me, right?…I use'ta win.

ALFRED: Your sister?…Your sister was Margaret? Lynchie? *That* Lynchie? You're Margaret's brother? The brother that's my age…roughly?

LYNCH: *(Deadly serious now.)* Yuh, Your age, roughly. I'm six weeks older than you. Six.

ALFRED: My God…I just…Well, look at you!

LYNCH: *(After a long pause; with tremendous hostility.)* How's your pecker?

ALFRED: Excuse me?

LYNCH: *(Smiles.)* We'll talk about Margaret in due course, huh? *(Attitude changes drastically; he laughs.)* You're lookin' great, Alfred…just great!

ALFRED: *(Half laughs.)* You don't look so bad, yourself, Lynchie. Good ta see ya… *(Smiles; looks around.)* What is this place, anyway? Some kind of…prison?

LYNCH: Yuh, 'tis.

ALFRED: Where are we, anyway? Are we in Wakefield?

LYNCH: What kind of dumb question's that s'posed ta be?

ALFRED: What kind of dumb question? I don't actually *know* what kind. Are we, Lynchie? Are we in Wakefield?

LYNCH: Yuh. We are. We're in Wakefield. In the storage room for park benches, under the bandstand, center of the Common, right overlookin' Lake Quannapowitt. I built this on commission…

ALFRED: *What?*

LYNCH: The pen. Your cage. I built it on commission. Specially built prison, just for the occasion. No expense spared. Pretty good, huh?

ALFRED: *(Looking at his cage; feeling bars to it.)* You did this, huh? You seem to know your way around a tool. *(Smiles at Lynch.)* You in construction?

LYNCH: In what?

ALFRED: Your line of work: construction?

LYNCH: Opposite.

(Alfred looks at Lynch blankly.)

LYNCH: *De*struction. *(Smiles.)* I take things down.

ALFRED: But in the case of this…prison…you put things up?

LYNCH: Well, yuh. I mean, you can't learn one thing without learning the other…the opposite. Right?

ALFRED: Yes. I definitely agree. I wish I knew to what, exactly, but let's just move along… *(He pauses.)* We're in Wakefield, Massachusetts, under the bandstand, in the Common, underground? That's where we are?

LYNCH: Who told you that?

ALFRED: You told me that.

LYNCH: I've never been able to control my mouth. Yuh. It's true. Mother Earth is just above us.

ALFRED: Lynchie…uh?…Could I possibly risk another dumb one? Another dumb question? There's one burning inside me right now.

LYNCH: Shoot! It's a free country. Never let it be said I don't still have my sense of humor, huh? Remember?

ALFRED: *(Smiles.)* I sure do.

LYNCH: I remember takin' apart your 'thirty-seven Chevy Coupe…a two-seater, right?…and puttin' it back together again up on Buzzy Whatsis's barn roof… *(He laughs.)* That was hilarious!

ALFRED: *(Stares at Lynch awhile before speaking.)* Uh, Lynchie?

LYNCH: Yuh?

ALFRED: Am…uh…Am I inside the cell or are *you* inside the cell? *(Silence.)* It's a little difficult to tell from here.
(Lynch stares at Alfred.)

ALFRED: I knew you were going to think it was kinda a dumb question…

LYNCH: *(Astonished.)* Am *I* or *you?*… *(Laughs.)* That's really rich! *(Roars.)* You are one hilarious son of a bitch! No *wonder* Alfred L. Webber got rich and B. J. Lynch got nothin'!
(After laughter subsides, Alfred and Lynch stare at each other.)

ALFRED: My guess is me.

LYNCH: Right.

ALFRED: Could I ask you for how long?

LYNCH: How long you've *been?* Or how long you're *gonna be?*

ALFRED: Either, Lynchie. I'll take either.

LYNCH: You've *been* maybe three days now. Mostly sleeping. *(Pauses; scratches head.)* How long you're *gonna be*…depends.

ALFRED: On what?

LYNCH: Don't be a joker, Alfred. Not all the time. Air's getting foul… *(Pokes ventilator duct open.)* Some things are not laughing matters, huh?

ALFRED: Would you believe me if I told you I don't know a single bit of what's going on? This is a *total* blank to me…

LYNCH: That should be your case, then.

ALFRED: Case? I'm arrested? For what? Could I ask you for what?

(Lynch tries phone. As the men talk, Alfred, at first discreetly and then openly, tests the strength of the bars that define his cell. Neither will comment on this action.)

LYNCH: Insanity.

ALFRED: What?

LYNCH: Insanity. *(Tries phone again.)*

ALFRED: I've been arrested for insanity?

LYNCH: That should be your case.

ALFRED: Nobody gets arrested for insanity! *(Pauses.)* Most people are *rewarded* for insanity. Given better jobs: positions of leadership and control. *(Pauses.)* Political power. *(Pauses.)* Professions such as law and medicine: crawling with the demented and the insane. *(Pauses.)* It's a fact. *(Pauses.)* What case?

(The phone is dead. Lynch turns to Alfred.)

LYNCH: Here's what, if I was you…

ALFRED: Were.

LYNCH: Huh?

ALFRED: *(Steps back three steps and then runs his body into the upstage-left bars. They do not budge under the force of his weight.)* If I *were* you… *(Smiles.)* Subjunctive. *(Pauses.)* Sorry. It's the one case I tend to believe in… *(Smiles, embarrassed by his own digression.)* In which I tend to believe. Am I in danger?

LYNCH: Twenty years ago, you were as normal as any of us. That's what the city does to you, Alf…

ALFRED: *(Sits on floor; pauses.)* Uh…Lynchie?

LYNCH: Yuh?

ALFRED: Could you try never to call me that?

LYNCH: Huh?

ALFRED: What you just called me.

LYNCH: Alf? *(Pauses.)* Everybody calls you Alf.

ALFRED: I don't think so.

LYNCH: Are you kidding me?

ALFRED: No, I really don't like that so much: being called that.

LYNCH: Alf? You don't like "Alf"?

ALFRED: It really annoys me…

LYNCH: Alf? "Alf" annoys you?

ALFRED: …Runny.

LYNCH: What's'at?

ALFRED: Runny. Unless my memory fails me…Runny.

LYNCH: I wouldn't, Alf…

ALFRED: Runny Lynch…"The nose that flows like the Mystic River." Wasn't that the way you were known in some circles?

LYNCH: Okay, Alfred. Okay.

ALFRED: *(Smiling.)* Okay, Lynch. *(Suddenly.)* What the hell did I do? Who brought me here? When? I feel like I've been drugged! Or hit over the head? Did somebody hit me over the head? Huh? Huh? *(Leans in.)* Someone will be held responsible here…I warn you.

LYNCH: *You* warn *me?*

ALFRED: "Imbroglio" is the word that springs to mind.

LYNCH: What's that supposed to mean? Like a barbecue? You hungry?

ALFRED: Hungry? I am. Yes.

LYNCH: Well, I suppose I could go into town and try to scrounge something up…maybe at Hazelwood. Sun's up. They're open. What kind of food you like?

ALFRED: Could you just give me a hint?

LYNCH: You mean like pancakes?

ALFRED: What on earth are you talking about?

LYNCH: What on earth are *you* talking about?

ALFRED: I asked you first.

LYNCH: I'm talking about breakfast.

ALFRED: I'm talking about why I'm here. Just a hint, Lynchie?

LYNCH: What was the word that sprung to your mind?

ALFRED: I'll tell *you,* if you tell *me.*

LYNCH: C'mon, Alf…I'm not s'pose'ta be talking to you at all…

ALFRED: Runn*yyyy…*

LYNCH: C'mon, Alfred. I can't. I could get into real trouble.

ALFRED: For an old pal? What am I here for? How come I'm in jail?

LYNCH: I can't. I really can't.

ALFRED: I'm going to find out anyway, right? For an old pal, Lynchie. Come on…I'll count to three and you say your word and I'll say my word. Come on, Lynchie…

LYNCH: I dunno…

ALFRED: Lynchie. Lynchie-Lynchie. Lynchie-Lynchie-Lynchie…

LYNCH: At three. Okay. Count.

ALFRED: One…two…*three! Imbroglio!*

LYNCH: Didn't know you could count that high. *(Laughs.)*

ALFRED: You cheated me, Lynch. You goddamn cheated me.

(Lynch laughs.)

ALFRED: I gave you my word, Lynch. A deal's a deal…

(Lynch laughs again.)

ALFRED: You're welchin' out! *(Pauses.)* You're pullin' a Guinea-give… *(Pauses.)* You're Scotchin' me… *(Pauses.)* You're Jewin' me…You're Jappin' me… *(Pauses.)* I'm gettin' a Sheenie-screwin'…Baptist bee bop… *(Pauses.)* This is Polack pudding… *(Pauses.)* You're a nigger in a woodpile, Lynch… *(With sudden anger.)* Now, you open your dumb mouth and you speak words, dolt!

LYNCH: *(After a pause.)* I don't like your attitude. I would try a little more respect, if I was—were—you. *(Smiles.)* You ain't exactly able to call your position *prime,* ya know.

ALFRED: Have I been charged?

LYNCH: For what? For *this?* *(Pauses.)* This is being paid for… *(Laughs.)*

ALFRED: Have I been charged *with something* is what I meant. Not *for something.* *(Pauses.)* The state's paying for this, right? There'll be a judge, right? *(Pauses.)* Lynchie, for the love of God, *I really don't know!*

LYNCH: I'm not supposed to be talking to you, Alfred…I'm even a little sorry I mentioned the bandstand to ya…Maybe that was a mistake, ya know?

ALFRED: But I'm in trouble…

LYNCH: That's an understatement, if I ever heard one…

ALFRED: Then the state *is* paying for this, right?

LYNCH: I can't talk.

ALFRED: I mean, that's just *assumed,* right?

LYNCH: Sorry, Alf. *(He crosses to desk and telephone; sits.)*

ALFRED: You mean that somebody else is?…Somebody else is footing the bill for this…? *(Pauses.)* A private person…party? *(No response.)* It is, isn't it? What's in the back room behind me? I can't see anything in there. Where does it lead to?

LYNCH: You're gonna haveta figure things out for yourself.

ALFRED: Sure. *(Pauses.)* Okay. *(Pauses.)* I don't mind at all…

(Alfred moves upstage and exits into the darkened room. Lynch watches a moment and then goes to telephone. He dials a number on the telephone, waits a moment, listens.)

LYNCH: What's'a matter here? *(Jiggles the receiver on and off the cradle, breaking the connection; he listens for a dial tone. There is none.)* What's'a matter here?

ALFRED: *(Calling from darkened room, upstage.)* Hello? Anybody here?

LYNCH: *(Looks up to cell. Moves from telephone to bars and tries to look into darkened room. Calls into room.)* Alfred!

ALFRED: *(Calling from room, offstage.)* Hello? *(There is a silence. Alfred reenters cell, onstage. He shields his eyes from the bright onstage light.)* Where's the door? I've just felt my way around in there. No door... *(Moves around cell, feeling bars.)* No breaks in bars... *(Stops; looks at door.)* Just one door between room and cage... *(Looks at Lynch; smiles.)* You must have rebuilt this whole room for me, huh? All this welding...all those bricks laid in there... *(Motions to back room.)* Highly skilled work...backbreaking, too, I should think...

LYNCH: Not too bad...

ALFRED: Somebody must be very anxious to...well...hold me down.

LYNCH: You hungry?

ALFRED: I believe we've been through all that...

LYNCH: You didn't give me your order...

ALFRED: Do I have choices?

LYNCH: How do you feel about meat?

ALFRED: Meat? *(Pauses.)* Neutral. *(Pauses.)* I am quite neutral on the subject of meat. *(Pauses.)* It's Emily, isn't it?

(Lynch turns to Alfred and smiles. Lynch walks to telephone and tries to dial a number.)

LYNCH: What the hell's the matter here? *(Slams receiver down on its cradle.)* Phone's outa whack! Three days, now. The whole goddamn week before the goddamn Fourth of July is a waste, far's I'm concerned...They oughtta just skip from June Thirtieth ta July Eighth...and that'd be it!...How da they expect me ta operate without a phone?

ALFRED: Two Whiting's milk cartons and string? Semaphore flags? Finger-taps in Morse Code. *(After a stare from Lynch.)* Where is she, Lynch? I'd sure hate to celebrate Independence Day without my Emily close by...

LYNCH: *(Moves again to the telephone, made nervous by the mention of the name Emily. He picks up the phone, but it is dead.)* Crappola! *(Lynch violently rips the phone from the wall and throws it onto the floor.)* Conditions are wicked awful nowadays!

(Alfred stares incredulously at Lynch, who kicks the fallen telephone, crosses to the crates, stage left; sits. Alfred stares after him awhile.)

ALFRED: *(Smiling.)* You've grown into quite an ignoramus.

(Lynch turns to him; stares.)

ALFRED: You were kinda a dumb, but likable kid. *(Pauses.)* I remember. *(Pauses.)* It's amazing how the worst multiplies. Whatever was likable was probably beaten down and out…Was that it? Beaten? *(Pauses.)* What's left is really horrifying, Lynch. *(Pauses.)* You've become a veritable mutant. You've become to man what margarine has become to butter… you are decaf, the anti-christ to coffee. You are Sweet 'n' Low! *(Pauses.)* It is incredibly difficult to believe that we're even close to the same age, Lynch. Incredibly difficult to believe…You look just awful, Lynch. Awful. What did they *do* to you…to make you look so awful?
(Lynch bows his head.)

ALFRED: Where is she, Lynch? Where's Emily? I want to know where Emily is, Lynch. I want to see Emily.

LYNCH: *(After a pause, looks up.)* I don't know what you're talking about, Alfred. *(Pauses; smiles.)* You're not making any sense… *(Pauses. Stands.)* I don't know any Emily. *(Smiles again.)* She someone local or is she a visitor? *(Moves to door.)* I don't know what you're talking about, Alfred… *(Hand on doorknob.)* You're not making any sense.
(There is a silence in which Alfred and Lynch look at one another.)

LYNCH: *(Moves to cage. Uses confidential tone.)* Alfred?

ALFRED: *(Moves to him, thinking he will get information.)* What do you want?
(Lynch spits at Alfred, wetting Alfred's face. There is a pause. Alfred smiles, stares at Lynch.)

ALFRED: Nice. Really nice.
(The two men stare at each other. Tableau. Blackout.)

SCENE II

Later. Stage in darkness. Three sharp knocks are heard. First words of scene—Alfred's—are heard in darkness.

ALFRED: It's very comforting for me to know that you're out there…
(Lights to full, suddenly. Alfred, in cell, standing, leaning against bars of stage right wall. He stares at Emily, who sits in middle bench, outside of cell. Her legs are up on bench in front of her. There is a brown-paper bundle of food in cell, stage left. Alfred's beard has begun to fill in.)

ALFRED: I feel quite comfortable, really, knowing you're out *there* and I'm in *here*. *(Pauses.)* I'd always wondered why there were people who insisted on being jailed, time and time again. *(Pauses.)* Now I know. *(Pauses.)* It's the comfort of the situation. *(Moves to food bundle.)* Food? *(Lifts it as best he can.)* Yes, it certainly is. You're too kind to me, Emily. Far too kind. *(Sniffs. Opens bag: a cheeseburger.)* Something Oriental? I think it is! Quite a change of pace from what I've been eating… *(Looks at Emily.)* You do know what I've been eating, don't you? *(Smiles.)* Nothing.

(Emily sits, watching, silently. Alfred eats voraciously; ravenously. When he is again aware of Emily's presence, he is embarrassed.)

ALFRED: Look at *me*: eating like a bird: a raven…a vulture…a condor… *(Pauses; smiles. He stands; faces Emily.)* Look at *me*…awful. Needing a shave, as I do. Very sloppy… *(Bows head.)*

(Emily's feet down now; replaced by her hands, as she leans in against bench in front of her.)

ALFRED: Been quite a while, hasn't it, Emily? *(Pauses.)* I hope you take this remark in the right spirit… *(Pauses.)* You look…older. *(Without warning.)* Is this your idea of a *joke*? Is this your idea of something *funny*? *(Angrily.)* This is hardly a joke, Emily! This is hardly funny! *(Pauses.)* What is it about you that moves me to such…anger? To such heights of rage and revulsion? *(Pauses.)* Maybe it's the funny little way you wear your hair. Or the way you have me hit over the head and tortured. The way you build jails and have me locked up like some sort of criminal. Maybe that's it. Or maybe it's just your face, which I suddenly discover I can't…stomach.

(Emily stands; walks to door, exits. There is a long pause.)

ALFRED: *(Calls after her.)* Em-i-leee!

(Lights quickly fade to black.)

SCENE III

Later. Stage in darkness. Three sharp knocks sound as soon as lights have gone to black at end of preceding scene. First words of scene—Lynch's—are heard in darkness.

LYNCH: You're gonna haveta pay some attention!

(Lights to full, suddenly. Alfred, on floor, dozing in cell. Lynch, standing at bars to cell, poking inside at Alfred with ten-foot pole. Alfred, struck by the

pole, stirs. Lynch pokes him violently. Alfred raises his head, suddenly. His beard is filling in now, considerably.)

LYNCH: Shake a leg!

ALFRED: Huh?

LYNCH: Wiggle it! *(Pokes him.)* Move your ass! *(Pokes him again.)* Get a move on!

ALFRED: What do you want?

LYNCH: Let's have a little hustle.

ALFRED: What for?

LYNCH: It's morning… *(Pauses.)* Rise and shine…

ALFRED: Stuff it closed, will ya, Lynch?…

LYNCH: *(Poking at Alfred with the pole.)* Up and Adam and Eve!

ALFRED: *Lynch, God damn it! Knock it off!*

(Lynch pokes Alfred again.)

ALFRED: C'mon!

(Lynch pokes him again.)

ALFRED: Knock it off!

(Lynch pokes him again. Alfred leaps to his feet.)

ALFRED: Okay, *okay,* I'm up!

LYNCH: *(Removes pole from cell and leans it against wall, next to his desk.)* I got some duties for you. *(Pauses.)* Boss's orders… *(Produces leather travel kit with shaving cream, towel, razor. No mirror.)* You gotta shave.

ALFRED: Shave? *(Pauses.)* Why? *(Pauses.)* For whom? For you?

LYNCH: I only deliver the messages, Alfred. *(Pauses.)* C'mon, you gotta… *(Hands razor, shaving, cream, etc. through bars.)*

ALFRED: *(Taking supplies.)* Maybe if you didn't start off with "You gotta"… *(Pauses.)* I don't "gotta"… *(Pauses.)* Nobody's "gotta"…

LYNCH: Now that's where you're wrong, Alfred… *(Moves to other side of room.)* Everybody's gotta… *(Finds broom against wall.)* That's the truth… *(Begins sweeping room.)* You think I wanna do this? *(Pauses.)* I gotta. *(Pauses.)* You think I wanna spend my time poking you with a pole?

ALFRED: Call me crazy for saying this, Lynchie, but I do. I really do. I really think you enjoy spending your time poking me with what appears to be the legendary ten-foot pole. I think it pleases the living piss right outa you.

LYNCH: Yuh… *(Smiles.)* That's true, too. *(Laughs.)* I gotta admit, you got me there, Alfred. *(Laughs.)* You've got a hell of a way with words, too… *Ten-foot pole! (Laughs.)* I'm enjoyin' this all right. *(Pauses.)* But I don't enjoy working for a woman. I've got to tell you that. I don't enjoy working for a woman at all.

ALFRED: Especially *that* woman.

LYNCH: Yuh. True, again. You've got a knack for hitting the nail right on the head.

ALFRED: And you've got a knack for hitting *me* right on the head.

LYNCH: Hey, listen…It's my job, you know?

ALFRED: Hey, listen…I can remember when you did it without pay.

LYNCH: Times change.

ALFRED: "Times change"? You've got quite a way with the word yourself, Lynchie. Quite a way.

LYNCH: How'd you ever get stuck with her, Alf?

ALFRED: Me? *(Smiles.)* Stuck with Emily? *(Pauses.)* I forget. We've been stuck together for so long, I actually can't remember the first sticking…

LYNCH: I gotta.

ALFRED: Huh?

LYNCH: Work for her.

ALFRED: Oh. *(Shaving now.)* Could I ask you something, Lynch?

LYNCH: *(Sweeping.)* Sure.

ALFRED: Isn't there something better I could do with my shit? *(Pauses.)* Maybe if you put a light in there…so I could at least *see* where it was going… *(Pauses.)* *Could* we get a light back there? It would be a hell of a lot better if I could…you know…Could you ask Emily for a light?

LYNCH: I'm not even supposed to be talking to you, ya know, let alone askin' favors…

ALFRED: Oh, you're supposed to be talking to me, all right… *(Pauses.)* Emily's too smart to trap me in a place with somebody like you and have you not talking… *(Pauses.)* I should not worry, if I were you, Lynch: You're doing good work.

LYNCH: Thank you.

ALFRED: Don't mention it.

LYNCH: God knows I try.

ALFRED: I said "Don't mention it."

LYNCH: Huh?

ALFRED: By my calculations, today is Thursday, right?

LYNCH: I can't tell you.

ALFRED: Am I at least warm? July Fourth will be Friday this year, right?

LYNCH: Can't say.

ALFRED: Cold then? July Fourth isn't Friday? It's Monday? Thursday? *(Pauses.)* Today is Monday, isn't it? Those are my two guesses: Thursday and Monday. *(Pauses.)* C'mon, Lynch…Give me a break, huh?

LYNCH: Sorry, Alfred…I ain't fallin' for it. *(Pauses; smiles.)* You must figure me for a dope…a real dumbbell.

ALFRED: You have uncanny perceptiveness… *(Wipes remainder of lather from his face with towel.)* No mirror, huh? *(Smiles.)* Just as well *(To Lynch.)* Any nicks?

LYNCH: *(Studies Alfred's face.)* Couple of suds still… *(Points.)* There. *(Alfred wipes his face.)*

LYNCH: You got 'em.

ALFRED: Thanks.

LYNCH: Pleasure.

ALFRED: I'll just bet.

LYNCH: You'll have to give me back the razor now…

ALFRED: That's ridiculous…

LYNCH: Sorry…

ALFRED: My beard's just going to appear again tomorrow… *(Pauses; smiles.)* That's the way a beard works, Lynch…

LYNCH: You bet. *(Pauses.)* Gimme the razor. *(Pauses.)* Give it over, Alfred!

ALFRED: The actual mechanism of a man's beard is quite fascinating… *(Smiles.)* Don't you think?

LYNCH: Razor.

ALFRED: How the good Lord can be so divinely and supremely clever, God only knows! To have the skill and cunning to insert exactly the right length of hair for sixty, seventy, eighty, a hundred years of life…

LYNCH: Huh?

ALFRED: All coiled in the jawbone…

LYNCH: What the hell are you talking about?

ALFRED: …serpentine… *(Pauses.)* Didn't you know? A head is full of curled hair.

LYNCH: You're cracked…you're mental…

ALFRED: Where'd ya think your beard was comin' from, Lynch? Your underarms and your crotch as well? *(Pauses.)* Thin air? Magic? Religious fervor? Patriotic passion? A vehement belief in order, such as in the old Quaker quantum: the tidier the house, the longer the beard; the sloppier the house, the more pubic the beard… *(Smiles.)*

LYNCH: Gimme the goddamn razor, Alfred!

ALFRED: *(Suddenly.)* Why'd she want me clean today, Lynch?

LYNCH: Just gimme!

ALFRED: *Plans today? Big boggling plans today? (Leans in.) What are they, Lynchie? What? What? What?*

LYNCH: *Gimme the goddamn razor!!!*

ALFRED: Frightened of an untimely end, are you? Frightened of suicide? Wouldn't you just be in the shit for that, huh?

LYNCH: Just gimme the goddamn razor, Alfred!

ALFRED: No! *(He smiles; walks to back wall holding razor.)* No.

LYNCH: *(Tries a new tone; a new tactic to get razor from Alfred.)* This doesn't give me any pleasure, you know?

ALFRED: I should think not.

LYNCH: I mean you...you were kinda my...well...you were kinda my *ideal*...when we were younger, I mean. When you were getting your picture in the papers...when you were always bein' mentioned on the television...practically every night...back then. *(Pauses.)* I used to be able to say to people: "Alfred and I played together as kids." *(Laughs.)* "I used ta beat him up!" *(Pauses.)* I used ta get a kick outa feelin' close to you and all...My whole family did. Most of Wakefield did...You were a famous guy: eighteen years old and already a millionaire. Hey, didn't this town hate your guts when you sold the swamp by the lake, huh? Eighteen years old and already made a cool million... *(Whistles appreciatively.)* "Boy Wonder" is what they used to call you in these parts. "Boy Wonder..." *(Pauses.)* Look at you now.

ALFRED: Lynchie...There's something I really need to know for old time's sake, huh? Why does Emily want me shaved today? Why does she want me all cleaned up? You can tell me, sport, huh? Is there an event coming? A special day? Is there a dignitary visiting? A Saltonstall? A Lodge? A Lowell? A Kennedy? A Cushing? A Bishop? A Pope? A Dryden? A Swift?

LYNCH: You know I'd tell you if I could, Alf... *(Pauses.)* There's no dignitary comin' here... *(Pauses.)* Your days of gettin' dignitaries to visit are all over, Alf. *(Quietly.)* The razor. *(No reply.)* You know something, Alf? Once I was getting fired...I was workin' at Crystal Cement as a loader. It was Christmastime, and I was gettin' fired. *(Pauses.)* Sons a bitches! *(Looks up at Alfred; smiles.)* I'm sittin' 'cross the desk from old Kiley...He was running the crew assignments then. He's tellin' me how bad times are. I'm gettin' two and a half bucks an hour and not even half a weeks work and *he's* tellin' *me* how bad things are... *(Pauses.)* I'm lookin' at my shoes, 'cause I know what's comin'. The radio's on in the background. Kiley cryin' the blues...and the next thing I know, old Alfred—you—on Kiley's radio. You were being interviewed. *(Smiles.)* Kiley asks if you're the same Alfred who was my sister Margaret's sweetheart and I say "yes" and one thing leads to another and I get to keep my rotten job. *(Pauses.)* You saved my ass, Alfred. *(Quietly.)* The razor.

ALFRED: Why am I being cleaned and shaved today, Lynchie? What's going to happen? *Please!*

LYNCH: You're being charged today. Your trial begins. Now, gimme…

ALFRED: Oh. I see. My trial. I'm being charged.

LYNCH: I shouldn't be telling you; you gotta pretend you don't know. I could get into awful trouble…

ALFRED: Don't you worry, Lynch. You don't have a worry in the world. *(Smiles.)* I swear to God. *(Pauses.)* Lynch?

(Lynch looks up.)

ALFRED: Charged with what? I'd really like to know. What crime, Lynch? Just give me the word.

LYNCH: I can't.

ALFRED: The word, please, Lynchie…

LYNCH: I can't. Really.

ALFRED: *(Screams, suddenly.)* I'll call Kiley! I will! You'll never work in the cement business again, Lynch! You'll be ruined in this town, Lynch. I gave you *my* word and you cheated me. You lied! Now, you…goddammit!…give me the word.

LYNCH: Razor, Alfred.

(Lynch reaches through the bars. Alfred extends the razor and they both hold the handle of same, as two young boys might hold a baseball bat in the air, waiting for the other to let loose.)

ALFRED: The word, Lynch.

LYNCH: Murder.

(Alfred lets loose his grip on the razor. Lynch takes it from him at once. Alfred repeats the following lines, moving his head from side to side, as through a machine.)

ALFRED: This is *déjà vu*… *(Repeats exactly the same tone.)* This is *déjà vu*… *(Again.)* This is *déjà vu*… *(Again.)* This is *déjà vu*… *(Smiles.)* That's French… *(Pauses.)* C'est *déjà vu*, mon cher Lynch… *(Repeats.)* C'est *déjà vu*, mon cher Lynch… *(Smiles.)* Of whom?

LYNCH: Of *whom?* As if you didn't know… *(Smiles.)* …of *whom*… *(Lynch moves to position in front of Alfred; stops. He smiles.)* Ten years, I worked on the cement trucks: you know that? I wasted ten years. *(Pauses.)* Your fault, Alfred. Your fault. *(Pauses.)* You wrecked my life. You ruined me. I was almost outa there too… *(Pauses; smiles.)* That's a fact.

ALFRED: I want a lawyer. I know my rights. I want a lawyer…

LYNCH: What rights? Rights, *here? (Laughs.)*

ALFRED: So. This is really happening, is it?

LYNCH: I know I shouldn't have talked, Alfred. I shouldn't have told you. *(Pauses.)* I shouldn't have spilled any beans… *(Pauses.)* But it was really worth it… *(Pauses.)* …to see your face… *(Pauses.)* I wish you could see your face…

ALFRED: I'm sure it's amusing…

LYNCH: Amusing? *(Smiles.)* Amusing? *(Smiles.)* Oh, it's much more than that, Alf. *(Pauses.)* It's the best thing I ever did. *(Pauses.)* In my whole life, this is the best! *(Pauses.)* By the time we're through with you, Alfred, you are gonna wish you never set foot back here in Wakefield, Massachusetts, again… *(Pauses.)* Really. *(Smiles.)* I give you my word.

(Lynch stands downstage left, near table, looking up at Alfred, who is in downstage-left-most position in cell. Alfred looks away and down. Alfred's head bows. Lynch watches a moment, then he too looks away and his head bows as well. Tableau. Lights fade to black.)

SCENE IV

Later. Stage in darkness. Three sharp knocks are heard. First words of scene—Emily's—are heard in darkness.

EMILY: I think you'd better start taking this seriously. *(Pauses.)* It's not going away.

(Lights to full, suddenly. Emily stands at table, downstage left. Beside her sits Roxy, an old woman, who records all dialogue on a courtroom stenography machine. Roxy is given to clearing her throat and her chest of bronchial mucus and phlegm. She is corpulent: obese. Lynch reclines on middle bench, with his feet dangling over bench in front of him. He appears to be sleeping. Alfred stands facing bars, upstage of Emily and Roxy, same side, looking away from them intentionally.)

EMILY: *(To Roxy.)* Did you get that?

ROXY: *(After a great deal of coughing and clearing of her throat and chest, looks at long tape that has been folding into stenography machine's tray. She tries to read same but cannot.)* I can't see without my glasses.

EMILY: *(After a long pause in which she and Roxy stare silently at each other.)* Do you have them?

ROXY: *(Pauses.)* My glasses?

EMILY: Yes, of course, your glasses…

ROXY: They're in my bag. *(Displaying oversized satchel pocketbook.)* Here.

EMILY: Put them on, please…

ROXY: Certainly. *(She does.)*

EMILY: Now have a look and read back what you've got…

ROXY: The whole thing?

EMILY: Just the last part, please…

ROXY: *(Reading.)* "I think you'd better start taking this seriously…It's not going away."

EMILY: Could you read before that, please…

(Alfred on his hands, feet against wall.)

ROXY: How afar before that?

EMILY: Use your own discretion…

ROXY: *(Rummaging through tape now, reading to herself. She coughs a great deal and then reads aloud.)* "Alfred? Are you paying attention to me?"…

ALFRED: *(Rights himself onto his feet.)* Huh?

ROXY: *(Still reading.)* "This is Roxy. Roxy, this is Alfred. Alfred, this is Roxy…"

ALFRED: Oh. You're reading… *(To Lynch.)* She's reading…

ROXY: *(Continuing.)* "How-dee-do," *I* said and "It's a pleasure, dear lady," *he* said. I then said, "I've heard a lot aboutcha," and he then said, "This is attractive, Emily…"

ALFRED: *(Interrupting.)* Wrong!

(Roxy and Emily turn to Alfred.)

ALFRED: "This is atrocious, Emily."…That's what I said.

EMILY: That's what he said.

ROXY: That's *not* what you said!

LYNCH: *(Calling across room.)* That's what he said!

ROXY: *(Calling to Lynch.)* You just keep your trap shut, okay?

LYNCH: Okay by me…

ROXY: *Do it, then!!!*

LYNCH: Okay…

ROXY: Don't answer me back!

(Lynch waves his hand at her in sign of disgust. Slouches back into chair.)

ROXY: That's better. *(To Emily.)* Where were we? *(Coughs a lot, clearing throat and chest of phlegm.)* Then Emily butted in here and says, "You remember Lynch, don't you, Alfred? His grandfather was the hangman who hanged his own son…for whom the very act of lynching was named."

LYNCH: *(Jumps up.)* Come on, God damn it!

ROXY: Then Lynch jumps up and yells, "Come on, God damn it!" Then Emily continues here with "Lynch will be chief guard, custodian-at-large, trochee judge, and executioner."... *(Pauses.)* Emily butts in again here with "Not a *trochee* judge, but a..." *(Looks at Emily.)* Still can't read the word.

EMILY: Troika judge... *(Smiles; to Alfred.)* Three judges, one judgment. *(Pauses; to Roxy.)* Troika...

ROXY: That's what *I* said!

EMILY: You said *trochee*...

ALFRED: *(Standing; watching.)* Too poetic... *(Smiles.)* Trooche. *(Pauses.)* A trochee is a foot of two syllables...

ROXY: What's he saying?

ALFRED: Metrical measure. The word "trochee" is from the Greek. You've heard of the Greeks, Roxy. They're the folks who put white cheese next to black olives and call it salad.

(Roxy laughs.)

ALFRED: A trochee, Rox, is a foot of two syllables. A long followed by a short in quantitative meter...such as "Soooooo-eeee-sooooooo-eeee." *(Makes the sound of a hog caller.)*

(Lynch laughs.)

ALFRED: Or a stressed followed by an unstressed in accentual meter, like Emily and me; the unstressed following the stressed...Are you paying attention, Roxy?

EMILY: Just write the word "Babble" into the record.

ROXY: Thank God.

ALFRED: "Thank God" is unnecessarily reverential, Roxy, but I'm sure Emily accepts your gratitude.

EMILY: I call your attention, Roxy...and Mr. Lynch...to Alfred's inability to stop his incessant—continual and repeated—babble. *(Pauses.)* It gets a bit tiring, Alfred, after fifteen or twenty years. *(Pauses; smiles.)* I hope you understand. *(Pauses; to Roxy. Her attitude changes.)* Skip ahead, now, Roxy. Skip ahead and read, please...

ROXY: From where.

EMILY: From the charges against Alfred. I read them into the record yesterday morning.

ROXY: The what?

EMILY: The charges.

ALFRED: For what? *(Pauses; smiles.)* The amusement?...I'm being charged for

the amusement?…How much you chargin' for this animal act, Emmy?…
A buck an hour?

EMILY: Mr. Lynch!

ALFRED: Emily, come on, now…Emily?

EMILY: Mr. Lynch! I would like Alfred touched…deeply.

LYNCH: *(Stands.)* Okay.

(Lynch moves to wall behind bench, from which he removes the long pole. He inserts the pole into the cell and chases Alfred down, tripping him and then finally punching him to floor with end of pole. When he has finished beating Alfred, he returns to bench, where, after setting pole back into its position against wall, Lynch rests again on bench in recline. Alfred lies in pain, on floor of cell.)

EMILY: Roxy?

ROXY: *(Continues to read.)* "…because he has murdered…" *(Looks up.)* Anywhere here?

EMILY: Alfred, are you paying close attention?

ALFRED: *(Looking up from floor.)* Rapt.

EMILY: What was that?

ALFRED: Rapt attention.

EMILY: *(To Roxy.)* His mother… *(Nods.)*

ROXY: *(Repeating Emily's words.)* …his mother…

EMILY: …his father…

ROXY: …his father…

EMILY: …his friends…

ROXY: …his friends…

EMILY: …his children…

ROXY: …his children…

EMILY: Are you reading?

ROXY: Reading… *(Roxy has been staring at Alfred and repeating Emily's words, not reading.)*

EMILY: I asked you to read, please…

ROXY: Huh? Oh. I was just watching him…I'll read.

(Lynch stands at attention.)

ROXY: *(Reads.)* "Because he has murdered his mother, causing the curse that fell upon the people of his town…because he has murdered his father, and his close friends… *(Pauses.)* Because he is responsible for the deaths of those who have died… *(Pauses.)* He then too must…die."

ALFRED: Emily, could I have a moment with you?

EMILY: What?

ALFRED: Could I possibly have a moment with you?

EMILY: But you've already had *years* with me…

ALFRED: Alone?

EMILY: That too. *(Pauses.)* I don't think so, Alfred. *(Smiles.)* A person's got to know where to draw the line… *(Pauses.)* I've drawn mine.

ALFRED: *(To Emily.)* How far are you planning to take this, Emily?

EMILY: How far? *(Pauses.)* All the way.

ALFRED: Don't you find all this a trifle…suburban?

(Emily sits with her back to Alfred.)

ALFRED: Excuse me. Emily? *(Still no reply; louder.)* Excuse me…Emily? Lynch, poke Emily.

LYNCH: *(Starts for pole; realizes. Calls across to Emily, who is lost in a memory.)* Emily! Alfred's calling you!

EMILY: *(To Alfred.)* What?

ALFRED: I'm going to have to leave you all for a while…

EMILY: You're what?

ALFRED: Going to have to say "Excuse me," *Je m'excuse,* but I'm…well…going off for a while. *(Smiles.)* Into the other room.

EMILY: To do what?

LYNCH: To do what?

ROXY: To do what?

ALFRED: Rest.

EMILY: Rest?

LYNCH: Rest?

ROXY: Rest?

EMILY: In there?

LYNCH: In there?

ROXY: In there?

ALFRED: You three should really work on that routine… *(Pauses.)* Rehearse it. *(Pauses.)* Perfect it. *(Pauses.)* It's quite amusing. Nearly funny. *(Pauses.)* Makes me…happy… *(Pauses.)* It really does: I'm happy… *(Pauses; smiles.)* Especially now that you've added the hog to your animal act. *(To Emily.)* The gorilla made me smile, but not laugh… *(To Lynch.)* No offense. *(To Emily.)* The addition of the hog was a sensational touch…A masterstroke… *(Moves back three steps.)* Look at you three: the perfect blend of python, gorilla, and hog… *(Backs up a few more steps; smiles and points finger in schoolteacherish manner.)* Practice: That's the ticket… *(Smiles.)* You kids have got it!…The goods! The stuff! The talent! That magic quelque chose! *(Alfred exits into the back room, closing door tightly shut behind him.)*

(There is a ten count of silence. Emily nods to Lynch.)

EMILY: Mr. Lynch?

LYNCH: Huh?

EMILY: Secure the lock.

LYNCH: Hmm?

EMILY: Alfred's door. Lock it.

(Lynch stands, takes pole, reaches into cage, pokes door latch closed. He returns to his seat; sits. There is another ten count of silence. Alfred's coughing and retching is heard from back room. The sound grows more sonorous. Alfred is now pounding on the inside of the back door, trying to open same. Lynch looks at Emily; smiles. Roxy looks at Emily; smiles. Tableau. Emily bows her head. The lights fade out.)

End of Act I.

ACT II
SCENE I

Later. Stage in darkness. Three sharp knocks are heard. The first words of this act—Alfred's— are heard in darkness.

ALFRED: *(Screams; offstage.)* If I have to break it down, *I God damned will!* *(Louder.)* Do...you...hear...me???
(Lights to full, suddenly. At same moment, door bursts open and Alfred bursts with it, onto stage, into visible portion of cell. Emily sits in cell with her back against upstage-right section of the wall that is now covered by door (door opens in against wall). Alfred will not see Emily until she slams door closed and noise of door slamming will startle him. Lynch reclines in center bench. Roxy is at her machine. Both are dozing.)

ALFRED: *(Adjusting eyes to light; to Roxy.)* Where is she? Where is she? *(Pauses; screams.)* Where...the hell...is she.???

LYNCH: She's right in front of you, Alfred.

ROXY: Here I am, Alfred.

LYNCH: You're all hot and bothered, Alfred...

ROXY: You oughtta calm down... *(Pauses.)* You could have yaself a stroke...

ALFRED: *(Screams.)* Where is she??? Answer me!!! *(Leans in toward Roxy and Lynch.)* God damn you!!! Where...is...she???

LYNCH: You better learn ta calm down, Alfred. Bad for the ticker.

ROXY: *(Giggles.)* What a temper!
(Emily slams door closed, revealing to Alfred that she is where she is. There is a long pause. Alfred turns, slowly, and stares at her. Emily smiles.)

EMILY: Here I am, Alfred.

LYNCH: There she is, Alfred.

ROXY: There she is, Alfred.

ALFRED: What the hell *is* this? You, too? Did they lock *you* up, too?

EMILY: Oh, nooo. I'm just visiting. Today is visitors' day.

ALFRED: I could kill you now, if I wanted to...

EMILY: Well, there it is: The first thought-out sentence you've spoken. The first premeditated thought expressed. *(Smiles.)* The killer returns to the sense of the crime. *(Pauses.)* Irrefutable witnesses, this time, Alfred. *(To Roxy and Lynch.)* Repeat Alfred's threat, please.

ROXY: He said he could kill you now.

LYNCH: *(Correcting Roxy.)* No. He said he could kill her, now...if he wanted to.

ROXY: That's exactly what *I* just said!

EMILY: Type it into the records, please. I want all threats of physical harm in the record…I must insist.

ROXY: *(Stands; shuffles to her stenography machine and types statement.)* Okay. Done.

LYNCH: Did you get the "if I wanted to" part?

ROXY: I really think we could keep things straighter if you'd just let me use a tape recorder…

EMILY: No. I want all the twistings and turnings of a human touch. Those are the rules, Roxy.

ALFRED: Emily, I am so completely traumatized, I think what I think is that I've stopped thinking… *(Pauses.)* I've stopped all thought. *(Pauses.)* I… *(Stops; looks at Roxy.)* You needn't copy down any of this… *(To Emily.)* I'm a little self-conscious about things being written down… *(Pauses.)* I guess that's your idea… *(Pauses.)* It's working… *(Bows head.)*

EMILY: Rap the gavel, Roxy.

(Roxy crosses to table, picks up a wooden gavel; raps three times. Alfred looks up.)

EMILY: Better. Wonderful gavel. Burled walnut. *(To Alfred.)* You're going to face it all, Alfred. All the twistings and turnings, all the amazing details, all the surprises, all of your absolutely incredible lies…They're all coming back.

(Alfred looks up at her.)

EMILY: Roxy, Lynch and I all have…complaints. *(Pauses.)* Mr. Lynch?

(Lynch looks up.)

EMILY: Your complaints now. Briefly, please.

LYNCH: Briefly? Sure. *(Officious tone; clearly.)* Sister, father, family name…Alfred killed them all. *(He glares at Alfred.)*

ALFRED: Lynch…You can't be serious.

EMILY: I'd suggest that you just listen, Alfred. Roxy?

ROXY: How much of it?

EMILY: The barest bones for now, please…

ROXY: Let's see…barest bones? Okay. All of my husbands, several of my children, and, of course, me. Alfred killed us all.

ALFRED: Emily, it is somewhat anxiety-producing to realize that the entire world's gone berserk…I really don't know what anyone here is saying. None of you…

EMILY: Alfred, I suggest you listen carefully to my complaints.

ROXY: Ready. *(She sits at stenography machine.)*

EMILY: Four stillbirths, Alfred. Your fault. *(Pauses.)* If four stillbirths sound like a lot, you ought to try *feeling* them. They *feel* like a *hell* of a lot.

(Pauses.) Four. Each one dead in the seventh month. Twenty-eight months of feeling your children inside of me...kicking...punching...sucking away...until they stopped...And stop they did, didn't they? Had to. Every last one of them. *(Suddenly; her tone changes.)* I know the truth, Alfred. I know exactly why...why they died.

ALFRED: *(Quietly.)* Emily, I...

EMILY: Did you say "Emily, I..."? *(Smiles.)* How like you. Generous to the last. *(Pauses; attitude changes again.)* I was always shamed. You did that, Alfred. You shamed me. *(Pauses.)* I remember, 'round about our fourth or fifth child, I had a real catastrophe...both a miscarriage *and* a still-birth: a double treat. I remember...how it was to watch you be not able to face it...to join me. *(Quietly.)* I took a taxi, alone, to the hospital. I didn't have any money with me for the fare. I just didn't *have* any. I had probably a hundred different credit cards, but not a dime in hard cold cash. The driver was furious. Thanks to my prior annual visits, the old doorman knew me...remembered me. He coughed up the money... Quite a lot, I recall. Ten or twelve dollars... *(Pauses; smiles.)* The back seat of the cab was ruined, Alfred. Drenched with blood. You should have seen the driver's face, when I lifted my seat from *his* seat. "You wrecked my goddamn seat, lady! What the hell's the matter with you?" *(Pauses.)* I asked the doorman for enough money to replace the seat. The driver yelled at me "That'll be a hundred bucks, you know that?" *(Smiles.)* I didn't know that. The doorman told me he only earned a hundred a week. Can you imagine that? A hundred for one whole week of opening doors for women like me: bleeders, sufferers, complainers. I'd spent more than a hundred on my pocketbook...almost that for my credit-card case. *(Pauses. She is smiling.)* I was ashamed I'd bled on his seat...ashamed I asked the doorman for the fare...ashamed to have had the doorman have to tell me his salary...ashamed to own my pocket-book...my wallet...my shoes...my dead baby in my broken stretched-out bleeding body. I was ashamed! I was ashamed! *I...was...ashamed!* *(Pauses; attitude changes.)* Looking at you now, Alfred...knowing what I know about us...what you've done...*what you've done!*... *(Screams.)* I...am not...ashamed!!! *(After a long pause, she smiles.)* Mr. Lynch, I'd like to leave the cage, now.

LYNCH: Right.

(Lynch stands, gets long pole. Alfred backs up; frightened.)

ALFRED: Don't, Lynch! Emily, tell him "Don't!"

(Lynch moves to edge of cell with pole.)

EMILY: Stand with your face against the wall, Alfred. *(Motions to back wall.)*

ALFRED: *(Looks first to wall and then to Emily.)* I… *(Stops his voice.)* Okay.
(He walks to back wall, faces same. Lynch places end of pole just behind Alfred's head.)

LYNCH: Any kind of funny business, I push. If I push, your face ain't gonna look like much in tomorrow's paper…if ya know what I mean.

ALFRED: This is the most extraordinarily infantile and sick…

EMILY: You may be wondering why, out of all the possible Wakefieldians I could have employed, I've employed Roxy and Lynch. Roxy, Lynch, and I have made an amazing pact. Remember the word "pact," Alfred… You'll be hearing it again. *(Moves to cell door, unlocks it. Moves to Roxy, inspects tape.)* This tape will be history, Alfred. Every word Roxy writes here will get out of this room…will be read and reread…will be discussed and chewed over and digested. It's a fact. You're a famous fellow. People will be interested in what's gone on here…now…and *before* now. What you've done. *(Pauses; with hostility.)* Mr. Lynch, see to it that he doesn't sleep. I want him standing, face to the wall…No rest. *(To Roxy.)* Take a break, Roxy. Work begins at nine. Did you get that?

ROXY: First you said for Lynch to smash his face into the wall and get some sleep…and then you said…let's see… *(Reads.)* You said, "Work, Roxy. We'll take a break at nine." Then you asked, "Did you get that?" *(Looks up at Emily.)* And I answered, "Yup."
(Lynch is disgusted. Alfred turns helplessly; his eyes meet Emily's. Alfred bows his head. The lights fade out.)

SCENE II

Later. Stage in darkness. Three sharp knocks are heard. The first words of the scene—Emily's—are heard in darkness.

EMILY: Mr. Lynch, I blame you for this!
(Lights to full, suddenly. Roxy sits center stage, at stenotype machine, staring into cell. Lynch is sitting, on bench across from Roxy, asleep. Emily is standing at table, gavel in hand, staring angrily at Lynch. Alfred is sitting asleep on floor of cell, his back against the back wall. His clothing is somewhat scruffier; his beard fuller. Emily calls Lynch's name again and raps gavel on table.)

EMILY: *Mr. Lynch, dammit!*

LYNCH: *(At once alert.)* What? What is it?

ROXY: *(Typing and talking at same time.)* You're being blamed.

LYNCH: For what? *(To Emily.)* For what? *(Sees Alfred asleep on cell floor.)* Again? *(To Emily.)* Sorry. I'll fix it… *(Lifts pole, walks to cell, pokes Alfred forcefully, waking him.)* Get up, you.

ALFRED: What?…Ughh…*Hey!*…Emily…heyyy! *(Rises to his knees.)* Heyyy!

LYNCH: *Up!*

ALFRED: *Heyyy, c'mon…*

LYNCH: I don't wanna hurt you, Alfred!

ALFRED: But you are! You really are!

LYNCH: Then, stand up!

ALFRED: *(Rising.)* Okay!

LYNCH: *(Screams.)* Do it!

ALFRED: *(Stands and screams.)* Okay!
    (Lynch stops; Alfred faces him.)

ALFRED: Okay. *(To Emily.)* Okay?

EMILY: Good afternoon, Alfred.

ALFRED: Afternoon?

EMILY: Put your pole back now, Mr. Lynch. And thank you…

LYNCH: Sorry I dozed. I got dozy.

ROXY: The nose that flows dozed.

LYNCH: What's that s'pose'ta be, blimp? A name-joke? *(To Alfred.)* You remember her name when she was substitute-teachin'? They called her Graf Zeppelin: the blimp that burned. *(Laughs.)* Graf Zeppelin…quite a catastrophe.

EMILY: *(To Alfred.)* We're ready to continue our interview, Alfred.

ALFRED: Is it really afternoon, Emily? I really don't know. I can't tell…I'd like to know.

EMILY: *(To Roxy.)* Did you get that?

ROXY: *(Reads.)* "Is it really afternoon, Emily? I really don't know."

ALFRED: *(Interrupts Roxy's reading.)* It makes me terribly nervous to have her writing all of this down…

EMILY: If interviews made you nervous, you certainly opened yourself up for a lot of anxiety over the years! *(To Lynch.)* He was interviewed every five minutes. He set them up himself.

LYNCH: I don't blame you, Alfred. If you don't push yourself, who's gonna, right? I don't blame you…

ALFRED: Why is it that all the uninterviewed are always telling all the interviewed "I don't blame you"? *(Pauses.)* Who do you blame, Lynch?

LYNCH: For what?

ALFRED: For your being nobody... *(Pauses.)* A man of your years, too...being nobody. *(Pauses.)* Who's ever heard of you, Lynch? *(Pauses.)* Hardly a soul. *(Pauses.)* You almost never happened, Lynch. *(Pauses.)* Must be awful, huh?

LYNCH: It is. *(Sadly.)* It's awful.

EMILY: Who do you blame? Roxy, write Lynch's answer, please.

LYNCH: Myself. *(Pauses.)* I do. I blame myself. *(Pauses.)* I shoulda listened...

EMILY: To whom?

LYNCH: Everybody...my teachers...my father...

ALFRED: Who was he, Lynch? Your father: Who was he?

LYNCH: Are you kiddin' me?

ALFRED: I mean *really*...who was your father, *really?*

LYNCH: *He was somebody!*

ALFRED: You don't say?

LYNCH: Write this down! Greasy-pole champion, two times. *(To Roxy.)* Write this...

(All are staring at Lynch; he continues, nervously.)

LYNCH: Gloucester. Every June. They run a greasy-pole contest. The St. Peter's Club...mostly Italians...They nail a telephone pole down to a floating wharf out in the harbor...and grease it. *(Pauses.)* Any man who can make it out to the end of the greasy pole and grab the red flag—they have a red flag at the end—wins.

ALFRED: Wins what?

LYNCH: Wins. *(Pauses.)* Wins. *(Pauses.)* My father won once and then he actually won again, five years later. *(Pauses.)* I was five the first time; ten, the second. *(To Roxy.)* Don't smirk! It ain't that easy, ya know. Damn near impossible.

ALFRED: You ever try it yourself, Lynchie?... *(Pauses.)* You know: After he... your father...died?

LYNCH: I...well...yuh, I did.

ALFRED: Tried for his record?

LYNCH: It woulda made him proud, yuh.

ALFRED: After he was dead?

LYNCH: What are you sayin'?

ALFRED: Do you think it would have made him proud after he was dead? *(Pauses.)* Was that an important...consideration?

LYNCH: What?

ALFRED: Paternal pride after death!

LYNCH: I don't have to take this kind of guff from anybody, bub. Especially *you!* (To Emily.) My father was *somebody* and that's the truth!

EMILY: *(After a long pause.)* I don't think you'll have to transcribe any of that.

LYNCH: *(To Roxy.)* Write it.

EMILY: Mr. Lynch, really…

LYNCH: I want my father's story written here: Willie-Boy Lynch: a champion.

EMILY: All right. Write out your statement in longhand and I'll see to it that Roxy types it into the record later. I think that's fair, Lynch.

ROXY: Fair's fair, Lynch.

LYNCH: Don't "fair's fair" me, blimp, or you'll have a fat lip to worry about!

ALFRED: I believe that Emily requires that all threats of physical harm go into the record as well…Fair's fair, Emily. You had her type mine…

ROXY: That's right! I'm putting that right in, Lynch! *(Types.)* "Fat lip ta worry about." It's all in there now to hang you.

LYNCH: It's all in there to *what* me, bitch?

ALFRED: Whoops! I think you said the magic word, Rox!

ROXY: What magic word? *(Realizes.)* I get it!

LYNCH: You get what? Bad breath in the morning? A cruller with your coffee? No kicks from champagne? What? What do you get?

ROXY: *(Smiling into Lynch's remarks, and then.)* "Hang" is the magic word. Isn't it?

LYNCH: I'm gonna rip her tits off!

ALFRED: *(Nodding up and down.)* Another threat, Em!

LYNCH: I'm gonna unscrew her head and flush it down the hopper!

ALFRED: A *definite* threat there, Em.

LYNCH: I'm gonna take a greasy pole and shove it right up.

EMILY: *(Interrupting.)* That will be *quite* enough, Mr. Lynch!
(Lynch makes a slow deliberate move toward Roxy.)

EMILY: I want some order here…Sit down, Mr. Lynch!

ALFRED: Emily has an order, Lynch!

LYNCH: What's that? *(He stops, in front of Roxy.)*

ALFRED: She orders you to sit down, Mr. Lynch.

LYNCH: *(Amazed. To Emily.)* You *what* me?

ALFRED: Emily wants you to take her order. She used to be an absolute fiend for a Brigham's sundae…Chocolate mint chip, wasn't it, Em?

EMILY: You seem to be losing some of your reticence.

ALFRED: You seem to be losing some of your control. Just helpin out… *(Nods toward Roxy and Lynch.)*

LYNCH: *(Stands in front of Roxy now.)* Say you're sorry!

ROXY: When I grow a head under my arm is when I'll say I'm sorry!

LYNCH: You've already got a head growin' under your arm! You want another head there? Like Siamese twins?

EMILY: Mr. Lynch!

LYNCH: What?

EMILY: You can be easily replaced.

LYNCH: What's that s'pose'ta mean?

EMILY: Guess. *(Smiles.)* In or out?

LYNCH: Of what?

EMILY: This…bit of history… *(Pauses.)* Our…trial…The trial of Alfred L. Webber, boy wonder. *(Pauses.)* In or out?

LYNCH: In.

EMILY: Sit.

(He sits.)

EMILY: Stand.

(He stands.)

EMILY: Sit.

(He sits.)

EMILY: Stand.

LYNCH: Come on, lady…

EMILY: Mr. Lynch…? Alfred doubts my control here. *Stand!*

LYNCH: *(Stands.)* You got yourself quite a little wife here, Alfred…My heart goes out ta ya…

ALFRED: Emily? She's all right…

LYNCH: You got the prize here! I gotta admit it: You get the goddamn prize…

EMILY: *(To Lynch.)* Sit.

(He sits.)

EMILY: Not there. *(Points to step near door.)* There.

LYNCH: *(Moves to step; sits.)* No wonder you got rich. Bein' married to her, you probably never came home. Probably worked 'round the clock, twenty-four hours a day at four bucks an hour, that's nearly a hundred every day…seven hundred a week… *(Pauses.)* No wonder. *(Pauses.)* I guess what they say is true: It's the woman behind the man…

ALFRED: *(To Lynch.)* Stand.

(Lynch stands.)

EMILY: Sit!

LYNCH: C'mon, *goddammit!*

EMILY: Sit!

LYNCH: *(Sits.)* As far as I'm concerned, you two should split the trophy right down the middle…The Most-Likely-Ta-Drive-Everybody-Nuts Award… The gold cup for Alfred, and the brass balls for you, lady!

EMILY: Mr. Lynch?

LYNCH: *(Stands.)* Okay?

EMILY: Why are you standing?

LYNCH: You just told me to…

EMILY: I most certainly did not…
(Lynch sits.)

EMILY: Now then, Alfred. Roxy's testimony is first. The subject is Alfred's mother.

ALFRED: I beg your pardon?

ROXY: It's not just his mother. It's his mother, her murder by him…and the curse it put over this town. Also, the other people he slaughtered along the way… *(Smiles.)* I'm ready.

EMILY: Tell us what you saw…No interruptions, please, Alfred.

ROXY: I was hemming one of her just-below-the-knee skirts…a very bold plaid, if I recall… *(Smiles.)* I had one of those chalk markers with a squeegee on a stand…Alfred's mother—Sophie—stood on a little platform and I knelt down below with my chalk marker. *(Roxy has been staring at Alfred, absent-mindedly. Smiles to Emily.)* I haven't really seen his face close-up like this…not for a long time…He looks older. *(Clears her throat.)* There was a clickety-clickety at the window. Him.

EMILY: Him? Alfred?

ROXY: Oh, no: him…Willie-Boy Lynch. *His* father. *(Nods to Lynch.)* My boyfriend…

LYNCH: I don't like this…

ROXY: Breaks my heart to type it in the record, but it's true. My boyfriend was having a love affair with Alfred's mother…

ALFRED: *(Quietly.)* Emily, I hope you don't take this as misbehavior on my part, but I am incredibly angered to have you drag my mother's memory through this little mudwrestle of yours!

LYNCH: And my father's memory, too! I don't like the mud thrown there either, ya know! I've heard some wicked crap in my life, but nothin' never…*ever*…like the dung she's dumping now!

EMILY: Mr. Lynch, either you shut that halitositic mouth of yours once and for all, or you leave! Now which will it be: shut or leave?

LYNCH: *(After a pause, he goes to door, stands a moment.)* Shut.
(He settles back; disgusted, beaten. Alfred smiles.)

EMILY: As for you, Alfred, the more humiliated Mr. Lynch becomes, the more enraged he becomes. The more enraged he becomes, the more likely he is to hurt you.

LYNCH: I wouldn't mind.

ALFRED: I understand.

EMILY: Please, go on, Roxy. You won't be interrupted again.

ROXY: They went off upstairs together. I followed. I know I shouldn't have. I should have just let them go. But I was young and hurt…We were in love, me and Willie-Boy Lynch. *(Suddenly; to Emily.)* I was young once, too, ya know. You're not the only one ever had looks and youth. I had 'em… *(Quietly.)* He was handsome. *(To Lynch.)* Not like his children. The tree don't necessarily fall anywhere near the apples, ya know… *(To Emily.)* I was a simple dressmaker and Willie-Boy was a simple bread-truck driver…and *by God!* we had something good… *(Pauses.)* I followed. Alfred was in the hallway, hiding. I saw him. He had his Boy Scout knife open. Ten years old, and ready to kill. And kill he did. Killed 'em both… *(Pauses.)* The rest is history.

LYNCH: *(Has had his back turned to Roxy; suddenly turns toward her, enraged.)* The rest is horseshit! *(To Emily.)* She's lyin' about my father. I want this record straight, you get me? My father, Willie-Boy Lynch, never *ever* went near this fat bitch…not unless he had her price in his hand. Quarter, fifty cents… *(To Roxy.)* Now I want this goddamn record straight and I want it straight, *now! YOU TYPE THIS!* "I have never in my miserable life heard such horseshit!" *(To Emily.)* She was a hooker, down in Reading, near the head of the lake. Once they threw her outa Nazareth, she hooked full-time. *(To Alfred.)* Alfred killed my father and his own mother…that's true…and it was in *his own* house: That's true, too. But as far as my father goin' near this fat old bitch…old Graf Zeppelin Roxy…well, that's just a crock of you-know-what…unless he had the quarter in his hand and was in the you-know-what house, down in Reading. *(To Emily.)* Cheap! That was Roxy's main quality: cheap. Simple dressmaker? *Horseshit!* You think somebody named Roxy's gonna turn out ta be a simple dressmaker? Horseshit! That's a definite hooker name. A prostie. A lovelady. *(To Roxy.)* A *whooore*…

(Roxy stands up and faces Lynch, who faces her. A moment of silence. Lynch smiles.)

LYNCH: If you raise so much as a pinky to me, you're gonna be a flabby pancake.

(Roxy stops.)

LYNCH: Think about it.

(Roxy returns to table. She sits. Lynch turns to Alfred.)

LYNCH: If I remember correctly, it was a certain Tommy Webber who was truly nuts over *this* one, right? *(To Roxy.) RIGHT???*

ROXY: I did have an uncontrollable romantic streak. I still do.

ALFRED: *(Shaken.)* Did...uh...? Roxy, did Lynch say you got thrown out of Nazareth?

LYNCH: Yuh. That's what I said, Alfred.

EMILY: I've done my homework, Alfred. Nazareth Academy is Wakefield's Catholic girls' school, remember? Nuns with sticks and other famous catechetical methods. Teachers and pupils together, so to speak, sailing one holy ship of clitoridean panic. Girls in little blue uniforms, Alfred? How can you have forgotten?

ROXY: He didn't forget...

LYNCH: He didn't forget.

ROXY: He didn't forget.

LYNCH: He didn't forget.

ALFRED: Roxy, I...If you're *that* Roxy, you must be nearly a hundred...

ROXY: Thanks to you.

ALFRED: It's hard to believe I could have forgotten you...your face...

LYNCH: Stops your clock, doesn't it? It's true! That fornicating bitch was supposed ta be substitute-teaching my sister Margaret. My Margaret was a Nazarite, studyin' to become a nun. 'Stead of teachin' her the Catechism, she taught her the oldest profession of them all: hookin'...*hookin!* *(Enraged.) WRITE THIS IN!!!...WRITE THIS IN!!!* Between them... your Alfred and your Roxy, they took my Margaret...a seventeen-year-old virgin so pure you could show her to God himself...and they ruined her! *RUINED HER!* They made a fornicating bitch of a whore of her! *(To Roxy.) YOU WRITE IT! YOU WRITE EVERY WORD!!!*

ROXY: *(Frightened Lynch will hit her; she transcribes, looking to Emily for help.)* Okay, Lynch. Okay...

LYNCH: Better.

EMILY: I'm glad you're starting to remember, Alfred. How much of this sounds familiar?

(No reply. Alfred stares at Emily.)

EMILY: Okay then. How much of this sounds fami"l"*ial?*

ALFRED: Why is it that at the center of even total lunacy, there's always a scrap, a shard, a remnant, a vestige of something that was...well...true? *(Pauses.)* Most of what Roxy said was absolute first-level crap... demented...But some of it was true. *(Pauses.)* My mother certainly did have a friend and it certainly was Lynch's pop: Willie-Boy. And Roxy did make my mother's skirts…And I *was* just ten when it all…happened… *(Alfred pauses; bows his head. There is a short silence in which Emily, Roxy, and Lynch all stare at Alfred. Alfred faces them again.)*

ALFRED: Most of what Lynch said was crap, too. But, some of it was true. My father, Tommy Webber, did have a fling with Roxy. And Lynch's sister Margaret and I did have a high school indiscretion. She did have to leave Nazareth before graduation. It was taken care—aborted—up in New Hampshire. Route one-twenty-eight, Lynnfield way, then straight up the Newburyport Turnpike…

EMILY: Alfred, I think your mind is slipping.

ALFRED: You *think* my mind is slipping? You *think* my mind is slipping??? Climb into my mind awhile if you want to know what slippage *is!* My mind is the quintessence of slip!

(Alfred reaches to grab Emily through the bars. Lynch moves for the pole.)

ALFRED: No, Lynch! Don't poke me! Tell him not to poke me, Emily! I'm sorry, sorry. I apologize. I know you're angry. I'd forgotten that you were so deeply involved with your sister. I'm sorry. *(To Emily.)* Lynchie and Margaret were close. I forgot. I'm sorry.

LYNCH: You ain't payin' off the kind of debt you owe to me with no "I'm sorry" pally-pal. Believe you me…

ALFRED: I'd forgotten. Willie-Boy's family…Lynch…Margaret…all of them… intertwined. It slipped my mind. They lived in the Italian section of town: Guinea Gulch the kids called it. We all passed the Lynch house on the bus every day…on the bus to Woodville school. The kids all held their noses and made farting sounds…Kids are wonderful… They called the Lynch house "The Town Dump"! Margaret, God bless her, they called her "The Town Pump." Willie-Boy Lynch was the town's leading lunatic. That's why it was so upsetting to me when my mother found him to be so…well…attractive. So did Roxy…I forgot… *(Pauses.)* Roxy and Willie-Boy had a child together…

ROXY: Two. We had two. I told you we were in love…

ALFRED: My mind. I forgot it all. All intertwined…The word was that Margaret and her husband had blood between them: incest. All through their family. Before she married her husband…so the word went… Margaret and her brother, Lynchie, were…well…doin' it.

LYNCH: This is stoppin' and it's stoppin' right now! *(Moves to cell, unlocks door.)*

EMILY: What are you doing, Mr. Lynch?

LYNCH: There's no way I'm lettin' history get written the way it's gettin' writ-ten here. *(Enters cell.)* I'm s'pose'ta be settin' the history books straight on Lynches and lynchin', right?

(He moves to Alfred, who backs to wall.)

LYNCH: *You know what? You know what?* I think the record's lookin' *worse*…every minute…not better…*WORSE! (To Alfred.)* No more talk, Alfred. No more waitin'!

ALFRED: Emily?

EMILY: Mr. Lynch, you're highly overwrought. I must demand you back off…*Get out of there, Lynch!*

(Lynch removes his belt and moves to Alfred.)

EMILY: God damn it, You agreed! If you wanted, to just kill him, you should have done that weeks ago! We have a pact here!

LYNCH: *(Ties belt around Alfred's neck.)* Shove your pact.

EMILY: You're a greedy son of a bitch!

(Alfred stumbles out of cell, belt around his neck, end dangling. Alfred runs to door. Lynch follows. Alfred pulls at the door. It is padlocked closed.)

LYNCH: It's locked, Alfred. Locked it myself. *(Laughs; turns to Emily.)* This isn't for me: This is for my father…Willie-Boy Lynch: a champion…and for my sister, Margaret…a saint…a virgin and a saint and a Nazarite, too…And for Lynch, itself—the sacred family name…*ARE YOU WRITING THIS IN?*

(Roxy does. Alfred crawls to position behind cell door. He pulls himself to his feet; smiles at Lynch.)

LYNCH: What the hell are *you* doing?

ALFRED: Stay back, Lynch! *(Hops behind open cell door, thinking he has moved into cell itself.)* I'm just going back inside…

LYNCH: *(Confused.)* What the hell do you think *you're* doing?

ALFRED: *(His back is against front of cell. He has pulled the cell door against his belly and peers through the bars of cell door at Lynch. Alfred seems relieved.)* Better inside. It's better. More relaxed. Safer… *(Alfred exhales, relieved. He smiles.)*

LYNCH: This is the fuckin' one-time-only *limit!* *(Moves to Alfred; faces him through bars of door.)* Look at me, Alfred; Lynchie. We were kids together, Alfred…Bottom of West Ward School hill…I know every detail, Alfred, don't I? *(Screams.)* LOOK…AT…ME! LOOK! LOOK! LOOK!

(Lynch bangs on the bars, as he screams. Lynch slams cell door closed. Alfred

stands facing Lynch now, his back against bars, front of cell. Lynch tightens loop of belt around Alfred's neck.)

LYNCH: *C'MON! C'MON! C'MON! C'MONNNNNNN!*

(Emily arrives at desk, opens drawer, removes gun.)

ROXY: Jesus, it's *the* gun...*the* gun.

EMILY: Yes. It is. Thirty-two-calibre. Not a lot, but enough... *(Calls across.)* Mr. Lynch?

(Lynch laughs. He pulls Alfred between Emily and himself, so that if Emily shoots gun, she must first hit Alfred. Lynch holds belt tightly, choking Alfred.)

LYNCH: You want to shoot me, Emily? Great! Terrific! Do it! Only thing is, you're gonna have to send the bullet through Alfred to get to me. Okay? Come on. Do it! Save me some trouble!

EMILY: You bricked up the door. How do you plan on leaving here?

LYNCH: Any man who knows how ta brick a door, knows how ta unbrick a door. Can't learn one without learnin' t'other. The opposite.

EMILY: We have a pact, Mr. Lynch: a firm and solid pact...

LYNCH: *(To Alfred.)* She's got us down here on a suicide pact. Can ya believe it? A suicide pact. She thinks I'm s'posed ta die in here with you...*I'm* goin' out: I've got a great hiding; place...my house. Nobody's gonna find me there 'cause nobody even know's I exist. That's what forty years in Wakefield did for B.J. Lynch: He's safe in his own house... *(To Alfred.)* I'm going to kill you now, Alfred. *(Begins to choke him. To Emily.)* If you had the guts to shoot me, Emily, you would've done it as soon as you picked up the gun...

(There is a pause. Emily is unable to kill Lynch.)

EMILY: Why...can't I...pull the trigger?

ALFRED: Emily, please...

EMILY: I can't, Alfred...

(Roxy moves to Emily: takes Emily's hand with gun in it in her own hand. Lynch begins choking Alfred. GUNSHOT. Both Alfred and Lynch fall, at once. Lynch is dead. Emily steps back, three steps. Roxy stands alone, holding pistol in hand. Alfred is unable at first to open his eyes. He lies next to the dead Lynch, eyes clenched closed.)

ALFRED: Emily? Are you hurt? Emily? *(He opens his eyes.)* Lynch...all bloody... he's dead, Emily...Emily?

ROXY: Silly to worry, right? Silly to think of a woman of my age getting punished for anything, right?

ALFRED: I...I don't know why you did what you did, Roxy...but...thank you.

EMILY: I...I...thank you...

ALFRED DIES 365

ROXY: After all, a mother has certain obligations, right? A mother has an obligation to protect her daughter. No matter what… *(She looks at Alfred, then to Emily. She touches Emily's arm.)* No matter what.
(Emily and Alfred look at Roxy; then at each other. All bow heads. Tableau. The lights fade to black.)

End of Act II.

ACT III

Later. Stage in darkness. Three sharp knocks are heard. First words of this act—Roxy's—are heard in darkness.

ROXY: I blame you, Alfred.
(Lights to full, suddenly. Cell door is open. Roxy in chair pulled in front of cell. Her stenotype machine is in front of her, as she gives testimony and records her words simultaneously. Emily sits on desk, watching. Lynch's body is gone from room. Alfred in cell. His clothing is scruffy. His beard quite full again. He is groggy. Roxy turns to Emily.)
ROXY: He's not listening to me.
EMILY: *(Raps with the wooden gavel on the desktop: three sharp raps.)* Alfred! Look at my mother, Alfred!
(Alfred looks up, meekly.)
ROXY: It's true. *(Pauses.)* It is true, too.
EMILY: *(To Alfred.)* Look at her. *(Pauses.)* She's telling the truth. *(Pauses.)* Look at her!
ROXY: It's *you* who's responsible for our troubles here…and that's the truth of it. *(To Emily.)* It's him. *(Pauses; to Alfred again.)* Old folks livin' way beyond their prime…way beyond their wildest dreams! *You* did that! *(Pauses.)* Look at me: nearly a hundred and sunk since the age of fourteen. Is that a life? Is that a pleasure? Is that any goddamn reward for my suffering? *(Pauses.)* I blame *you* Alfred. *(Pauses.)* No one else.
ALFRED: *(Lies down on floor.)* …so tired, Emily…want to rest…want to sleep… please…no more of this…so tired…no more…let me rest…
(Emily stands, takes long pole. Alfred looks at her. He recoils.)
ALFRED: No! Don't! *(Looks up at her again.)*
EMILY: Stand up Alfred. You're on the ground.
(He does.)
EMILY: Better.
ALFRED: Emily I can't be responsible for what I did when I was ten. Ten, Emily. Ten. Surely, you can see. I forgot. I'd forgotten. I'd blocked it out… pushed it under…
EMILY: You are responsible…
ALFRED: I…yes. I am. *(Pauses.)* I thought it would please him…my father… to punish her…my mother. I did it for him… *(Looks at Emily.)* I did do that…my mother…killed her…I did do that…but the rest, Emily, the

rest…didn't…didn't…don't know why I'm being punished…not for the rest…

EMILY: Your father.

ALFRED: My father? No. You mean my mother…

EMILY: Father.

ROXY: Who killed him, Alfred?

ALFRED: Who killed my father? Is that what you're asking me?

ROXY: That's it.

ALFRED: Emily…Over and over…I can't take it…

EMILY: Each crime must be counted…over and over again. *(Pauses.)* Your father. Who killed him? Who put him in a home and let him rot for thirty years?

ALFRED: I… *(Pauses.)* For the love of God! *(Pauses.)* I…I feel responsible.

EMILY: *(To Roxy.)* Did you get that? In the record?

ROXY: *(Stops typing; reads.)* "I…for the love of God…I did it…I killed my father."

ALFRED: I feel responsible! I did not say I killed him. I said I feel responsible.

ROXY: *(Pointing gun at him. To Alfred.)* What's the difference? *(To Emily.)* What's the difference? *(To Alfred.)* I don't see any difference.
(Alfred bows his head.)

ROXY: Do you? *(To Emily.)* Do *you?*

EMILY: There seems to be an entire family to account for, Alfred…

ALFRED: For which to account.

EMILY: *(Pauses.)* Everyone who died, Alfred. What of them?

ALFRED: *(Angrily.)* Yes. Me. My fault. I…All of them. Me… *(Pauses.)* My fault.

EMILY: I'd like now to point to the family tree, Alfred. I know it well. I've studied it. Become an expert. I've actually climbed it and a hard climb it was, too. Once I started climbing the tree, Alfred, I…well…you know me…sooner or later, I had to find the absolute top.

ALFRED: Yes, I do know, Emily. When she said it…Roxy your mother…it all fit. *(Pauses.)* Roxy, your mother: Willie-Boy, your father… *(Pauses.)* It all fit together. *(Pauses.)* My fault. I killed your father, didn't I? I did that.

ROXY: What?

ALFRED: My fault.
(Roxy laughs; Alfred looks up at her.)

EMILY: Sorry, Alfred. You can't close your eyes to it, anymore… *(Pauses.)* Wrong father.

ROXY: Wrong father.

EMILY: Tommy. Tommy. My father...our father. Pa. Tommy Webber. We share the same Pa. Remember?

ALFRED: *(After a pause. He is shocked; shaken.)* Emily, I...I didn't know. Emily, I... *(He looks away.)*

ROXY: He's known that all along, Emily. No way he could have forgotten: not known.

ALFRED: I...didn't...know.

EMILY: One child after the other. *(Pauses.)* I always wondered why. *(Pauses.)* One child after the other. *(Pauses.)* So close to being born. But, never quite. *(Pauses.)* Always spared the shame. *(Pauses.)* I always wondered why. Didn't you?

ALFRED: Yes.

ROXY: Nobody could ever keep the family ties straight... *(Laughs.)* The ties that bind, they say. Well, that's true enough, isn't it? *(Pauses.)* We could never keep them straight...unknotted. *(Pauses.)* We used to pretend it didn't matter. But we were all old enough to know better...to know it did matter...but we closed our eyes to it...pretended. *(Pauses.)* We couldn't stop it anyway. Nothing we could do. Not after *you* started it, Alfred. Not after you killed your mother. It seemed to me, at the time, like the end of something... *(Pauses.)* I was wrong. It wasn't. *(Pauses.)* Opposite. *(Pauses.)* It was the start of something. A curse! *(Pauses.)* Thirty years, no births, no deaths...We grew older. That's for sure. But no one...got out. Only those without our blood. That's what you started. *(Pauses.)* Awful thing to watch. *(Pauses.)* Awful thing to watch. *(Pauses.)* Awful thing to watch. *(Pauses.)* I never could keep it straight...who was family...who was even mine... *(Pauses.)* Seein' Emily, again...here... now...suffering, as she is...seeing my face on hers...that face...that face... *(Pauses.)* I know it well. *(Pauses.)* I love her, Alfred. I love my daughter... *(Pauses.)* I love you, Emily... *(Pauses.)* Oh, God! Oh, God! Oh, God, forgive us... *(Bows her head; weeps. Looks at Alfred.)* Lynch's grandfather tried to stop it...the incest...His children, all mutant. Awful thing to watch. *(Pauses.)* Hanged one of his own sons...He got caught doin' it... *(Pauses.)* There was no way of stoppin' the incest...So it seemed. *(Pauses.)* I knew what we were. My own father told me. He gave me over to the Carmelites, down in Ipswich, but I talked. They gave me over to the Sisters of Charity and I tried to stick it out...to never *ever* have babies. *(Pauses.)* But I couldn't resist the pull. *(Pauses.)* I wanted to. I couldn't. I couldn't resist the pull. *(Pauses.)* Baby after baby, they just kept comin'. *(Pauses.)* I gave them away...each of them...I couldn't *look* at them. I'm in the Guinness Book of World Records. Oldest Living Mother. Fifty-seven when I had Emily. *(Pauses.)* You're the first I've had to look at in all these years now, Emily…Having to sit across from you, Alfred, lookin' exactly as your Pa…and Lynch, Jesus-God forgive him, lookin' exactly like *his* Pa…and Emily, all the look of me, when I was…well…*then. Such a thing! (Pauses.)* I never thought it could grow worse, Alfred, but you saw to it it did. *(Pauses.)* The day you killed your mother, we were cursed. I swear we were. Thirty years…no births, no deaths, unless by murder. *(Pauses.) It's you I blame!*

ALFRED: I can't be blamed.

EMILY: Not true.

ALFRED: I didn't know.

EMILY: Not true.

ALFRED: I was led to it…Out of my control…

EMILY: Not true…

ALFRED: Emily, please…

EMILY: You chose me. You tracked me down. You forced me. You stopped me. You forced me. You forced me. You forced me.

ROXY: You must be blamed, Alfred.

EMILY: You knew *before* you ever married me, Alfred. You wanted us to be married in spite of what you knew… *(Pauses; then pleading.)* For God's sakes, Alfred…don't close your eyes to it. Not now! Give…me…*some*-thing!

ALFRED: *(After a pause.)* I did. I knew. I'd blocked it out…forgotten. *(Pauses.)* I lied. *(Pauses.)* You'd just returned from the hospital…another still-birth…another one lost…We were sitting in a restaurant…only us… staring…lost in a memory… *(Pauses; quietly.)* I thought I was looking into a mirror but my hair seemed too long…extraordinarily so…hanging over my eyes… *(Pauses.)* I moved it up, across my forehead wedging it behind my ear… *(Pauses.)* My reflection didn't move, Emily…It was you…me…*us… (Pauses.)* Same face…same eyes…same lips…all the same. I remembered. I knew. *(Pauses.)* I'd grown up with a photograph of you…large…tinted with pastels…hanging in the hall outside my room. *(Pauses.)* It was the kind of hall that was taken for granted. Pictures and photographs on the walls…never really looked at…taken for granted…forgotten. *(Pauses.)* Your hair was brown…your loose blouse white. *(Pauses.)* You were looking at a bird: a robin. *(Pauses.)* I knew you were my father's child…The photograph was his. My mother forgot to take it down…She'd told me that you were his…and that your mother had...given you away...to a home...in Boston. *(Pauses.)* I was so frightened that my mother would give me away, too... *(Pauses; smiles bravely.)* She didn't. *(Pauses.)* When I was ten, I murdered my mother. Found her in bed with Willie-Boy Lynch: a champion. I killed them both with my Boy Scout knife. I thought it would please my father. I thought she'd betrayed him and had to be punished. *(Pauses.)* My father took the blame...told the police he did it. He was too old for jail...too crazy. He went to the asylum on the hill...Rotted there...thirty years, before he died. He took the blame...held it for thirty years. He protected *me* from it...protected me from the blame. He felt responsible. Almost every memory I had before the day I killed my mother... well...disappeared. The day itself was a complete blank. *(Pauses.)* Emily, you were the most exciting creature I'd ever laid eyes upon. *(Pauses.)* It *had* to be that way. Our whole family punished for what I did. *(Pauses.)* It had to be that way. *(Pauses.)* When I did finally remember, that was the start of it. From the moment of remembering, things...well... changed between us. I found you revolting. I began to remember...all of it. *(Pauses.)* I'd forgotten my father was alive...Forgotten I'd killed my mother...all of it. The first fact that came back to me was you: that we were brother and sister, husband and wife. *(Pauses.)* I feel responsible. I *am* responsible. I shouldn't have lied. I should have told you. Who did?

EMILY: Pa. Our father. Pa.

ALFRED: *(After a long pause.)* God... *(Pauses.)* Let me...be...dead. Let me die!

EMILY: He will, Alfred. He'll let you die. There are just a few interesting steps to go: to take...I have it all planned...beautifully planned. *(Smiles.)* It's rare, in this life, that it becomes really and truly possible to blame *any*-one for *any*thing...In the matter of twenty years of my life, Alfred, I blame you. I hold you responsible...*accountable. (To Roxy.)* It's your time, Mother...

(Roxy stands, moves to Emily. They embrace. They kiss.)

ROXY: If I had to live my life over, Emily, I would try hard to make it differ-ent... *(Pauses; moves to cell.)* If I had to live my life over...I would.

(She faces Alfred, stares a moment, kisses him. She moves into back room, behind the cell. Alfred waits a moment and then turns, facing Emily.)

ALFRED: Where's she going? There's a door? All the time, there was a door?

(He moves into back room. There is a pause. Alfred's voice heard offstage.)

ALFRED: *(Offstage.)* Roxy? I can't see anything! Roxy?...

(The sound of a gunshot. Silence. Emily, alone on stage, staring at door to back room. Alfred staggers out of door into cell.)

ALFRED: Emily! Your mother…

(He stops at bars to cell; stares at Emily. There is a moment between them.)

EMILY: I know. We have a pact: Lynch, my mother, and I.

ALFRED: She had this with her…this gun…I didn't… *(Frightened that Emily will think he killed Roxy, Alfred tosses gun onto floor near Emily's feet.)* Emily, I…

EMILY: *(Pauses.)* It has to stop, Alfred…this path for me…It has to stop…I've had all I can bear… *(She moves to cell.)* The lock.

ALFRED: *(Clicks the lock closed.)* Done.

EMILY: There's one more, Alfred. One to go.

ALFRED: One more what, Emily?

EMILY: Murder. *(Pauses.)* The supreme kill…the over-the-top kill… *(To Alfred.)* the *risus puris*. *(Pauses.)* Alfred?

ALFRED: *(Accepting his fate; quietly.)* Yes.

EMILY: Me. *(Moves to stage-right door.)* There is something special about this door… *(Smiles.)* Something you should know… *(Opens the stage-right door. It opens onstage, hinged on the upstage edge of door. It is now revealed that opening that was doorway has been cemented, space is filled in. Cement blocks and stucco form a solid impenetrable wall.)* Like it? I do. Expensive, but well worth the price…

ALFRED: I…

(He moves slowly to stage-left lower wall of cell, gripping bars for support as he goes. He stops: stares at plugged doorway. Emily leaves door opened, against stage-left wall.)

EMILY: *(Moves to table: picks up gavel again, raps three knocks on tabletop.)* Like it? Guaranteed impenetrability. I asked for granite… *(Pauses.)* From Rockport… *(Pauses.)* Had to settle for cement…from Wakefield… native… *(Pauses.)* The price of granite has, as they say, mushroomed. *(Smiles.)* Mr. Lynch did this. He bricked the door. Good worker, Mr. Lynch. Pity. He died.

(Emily raps the gavel against the tabletop sharply; three knocks. Alfred blinks three times, clenching his eyes closed, and then open.)

EMILY: Stop blinking…

(Alfred's eyes open and close, rapidly.)

EMILY: Stop blinking!

(Alfred clenches his eyes closed.)

EMILY: You've closed your eyes…Fine…just fine. *(Pauses; coughs.)* The air is awful already. Awful.

(Alfred moves from side to side of his cell, feeling his way along the front edge,

eyes clenched closed. When he has completed traveling the full surface and has returned to his starting position, center of cell's downstage wall, he stops, gripping the bars above and outside his shoulders. He opens his eyes. He looks at Emily a moment in silence. Speaks again, rapidly now.)

ALFRED: I tried to tell you before this…I did: I really did. You wouldn't listen. Wouldn't hear it. *(Pauses.)* I never thought it was natural: pairs. You and me, you and anybody, me and anybody. In alone, out alone.

EMILY: Alfred. I am…somebody.

ALFRED: *(After a long pause.)* Never, not in my entire life, did I ever have to *say* I was somebody. *(Pauses.)* I just…was. *(Pauses.)* Sorry, Emily…

EMILY: Alfred, *I am somebody.*

ALFRED: How can we get out of here? *(Pauses.)* How can we get out of here? *(Pauses.)* How can we get out of here?

EMILY: *(Slowly.)* How can you be so…hopeful?

ALFRED: I have no intention of ending it here, Emily. Not in Wakefield, not in this room, not in front of you… *(He circles the cell, furious, finally comes to rest. Pauses.)* How?

EMILY: Neither of us can or will leave this room. *(Pauses.)* Not you nor I. Neither. *(Pauses.)* It's possible, of course, in a few months' time, someone might blast a way in…just to have a peek…and pull us out. Maybe, in November, to put the park benches away for winter. *(She begins packing tapes into box.)* For the moment, polymer…a sealed tomb: the perfect compound…us and our history: Roxy's report. It'll be quite a find: big news. *(Pauses.)* An average man of average weight and height could stay alive, say, one month. *(Pauses.)* You are, of course, not average. *(Pauses.)* You are, at this particular juncture in your life, less than average. *(Pauses.)* Three weeks I'd say. Three weeks. Your body can devour itself, in place of food, for three weeks. *(She stacks bottles near cell.)* Without water, less. That's why you'll notice that there is an adequate supply of water set in these bottles. *(There are now eight bottles of water, set against the upstage wall of the cell.)* If you have the…you know…desire to hurry… *(Smiles.)* If you…well… *(Pauses.)* …find the courage… just… *(Pauses; smiles.)* …don't drink the water. *(Pauses.)* I have no doubt as to the outcome… *(Pauses.)* You'll sip away… *(Pauses.)* You'll remain… hopeful…until the last… *(Pauses.)* One day…in the next twenty or twenty-one…you'll understand…It will all become comprehensible… *(Smiles.)* Coherent.

(The sound of explosions from above: dull thuds, as though bomb were exploding somewhere a great distance away.)

EMILY: The fireworks have started, Alfred. *(Looks up to ceiling; smiles.)* It's the night before the Fourth. Tomorrow is Independence Day…Parade floats… majorettes twirling their aluminum sticks…senators, marching…All above us. Everyone…smiling… *(Pauses.)* I don't have what it takes to kill you…not directly, not face-to-face; I knew that when I stood facing Lynch. I wanted him dead. I couldn't. *(Pauses.)* It seems that I'm just not…allowed. *(Pauses.)* I've figured this way instead: *My* death will kill you, too. *(Pauses.)* It *will,* you know.

ALFRED: Emily…Forgive me. I shouldn't have lied…forgotten…

EMILY: I forgive you, Alfred. I do. *(Pauses.)* Forgiveness is all I have for which to be proud…of me. Forgiveness is my last and final right on this habitable earth…I know you'd love to go on and on…to live. I know you'll hope for it…struggle…fight it out until the end… *(Pauses.)* But you can't go on, Alfred. You have to die. Both of us. It has to end with us. *(Pauses.)* Really, Alfred. Trust me. Somebody has to stop it, here and now. There's always a possibility that one child might make it all the way…be born…start it again. I can't take the chance. I have to be certain. You're going to be so much happier…I promise you. *(Walks to desk and takes revolver from desk drawer.)* Look at me, Alfred…

ALFRED: Emily, for the love of God… *(Panic now.)* Emily!
(Emily places the revolver against her breast. She turns from desk and moves directly to Alfred, smiling. She stops at bars in front of him.)

EMILY: Sorry it's a gun. *(Pauses.)* Sorry it couldn't be something more…you know…imaginative… (Pauses.) …something less…modern. *(Pauses.)* These are inferior times… *(Pauses.)* I have to be…certain. *(Pauses.)* Alfred?

ALFRED: *(Stares at Emily.)* Don't, Emily…please don't…

EMILY: *(Slowly; clearly.)* Emily…dies.
(She fires the revolver into her breast: one sharp report; Emily's body jerks backward against desk and she slumps into chair. Drops gun. Clutches chest. She is dead. Alfred stares at Emily's body.)

ALFRED: I wish you hadn't done that, Emily. I do wish that.
(He walks to back wall, presses face against same, clenching eyes closed. He suddenly turns, blinks eyes open, as if Emily might be gone.)

ALFRED: Still there.
(He inhales and exhales through his nostrils. He walks to water bottles, lined in a row at edge of cell. He nonchalantly opens one, drinks from it, relids bottle, replaces same in row, but at other end: closer to Emily. He bends, reaches across, touches Emily's hair.)

ALFRED: This is attractive, Emily. Wrong! This is *atrocious,* Emily. That's what

I said. That's *not* what you said! *That's what I said! (Pauses.)* Losing my grip.

(He takes gun from beneath Emily and stands. Alfred places barrel of gun in his mouth. He holds his breath, weeps. He cannot pull the trigger. He places the gun's barrel against the palm of his hand, walks to back wall, stoops, pulls trigger twice: two reports. He turns, faces front, blood dripping from his wounded hand. He looks at Emily, smiles.)

ALFRED: Better. *(Kneels on floor, next to her, carefully.)* I would like this in the record, please: I feel somewhat better I have taken positive steps to ensure the loss of my grip... *(Looks at Emily. Pauses; stands, looks at hand dripping blood.)* What have you done, Alfred? *(Smiles.)* Look at us. *(Pauses.)* You are Emily and I am Alfred. *(Pauses.)* We were cursed, Emily. Your mother was right. We were cursed. *(Pauses.)* By whom?

(He is weak now. He looks at his hand dripping blood.)

ALFRED: My hand. *(Pauses.)* What have you done, Alfred? *(Tries to stand; cannot.)* Too weak.

(The sound of Fourth of July celebration—faintly, dully—overhead. The dull thuds of the final fireworks display, overhead.)

ALFRED: Finished.

(Alfred, sitting on floor next to Emily. Only the bars of the cage separate them. He now hears the music. He looks up, suddenly. He is hopeful. Tableau. The lights fade to black.)

The play is over.

Paris, New York, San Francisco, Milford, Gloucester—1971–1978